Lecture Notes in Artificial Intelligence 1435

Subseries of Lecture Notes in Computer Science
Edited by J. G. Carbonell and J. Siekmann

Lecture Notes in Computer Science

Edited by G. Goos, J. Hartmanis and J. van Leeuwen

T0223316

Springer
Berlin
Heidelberg
New York
Barcelona
Budapest
Hong Kong
London
Milan
Paris
Singapore
Tokyo

Matthias Klusch   Gerhard Weiß (Eds.)

Cooperative Information Agents II

Learning, Mobility and Electronic
Commerce for Information Discovery
on the Internet

Second International Workshop, CIA'98
Paris, France, July 4-7, 1998
Proceedings

Springer

Series Editors

Jaime G. Carbonell, Carnegie Mellon University, Pittsburgh, PA, USA
Jörg Siekmann, University of Saarland, Saarbrücken, Germany

Volume Editors

Matthias Klusch
Carnegie Mellon University, The Robotics Institute
3317 Doherty Hall, 5000 Forbes Ave., Pittsburgh, PA 15213-3891, USA
E-mail: klusch@cs.cmu.edu

Gerhard Weiß
Institut für Informatik, Technische Universität München
Arcisstr. 21, D-80290 München, Germany
E-mail: weissg@informatik.tu-muenchen.de

Cataloging-in-Publication Data applied for

Die Deutsche Bibliothek - CIP-Einheitsaufnahme

Cooperative information agents II : learning, mobility and
electronic commerce for information discovery on the internet ;
second international workshop ; proceedings / CIA '98, Paris, France,
July 4 - 7, 1998. Matthias Klusch ; Gerhard Weiß (ed.). - Berlin ;
Heidelberg ; New York ; Barcelona ; Budapest ; Hong Kong ;
London ; Milan ; Paris ; Santa Clara ; Singapore ; Tokyo : Springer,
1998
    (Lecture notes in computer science ; 1435 : Lecture notes in artificial
    intelligence)
    ISBN 3-540-64676-0

CR Subject Classification (1991): H.2, I.2, H.3.3, H.4.4, C.2.4

ISBN 3-540-64676-0 Springer-Verlag Berlin Heidelberg New York

© Springer-Verlag Berlin Heidelberg 1998
Printed in Germany

Typesetting: Camera ready by author
SPIN 10637697   06/3142 – 5 4 3 2 1 0   Printed on acid-free paper

Foreword

These are the proceedings of the Second International Workshop on Cooperative Information Agents, held in Paris, July 4–7, 1998.

The research and application area of cooperative information agents is of rapidly increasing importance. Information agents are computational software systems that have access to multiple, heterogeneous and geographically distributed information sources. These agents have to face up to the increasing complexity of modern information environments ranging from relatively simple in-house information systems, through large-scale multidatabase systems, to the visionary Infosphere in the Internet. Cooperative information agents work together in order to achieve private or global goals. One of their main tasks is an active search for relevant information in non-local domains on behalf of their users or other agents. This includes retrieving, analyzing, manipulating, and integrating information available from different information sources. The development of cooperative information agents requires expertise from several different research areas, especially AI, DAI, databases, and CSCW. It is particularly important to investigate to what extent AI methods can be applied for information discovery by groups or teams of cooperative information agents in the Internet. This concerns, e.g., the use of efficient techniques from machine learning, evolutionary computing, and symbolic or numerical approaches for uncertain reasoning. Moreover, commercial aspects of information gathering in the Internet are becoming more and more relevant, e.g., agents are paid and have to pay for services. Thus, methods for rational, utility-based cooperation among the agents are needed. In addition, mobile information agents seems to be attractive for flexible and efficient information discovery in constrained environments.

The interdisciplinary CIA workshop series covers the whole thematic range of cooperative information agents. In addition, each workshop in this series focuses on a few selected themes of particular relevance and actuality. The CIA-98 workshop, building on the success of CIA-97 ('DAI meets Databases', LNAI Series Vol. 1202), mainly concentrates on the themes learning, mobility, and electronic commerce in the context of cooperative information discovery. CIA-98 features 10 invited research and industrial lectures, and 14 contributed regular papers selected from 54 submissions.

Acknowledgements. First of all, we gratefully acknowledge the financial support from our Co-Sponsors

DAIMLER-BENZ AG, Stuttgart (Germany) and
GEORGE MASON UNIVERSITY, Fairfax VA (USA).

The workshop was organized in cooperation with the special interest groups on

Distributed Artificial Intelligence,
Database Systems, and
Information Retrieval

of the German Society for Computer Science (GI), and the

Institute for Integrated Publication and Information Systems

of the German National Research Center for Information Technology (GMD). We are especially grateful to the authors and invited speakers for contributing to this workshop. Last but not least, we thank the members of the program committee and the external referees for very carefully reviewing the submitted papers.

Paris, July 1998   Matthias Klusch & Gerhard Weiß

Program Committee

Gilbert Babin	(Laval University, Canada)
Wolfgang Benn	(University of Chemnitz, Germany)
Sonia Bergamaschi	(University of Modena, Italy)
Hans-Dieter Burkhard	(Humboldt University Berlin, Germany)
Brahim Chaib-draa	(Laval University, Canada)
Sharma Chakravarthy	(University of Florida, USA)
Keith Decker	(University of Delaware, USA)
Misbah Deen	(University of Keele, UK)
Yves Demazeau	(Leibniz/IMAG/CNRS, France)
Frank Dignum	(University of Eindhoven, Netherlands)
Edmund Durfee	(University of Michigan, USA)
Carl Hewitt	(MIT AI Lab, USA)
Toru Ishida	(University of Kyoto, Japan)
Leonid A. Kalinichenko	(Russian Academy of Sciences, Russia)
Takashi Kido	(NTT Information Systems Labs, Japan)
Ami Motro	(George Mason University, USA)
Erich Neuhold	(GMD IPSI, Germany)
Aris Ouksel	(University of Illinois at Chicago, USA)
Tuomas Sandholm	(Washington University, USA)
Sandip Sen	(University of Tulsa, USA)
Munindar P. Singh	(North Carolina State University, USA)
Michael Stillger	(Humboldt University Berlin, Germany)
Kurt Sundermeyer	(Daimler-Benz Research, Germany)
Katia Sycara	(Carnegie Mellon University, USA)
Robert Tolksdorf	(Technical University of Berlin, Germany)
Markus Tresch	(ETH Zurich, Switzerland)
Mike Wooldridge	(QMW College London, UK)

General Chair

Matthias Klusch (Technical University of Chemnitz, Germany)

Co-Chairs

Larry Kerschberg (George Mason University, USA)
Gerhard Weiß (Technical University of Munich, Germany)

External Reviewers

Davide Brugali	Terrence G. Harvey
Prasad Chalasani	Ralf Kühnel
Liren Chen	Anandeep Pannu
Feodor Fomenko	Onn Shehory
Ottmar Görlitz	Fernando Tohme

Table of Contents

Cooperative Information Agents – Systems and Applications

Cooperative Information Agents – Issues of Design, Querying, and Communication

Rational Collaboration and Electronic Commerce

Adaptive and Collaborative Information Gathering

Mobile Information Agents in the Internet

What Can Agents Do in Industry, and Why?
An Overview of Industrially-Oriented R&D at CEC

H. Van Dyke Parunak

Industrial Technology Institute
PO Box 1485
Ann Arbor, MI 48106 USA
van@iti.org

Abstract

The Center for Electronic Commerce (CEC) embodies over fourteen years of experience in applying agents to industrial problems. We have found such a fit in three areas: coordination of industrial designers, simulation and modeling of complex products and processes, and scheduling and control of production systems. This presentation outlines several trends in modern manufacturing, describes how these trends affect the three problem areas, discusses the features of agents that make them attractive candidates for implementing such systems, and reviews example applications from CEC's portfolio in each of these areas.

1. Trends in Manufacturing

Three trends in modern manufacturing present challenges that agent technologies can address. Manufactured products and the systems that produce them have become more complex. The manufacturing process is increasingly spread out over a supply network rather than being concentrated in a single firm, and the variety of products that a firm must offer is increasing while the time to bring them to market is decreasing.

1.1 Increased Product Complexity

A comparison of the features available in a modern automobile with those in a Model T illustrates how the functionality of products has increased. A modern vehicle may include air conditioning, automatic transmission, power steering, power brakes, roll-up windows, turn signals, cruise control, seat belts, air bags, radio and tape player, adjustable seats, and a host of other features that did not exist or could not be installed in an automobile earlier in this century. Similar technical enhancements have enriched many other products, including appliances, machine tools, and aircraft.

1.2 Supply Networks

Modern industrial strategists are developing the vision of the "virtual enterprise," formed for a particular market opportunity from a collection of independent firms with well-defined core competencies [13]. The manufacturer of a complex product (the original equipment manufacturer, or "OEM") may purchase half or even more of the content in the product from other companies. For example, an automotive manufacturer might buy seats from one company, brake systems from another, air conditioning from a third, and electrical systems from a fourth, and manufacture only the chassis, body, and powertrain in its own facilities. The suppliers of major subsystems (such as seats) in turn purchase much of their content from still other companies. As a result, the "production line" that turns raw materials into a vehicle is a "supply network" (more commonly though less precisely called a "supply chain") of many different firms.

Figure 1 illustrates a simple supply network [1, 7]. Johnson Controls supplies seating systems to Ford, General Motors, and Chrysler, and purchases the components and subassemblies of seats either directly or indirectly from at least twelve smaller companies, some of which also supply one another. Issues of product design and production schedule must be managed across all of these firms in order to produce quality vehicles on time and at reasonable cost.

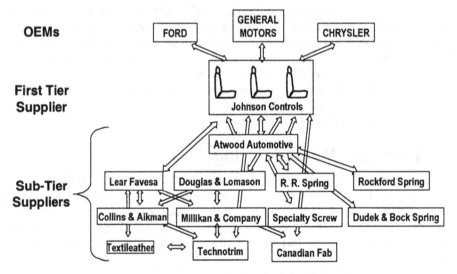

Figure 1: A Simple Automotive Supply Network

1.3 Increased Product Variety over Time

In manufacturing, the product that pleases the most customers has a tremendous advantage, and one of the most effective means known to determine what product features customer like is to turn out as many different product variations as quickly as possible. Customers tend to favor a company offering many product variations, because they can choose the model most closely meeting their desires. In addition, if a company can bring new products to market quickly, it can shift its offerings to reflect customer preferences and thus capture even more of the market. This strategy is responsible for the precipitous drop in the time-to-market for many products. The time from product concept to first production in automotive used to be 60 months. Now world-class performance requires 30 months, and some vehicles have been produced in even less time.

From an AI perspective, a product represents a particular point in the space of product characteristics, and its market performance measures the desirability of that point to customers. The more variations a company can offer and the faster it can bring them to market, the more thoroughly it can sample the space of customer demand, and the more satisfaction it can deliver to its customers.

2. What Needs to be Done in Industry?

Industry creates wealth and enriches people's lives by conceiving new products and services and bringing them from vision to reality. In manufacturing, two essential steps in this process are design (working out the details of the product and the systems needed to manufacture it) and operation (of the manufacturing system that produces the product). Increasingly, simulation and modeling tools support the design process. The CEC's experience in applying agents to industry focuses in these three areas.

2.1 Design

Manufactured products do not just happen. They and the systems that make them must be designed, planned out in great detail to guide the expenditures of capital and effort necessary to realize them.

The movement toward supply chains means that each supplier shares in the design of the overall product by helping design the subsystems it supplies. In addition to product design, much of the design of the production system is routinely assigned to vendors of production equipment or third party "system integrators" responsible for assembling this equipment into a working factory. This strategy poses difficulties of communication and coordination. Design is difficult enough when the participants come from different technical disciplines. When they belong to different companies, they often have divergent corporate cultures and proprietary needs to keep certain information confidential, and information movement between designers can be much slower than between members of a single company. As a result, the cost of design can easily increase, while the coherence of the overall design suffers. Three challenges, difficult enough when design is done by a single-firm, become daunting in the distributed environment of a modern supply chain.

Planning. Design tasks cannot be sequenced in detail. Because of the complex dependencies among components and subsystems, early decisions often have to be changed in the light of later ones. Such backtracking is much easier for closely-linked designers in a single firm than for a widely distributed team.

Coupling. Designers think locally, focusing on their own subsystems, but the complexities of the product couple them with other designers. This challenge and the previous one can lead to infinite loops: designer A's decision on one feature leads to a decision by designer B that invalidates designer A's decision on another feature, but when designer A revises this feature, it invalidates B's earlier decision, and so forth. Distributing the designers across multiple firms only increases the time lag in such loops and makes their resolution more difficult.

Prioritizing. Designers have no common language for comparing the importance of issues. For instance, every subsystem in a vehicle contributes mass to the overall vehicle, and if one weighs more, others must weigh less to keep the entire vehicle in a reasonable range. However, the decision of which components can have more mass and which must make do with less is typically resolved politically, on the basis of whose supervisor is more powerful. In a supply network, this dynamic requires the

OEM to adjudicate conflicts between the suppliers, forcing the OEM to make design decisions about purchased subsystems that it would rather defer to its suppliers.

2.2 Simulation and Modeling

A design for an industrial system or manufactured product is a plan, and like other plans, it can sometimes fail. The modern manufacturing trends discussed above make failure both more likely and more costly than in earlier days. Thus it is increasingly important to test the design before incurring the expense of implementation.

The increased complexity of modern products raises the risk of design failure through the possibility of unanticipated interactions among subsystems and components. Pressures toward distributed manufacturing and design result in a more heterogeneous product. Shorter product life cycles leave less time for design. All of these issues raise the risk that the physical product or system will not satisfy the expectations of the design. The increased scope of the venture also raises the investment necessary to bring the product to fulfillment. An automotive manufacturer must spend between $1*10^9$ and $3*10^9$ to bring a new vehicle to market, an investment that can be compromised at many points by design failure.

The increased risk and cost of manufactured products is leading to increased use of simulation and modeling technology to assess the performance of a design before its physical implementation. Product simulation (for example, to determine the crash-worthiness of a vehicle) usually relies heavily on finite element analysis, while process simulation (such as establishing the capacity of a production line or the behavior of an inventory system) depends traditionally on stock-and-flow models such as queueing systems or differential equations.

A number of requirements constrain the value of a simulation and modeling environment. A simulation is easier to develop and use if the modeling formalism maps naturally onto the problem domain both structurally (so that model elements correspond to domain entities) and semantically (so that the model language covers the ontology of the domain). The more accurately the model predicts the behavior of the real world, the more risk it will remove from the development process and thus the more value it contributes to the enterprise. The model is not an end in itself, but a step in a larger life cycle that begins with design and moves on to operation of the resulting product, and a model that can support operation will be more valuable than one that serves only the modeling activity.

2.3 Scheduling and Control

Design and simulation can be applied both to the consumer product being manufactured and to the tools and system that will manufacture it. Scheduling and control apply mostly to the manufacturing system. They monitor its trajectory through state space over time and adjust operating parameters to make that trajectory satisfy some overall criterion.

Scheduling and control differ in their characteristic time constants and the kind of information manipulated [19]. Scheduling is longer-term, usually on a scale to which humans can respond, and involves the manipulation of concepts through semantically-grounded symbols. Control manipulates scalar- and vector-valued physical variables, and usually happens too fast for direct human supervision.

In manufacturing, scheduling ranges from long-range plans that support delivery promises to customers, to shop-floor scheduling that determines what happens when at which resources on the factory floor. The objective is to produce the most product possible with the lowest capital investment, while satisfying customer requirements for quality and delivery time. Control deals with turning devices on and off to execute the processes that transform input materials into a finished product.

Increasing product variety challenges both scheduling and control. Scheduling is essentially a search through a combinatorially complex space (roughly, the Cartesian product of the set of parts being manipulated, the set of resources that manipulate them, and the time line). The more products or product variations one manufactures, the larger this space, and the more difficult the scheduling problem. Increased product variation also makes control more difficult, since it increases both the number of devices that must be coordinated and the range of behaviors that those devices must support.

Scheduling is also aggravated by the shift toward supply networks. By passing manufacturing of critical components to suppliers, an OEM relinquishes direct control on when they are produced, and thus increases the uncertainty in the timing of the processes by which it integrates these components into the overall product.

Traditionally, both control and scheduling are done with centralized processes. The combinatorial explosion of scheduling possibilities taxes the ability of a centralized program to compute an optimal schedule. The constant change of product mix needed to respond to customer orders against an increasingly varied set of product offerings means that the factory may never even reach a steady state in which an optimal schedule is well defined. The increased distribution that product complexity brings to control and that supply networks bring to scheduling makes centralization awkward. For both scheduling and control, increased product complexity and supply networks greatly increase the size and complexity of traditional monolithic systems, increasing the cost of software engineering and maintaintenance.

3. What Can Agents Do?

Agents are not a panacea for industrial software. Like any other technology, they have certain capabilities, and are best used for problems whose characteristics require those capabilities. Five such characteristics are particularly salient: agents are best suited for applications that are modular, decentralized, changeable, ill-structured, and complex.[1] The tasks of design, simulation, and scheduling and control manifest many of these characteristics, particularly under the impact of modern manufacturing trends, suggesting that agents are a natural way to address them.

3.1 Modular

Agents are pro-active objects, and share the benefits of modularity that have led to the widespread adoption of object technology. They are best suited to applications that fall into natural modules. An agent has its own set of state variables, distinct from those of the environment. The agent's input and output mechanisms couple its state

---

[1] These are an extension of the categories described by [8].

variables to some subset of the environment's state variables. An industrial entity is a good candidate for agent-hood if it has a well-defined set of state variables that are distinct from those of its environment, and if its interfaces with that environment can be clearly identified.

All three of the modern manufacturing trends we are discussing lend themselves to modular analysis. Engineers manage increased product complexity by refining the overall product into subsystems with well defined interfaces. Supply networks assign these subsystems and components to different companies, each with its own organizational identity, operational boundaries, and procedures for interfacing with its environment. The proliferation of product varieties leads to the definition of a product as a base platform and a set of modular options.

3.2 Decentralized

An agent is more than an object; it is a pro-active object, a bounded process. It does not need to be invoked externally, but autonomously monitors its own environment and takes action as it deems appropriate. This characteristic of agents makes them particularly suited for applications that can be decomposed into stand-alone processes, each capable of doing useful things without continuous direction by some other process.

Many industrial processes can be organized in either a centralized or a decentralized way. Centralized organizations go back to the governments of ancient Egypt, Assyria, China, and Babylon, with their focus on a central demigod and an elaborate bureaucracy to manage the flow of control down and information back up. The popularity of this structure can be traced through the army of Alexander the Great, the Roman legions, and the rival empires of pre-modern Europe down to the structure of modern Fortune 500 companies and industrial control architectures [2].

This approach is not the only alternative. The power of decentralization has been made clear in recent years in the contrast in performance between a centralized economic system (the former Soviet Union) and a decentralized one (free-market capitalism). Supply networks are an expression of the decentralized approach, and agent-based architectures are an ideal fit to such an organizational strategy. In fact, a European observer suggests that one of the forces leading to the growing popularity of multi-agent systems is "the rise of the American style of liberalism and individualism" [26]. In addition, the increase in product variation leads to a proliferation of manufacturing devices across increasingly larger factories, so that even within a single company problems of control and scheduling may be more naturally considered from a decentralized point of view.

3.3 Changeable

Agents are well suited to modular problems because they are objects. They are well suited to decentralized problems because they are pro-active objects. These two characteristics combine to make them especially valuable when a problem is likely to change frequently. Modularity permits the system to be modified one piece at a time. Decentralization minimizes the impact that changing one module has on the behavior of other modules.

Modularization alone is not sufficient to permit frequent changes. In a system with a single thread of control, changes to a single module can cause later modules, those it invokes, to malfunction. Decentralization decouples the individual modules from one another, so that errors in one module impact only those modules that interact with it, leaving the rest of the system unaffected.

The modern trend toward increased product variety and shorter time to market makes the manufacturing environment much more changeable than it was previously. Much of the cost of a new factory is in its software. Agent-based architectures permit reuse of much existing code and self-configuration of large portions of the system, reducing both the cost and the time needed to bring up a new factory.

3.4 Ill-structured

An early deliverable in traditional systems design is an architecture of the application, showing which entities interact with which other entities and specifying the interfaces among them. For example, installation of a conventional system for electronic data interchange (EDI) among trading partners requires that one know the providers and consumers of the various goods and services being traded, so that orders can be sent to the appropriate parties.

Such a structure could be defined in advance in the days when a company made most of each product itself and dealt only with its own internal divisions and selected suppliers. The structure of modern supply networks can be dynamic, changing many times over the lifetime of an information system. Consider an electronic system to support open trading, where orders are open to any qualified bidder. Requiring the system designer to specify the sender and recipient of each transaction would quickly lead to "paralysis by analysis." From a traditional point of view, this application is ill-structured. That is, not all of the necessary structural information is available when the system is designed. Agents can discover this structure as the system operates, rather than requiring it to be designed into the system initially.

Some applications are intrinsically under-specified and thus ill-structured, and agents offer the only realistic approach to managing them. Even where more detailed structural information is available, the wiser course may be to pretend that it is not. A system that is designed to a specific domain structure will require modification if that structure changes. Agent technology permits the analyst to design a system to the classes that generate a given domain structure rather than to that structure itself, thus extending the useful life of the resulting system and reducing the cost of maintenance and reconfiguration.

3.5 Complex

All three of the modern manufacturing tendencies that we have identified increase the complexity of the manufacturing problem. Increased product complexity explodes the size of the space that designers must search and the number of machines that must be scheduled and controlled, and makes the task of mapping between design and simulation model more daunting. Supply networks and increased product variability push traditional optimal scheduling against the wall of computational complexity.

As is often the case, the complexity in this example is combinatorial in nature, resulting from the fact that the number of different interactions among a set of elements increases much faster than does the number of elements in the set. By mapping individual agents to the interacting elements, agent architectures can replace explicit coding of this large set of interactions with generation of them at run-time. Consider 100 agents, each with ten behaviors, each behavior requiring 20 lines of code. The total amount of software that has to be produced to instantiate this system is 20,000 lines of code, an extremely modest undertaking. But the total number of behaviors in the repertoire of the resulting system is on the order of ten for the first agent, times ten for the second, times ten for the third, and so forth, or 10^{100}, an overwhelmingly large number. Naturally, not all of these will be useful behaviors, and one can imagine pathological agent designs in which none of the generated behaviors will be appropriate. However, appropriately designed agent architectures can move the generation of combinatorial behavior spaces from design-time to run-time, drastically reducing the amount of software that must be generated and thus the cost of the system to be constructed.

Just as well-structured systems can become ill-structured when viewed over their entire life span, so a system that appears to require only a few behaviors can become more complex as it is modified in response to changing user requirements. By adopting an agent approach at the outset, systems engineers can provide a much more robust and adaptable solution that will grow naturally to meet business needs.

4. What Has the CEC Done with Agents in Industry?

The Center for Electronic Commerce has been active in applying agents to industrial problems since the early 1980's. These applications cover all three of the tasks described above, and illustrate many of the benefits of agents in industry.

4.1 Design

The CEC's major initiative in applying agents to design is in the context of RAPPID (Responsible Agents for Product-Process Integrated Design)[2] [22-24].

A designer seeks to embed a set of *functions* (e.g., optical, electromechanical, control) in an artifact with specified *characteristics* (e.g., weight, color, complexity, materials, power consumption, physical size). The functional view drives most designs, since it distinguishes the disciplines in which engineers are trained and in support of which design tools are available. Conflicts arise when different teams disagree on the relation between the characteristics of their own functional pieces and the characteristics of the entire product. Some conflicts are within the design team: How much of a mechanism's power budget should be available to the sensor circuitry,

---

[2] RAPPID was sponsored by the Rapid Design Exploration and Optimization (RaDEO) program (formerly MADE) of DARPA, managed successively by Pradeep Khosla and Kevin Lyons, and administered through the AF ManTech program at Wright Laboratories under the direction of James Poindexter. The project team includes Steve Clark, Mike Davis, Mitch Fleischer, Bob Matthews, Van Parunak, and John Sauter (all ITI), Al Ward and Tzyy-Chuh Chang (Ward Synthesis), and Mike Wellman (University of Michigan). The RAPPID prototype is being tested on the design of military land vehicles at the U.S. Army's Tank and Automotive Command (TACOM) in Warren, MI, with the support of the Technology Integration Division.

and how much to the actuator? Others face design off against other manufacturing functions: How should we balance the functional desirability of an unusual machined shape against the increased manufacturing expense of creating that shape?

It is easy to represent how much a mechanism weighs or how much power it consumes, but there is seldom a disciplined way to trade off weight and power consumption against one another. The more characteristics are involved in a design compromise, the more difficult the trade-off becomes. The problem is the classic dilemma of multivariate optimization. Analytical solutions are available only in specialized and limited niches. In current practice such trade-offs are sometimes supported by processes such as QFD (Quality Functional Deployment) or resolved politically, rather than in a way that optimizes the overall design and its manufacturability. The problem is compounded when design teams are distributed across different companies.

RAPPID uses a marketplace to set prices on each characteristic of a design. Agents representing each component buy and sell units of these characteristics. A component that needs more latitude in a given characteristic (say, more weight) can purchase increments of that characteristic from another component, but may need to sell another characteristic to raise resources for this purchase. In some cases, analytical models of the dependencies between characteristics may help designers estimate their relative costs, but even where such models are clumsy or nonexistent, prices set in the marketplace define the coupling among characteristics.

Figure 2 shows a design decomposed into Component Agents (rounded rectangles), each with one Characteristic Agent (ovals) for each dimension in the design space. For example, the "SS.Weight" Characteristic might represent the constraint that the entire product weigh between 5 and 10 kg. The topmost

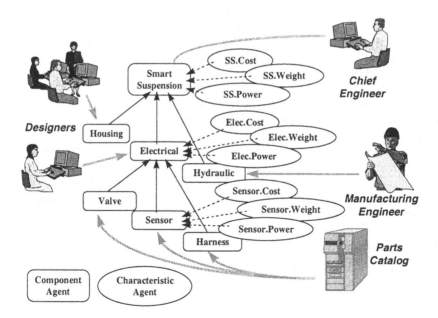

Figure 2: The RAPPID Design Ecosystem for a New Tank Suspension

Component represents the complete product (in this case, a new suspension for a tank), and is the concern of the Chief Engineer, who reflects the Customer's requirements in the initial allocation of design space. The bottom-most Components are either custom-manufactured or (in the Figure) selected from an on-line Parts Catalog. Designers, who typically have responsibility for intermediate levels of the product tree, propagate the constraints from the top and bottom of the tree toward each other. Each Component (either automatically or under guidance from its Designer) buys and sells allocations on its Characteristics to and from other Components.

RAPPID rests on three basic concepts: markets as a mechanism for coordinating distributed decision-making, set-based design, and the use of computer agents in partnership with human agents rather than as a replacement for them.

Market-Based Control.—Researchers addressing distributed problems in a wide range of domains have recently begun to turn to market-based mechanisms for coordination. [3] offers a convenient collection of applications to fields as diverse as computer network control, memory allocation, factory scheduling, pollution management, and air-conditioning load balancing. In all of these areas, competitors for scarce resources can efficiently express their needs in terms of a common currency, and the balance between supply and demand can set prices for those resources that rationalize the distribution of resources across competitors.

Set-Based Ideas.—A product's characteristics can be thought of as dimensions of a Cartesian space within which the product is defined. Traditionally, designers seek to *build* a design to fit a predefined subspace of characteristics, without knowing in advance whether any acceptable design fits. Toyota has pioneered a more promising vision that begins with a design space much larger than necessary, and then shrinks it incrementally to *discover* the subspace occupied by the desired design [29].

Current design tools do not support this vision. With a market in design characteristics, low prices identify slack characteristics (dimensions of the space) that the chief engineer can collapse by buying up allocations of that characteristic. This action simultaneously reduces the amount of that characteristic available for use by designers and increases the funds in the system available to purchase other characteristics to compensate for the decrease in the given characteristic. As designers buy and sell, the relative prices of the various characteristics change, identifying a new slack dimension that can further shrink the design space.

Silicon and Carbon Agents.—RAPPID does not automate the entire design problem. Its market mechanisms function alongside conventional interactions, which we describe as SLOWH (Standard Legacy-Oriented Work Habits). The market mechanisms themselves are not entirely automated, but are implemented partly in computer algorithms and partly in human behaviors, a mixture that we describe as "hybrid carbon-silicon systems."

4.2 Simulation

The CEC's research in agent-based simulation and modeling includes the development of XSpec (a modeling tool specifically equipped for industrial controls) and the DASCh project (applying the SWARM modeling environment [11] to industrial supply networks).

4.2.1 XSpec

XSpec ("eXecutable Specification")[3] [28] is a simulation environment designed specifically for modeling industrial control systems. It develops three techniques that are critical for success in this domain: pairing of physical and control models, the use of wrappers to integrate existing applications, and a technique for synchronizing time across such integrated applications.

Pairing of Physical and Control Models.—Design of a manufacturing mechanism typically requires close coordination between a mechanical engineer who designs the physical components and an electrical engineer who designs the control algorithms that manipulate it. Conventionally, these distinct aspects are often developed in isolation from one another, using separate engineering tools, and then brought together in an integration task when inevitable inconsistencies are discovered. XSpec promotes the integrated development of physical and control models with a class of agents, "components." Each component includes both physical and control models and the interfaces between them for a specific element of the system, and defines the interfaces that this combined model presents to other components. These external interfaces include not only control signals but also physical interactions. The discipline of defining both physical and control sides of each component before tying these components together into a system forces engineers to work closely together, resolving inconsistencies at the level of an individual device rather than after devices have been elaborated into two complete but incompatible systems.

Wrapping of Existing Applications.—Integrating physical and control models device-by-device runs contrary to the grain of existing modeling tools, which focus either on the physical behavior of the system (e.g., a kinematic modeler such as Robcad) or on its control behavior (e.g., a DEDS modeler such as Flexis). Because these tools divide the world by discipline (mechanics vs. control) rather than by device, they discourage engineers from the close integration of disciplines on a device-by-device basis. To overcome this pressure, XSpec enables individual tools to be wrapped so that they can automatically exchange their results with one another, much along the lines of ARCHON [4, 9, 25]. In the applications we have modeled, we use XSpec to integrate Robcad (for the kinematic behavior of individual mechanisms), SIMAN/Cinema (for queueing behavior) and Flexis (for control algorithms).

Synchronizing Time.—A major challenge in integrating different models of real-time behavior is maintaining a common view of time across the various applications. The XSpec wrapper for modeling packages includes a special synchronization protocol and a time server, or "Syncer." These mechanisms coordinate the temporal execution of models constructed in different tools so that their integrated behavior is causally meaningful and useful as an overall model of the system [10]. The Syncer supports the integration of different time models, including discrete events, continuous time, and the special case of zero time between two events on different tools.

The power of XSpec was demonstrated in its application to a gear weld cell for a major automotive manufacturer. The cell, designed and constructed with conventional

---

[3] The XSpec team includes Mark Brown, John Sauter, Ray VanderBok, and Jack White of ITI, and Bob Judd of the University of Ohio.

technologies, was only producing 75% of its rated capacity. The XSpec team modeled the line, and then tested various modifications on the model without the constraint of working around daily production use of the cell. When the modifications recommended by the model were installed in the cell, its production rose to 125% of its rated capacity.

4.2.2 DASCh

Supply networks, like most systems composed of interacting components, support a wide range of dynamical behavior that can interfere with scheduling and control at the enterprise level. Data analytic approaches are not effective in understanding these dynamics, because the commercial environment changes too rapidly to permit the collection of consistent data series long enough to support statistical requirements. The DASCh project (Dynamical Analysis of Supply Chains)[4] [16, 17] explores the dynamical behavior of takes the approach of constructing and experimenting with an agent-based emulation model of the system that can maintain a given set of conditions as long as desired.

Following the pioneering work of Jay Forrester and the Systems Dynamics movement [6], virtually all simulation work to date models the supply chain as a set of partial differential equations and then integrates these equations over time. DASCh uses agent-based emulation, representing the various components of the supply chain by software agents that emulate their actual behaviors. The DASCh approach is more faithful than numerical simulation, better supports the increasingly decentralized nature of supply chains and the need to protect proprietary information, and provides a much closer interaction between model and real system [17].

DASCh includes three species of agents. *Company agents* represent the different firms that trade with one another in a supply network. They consume inputs from their suppliers and transform them into outputs that they send to their customers. *PPIC agents* model the production planning and inventory control algorithms used by company agents, and currently support a simple MRP model. *Shipping agents* model the delay and uncertainty involved in the movement of both material and information between trading partners.

The initial DASCh experiments involve a supply chain with four company agents (a boundary supplier, a boundary consumer, and two intermediate firms producing a product with neither assembly nor disassembly), illustrated in Figure 3. The two intermediate company agents each have PPIC agents to convert incoming orders to orders for their inputs, and shipping agents manage all movement of both material and information among company agents.

This simple structure was intended as a starting point. It was expected to yield relatively uninteresting behavior, on which the impact of successive modifications could be studied. In fact, it shows a range of interesting behaviors in terms of the variability in orders and inventories at the various company agents.

---

[4] DASCh was funded by DARPA, and administered through the AF ManTech program at Wright Laboratories under the direction of James Poindexter. The DASCh team includes Steve Clark and Van Parunak of ITI, and Prof. Bob Savit and Rick Riolo of the University of Michigan's Program for the Study of Complex Systems.

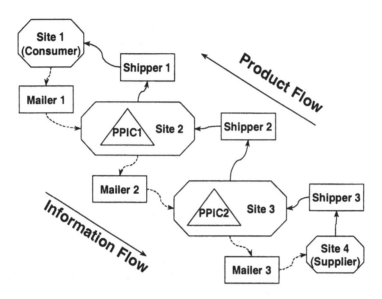

Figure 3: The DASCh Supply Chain

• As the demand generated by the top-level consumer propagates to lower levels, its variance increases, so that lower-level suppliers experience much more variability than higher-level ones. This phenomenon is widely discussed in the literature.

• Not as well recognized is the correlation imposed on an originally uncorrelated series of random orders by the PPIC algorithms in the supply network.

• A single modest change at the top of the chain generates disturbances in the order sequences of lower tier suppliers that persist long after the original change.

• Even when top-level demand is constant and bottom-level supply is completely reliable, intermediate sites can generate complex oscillations in inventory levels, including period doubling, as a result of capacity limitations.

The unexpectedly complex behavior of the DASCh model holds a lesson not only for industrialists with supply chains but for researchers in multi-agent systems generally. The interactions of agents with one another can generate complex behaviors, even when the agents and their organization seem simple and straightforward. This complex emergent behavior is both a challenge and a benefit. It is a benefit because it means that complex problems can in principle be addressed with sets of relatively simple agents, if their complex interactions can be harnessed. It is a challenge because it requires agent engineers to pay close attention to system behaviors as well as agent behaviors, rather than assuming that the whole will equal the sum of the parts.

4.3 Scheduling and Control

Shop-floor scheduling and control is one of the more mature application areas for agent technology, and CEC has executed several projects in this area. This summary will highlight major lessons from each of these.

YAMS ("Yet Another Manufacturing System") [14] applied a contract net to a hierarchical model of manufacturing system, including agents representing the overall shop, each of several workstations in the shop, and each of several devices in each workstation. The hierarchical model followed the widely-circulated NASREM architecture promoted by the US National Institute for Standards and Technology [2]. Our experiments using this system to control an actual shop in our laboratory led to two major conclusions. First, hierarchies are in general a poor way to organize agents. While most physical interactions were between peers in the hierarchy, the use of a rigidly hierarchical model forced messages to travel up to the lowest shared node and then back down. The resulting flood of messages rapidly overwhelmed the communication network. Second, messages can be physical as well as electronic. In spite of careful analysis to prove that the protocols were deadlock-free, the system deadlocked. Further analysis showed that the movement of a physical part from one station to another, and the signal generated when it encountered a sensor at its destination, provided a "message" from the sending station to the receiving station that had not been included in the protocol analysis and that compromised the system's liveness.

CASCADE[5] (not an acronym, although usually spelled with upper-case letters) [20, 21] focused agent methods on the specific domain of material handling. Our objective was to develop a distributed control mechanism for a Weldun-Bosch modular conveyor system, so that configuring the control software could be as straightforward as plugging together the physical components of the conveyor. We began by modeling the protocols as a contract net between conveyor segments. Because of the simple semantics involved ("Give me a pallet." "Here, take a pallet."), we were able to streamline the ontology and protocol considerably, using reinforcement learning in the individual segments to yield a self-routing system. During our work, the work of the Parallel Distributed Processing group [12, 27] came to our attention, and we noticed that our reduction of the contract net had led us to a structure isomorphic to a back-propagation neural network. We articulated the experience as the "marching-band syndrome," in which agents of considerable sophistication (such as the members of a marching band) sometimes achieve their objectives best by adopting a greatly reduced interaction protocol based on the requirements of the domain (in the case of the marching band, match one's velocity and separation to one's neighbors, a mechanism successfully executed by flocks of birds and schools of fish). CASCADE drew our attention to the power of fine-grained agent solutions and led to our advocacy of synthetic ecosystems, agent architectures that depend for their functionality on the emergent dynamics of interaction among agents as well as the explicitly defined behaviors of individual agents.

SFA (Shop Floor Agents)[6] [15] is a collaborative project in which several industrial firms are sharing their experiences in constructing agent-based shop floor systems. The project has highlighted the difference between a research environment (in which every developer is an agent researcher, capable of devising new architectural solutions in mid-stream to fit emerging challenges) and an industrial one

---

[5] YAMS and CASCADE were funded in part by the Kellogg Foundation. Participants included Bruce Irish, Jim Kindrick, Peter Lozo, and Van Parunak.
[6] Sponsored by the National Center for Manufacturing Sciences, directed by Tony Haynes, and executed at ITI by Steve Clark, Mike Davis, Jorge Goic, Van Parunak, and John Sauter.

(in which developers are general software engineers without any deep knowledge of agent theory). This experience shows that effective deployment of agents in industrial settings requires the articulation of a teachable methodology for specifying and designing multi-agent systems and the availability of development tools that package best practice for implementation. The project's deliverables address these needs with extensions to standard object-oriented development methods and a sophisticated implementation environment within the Gensym G2 system.

AARIA (Autonomous Agents at Rock Island Arsenal)[7] [18] developed an architecture for manufacturing scheduling in which resources, processes, and parts are peer agents. In most previous work on agent-based scheduling, resources (such as machining workcenters) are agents, negotiating with one another for access to input parts and the disposition of output parts. This architecture is acceptable in a classical job shop in which parts compete for access to resources, but does not fit as well in block-build environments such as airframe fabrication or ship drydocking, in which the product is stationary and resources must compete for access to it. The basic idea of a multi-species approach to agent-based scheduling and control emerged from a conversation with Jean-Pierre Müller in Neuchâtel in September of 1992. The resulting ecosystem (Figure 4) includes three main species: resources (including machines, tools, and operators), part types, and unit processes (the basic production steps into which manufacturing is divided [5]). The dynamic of this system can be viewed as two flows, one of resources and one of parts, intersecting at the unit process.

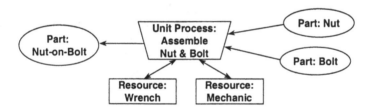

Figure 4: A Shop-Floor Ecosystem

By maintaining the orthogonality of these three species, the framework can support industries such as aerospace and shipbuilding that require integration of job-shop and block-build environments. In addition, these flows support mechanisms that permit different scheduling modalities to emerge dynamically at different resources as the system runs. Conventional shops are scheduled either by dispatching based on local equipment constraints, dispatching against an advance schedule, or Kanban (response to a demand pull). These techniques can be distinguished on the basis of the

[7] Initial research on AARIA was funded by the DARPA Agile program under contract F33615-95-C-5524, managed by USAF ManTech. The prime contractor is Intelligent Automation, Inc. (Len Haynes, Kutluhan Erol, and Renato Levy). Other contractors are the Industrial Technology Institute (Van Parunak, Steve Clark, Jorge Goic), the University of Cincinnati (Albert Baker, Bradley Matthews, Ben Moore, Brian Birtle, Veena Pandiri), Flavors Technology (Howell Mitchell), and Rock Island Army Arsenal (Greg Peters, Don Tice).

degree to which they are constrained by advance commitment and by customer demand (Figure 5). Dispatch is the least constrained modality. Advance scheduling is highly constrained by earlier promises, but unresponsive to changes in demand while the system operates. Kanban requires both advance commitment and current demand.

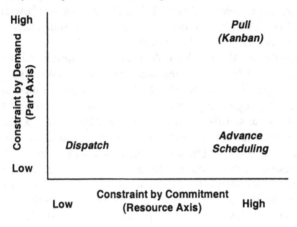

Figure 5: Emergent Scheduling Modalities

In a conventional shop, every workstation is driven by the same modality. In the three-species ecosystem, different portions of the shop can behave according to different modalities, and can change their modality over time as conditions change. The degree to which a given unit process is constrained by demand is determined by the behavior of part type agents, while the degree of constraint by commitment is determined by the behavior of resources. The result is a highly flexible architecture that is readily adaptable to a wide range of manufacturing applications.

Growing out of this long experience, the CEC is currently a subcontractor in three different industrial projects in the domain of manufacturing scheduling and control. One applies agents to scheduling problems in the domain of semiconductor manufacturing, another deals with scheduling in shipbuilding, and a third addresses dynamic reconfiguration of the equipment in a manufacturing line in the event of device failure. For proprietary reasons, details of these projects cannot be revealed at this time.

5. Summary

Manufacturing is a rich domain for application of software technology. Modern pressures toward increased product complexity and diversity and the use of supply networks to produce these products produce problems characterized by modularity, decentralization, changeability, poor structure, and high complexity, a set of characteristics that agents are uniquely suited to address. These problems impact the design of products and the systems that manufacture them, the simulation and modeling of these systems, and their scheduling and control during operation. The CEC's extensive experience in applying agents to such problems confirms the importance and appropriateness of agent technology in modern industrial applications, and demonstrates that this technology is mature enough for wide-spread deployment.

6. References

[1] AIAG. Manufacturing Assembly Pilot (MAP) Project Final Report. M-4, Automotive Industry Action Group, Southfield, MI, 1997.

[2] J. S. Albus, H. G. McCain, and R. Lumia. NASA/NBS Standard Reference Model for Telerobot Control System Architecture (NASREM). NBS Technical Note 1235, National Bureau of Standards, Gaithersburg, MD, 1987.

[3] S. H. Clearwater, Editor. *Market-Based Control: A Paradigm for Distributed Resource Allocation.* Singapore, World Scientific, 1996.

[4] J. M. Corera, I. Laresgoiti, and N. R. Jennings. Using ARCHON, Part 2: Electricity Transportation Management. *IEEE Expert*, 11(6):71-79, 1996.

[5] I. Finnie, Editor. *Unit Manufacturing Processes: Issues and Opportunities in Research.* Washington, DC, National Academy Press, 1995.

[6] J. W. Forrester. *Industrial Dynamics.* Cambridge, MA, MIT Press, 1961.

[7] T. Hoy. The Manufacturing Assembly Pilot (MAP): A Breakthrough in Information System Design. *EDI Forum*, 10(1):26-28, 1996.

[8] N. Jennings. Applying Agent Technology. Plenary presentation at PAAM'96. 1996.

[9] N. R. Jennings, E. H. Mamdani, J. M. Corera, I. Laresgoiti, F. Perriolat, P. Skarek, and L. Z. Varga. Using ARCHON to develop real-word DAI applications, Part 1. *IEEE Expert*, 11(6):64-70, 1996.

[10] R. P. Judd, J. F. White, P. K. Hickman, M. E. Brown, and J. A. Sauter. System for combining originally software incompatible control, kinematic, and discrete event simulation systems into a single integrated simulation system. , Industrial Technology Institute, U.S., 1993.

[11] C. Langton, R. Burkhart, and G. Ropella. The Swarm Simulation System. http://www.santafe.edu/projects/swarm/, 1997.

[12] J. L. McClelland and D. E. Rumelhart, Editors. *Parallel Distributed Processing: Explorations in the Microstructure of Cognition. Volume 2: Psychological and Biological Models.* Cambridge, MA, MIT Press, 1986.

[13] R. N. Nagel and R. Dove. *21st Century Manufacturing Enterprise Strategy.* Bethlehem, PA, Agility Forum, 1991.

[14] H. V. D. Parunak. Manufacturing Experience with the Contract Net. In M. N. Huhns, Editor, *Distributed Artificial Intelligence*, pages 285-310. Pitman, London, 1987.

[15] H. V. D. Parunak. Workshop Report: Implementing Manufacturing Agents. http://www.iti.org/~van/paamncms.ps, Industrial Technology Institute, 1996.

[16] H. V. D. Parunak. DASCh: Dynamic Analysis of Supply Chains. http://www.iti.org/~van/dasch, 1997.

[17] H. V. D. Parunak. Agent-Based Behavioral Emulation vs. Numerical Simulation: A Users' Guide. In *Proceedings of ICMAS '98 Workshop on Multi-Agent Systems and Agent-Based Simulation*, Springer, 1998.

[18] H. V. D. Parunak, A. D. Baker, and S. J. Clark. The AARIA Agent Architecture: An Example of Requirements-Driven Agent-Based System Design. In *Proceedings of First International Conference on Autonomous Agents (ICAA-97)*, 1997.

[19]   H. V. D. Parunak and R. Judd. Sharpening the focus on intelligent control. *International Journal of Computer Integrated Manufacturing*, 3(1):1-5, 1990.

[20]   H. V. D. Parunak, J. Kindrick, and B. Irish. Material Handling: A Conservative Domain for Neural Connectivity and Propagation. In *Proceedings of Sixth National Conference on Artificial Intelligence*, pages 307-311, American Association for Artificial Intelligence, 1987.

[21]   H. V. D. Parunak, J. Kindrick, and B. W. Irish. A Connectionist Model for Material Handling. *Robotics & Computer-Integrated Manufacturing*, 4(3/4):643-654, 1988.

[22]   H. V. D. Parunak, A. Ward, M. Fleischer, and J. Sauter. A Marketplace of Design Agents for Distributed Concurrent Set-Based Design. In *Proceedings of ISPE/CE97: Fourth ISPE International Conference on Concurrent Engineering: Research and Applications*, 1997.

[23]   H. V. D. Parunak, A. Ward, M. Fleischer, J. Sauter, and T.-C. Chang. Distributed Component-Centered Design as Agent-Based Distributed Constraint Optimization. In *Proceedings of AAAI Workshop on Constraints and Agents*, pages 93-99, American Association for Artificial Intelligence, 1997.

[24]   H. V. D. Parunak, A. Ward, and J. Sauter. A Systematic Market Approach To Distributed Constraint Problems. In *Proceedings of International Conference on Multi-Agent Systems*, pages (submitted), AAAI, 1998.

[25]   F. Perriolat, P. Skarek, L. Z. Varga, and N. R. Jennings. Using ARCHON, Part 3: Particle Accelerator Control. *IEEE Expert*, 11(6):80-86, 1996.

[26]   J.-F. Perrot. Preface. In J. Ferber, Editor, *Les Systèmes Multi-Agents: Vers une intelligence collective*, pages xiii-xiv. InterEditions, Paris, 1995.

[27]   D. E. Rumelhart and J. L. McClelland, Editors. *Parallel Distributed Processing: Explorations in the Microstructure of Cognition. Volume 1: Foundations.* Cambridge, MA, MIT Press, 1986.

[28]   J. A. Sauter and R. P. Judd. XSpec: The Modeling and Design of Complex Systems. In *Proceedings of DARPA Manufacturing, Engineering, Design, Automation Workshop*, pages 125-132, DARPA SISTO and DSO, 1992.

[29]   A. Ward, J. K. Liker, J. J. Cristiano, and D. K. S. II. The Second Toyota Paradox: How Delaying Decisions Can Make Better Cars Faster. *Sloan Management Review*, (Spring):43-61, 1995.

The InfoSleuth Agent System

Marian Nodine

Microelectronics and Computer Technology Corp. (MCC)
3500 West Balcones Center Dr.
Austin, TX 78759
phone (512)338-3719
email nodine@mcc.com.

The InfoSleuth architecture consists of a set of collaborating agents that work together at the request of the user to:

1. gather information via complex queries from a changing set of databases and semi-structured text repositories distributed across an internet,

2. perform rudimentary polling and notification facilities for monitoring changes in data,

3. automatically route location-independent requests to update individual data items, and

4. analyze information using statistical data mining techniques and/or logical inferencing.

Users make requests to InfoSleuth from a domain-independent or domain-specific applet. Requests are made against an ontology specifying his domain of interest. The applet forwards the request to the agent system. Within the agent system, agents cooperate to satisfy the request on behalf of the user. Each request is processed by the available agents at the time of the request. Results are presented either within the user's applet or within a specialized result applet.

Figure 1 on page 2 shows the basic structure of the InfoSleuth agents. Together, the ontology agent and the broker agent provide the basic support for enabling the agents to interconnect and intercommunicate.

* *Ontology agents* maintain a knowledge base of the different ontologies used for specifying requests, and returns ontology information as requested.

* The *Broker agent* maintains a knowledge base of information that all the other agents advertise about themselves, and uses this knowledge to match agents with requested services. Thus, technically, the broker does semantic matchmaking. When an agent comes on-line, it advertises itself to the broker and thus makes itself available for use. When an agent goes off-line, the broker removes the agent from its knowledge base.

We provide several different types of agents for processing information within InfoSleuth.

* *User agents* act on behalf of users to formulate their requests and pass them in for execution, and to match the responses with the requests and pass them back to the requesting applet.

* *Resource agents* wrap and activate databases and other repositories of information. We consider any source of information a resource.

* *Task Execution agents* plan how the request should be processed within InfoSleuth, including result caching. Task Execution agents may also be specialized to monitor for complex events that include changes over time and simple events detected within individual resources.

- *Deviation Detection agents* monitor streams of data for instances that are beyond some threshold, where the threshold may be hardwired or may be learned over time.
- *Multiresource Query agents* process complex queries that span multiple resources. They may or may not allow the query to include logically derived concepts as well as slots in the ontology.

Within the InfoSleuth system, the agents themselves are roughly organized into layers, with the broker and ontology agents serving all of the other agents. Users access resources via a middle set of layers that acquire and process the information from the resources as requested. Within the two middle layers, the upper, "planning/temporal" layer deals with processes that occur over time, such as the planning of tasks and the detection of complex events that may be composed of sequences of simpler events. The lower, "query/analysis" layer executes one-time subtasks such as the retrieval of a current snapshot of some related information or the detection of an anomaly in the data stream as it occurs.

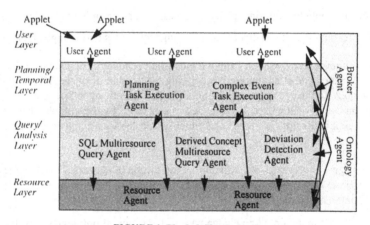

FIGURE 1. The InfoSleuth Agents

Agents for Hypermedia Information Discovery

Vasilios S. Lazarou and Keith L. Clark
Department of Computing
Imperial College, 180 Queen's Gate, London SW7 2BZ
{V.Lazarou, K.L.Clark}@ic.ac.uk

Abstract

In this paper, a Multi-Agent System for Distributed Information Discovery and Retrieval is presented. Data mining enables extraction of hypermedia information from heterogeneous information sources existing on the World Wide Web. The goal is to construct a distributed deductive database system of meta-information about these sources using an open architecture and an extensible ontology of descriptive attributes. Each component database is maintained by an information source agent. Prolog-style queries, entered via a user agent, express user requests for information items of interest. The query evaluation is performed utilising intermediary architectural layers of facilitator, matchmaker and descriptor agents that enable intelligent query routing exhibiting co-operative answering behaviour.

1 Overview of the system's architecture

The advent of large wide-area networks, Internet is the most characteristic example, has caused a vast increase both in the information availability and in the number of the information sources. This evolution offers great promise for obtaining and sharing diverse information conveniently. However, the multitude, diversity and the dynamic nature of on-line information sources make accessing any specific piece of information an extremely difficult task.

One way to address these issues is to use information agents. These Distributed Information Retrieval agents should be able to:

- Accept a request from a human or agent client
- Translate this request into a language understood by the information sources
- Identify the information sources that contain information relevant to the request
- Pose the request to these sources
- Collect and process the corresponding results and present them to the client

We have followed this approach in developing our information retrieval system for the WWW. The overall agent architecture is as follows (see Figure 1: info. req., prov. stand for information request and supply accordingly). The inter-agent communication is based on standard Knowledge Query Manipulation Language (KQML) performatives. Our system supports a collection of information sites. The notion of an information site is used to describe a logical entity that contains a set of information sources. It is a logical clustering of actual-physical WWW sites.

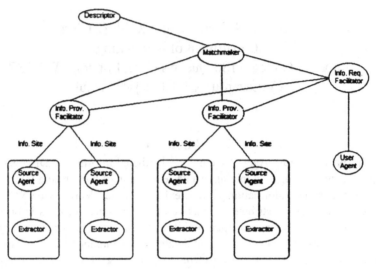

Figure 1

In each information site, we have an *extractor agent* and an *information source agent*. The tasks to be performed by the extractor include detecting which web pages contain relevant information, extracting this information and representing it in a standard attribute-based format. For a technical documents application, the attributes that we seek to extract are **authors**, **title**, **topic**, **keywords**, **document location**, **document abstract location**, **referred titles** and **referred authors**.

The extractor elicits the links-references of each page, discards the ones referring to other sites and fetches the next page. The process stops when all the pages of the site have been traversed. The extractor goes through the pages of interest to spot any textual portions that are used to describe some technical paper for example. First, the page is partitioned into smaller textual parts. Then each small textual part is examined to detect the desired attributes. HTML formatting information and appearance of importantly relevant terms is utilised to perform the above operations.

It is essential to note at this point the effect of XML (eXtensible Mark-up Language). XML is the emerging standard proposed by W3C to complement HTML by managing the semantic structure of WWW pages. XML allows authors to specify their own document syntax, hypertext link semantics, and presentation style. Once new tags and elements can be created with new attribute-value metadata, they can be re-encoded in a systematic, structured document format using XML.

The primary achievement of XML is that by defining a custom mark-up language, anyone can encode the information of his documents much more precisely than is possible with HTML. This means that the extractor could use straightforward string parsing to produce the required attribute-based representation. XML parsing capabilities have just been incorporated to the extractor.

Finally, after all the pages have been examined, this attribute-based, relational information is passed to the information source agent. The information source agent handles the query answering process. It accepts retrieval enquiries and attempts to evaluate them against the attribute-based information. It acts as an information gateway to the information sources it manages.

Before any request processing, during the set-up of the system, an *information supply facilitator* accepts registrations from source agents. When they register, the source agents send an abstracted form of the information they contain. This summary information includes the attribute values that occur in a frequent manner in their information bases. These attribute values will be utilised by this agent in order to forward queries to appropriate source agents. Finally, each information supply facilitator, in turn, advertises its capabilities with a *matchmaker*, the corner stone of the distributed retrieval system.

In contrast to the above, the *user agent* is the one that the end user interacts with. The user enters the query in a Prolog-like form using application-specific predicates (the ontology of the retrieval system) and sets various parameters in order to customise the retrieval operation. The query predicates correspond to the most significant information attributes. A web browser interface gives access to the ontology of query predicates including attribute-value names and information about query syntax. For the domain of technical documents, we use the following predicates: *document-location, abstract-location, author, title, topic, document-type, keyword, referred-author and referred-title*. An example query is:

```
document-location (?DL,?D) and {(author("Michael Huhns", ?D)
and topic(["DAI"],?D)) or (referred-author("R. A. Kowalski",
?D) and topic(["Databases, Logic"], ?D))}
```

The query strings such as *DAI* will be matched (in a "fuzzy" way) against information mined from the data sources. Thus, the query is a request for URL-locations of papers authored by *Michael Huhns* on the topic of DAI or for papers on the topic of *Databases* and *Logic* that refer to a paper by *R. A. Kowalski*. After the query submission, the user agent transforms it into a KQML-style message structure. The results (URLs of documents that satisfied the query) are displayed through a web browser in an HTML page.

The user agent makes use of the services of a corresponding *information request facilitator agent*. The information request facilitator is in charge of organising the query answering process. It accepts queries from user agents and attempts to find which information supply facilitators may potentially answer it; in other words, it acts as a query-answering planner. Some of the other activities it performs include query reformulation, consulting and subscribing to the matchmaker, and metadata caching.

The request facilitator maintains cached information about the answering capabilities of supply facilitators. This is based on queries (from various user agents) that have been successfully answered by them. In addition, it subscribes to the matchmaker for frequently requested attribute values in order to receive information about supply facilitators supporting them. The request facilitator first attempts to determine to which supply facilitators to send the query using this cached information. However, for incoming queries mentioning attribute values that the facilitator has previously encountered, it will ask the matchmaker to recommend supply facilitators based on advertisements it has received from all the supply facilitators.

The *matchmaker agent* serves as an advisor agent that facilitates the diffusion of requests to agents that have expressed an ability to handle them. This is performed by accepting advertisements from supply facilitators and recommendation requests from request facilitators.

The overall architecture is completed by the *descriptor agent.* This agent holds terminological knowledge capable of identifying synonyms, hypernyms and hyponyms of a specific term by accessing an external thesaurus (Wordnet). The topic attribute is a characteristic example. A topic for example can have synonym topics, several subtopics (topics used to describe a subject more specific than the current one) and higher level topics (topics used to describe a subject more general than the current one). The descriptor agent provides this terminological information to be used by the request facilitator during query reformulation (see next section).

The matchmaker answers recommendation-requests for certain authors or topics by identifying suitable supply facilitators. The suitable facilitators are those that advertised they support one of the authors, or one of the topics or a closely related topic. Moreover, the matchmaker will indicate how the advertised topics are related to the enquiry ones. For example, consider that the matchmaker finds a supply facilitator (SF1) that supports the "Mobile Agent Languages" topic (subtopic of "Agent Languages") and another (SF2) that supports the "AI Languages" topic (higher level topic of "Agent Languages"). In such a scenario, the request facilitator will point this out when responding to a recommendation request concerning "Agent Languages" and will reformulate the original query. The reformulation will result in replacing the "Agent Languages" topic by "Mobile Agent Languages" for the query to be sent to the SF1 facilitator and replacing it by "AI Languages" for the query to be sent to SF2.

For a more detailed discussion about the activities of the agents regarding search for technical documents, refer to [Lazarou 97a] and [Lazarou 97b]. In the remaining of this paper we will highlight the aspects of co-operative answering and data mining as exhibited in our system (section 2) and its extension to support searching for multimedia information (section 3). This extension requires adding support for an extensible ontology of query predicates and descriptive terms (section 4). We will end our presentation by giving a summary, some notes about related work and some concluding comments (sections 5-7).

2 The role of Co-operative Answering and Data Mining

The co-operative answering behaviour of our system is illustrated by the activities of the information request facilitator. The goal is to provide useful responses to user queries. In other words, to provide associated information that is a relevant to a query. A query answering system should collaborate with the user since the latter does not always know enough to ask accurate queries. Consequently, queries can be either too general or too specific.

In order to address these issues, one form of co-operative behaviour involves transforming a query to capture neighbouring information. A standard approach as described in [Gaasterland 97], is *query relaxation* where a query is generalised by making use of *taxonomy clauses*. These define hierarchical type relationships between predicates and constants. In our system, a form of query relaxation is performed by the request facilitator when attempting to find appropriate supply facilitators. In this case, conjunction is replaced by disjunction leading to a more general form. However this transformation is related to query routing; the answering process will be performed on the original query.

In contrast, a query transformation more relevant to co-operative answering behaviour also appears in our system. It has to do with the replacement of query terms after the request facilitator (possibly after interacting with the matchmaker) receives terminological information from the descriptor. As already mentioned, a topic can be replaced by a synonym topic, a higher-level topic or a lower-level one (up to a certain level). Hence, this transformation makes use of the terminological hierarchy (instead of built-in taxonomy clauses) maintained by the descriptor. In contrast to the query relaxation method, this transformation can be exposed in three different ways. It can have the form of equivalent query reformulation (when a term is replaced by a synonym one) or query specialisation (when a term is replaced by a lower level one). Query generalisation (when a term is replaced by a higher level one) is also an option. Moreover, equivalent reformulation has precedence over specialisation that has precedence over generalisation in order to preserve precision where possible. A final form of user-defined query relaxation will be presented later in this paper in the section for non-standard predicates and the use of a meta-predicate.

The data mining features of our system are demonstrated by the activities of the extractor agent. This one metamorphoses the raw data (both hypertext and hypermedia) into an attribute-based information. Under this format, the information is both understandable and effectively processed by the agent system and the users. Since our underlying platform is the WWW and the data sources are arbitrary web pages, the information is entirely unstructured conceptually. However, HTML provides intra-document formatting structure assistance that is utilised to gain some understanding about the conceptual role of textual portions. As already noted, the arrival of XML will alter the picture dramatically. The attributed-based information specification will be embedded directly into XML documents simplifying the data mining activities into XML pattern parsing.

3 Support of multimedia information

We have considerably extended the system to support hypermedia information including images, video and audio. This extension does not affect the architecture of the system. Primarily, we need only to add extra capabilities to the extractor to elicit information from different types of information sources. The user agents, unaltered, act as information consumers transmitting user requests for multimedia objects and filtering the responses according to user preferences.

The source agents act as providers that additionally advertise their multimedia capabilities. They need to store descriptions of the multimedia items just as they keep descriptions about the technical paper data. The source agents provide the logical locations of the documents that contain multimedia objects and return these locations whenever a query is encountered. In a slightly different scenario, where the query indicates direct transmission of the document, the document would be fetched from the information site repository.

There are some fundamental assumptions made for the multimedia information sources. We assume that there is some metadata associated with each multimedia item. This metadata describes the content of multimedia items. It contains information about the item's objects, their properties and the relationships among them. For example, consider an image where a man kicks a ball that is in front of him. Metadata that might be associated with this image would identify two objects (man, ball), an action relationship (kick) and a spatial relationship (in front of). In a relational form, we would record the metadata as "(kicks man, ball)" and "in-front-of (man, ball)". Another representation under consideration is to record them as: *"transitive-action (kicks, man, ball)"* and *"object-relationship (in-front-of, man, ball)"*. The latter corresponds to a more generic approach for outlining actions and relationships.

We assume that this metadata is generated a priori. One target of our research is to determine multimedia items where automatic metadata generation is attainable by the extractor agent. Two cases exhibiting this property include portrait images and images that represent covers of music item releases where associated descriptive text (e.g. anchor text) provides the means for metadata elicitation. Alternatively, we can create metadata from a textual description of the multimedia item existing in the web page that references it. A last resort is to utilise human assistance.

The metadata (in a relational form) is maintained by the source agent and will be used during the query processing to determine the items that satisfy a query description. The application that is used as a testbed for our multimedia support effort deals with the retrieval of images from music-related information sources. However most of the issues to be mentioned are application-independent.

An important decision has to do with the adoption of a retrieval model. A retrieval model encompasses a query language and a retrieval strategy. A query language expressing the features (as constants) and their relationships (as predicates) is sufficient for our modelling needs. In our case, we adopted retrieval by attribute strategy. In this strategy, a query is formulated using a combination of attributes, meta-attributes, logical attributes or semantic attributes as discussed below.

3.1 Multimedia information attributes

A multimedia object is defined as a semantic entity (contained in a multimedia item) that is meaningful in a specific domain. For example in a music image database, <u>musical instruments</u> are multimedia <u>objects</u>. Following [Gudivada 96], we first distinguish objective and semantic attributes (of multimedia items). Objective attributes are further categorised into meta-attributes and logical attributes. Meta-attributes are the ones that are derived externally and are content-independent. For example the creator of an item or the acquisition date are meta-attributes since we expect them to exist independently of what the item portrays, and they can be identified without examining the item content.

Logical attributes are the ones used to describe the properties of a multimedia item. They differ from the meta-attributes since they have to be derived directly from the item itself. For example, rivers, lakes and seas in a geographical picture are logical attributes. Semantic attributes are the ones used to describe high-level domain concepts exhibited by the multimedia item. For example characterisation of attributes like rock, pop and soul audio clips in a music database.

Compared to logical attributes, semantic attributes are less precise and require domain expertise for their identification and/or quantification. In addition, the specification of semantic attributes frequently involves subjectivity, uncertainty or imprecision. Subjectivity may appear because of differing view points of the users about various domain aspects. Uncertainty arises due to vagueness in the retrieval needs of a user. Imprecision arises due to difficulties in the measurement and specification of the accompanying features. The existence of these semantic attributes in a query makes its processing much harder. The system has to cope with domain-dependent semantics as well as diverse user interpretations of these semantics.

In our system, all of the above attribute types are supported. Meta-attributes like the provider, the date, the physical representation format (JPEG, GIF, TIFF among others) and the size are among the standard predicates that are supported. Their values are automatically identified by the extractor. Logical attributes are supported as well. For example the attributes used to express spatial relationships (in_front, upper, left_of) belong to the standard predicate set that can be used.

All the above attributes describe properties of an image without requiring high-level domain expertise; they can be used in any application. In contrast, the semantic attributes used are domain dependent and make sense for a specific application. In our application that is concerned with the retrieval of images from music-related information sources, semantic attributes such as *group_photo, release_cover, concert_photo, plays* and *wears* can be used.

3.2 Multimedia Information Retrieval

An important issue is to introduce a representation for the content of multimedia items. In general, in any item there is a set of objects related by some associations. An attribute/value representation is sufficient in capturing this information. Attributes are used in two ways: a) to express properties that characterise the objects (e.g. *colour (hat, red)* or *format (image, tiff)*), b) to express relationships among the objects. Furthermore, these relationships can be classified into two primal categories, action (e.g. *sings (Claus)* or *plays (Al, guitar)*) and spatial relationships (e.g. *in_front (drums, bass)* or *left_of (bass, piano)*).

Query processing involves finding items in the multimedia information sources that are expressed by attribute values highly similar to the ones existing in the user's query. A standard IR approach is to use approximate matching, where the similarity between queries and documents is computed. In a similar fashion, we compute the similarity between queries and multimedia items. Approximate matching has an apparent application when the user cannot provide a precise specification of his requirements; the lack of exact matches is another reason.

We need first to attempt to match the objects in the query to the ones in each multimedia item and if we succeed to determine which of these objects' relationships are satisfied by the objects of the multimedia item. Two objects are defined as similar when both the following hold: I) they are illustrated by identical attributes II) all the attribute values of the objects are identical or "close". Two relationships are defined as similar when both the following hold. First, they have identical or synonym names and second the existing objects can be placed in 1-1 correspondence such that each object in the first is similar to the one in the second. For example, the relationship "behind (boy, wall)" is similar to the "behind (male_teenager, wall)". The name (behind) is identical, the arity is the same, the second object (wall) is identical while the first ones are (boy and male_teenager) are considered similar.

If the attribute values can be represented in a scalar form (even approximately), the notion of closeness mentioned above depends on the existence of a predicate that determines the distance of any two given attribute values. If such a predicate does exist, then we can define closeness as a distance lower than a predefined threshold. If not, then the values have to be the same. For example, imagine a colour similarity predicate. Similarity can be calculated depending on colour characteristics like contrast and saturation.

In our current implementation, a closeness predicate is provided for all standard predicates that belong to the above category. The facility to enable the user/source agents to supply an appropriate closeness predicate for each non-standard predicate (see below) is under development.

When the values of a predicate cannot be represented in a scalar form, the only applicable method to compute similarity values is by consulting the descriptor agent. This agent, by performing a traversal of the vocabulary data structure, can calculate the distance between any two arbitrary terms. For example, consider two terms that are hyponyms of the same term without being synonyms. Their distance is small resulting in an adequate high similarity measure.

4 Use of non-standard attributes

In order to enhance the customisability of the overall system, both the users (through their user agents) and the source agents have the ability to introduce non-standard relations/predicates. There are two alternatives for the source agents. First, the site administrator can directly feed a new relation to the agent. Alternatively, as a result of a learning process employed by the source agent, attribute combinations that are frequently requested can be used to form a new retrieval concept. The source agents then seek human assistance to supply meaningful names to these induced relations. This functionality is very significant because we think it is unlikely that each information site supports every predicate that a user would like to use to express his retrieval needs.

The drawback of allowing new descriptions of relations is that the overall query management becomes more complicated. Whenever a human user or a source agent wants to make use of a non-standard relation, the other system agents have to be notified. Users will be eventually notified since there will be an update of the ontology they browse via the web interface. Another effect is that whenever a query that makes use of non-standard predicates has to be answered, only a subset of the source agents has the ability to support it and hence answer it. Nevertheless, this has a positive aspect since after semantic query optimisation we may detect that a query is guaranteed to fail if sent to agents lacking this support. Hence, the query routing procedure becomes more focused by pruning some branches of the search tree of the source agents to be probed.

The introduction of a non-standard relation involves a Prolog-like definition and a textual description. The source agents can maintain declarations of new primitive relations (with only a textual description). They also maintain declarations of defined relations (relations defined in terms of standard or other introduced relations).

The textual description is provided to help the users comprehend the role, the limits and the usage of a non-standard predicate. First, general information is displayed about what kind of retrieval requirements can be satisfied by the predicate. In addition, the arity of the predicate and the role of each argument are explained. The arguments are specified as input, output or any type. If the definition of a non-standard predicate makes use of another non-standard predicate, then its textual description is displayed as well.

As already mentioned, non-standard predicates can be introduced either by source agents or user agents. In both cases, the information related to these attributes is published to the matchmaker (passing via a facilitator agent). In this way, any agent can interact with the matchmaker to find information about new attributes. For the source agents, this functionality enables them to incorporate any new defined relations that can be expressed using already supported relations. Incorporating such new definitions is an aspect of co-operative behaviour by the source agent, co-operative because this is done to allow higher-level user queries.

When human users, through their user agent, define a higher level predicate, the definition uses only predicates that remote source agents already support. This leads to a more focused processing scenario that enables enhanced efficiency during the answering of user requests involving such a predicate. For example, if a site supports the **attributes** author and paperno the user agent could introduce the **defined relation**:

Productive-author (?A) if author(?A) and paper-number (?A, ?N) and ?N > 12.

The user, with his user agent, has also the option to be notified by the matchmaker about sites that support predicates of interest. He then formulates the queries according to the information that is received. This is especially true if the retrieval needs require the use of both standard and non-standard predicates. An example query could be:

> **image(?P) and appears ("R.Ratzinger", ?P) and
> appears(?X,?P) and assistant ("R.Ratzinger", ?X)**.

We assume that the "appears" relation is a standard one while the "assistant" one is not. The user can pose the above query for images where R. Ratzinger and another person appear, and it is explicitly required that the other person is his assistant.

However, the above query would not be sent to source agents where the "assistant" predicate is not supported (it would certainly be fruitless). If the user wants the request to be handled also by source agents not supporting this predicate he should reformulate the query. In this case, a special purpose meta-predicate understood by all source agents, the *"supports (predicate)"* has to be used. Therefore, instead of having the previous query, the condition *assistant (...)* would be replaced by *supports (assistant (...))*.

Wrapping any predicate using this meta-predicate has exactly the role to denote that a condition concerning the corresponding predicate has to be checked only if it is supported. This is another aspect of co-operative answering attempting to address a retrieval scenario tailored to more specialised user needs. Note also that in this case, query relaxation is entirely user-driven.

A final option targeting users with advanced expertise is to use two-phase query processing. The user has to decompose his enquiry into two disjoint sub-queries, one with the standard predicates and one with the others. In the first phase, the query sent contains the standard predicates together with *"supports"* conditions for each non-standard one. The answers to this query are not actual items but the addresses of the agents that satisfied the query conditions for the standard predicates indicating as well if they support the non-standard predicates.

In the second phase, the number of agents providing the required support and satisfying the other conditions drives any further actions. The user may send the full query using the non-standard predicates directly to the agents to be answered in a normal fashion. In addition, he may ask to receive the answers for the standard predicate relaxed version from the other agents. Finally, he may abandon the non-standard predicates and just receive answers for the relaxed version from all the agents.

5 Related Work

The existing Distributed Information Retrieval systems have a significant influence in the architectural as well as the implementation features of our system. The concept of some of the agent classes with a role similar to ours exists (among others) in: **a)** UMDL (such as the collection interface agents) [Birmingham 95] and [Vidal 95], **b)** IRA (such as userbots, corpusbots) [Voorhees 94], **c)** TSIMMIS (such as classifiers, translators) [Garcia-Molina 95], **d)** Information Brokers [Fikes 95], **e)** SHADE-COINS [Kuokka 95] and **f)** Knowledge Navigator (such as advisory agents) [Burke 95].

All the above systems tend to focus on specific aspects of both the system's architecture and the agents' responsibilities. The UMDL, IRA systems focus on the mid-level activities providing only agents similar to our source, user and facilitator agents. The TSIMMIS system examines mainly the retrieval procedure; it does not incorporate for example the basic user interface agent class. The SHADE-COINS is the only one that provides the high level class of the matchmakers but leaves an architectural gap caused by the lack of facilitators. The Knowledge Navigator has a different orientation since it adopts the browsing paradigm while the Information Brokers system appears inflexible by assigning all the activities into one agent class.

Research work on multimedia information ([Gudivada 95], [Marcus 95a], [Marcus 95b] and [Sistla 95]) is also very influential. For aspects specific to our agents' functionality, work from [Espinoza 96], [Goldman 96] and [Turpeinen 96] is directing some future aspects.

6 Summary

- Fully distributed, scalable and modular system; the information providers are not passive request servers. Hypermedia information is fully supported.
- Sites managed as local deductive databases and WWW as a distributed deductive one. Prolog-like query language provides expressiveness and accuracy concerning the user needs and answer precision.
- The predicate set for query formulation corresponds to salient information item properties or relationships. It includes semantic, logical and meta-multimedia attributes.
- Data mining activities. Unstructured site information is transformed in a relational, attribute-based representation permitting query processing.
- Integration between the query language and the site information representation enables efficient query answering. Straightforward mapping between the user's request and the one posed on the deductive database.
- Users and source agents can define extended relations based on existing ones. Moreover, they can incorporate any extended relation even if defined by other source or user agents. Meta-predicate support is also provided.
- The semantics behind the used terms is captured; polysemy and synonymy are tackled.
- Co-operative answering activities. Using terminological knowledge, the original query can be transformed into different equivalent ones. Answers can capture neighbouring (concerning the initial retrieval needs) information.

7 Conclusion

As already mentioned in this paper, the Distributed Information Retrieval task is a very complex task. The Internet as the underlying distributed environment, results to additional complication related to the vast amount of the available information, the lack of structure and the diversity in this information. In this paper we described a system that attempts to address the difficulties associated with this task. The agents are the active and intelligent components of the system that accomplish the activities concerned with the various aspects of the task. The complexity and the distributed nature of the task have shown that using an architecture of intelligent co-operating agents is a suitable, if not an obligatory, way to manage this problem.

References

[Birmingham 95] Birmingham, W. P., Durfee, E.H. 1995. The Distributed Agent Architecture of the University of Michigan Digital Library. In AAAI 95: Information Gathering from Heterogeneous, Distributed Environments.

[Burke 95] Burke, R., Hammond, K.J. 1995. Combining Databases and Knowledge Bases for Assisted Browsing. In AAAI 95: Information Gathering from Heterogeneous, Distributed Environments.

[Espinoza 96] Espinoza, F., Hook, K. 1996. A WWW Interface to an Adaptive Hypermedia System. In PAAM 96.

[Fikes 95] Fikes, R., Engelmore, R. 1995. Network-Based Information Brokers. In AAAI 95: Information Gathering from Heterogeneous, Distributed Environments.

[Gaasterland 97] Gaasterland, T. 1997. Co-operative Answering through Controlled Query Relaxation. In IEEE Expert Intelligent Systems, Sep/Oct 97.

[Garcia-Molina 95] Garcia-Molina, H., Hammer, J. 1995. Integrating and Accessing Heterogeneous Information Sources in TSIMMIS. In AAAI 95: Information Gathering from Heterogeneous, Distributed Environments.

[Goldman 96] Goldman, C. V., Langer, A., Rosenschein, J. S. 1996. Musag: an agent that learns what you mean. In PAAM 96.

[Gudivada 95] Gudivada, V. N., Raghavan, V. V., Vanapipat, K. 1995. A Unified Approach to Data Modelling and Retrieval for a Class of Image Database Applications. In Multimedia Database Systems, Springer-Verlag.

[Kuokka 95] Kuokka, D., Harada, L. 1995. Supporting Information Retrieval via Matchmaking. In AAAI 95: Information Gathering from Heterogeneous, Distributed Environments.

[Lazarou 97a] Lazarou, V. S., Clark, K. L. 1997. A Multi-Agent System for Distributed Information Retrieval on the World Wide Web. In WETICE97, Collaborative Agents in Distributed Web Applications, IEEE Computer Society Press.

[Lazarou 97b] Lazarou, V. S., Clark, K. L. 1997. Distributed Information Retrieval using a Multi-Agent System and the role of Logic Programming. In ICLP97, Logic Programming Tools for Internet Applications.

[Marcus 95a] Marcus, S., Subrahmanian, V. S. 1995. Towards a Theory of Multimedia Database Systems. In Multimedia Database Systems, Springer-Verlag.

[Marcus 95b] Marcus, S. 1995. Querying Multimedia Databases in SQL. In Multimedia Database Systems, Springer-Verlag.

[Sistla 95] Sistla, A. P., Yu, C. 1995. Retrieval of Pictures Using Approximate Matching. In Multimedia Database Systems, Springer Verlag.

[Turpeinen 96] Turpeinen, M., Saarela, J., Puskala, T. 1996. Architecture for Agent Mediated Personalised News Services. In PAAM 96.

[Vidal 95] Vidal, J. M., Durfee, E. H. 1995. Task Planning Agents in the UMDL. In CIKM95 Intelligent Information Agents Workshop.

[Voorhees 94] Voorhees, E. 1994. Information Agents. In AAAI 94: Software Agents.

Trafficopter: A Distributed Collection System for Traffic Information

Alexandros Moukas[1], Konstantinos Chandrinos[2] and Pattie Maes[1]

[1] Software Agents Group, MIT Media Laboratory, Cambridge, MA 02139
moux,pattie@media.mit.edu

[2] Institute for Computer Science, FORTH, Heraclion, Crete, Greece
kostel@ics.forth.gr

Abstract. We describe Trafficopter, a multi-agent system that collects and propagates traffic information in an urban setting using distributed methods. Agents into the vehicles themselves collect and propagate traffic-related information in a decentralized, self-organizing fashion with no single point of failure. The ideas in this system are the use of the vehicles/agents themselves as a way of collecting traffic data and the way those data are distributed to the interested vehicles. The tools used are a traffic simulator and a set of PDAs / WindowsCE-based terminals equipped with GPS and wireless transceivers. The simulator is used for the investigation of the validity of traffic control and information propagation algorithms in a distributed environment and the WindowsCE terminals for applying the above ideas into the real world.

1   Introduction

Trafficopter is a multiagent system that provides a fast and reliable way of assisting the driver of a vehicle in deciding the most convenient route to his/her destination without using any special road infrastructure. These suggestions change in regular time intervals according to real-time traffic conditions and do not require particular infrastructure for collection and dissemination of the relevant information. Our approach stems from the simple observation that the only reliable witness of the traffic conditions that lay ahead are the cars that are there now, or have been there recently. We attempt to exploit this by creating a virtual distributed network of intercommunicating agent nodes that pass along information (messages) that is enough for drawing conclusions on local traffic conditions. These traffic conditions are depicted on dashboard mounted map-viewing facilities. Extreme accuracy in the quantity of vehicles is not of paramount importance and the performance of the system gracefully degrades as the number of vehicles equipped with the system drops.

When driving, in order to find the fastest way to go somewhere one needs two things: a computer map with one's position on it (usually derived by a GPS) and the traffic conditions along the possible paths from the origin to the destination. The former already exists in a set of high-end vehicles. Current approaches to have a system that does the latter are stuck because of the huge costs associated with building a smart road infrastructure (digging up the road and putting magnetic coils beneath the pavement, sending all signals to data collection centers and then on to a centralized traffic management system which, in turn, sends everything back to the cars). In our proposal the vehicles themselves collect and distribute information about the traffic conditions they are experiencing to other interested vehicles.

To illustrate the potential use of the Trafficopter we include the following example: Let's say someone travels from Boston towards New York. His best source of information about traffic in front of him is the vehicle that is travelling in the opposite direction, from New York to Boston. It knows exactly what is happening further up the road on the opposite lanes. The first vehicle queries about traffic conditions near New York. If the other vehicle doesn't know how to answer the query, it propagates it to other vehicles until somebody responds or the query dies out.

An important feature of the architecture is the use of a *communication network built from nodes with dynamic topology*, which is itself not stationary but mobile (the vehicles are moving). On a layer above this virtual network, message objects are moving from node to node. These objects are unique in that they know their physical as well as their network position unlike conventional computer networks where the IP address is not related to the physical location. Moreover, instead of the nodes of the network (vehicle) "routing" the message objects, the message objects do that on their own, when they instantiate themselves in a node, behaving as "active packets". When a node broadcasts a message object, copies of this message object get instantiated into a number of different nodes in close proximity with the broadcaster. Unlike an IP packet, the different message objects decide for themselves whether to propagate further, when to expire and they try to minimize the number of hops between origin and destination (thus maximizing network efficiency).

As mentioned above each car is equipped with a commercial GPS receiver for acquiring position, speed and direction and a wireless transceiver for receiving and transmitting data to other cars. All the nodes (we are using the terms vehicle, network node and agent to describe the Trafficopter device that is installed inside each vehicle.) that comprise our system are equivalent and each broadcasts its information on a one-to-many basis. The main advantages of the proposed architecture are the following:

- Very cheap technology: the cost of the car-mounted device is not more that $200 in mass production.
- Car manufacturers can incorporate the system into their new car models without the need of an expensive supporting infrastructure.
- Not all carmakers need to have the system. Our experiments show that even if 25% of the vehicles are equipped with the system, the architecture performance is high.

This paper is organized as follows: in the next section we introduce our motivation and discuss related work. Section 3 analyses our implementation and discusses our experiment, and section 4 summarizes the paper and provides future research directions.

2 Motivation and Related Work

In recent years there have been a number of attempts to offer on-line traffic related information by combining cellular telephony with the Global Positioning System (GPS) technology. Most eminent among them is perhaps General Motors OnStar [13], a system that constantly communicates with several satellites orbiting the earth. The system triangulates the car's position, retains the information and, at the driver's request, transmits the vehicle's location to the OnStar Center via a cellular phone. An advisor at the OnStar center can send assistance if it is called for or use the cellular phone to guide the driver to his or her destination.

In late November 1997, a consortium of hi-tech companies in (IBM, DELCO, Netscape and Sun) have announced the Network Vehicle [11], which according to the respective press release during the COMDEX where a prototype was exhibited, aims at offering Web access to drivers and passengers inside a car through specially constructed panels and head-up displays. A similar prototype presented in October from the same initiative with the collaboration of Daimler-Benz Research and Technology Center comprised a set of computers in the trunk and was connecting to the Internet via an AT&T wireless digital cellular phone and a Metricom wireless modem. The system is briefly described to promise integration of voice-recognition for extra safety, ability to allow car mechanics to diagnose faults from afar, access to travel, weather and business information along with regular net-surfing and provision of games for the kids. Customized traffic updates and navigation help are also mentioned but the details given at the time of writing are geared towards the display of the data through custom-made browsing facilities and not on the actual collection of the traffic data.

Unlike on-board computer systems like Onstar, or similar products marketed in Europe by Philips, which link drivers to proprietary navigation wireless networks, the system we propose does not depend on any central authority, guaranteeing privacy. Also, it does not depend on external or internal infrastructure, other than the existence of a palmtop system to host the software and support the display. Although we use Microsoft Windows CE, during development, all our software is deployed in Java so as to achieve platform independence. Ideally, one should be able to use our navigation software whether he/she is using Windows CE, or any other personal-digital assistant (PDA). On the other hand, systems like the one proposed by the aforementioned consortium involve extensive interconnection with the mechanics of the actual vehicle a development that will require a great deal of time for standards to be established by automobile manufacturers. In our proposal a possible production cost, will be so low that will allow the construction and sale of add-on modules irrespective of the car make.

The majority of the research efforts in Traffic Coordination Systems evolve around efficient and optimize timing of traffic lights in order to maximize the average throughput of cars at major intersections in a given city setting using a centralized traffic control center. The work we are describing herein complements and augments the above-mentioned goal in the sense that it provides the centralized traffic control systems with a cheap way of collecting information. On top of that it provides the individual car drivers with information on the traffic condition of the road in front of them. It is important to realize that once we have a given number of vehicles operating on the road infrastructure, essentially the vehicles *are* the infrastructure and can be used as data collection mechanisms. A lot of research has been conducted on the area of automated traffic management and centralized traffic data acquisition. Traffic prediction patterns [17] and network flow theory [1] are recent examples. On the data acquisition frontier, sensors developed include sound-based systems [3],[5], laser-based systems [12] and vision-based systems [7]. Different intelligent transportation vehicle applications include data transmission models through cellular channels [19] but unlike this work have to rely on channels.

A very popular system in the DAI community DVMT [10] has a similar scope, and was used for conducting a series of experiments into a variety of DAI-related subjects, like approximation [4] and scheduling [6]. DVMT provides a collection of identical blackboard systems and its domain is the monitoring and interpretation of data from a set of distributed sensors.

In terms of network routing, the most common approaches to routing include link-state routing and source path routing. A typical example of link-state routing networks is the Internet that is based on regular IP routing [16]. In source-path routing the header of the message contains information of all the nodes through which it has to go through. A typical source-path routing protocol is UUCP.

3   Implementation and Experiments

3.1   The Simulator

The MIcroscopic Traffic SIMulator (MITSIM) has been developed by Qi Yang [18] for modeling traffic flows in networks involving advanced traffic control and route guidance systems. MITSIM represents networks at the lane level and simulates movements of individual vehicles using car-following, lane changing, and traffic signal response logic. Probabilistic route choice models are used to capture drivers' route choice decisions in the presence of real time traffic information provided by route guidance systems. The major elements of MITSIM are: network, traffic controls and surveillance sensors, incidents, travel demand, vehicle routing, and vehicle movements. The traffic simulation model is iterations of functions at specified frequencies (time-based) or when certain events occur (event-based). We are running MITSIM on an 8-processor SGI Onyx with 1GB of RAM. We simulate part of Boston area's new Central Artery and Amsterdam's major highway map and traffic conditions with around 4,000 vehicles.

3.2   Traffic data

Our objective is to have all the vehicles' agents know what the traffic conditions are in a metropolitan area by using data collected by other vehicles' agents. Each vehicle agent broadcasts a message object with its local data information (position, speed, direction). A set of other agents in nearby vehicles receives that message object. If all of them propagated each object they received our network would be very quickly saturated due to the exponential explosion of message objects. If we take into account the same-frequency communication model we are using (all vehicles share the same radio frequency: just one can broadcast at any given time in a given radius), it is evident that in the case of full propagation of all message objects, the network congestion would be eminent.

As stressed above, effort must be put into limiting what information each individual vehicle is going to transmit. We have different types of message objects:

- Beacon-like individual message objects, which are transmitted at regular time intervals by each vehicle. These are the data intrinsic to the vehicle itself (GPS_Position_X, GPS_Position_Y, GPS_Speed, GPS_Direction)
- Centroid message objects, which are again transmitted in regular intervals but contain information about a group of vehicles moving on the same direction with the vehicle that transmits them. Any given vehicle receives a number of individual message position objects (like the one described directly above) from a number of different vehicles. It filters out those that are not travelling in the same general direction that it is, and uses the rest to generate average data of "clusters" of vehicles (Centroid_Position_X, Centroid_Position_Y, Centroid_Speed, Centroid_Direction)
- Query message objects, which are requests for information about traffic conditions at specific points. Unlike the above two, the agents inside each vehicle decide when and where to send query message objects in order to fill-in spatial traffic knowledge gaps and find optimal vehicle paths from the point of origin to the point of destination.

3.3   Map: Grid-layered data

We divide the whole space of our map into a grid. Our vehicle is positioned in the center of the grid. The resolution of the grid is high near the vehicle and drops as it moves away from it. There are certain areas away from the vehicle with high resolution and these are in general areas critical between the point of origin and the point of destination. The data from the grid are superimposed on a map. The vehicles store each message object they receive into their cache and place it on the proper point on the grid. If they receive a more recent packet, they update that grid point. A half-time decay function of the traffic data on the grid is essential for refreshing the grid data.

3.4   Automatic Data Collection: Query Message Objects

In order to sample faster the traffic conditions on coordinates along its path, a vehicle in addition to *passively* listening to other vehicles' transmissions is able to *actively* request the support of other vehicles. Here is a scenario of how the querying system works:

In Figure 1, the vehicle in position A wants to go to its destination, Z. In order to find the fastest way to get there, the vehicle needs to know the traffic conditions in a bunch of points throughout the city (marked by asterisks) and evaluate the optimal path for the vehicle. Let's say that our vehicle wants to find out about position E in the map. It sends out a query request in the following form:

- (0) Unique ID
- (a) Originator Vehicle Position, Speed, Direction
- (b) Originator's Timestamp
- (c) Requested Position, Direction
- (d) Last Propagator Position
- (e) Last Propagator Timestamp
- (f) Hops Counter
- (g) Total Number of Hops

where (0), (a), (b), (c) and (g) are the initial data. (d), (e) and (f) are filled-in by other vehicles that propagate the information.

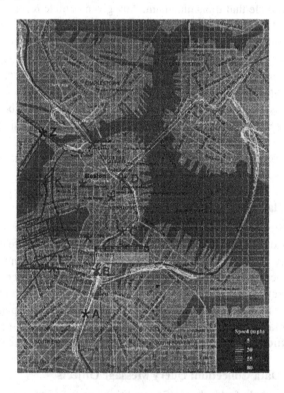

Figure 1   Figure 1A: Traffic data superimposed on a Boston Area Map.

Let's say that the vehicle at position A sends out a request. Vehicles south of A receive the request but ignore it since the vehicle at A is closer to E than they are. A vehicle a bit north of A listens to the request, realizes that it is closer to E and since it doesn't know the traffic conditions at position E, propagates it. The same happens with the vehicle in position C and D. A vehicle near position E receives the request and sends back a reply (i.e. at position E and direction North the average speed is 45 km/h.) A vehicle south of position E receives the request and propagates it south until it reaches the general area of where vehicle A was, adjusted for its new position. The vehicle that originated the query sends out a "received" message to indicate that it has its answer and that there should be no more propagation.

In case a vehicle out of range doesn't receive the cancellation notice and continues to propagate the query or the answer, there are two safeguard measures: the request dies off after a certain number of hops or after a specific time period. Note that the reply has been propagated through the main artery to position A and that all the vehicles on that highway know the traffic conditions at point E. Not all the vehicles that receive a request have to reply (more than one replies for redundancy purposes), but all of them saved the information into their grid and can use it later on, in case another query about E arises.

The query system is based on a stack of messages (a simple mailbox) present at each vehicle. When a vehicle receives a query, it appends the message to its stack and waits for a period of time. The waiting period before propagating the query is a function of its distance between itself and the last propagator of the message: the larger the distance, the shorter the delay. The aim is to minimize the amount of hops between origin and destination (i.e. increase the distance between two hops) as well as the "collisions" of transmitted queries propagated at the same time by everybody that received them.

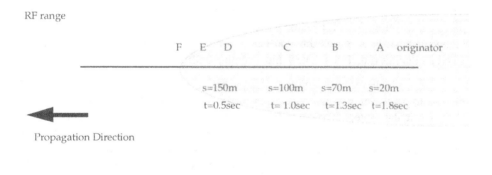

Figure 2   Hop minimization in a query object using positioning data

We described above that we don't want all vehicles to reply to a specific query. On the other hand, we don't want just one vehicle to reply/propagate a query because the message might be lost. In the future the number of the vehicles that re-propagate a query might be adaptive depending on the congestion of the network, but in the current implementation we chose to have each message propagated by at most three vehicles. Let's take the case where vehicle B originates a query on the traffic conditions ahead of F and vehicles A,C,D,E and F receive it (see Figure 2).

- Vehicle A ignores it because as mentioned above is farther away than the originator vehicle (B).
- Vehicles C,D,E and F all receive the same query and append a message to their stack.
- Vehicle F goes off and propagates the message first because it has the greater distance from the last propagator (which happens to be the originator) of the query
- Vehicles C,D and E receive the propagated query and now they all have the original query and the propagated query messages on their stack.
- Before vehicle F replied, the other three vehicles were planning on replying by each waiting for an amount of seconds (let's say t_C, t_D and t_E) inversely related to their distance from the last propagator.
- Now that vehicle F replied, C,D and E register the fact that somebody propagated the query they received (because both messages in their stack have the same ID.)
- Vehicle E goes off and re-propagates the query, and vehicles C and D now have three messages in their stack, all for the same query.
- After vehicle D propagates the query as well, vehicle C has four messages about the same query (the original and three propagations), so it realizes that already three vehicles propagated the query and it should not bother: it proceeds by deleting all four messages from its stack without taking any action.

3.5   Cached Data

If we review the process above, we would notice that a lot of bandwidth could have been saved if there was an efficient caching mechanism [8]. In our specific example, a car traveling from E towards A would know exactly what was happening on the highway ahead of A, on northbound lane. So A's request wouldn't have to be propagated all that far if there was one vehicle coming up from the opposite direction.

If a vehicle receives a more recent packet, it must certainly update the relevant map point. However, a weighting system tracks for the importance of that information to the particular route, otherwise we might had constant updating of irrelevant information. This leads to an architecture that resembles a multilevel hierarchical priority queue with the addition of information expiration along a half-time decay function. In other words, the system decides how up-to-date a piece of traffic information is based on factors like the importance of the particular route to the vehicle's path from origin to destination, the time that the information is kept in the cache, etc. [15],[9],[2]

3.6   RF Radio Communication

We are using short-range (~200m), low-power RF transceivers for communication between the vehicles' agents. In an ideal scenario, the effective range of the transceivers would be a perfect circle around the vehicle. However, due to practical limitations (namely buildings on the sides of the majority of urban streets), the real range area looks more like an ellipsis. In special cases, like major cross-sections the range area looks like a cross, with the remote edges extending along the crossing streets. The major characteristics of our network are the following:

- Low-power and limited range: Since the nodes are transmitting at the same frequency and the network is quite dense, we cannot afford to have long-range broadcast transceivers
- Position-based routing: The system uses only positioning information to forward its packets. The packets know their physical location and decide where to go next based solely on that. Since any node communicates only with its immediate neighbors, there can be no central controlling hub, and the burden of network controls falls upon individual nodes. Each node must play an equal part in routing messages and maintaining network state.

3.7 Experimental Results

We conducted a number of experiments to assess the validity of our architecture. We tried to address issues of overall feasibility and investigate the performance of agents sub-components like the cache and the hop minimizer mechanisms.

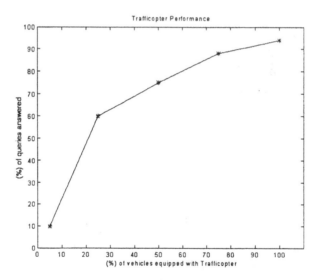

Figure 3   Trafficopter Query Performance

Figure 3 shows how the performance of the system improves when the percentage of vehicles equipped with the system increases. Trafficopter is able to perform quite well even in the case where just a quarter of the vehicles were Trafficopter-aware (60% of queries were answered). In our current implementation, when all the vehicles are equipped with Trafficopter, 94% of all the queries posed are answered. The above-mentioned experiment doesn't take into account the density of the vehicles in the region. In an urban setting the density is quite high and this enhances the performance of the system. In a low-traffic highway setting we believe that the performance curve would fall off considerably. We are currently conducting experiments where we correlate the percentage of queries answered, the percentage of the vehicles equipped with trafficopter and the density of the vehicles (3D chart). In parallel, we are trying to obtain a finer analysis of the system performance curve, especially in the small-percentage boundary cases. Figure 4a shows the performance of the traffic information caching mechanism. The vast majority of the vehicle queries are answered by other vehicles, without the query message object to have to reach its destination. We are currently performing experiments to better understand spatial patterns of cache hits and assess partial query propagation effects.

Figure 4b reports results from experiments on the validity of the objects "hop-minimizing" mechanism. When this technique is applied, the number of hops an object needs to reach its destination is substantially lower. This increases the bandwidth of our communications network. This is a representative result from our experiments pool. The actual number of hops shown in the figure varies depending on the size of the network, the average distance between each vehicle's origin and destination and other simulation factors.

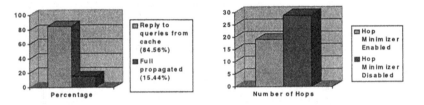

Figure 4   Initial experiments of vehicle cache performance (left) and Hop minimizing technique (right) in Trafficopter simulations

4   Future Work and Summary

In terms of future simulator development we would like to equip traffic lights with passive trafficopter receivers so we can assess the effect on traffic flow. At the same time, we are trying to use the same testbed for different types of architectures, where message objects are going to be the focus of the system. If we view each message object as a virus that tries to infect all the "un-infected" vehicle agents with its traffic information on a specific location, we could reach the same goal (traffic awareness) but from a completely different standpoint. We would like to implement and evaluate both approaches and try to find their strong and weak points.

In another set of experiments we are currently performing, the RF tranceiver range of the tranceivers is variable depending on the number of the Trafficopter-aware vehicles and the density of the vehicles. If the number of density of vehicles increases, the range goes down, in order to increase bandwidth. If on the other hand there are not many vehicles on the road, the tranceiver range increases.

We described Trafficopter, a multiagent system that collects, processes and distributes traffic conditions information in a completely decentralized and distributed fashion. The proposed architecture enables the agents to use message objects in order to request and propagate information about traffic. Results show that our hypotheses are valid and that such a distributed solution is feasible

5 References

[1] Ahuja R., Magnanti T, and Orlin J. (1993). *Network Flows: Theory, Algorithms, and Applications*. Prentice Hall, Englewood Cliffs, New Jersey, 1993.

[2] Bodin F., Seznec A. (1994), *Cache organization influence on loop blocking*, IRISA Internal Report, PI-803, 1994

[3] Chem S., Sun Z. and Bridge B (1997). Automatic traffic monitoringby intelligent sound detection. In *Proceedings of the 1997 IEEE Conference on Intelligent Transportation Systems*.

[4] Decker K., Lesser, V. and Whitehair R. (1990). Extending a blackboard architecture for approcimate processing. *The Journal of Real-Time Systems*, 2(1/2):47-79.

[5] Forren J. and Jaarsma D. (1997). Traffic monitoring by tire noise. In *Proceedings of the 1997 IEEE Conference on Intelligent Transportation Systems*.

[6] Garvey, A. and Lesser, V. (1993). Design-to-time real-time schediling. *IEEE Transactions on Systems, Man and Cybernetics*.

[7] Hancock T., Judd S., Novak C., Ricard S. (1997). Automatic vehicle location using cameras. In *Proceedings of the 1997 IEEE Conference on Intelligent Transportation Systems*.

[8] Handy, J. (1993). *The Cache Memory*, Academic Press.

[9] Hossain, A., Marudarajan A., and Manzoul M. (1991). *Fuzzy Replacement Algorithm for Cache Memory, Cybernetics and Systems*, v 22, pp. 733-746

[10] Lesser V. and Corkill D.(1983). The distributed vehicle monitoring testbed. *AI Magazine*, 4(3):63-109.

[11] NetVeh, 1997, The Network Vehicle, http://www.alphaworks.ibm.com/networkvehicle.

[12] Nishizawa S., Cheok K., Young W. and Zhao W. (1997) Traffic monitor using two multiple-beam laser radars. In *Proceedings of the 1997 IEEE Conference on Intelligent Transportation Systems*.

[13] Onstar (1997) General Motors Smart Car http://www.onstar.com

[14] Poor, R. (1997) Hyphos: A self-organizing, wireless network. Master's thesis, Massachusetts Institute of Technology.

[15] Przybylski, S. A., (1990). *Cache and Memory Hierarchy Design*, Morgan Kaufmann.

[16] Tanenbaum, A. (1996). *Computer Networks*. Prentice-Hall, NJ, 1996

[17] von Toorenburg J, der Linden R., van Velzen B.(1996). Predictive control in traffic management. Final Report AV-2468, Ministry of Transport, Public Works and Water Management, The Netherlands, 1996.

[18] Yang and Koutsopoulos (1996). *A microscopic traffic simulator for evaluation of dynamic traffic management systems*. Transportation Research C, 4 (3):-129, 1996.

[19] Zhao, Y. (1997) Efficient and reliable data transmission for cellular and GPS-based mayday systems, In *Proceedings of the 1997 IEEE Conference on Intelligent Transportation Systems*.

Agent-Supported Information Retrieval for Tracking and Tracing

Dominik Deschner, Oliver Hofmann,
Stefan Reinheimer, and Freimut Bodendorf

University of Erlangen-Nuremberg
Department of Information Systems
Lange Gasse 20, 90403 Nuremberg, Germany
Dominik.Deschner@wiso.uni-erlangen.de
Oliver.Hofmann@wiso.uni-erlangen.de
Stefan.Reinheimer@wiso.uni-erlangen.de
Freimut.Bodendorf@wiso.uni-erlangen.de
Tel.: +49 911 5302-450 , Fax.: +49 911 5302-379

Abstract. In recent years interorganizational communication and coordination have relied increasingly on the exchange of EDIFACT-messages. This is especially true for the logistics sector. In order for the sender to keep control over the forwarder's proper delivery process, status messages prove that certain milestones have been achieved. Taking into account that only a very small number of shipments face problems leading to a delay in delivery, this principle of pushed information causes a large amount of unnecessary EDIFACT-messages. In addition, many forwarders already allow their customers to request status information via WWW. A software agent based concept is presented to cope with the problem described, taking advantage of the WWW-services provided. The system called ECTL-Monitor (Electronic Commerce Transport Logistics) was developed in cooperation with a large company sending more than 10 million shipments per year. The main idea of the concept is to leave data of the transport process on the forwarders' computer systems and to access these remote system when necessary. On demand software agents collect status information of all forwarders involved in the transportation chain, which very often includes up to four different logistics service companies.

1 Introduction

In recent years interorganizational communication and coordination have relied increasingly on the exchange of EDIFACT-messages. Unfortunately, the design and implementation of EDIFACT connections between companies are quite expensive as long as EDIFACT interfaces have not penetrated the market completely. Therefore, an EDIFACT connection is affordable for only a limited number of long term partnerships [1, p.14].

In contrary, Electronic Commerce is directed to reduce transaction costs and – further on – to create the possibility of short term cooperation even on a single transaction base. Therefore, Electronic Commerce typically is not based on EDIFACT, but on more flexible Internet solutions [1, p.129].

In the logistics sector, in order for the sender to keep control over the forwarder's proper delivery process, status messages prove that certain milestones have been achieved. Taking into account that only a very small number of shipments face problems leading to a delay in delivery, this principle of pushed information causes a large amount of unnecessary EDIFACT-messages. Besides this, small forwarders hardly provide EDIFACT interfaces, but are extremely important for complete coverage of the logistics chain. As a result, the need for a system available for all forwarders is prevalent. Considering the new opportunities of the Internet and the fact that many forwarders – even smaller ones – already allow their customers to request status information via WWW, the platform for a cheap, reliable, and open system for all participants in the logistics chain seems to be the Internet.

In section 2 the problem and the concept are discussed in more detail. In section 3 an architecture, which will be implemented in the logistics department of a large company, using this concept is shown. In section 4 some aspects of further developments and further research are presented.

2   Tracking and Tracing in Interorganizational Logistics

Tracking (getting up to the minute information about the whereabouts of a certain load) and Tracing (evaluate the chain over a longer period) become more and more important in business since companies see the opportunity to offer value added services to their customers. For example, if a load is damaged and information is available without delay, the sender can resend the product by express. The customer will not notice that there have been any problems. If resending is impossible, the customer can at least be informed on time and reassign his processes. Both actions result in more customer satisfaction which in turn can increase the company's competitive advantage.

Having noticed the advantages of Tracking and Tracing, one faces several problems obtaining the relevant information which will be briefly shown in section 2.1. In section 2.2 an agent-based concept to cope with those problems will be discussed.

2.1   Problem

Due to the heterogeneous structure of the logistics chain (see Fig. 1, [5, p. 13]) senders and customers have difficulties obtaining information about the status of the transportation process. Not only are there different senders, but also several forwarders for a single transport [4, pp. 113].

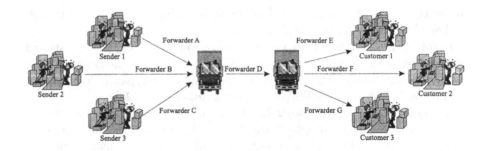

Fig. 1. Logistics Chain

One major problem is the fact that customers, senders, and forwarders are using different access keys for the same physical load in their databases. Therefore, it is necessary to transform keys in order to find the corresponding data in different databases. In addition to this problem, there is an even greater obstacle in the fact that depending on the request different access keys refer to different items in the entity relationship model (see Fig. 2). Information usually is obtained on the transportational level (e.g. scanning the packages at the forwarders' warehouse), whereas the search usually is done on the administrative level (e.g. searching for a customer order). Since there are several n:m relationships, the search for a delivery note of the sender can refer to a number of packages in the databases of the forwarders.

Generally, status information is relevant only if the package status is negative, e. g. the package is damaged or running late or a customer inquires about the scheduled arrival of his order. A negative status occurs about 3-5 times in a 100. Therefore, pushing the information to the sender or to the customer seems to be inappropriate due to the amount of "unnecessary" information which is transmitted. Pulling the information on request seems to be more adequate.

2.2 Concept

A new concept is introduced, where Tracking and Tracing is based on a pull principle, i.e., retrieving information out of decentralized databases. But in case of lost or damaged goods an exception message should be pushed to the sender.

Using the forwarders' databases for search activities requires on the one hand knowledge which forwarders to ask and on the other hand methods to transform the request from the context of the questioner to the context of the specific forwarder. Furthermore, the answer has to be translated vice versa.

Forwarder Identification Every delivery note describes goods that have to be routed from a sender (e.g. factory) to a receiver (e.g. customer). Typically, this transport task is divided into segments (see Fig. 1), resulting in several transportation orders for different forwarders.

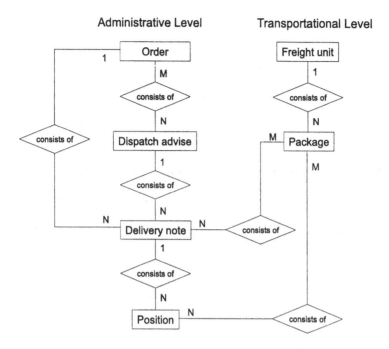

Fig. 2. Entity Relationship Model of Physical and Information Entities

In our case, the implementing company is using a static assignment of forwarders to geographical routes, so the identification of the forwarders of a specific logistics chain can be reduced to accessing master files manually entered by the office staff. These master files provide the sequence of the forwarders according to source and destination of the transportation.

Context Transformation The aim of Tracking and Tracing is to retrieve information about the location, the schedule of transportation, and the reasons for delayed or lost goods. Depending on the questioner, there are different ways to specify the goods of interest ("ontology"). The customer deals with its own customer order number, during the production process typically several additional references arise, the dispatcher places package numbers on barcode labels, forwarders create their own order numbers, etc. Tracking and Tracing of goods takes place in every listed context, so within the specification of a Tracking and Tracing request all types of references can occur.

Information retrieval in forwarders' databases must be based on specific forwarder keys exclusively. So, each Tracking and Tracing request needs a context transformation supplied by a cross reference database.

EDIFACT messages are still the backbone of information interchange. Even in the near future, forwarders will be put in charge by a DESADV message and accept the order by replying one or more IFCSUM messages. Within these messages different references are fixed. So, these message are used to fill the cross reference database assigning references of the forwarders to delivery notes and customer order numbers, etc.

Context transformation includes the risk of semantic inaccuracy. Especially the use of n:m relationships within the transformation path weakens the precision of the request and should be avoided (e.g. a retrieval based on a customer order number leading to several delivery notes which are compiled with other delivery notes to one shipment by a forwarder). While different transformation paths are possible sometimes, a suitable one must be identified.

Because transformation paths must be chosen deliberately, a formal representation of the data model itself with all relationships is part of the cross reference database.

2.3 Pulling and Pushing of Information

The widely available access to forwarders' databases via WWW meet the needs of pulling the information. Here, an easy to implement interface is specified based on already existing html pages. As a result, connecting even smaller forwarders is affordable.

Lost, damaged or delayed goods trigger an exception leading to an email message to the sender. Since the forwarder is in charge of providing those exception messages, a proactive messaging system based on forwarders' databases is implemented.

3 System Architecture

In this section the system architecture will be discussed in more detail. In section 3.1 the different components are introduced. Section 3.2 deals with agent interaction and in section 3.3 interfaces are shown.

3.1 System Components

A system of cooperating agents [10, p. 57] is designed to meet the requirements of distributed information retrieval (see Fig. 3, "distributed agent" approach [7]).

Three different types of agents (for an overview on the topic of software agents see [2, 3, 8]) can be identified:

- A user agent (UA) is located on the PC of the questioner. The user agent processes the user input, validates the entered requests, and assigns each request to a request agent. The results are transmitted back to the user agent to be displayed within an interactive graphical user interface. Because of the need for global acceptance, the user interface can be customized to the language of the user. Also the information itself will be translated to the user's language.

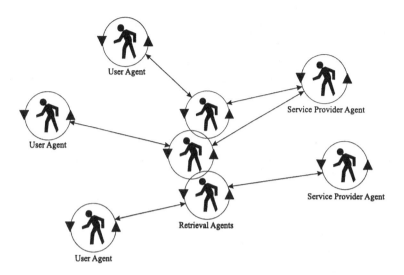

Fig. 3. Cooperating and Communicating Agents

- A retrieval agent (RA) is assigned to every request. Its lifetime is limited to the closure of the underlying request by the questioner. During its lifetime the RA is responsible for coordinating access to master files, interaction with the user agent, and assignment of decentralized retrieval tasks to service provider agents. The RAs are running on a dedicated server with fast access to the relevant master files and appropriate bandwidth to the Intranet/Internet.
- Each forwarder runs its own service provider agent (SA). A SA can be customized to the specific abilities of the forwarder with respect to both request and answer. In order to reduce communication load on the internet, the service provider agent should run on the forwarder's system. This allows the SA to handle the messages based on exception statuses like lost or damaged goods.

The procurement of information is based on an incremental approach. In a first step only information available at local master files is presented. Second, service provider agents at the affected forwarders are contacted for details (see Fig. 4).

In some cases an exceptional situation arises at a forwarder (goods are lost, delayed or damaged). The service provider agent recognizes this event and informs the sender by e-mail (step 3 in Fig. 4).

3.2 Software Agent Interaction

The agent interaction is shown in Fig. 5. Starting out with the request being sent from the UA to the RA (step 1), next steps are initiated: The retrieval agent forwards the request to the SA of the master file (step 2) which returns

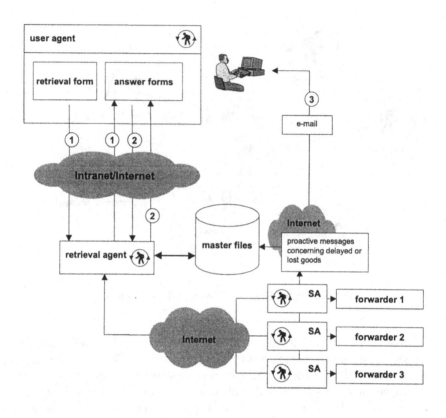

Fig. 4. System Architecture

data about the relevant forwarders (step 3). This information is sent to the UA (step 4) which presents the results to the user. Further information about specific forwarders can be obtained by repeating those steps (steps 5-8). The difference to step 2-3 lies in the fact that the requests are being sent to the SAs of the forwarders not to the SA of the master file. If requests are sent to the forwarders, the RA will convert the relevant data obtained from the master file to the context of the forwarder.

3.3 System Interfaces

There are three major interfaces to consider. First, the user interface, which allows the user to send his inquiries to the system. Second, the data base interface, which allows the retrieval agent to obtain necessary information about the forwarders of the logistics chain. Third, the interface to the forwarders, which allows the service provider agents to send a request to the forwarders' database and

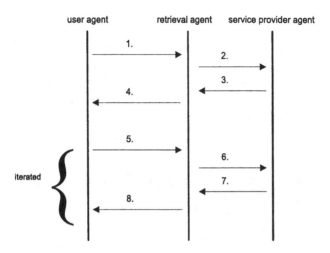

Fig. 5. Interaction Diagram

to receive the answer. Considering that the difference between the second and third interface is based only on the transferred information from the database to the agent, the in-house interface will be treated as a forwarders interface.

User Interface The user group of the Tracking and Tracing system consists of senders (e.g. staff), receivers (e.g. customers), and process controllers. This group is globally distributed and not willing to install and handle a dedicated software product. The 'smartness' of the user agent approach requires an active component on the retrieval client, so the usage of JAVA-applets within a web browser is almost compulsory.

Forwarder Interface The forwarder interface is technically based on a http connection between a service provider agent and a web server run by the forwarder. There are two services the forwarder's web server has to provide: a mailbox for requests and answer pages in a specific format.

The mailbox for requests is realized as an CGI interface with URL encoded request information (GET method) [6]. Structure and syntax of the request string correspond to an Extended Backus Naur Form (EBNF) description given to the forwarders.

The answer pages delivered as a result to a CGI request are also described in EBNF. In order to achieve a html page readable by agents, additional comments have to be inserted into the page tagging the information. Thus the effort of the forwarders can be reduced by reusing existing web pages.

4 Conclusions

The implementation of an agent based system is still quite unfamiliar in the business world. Therefore a phased realization concept was chosen. During the starting phase, all agent-oriented elements are kept local at the cooperating company, the search in the forwarders' databases is limited to a full context search (no joker letters allowed), and external customers cannot do the inquiries on their own (intranet solution, see Fig. 6 and Fig. 7).

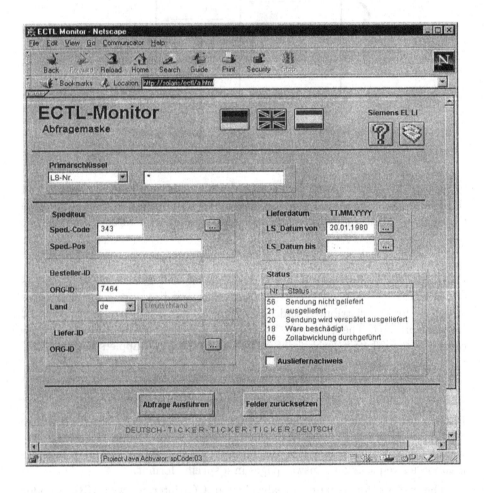

Fig. 6. Retrieval Form

In the subsequent phases a user concept will be introduced to allow customers to inquire on their own via Internet, to offer user profiles for widely used inquiries, and to allow different modes of inquiry for different users. Also a decentralization of the SAs is planned in order to have an even faster and proactive way to get

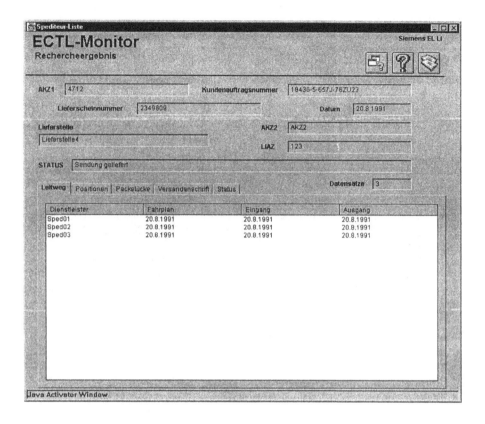

Fig. 7. Example of an Answer Form

the relevant information. In cooperation with the forwarders partially qualified inquiries within the forwarders' databases (e.g. for Tracing information) will be provided.

During analysis and design, the agent technology seems to be adequate to communicate certain aspects of a distributed system design to users who are not familiar with concepts of information system design.

The focus of the system discussed above was to offer an easy and inexpensive way to get Tracking and Tracing information for one company. The use of the Internet and the distributed databases of the forwarders offer the possibility to decentralize more business data, which can be retrieved in the same way. Besides that, the system allows other senders to develop a system which could use the forwarder's interface for automated information retrieval. Moreover, the system allows to adapt to dynamic changes in the logistics chain, i. e., the sender does not know all partners in the chain. This in turn would require the RA to find the relevant SAs for a given transport, which means, even more intelligence [9] on the RA's side.

As a result, further research is necessary with respect to those topics.

References

1. N.R. Adam and Y. Yesha. *Electronic Commerce: Current Research Issues and Applications.* Springer, Berlin, 1996.
2. W. Brenner. *Intelligente Softwareagenten.* Springer, Berlin, 1998.
3. F.-C. Cheong. *Internet Agents: Spiders, Wanderers, Brokers and Bots.* New Riders, Indianapolis, 1996.
4. F. Dordowsky and P. Kampmann. EURO-LOG, ein vernetztes Informationsverarbeitungssystem zur Unterstützung der unternehmensübergreifenden Transportlogistik. *Wirtschaftsinformatik,* pages 113–121, 1997.
5. G. Ihde. *Transport, Verkehr, Logistik, Gesamtwirtschaftliche Aspekte und einzelwirtschaftliche Handhabung.* Vahlen, München, 1991.
6. G. McComb. *Web Programming Languages.* Chichester Wiley, New York, 1997.
7. T. Mullen and M. P. Wellman. Some Issues in the Design of Market-Oriented Agents. In M. Wooldridge, J. P. Müller, and M. Tambe, editors, *Intelligent Agents II.* Springer, 1996.
8. J.-P. Müller. *The Design of Intelligent Agents.* Springer, Berlin, 1996.
9. F. v. Martial. *Coordinating Plans of Autonomous Agents.* Springer, Berlin, 1992.
10. H. Wedekind, editor. *Verteilte Systeme.* BI Wissenschaftsverlag, Mannheim, 1994.

The Dynamics
of the UMDL Service Market Society

Edmund H. Durfee, Tracy Mullen, Sunju Park,
José M. Vidal, and Peter Weinstein*

AI Laboratory, EECS Department, University of Michigan
1101 Beal Avenue, Ann Arbor, MI 48109-2110
{durfee, mullen, boxenju, jmvidal, peterw}@umich.edu

Abstract. One of our goals when building the University of Michigan
Digital Library (UMDL) has been to prototype an architecture that can
continually reconfigure itself as users, contents, and services come and
go. We have worked toward this goal by developing a multi-agent infrastructure with agents that buy and sell services from each other using our
commerce and communication protocols. We refer to the services and
protocols offered by this infrastructure as the Service Market Society
(SMS). Within the SMS, agents are able to find, work with, and even
try to outsmart each other, as each agent attempts to accomplish the
tasks for which it was created. When we open the door to decentralized
decision-making among self-interested agents, there is a risk that the
system will degenerate into chaos. In this paper, we describe the protocols, services, and agent abilities embedded in the SMS infrastructure
that combat such chaos while permitting flexibility, extensibility, and
scalability of the system.

1 Introduction

A library serves a community of users by making available information content
and services that are valued by that community. In a digital library, the information content and services are electronically available, and the user communities
are no longer geographically defined. Realizing a digital library therefore includes difficulties in digitizing contents, computerizing services, and networking
together users, services and contents. A tremendous amount of work has gone
into all of these areas, and while many challenges remain, increasing numbers of
digital libraries with interoperating components are appearing.

But even as these difficulties are being overcome, the result can well be an
overwhelming tangle of possible information sources without the structure and
selectivity that renders a library navigable. In other words, if the administration
of a traditional library is challenging, the administration of a digital library can
border on impossible due to the magnitude of content and services available,
the rate of change in what is available, the size of a user population that is not
bounded by physical proximity, and the evolving nature of that population.

* The authors are listed alphabetically. This work was supported, in part, by the
NSF/DARPA/NASA Digital Library Initiative under grant CERA IRI-9411287.

The focus of this paper is on meeting this challenge. That is, in this paper we take for granted a rich network of interoperating information providers, consumers, and services. We also assume that it is impractical to marshal all of the information sources and services to address every information need for every user. Choices must be made, such that services are applied where they are expected to yield the most benefit. Traditionally, these choices are made by administrators who: identify, characterize, register, and track a user community; seek out and include the content that will benefit that community; and provide the most valuable services for tasks such as organizing, searching, abstracting, and disseminating the content.

Because we see the pace of library evolution increasing in the digital age, we instead embrace an alternative approach where we want to move as much of the administrative overhead into the digital infrastructure as possible. Rather than requiring frequent and costly intervention by human librarians, the library should evolve guided by the policies dictated to the infrastructure. The infrastructure should encourage:

- **Flexibility**: It should be able to embody a wide variety of policies to realize different flavors of information economies (public libraries, corporate libraries, university libraries, personal libraries,...)

- **Extensibility**: Providers and consumers of information goods and services should have incentives to join the information economy and be able to find their counterparts.

- **Scalability**: As the plethora of users, goods, and services grows, the underlying, computerized administration of the library should not bog down.

- **Robustness:** The intrastructure should support resistance against any agent manipulating the system to its own benefit and at the expense of other agents.

Toward this end, the University of Michigan Digital Library (UMDL) is structured as a collection of agents that can buy and sell services from each other using our commerce and communications infrastructure. To many, the concept of commerce in a library is heresy, and conjures images of library patrons having to pay as they go. Before continuing, therefore, let us briefly dispel this misunderstanding. Treating a library as an information economy provides us with a well-studied framework for making decentralized decisions about the allocation of the limited information goods and services that are available. Poor allocation decisions can lead to users receiving poor service, or none at all! Yet, users need not necessarily be aware of the underlying economic decisions being made, just as they are generally shielded from the decisions library administrators must make as they weigh the pros and cons of subscribing to a particular monograph series versus hiring another reference librarian. Thus, in many cases, users will be unaware of the underlying infrastructure, though if it is working well they will reap the benefits.

Indeed, our initial agent infrastructure forms the core of the UMDL system that has been deployed to several schools in southeastern Michigan, where it is used by hundreds of students daily. For the most part, the services used by the students have been selected and added to the deployed UMDL system by project members, and with only hundreds of students performing similar tasks, issues of flexibility, scale, extensibility, and robustness have not been stressed. This has allowed our research efforts to begin developing answers to these issues and experimenting with our answers before they have become critical to the wider deployment of the system. In this paper, we outline the definition and design of the infrastructure for the UMDL information economy, and the kinds of agents that exist in it, that allow decentralized (scalable) ongoing configuration of an extensible set of users and services. We refer to the services/protocols offered by this infrastructure as the Service Market Society (SMS).

The SMS requires the integration of numerous agent technologies for knowledge exchange, commerce, learning, and modeling. Some of our earlier publications [1] have already explained the general agent architecture of the UMDL, along with the agents' communication system. In this paper we concentrate on the *dynamics* of the system (i.e. how agents find and interact with each other) and on the abilities and resources that the agents need in order to effectively participate in the economy. We describe our prototype SMS in which a changing population of agents can find each other, enlist each other's aid (for a price), decide on the terms of an interaction, and learn to differentiate among providers. We use our prototype to demonstrate how these technologies contribute to providing a flexible, extensible, scalable, and robust digital library. The agents and services we describe, unless otherwise noted, are implemented within the UMDL, but to avoid disrupting the use of the deployed system the experimental SMS agents are ignored by agents that are supporting the UMDL educational mission. As the kinks are worked out of experimental agents, therefore, deploying them has been trivial: an agent stops describing itself to the UMDL as experimental, and thus is available to the deployed system. Recently, for example, instances of many of the agents described in this paper (including auction agents, the auction manager, and the price monitor) have become part of the UMDL system used by the schools.

We start with an overview of the SMS, and its component technologies: the UMDL ontology and the auctions. Next, we illustrate how these technologies support resource allocation decision-making with a simple example of balancing load, and support the identification of resource needs based on supply and demand. We then turn to issues of whether our infrastructure encourages extensibility by looking at the impact of adding profit-seeking agents that reason about other agents into the mix. Finally, we summarize our work that shows how learning agents add a measure of robustness to the UMDL SMS. As the reader will surmise, the SMS brings together several related threads of work, and this paper attempts to summarize these pieces and how they fit together. The work addresses only one (high-level) facet of the digital library enterprise, concentrating on describing, finding, allocating, and evaluating services, and is as yet incomplete even for this aspect of digital libraries.[2] Yet, we hope to convince the reader of the promise of this approach for meeting some of the long-term challenges in managing large-scale, open, rapidly-evolving digital libraries.

1.1 Other Digital Library Infrastructures

There is a tremendous amount of work going on on many facets of digital libraries; entire conferences and journals are devoted to the topic, and surveying all of the excellent work in the field is beyond the scope of this paper. Here, we will only mention a few projects that directly address aspects of digital library infrastructures. The InfoBus [9] system extends the current Internet protocols with a suite of higher-level information management protocols. This work concentrates on the details of the communication protocols which are, in fact, quite similar to those used in the UMDL[3]. They have even implemented some commerce interfaces [4]. However, in contrast to the work in this paper, they do not address the higher-level problem of agents finding each other (i.e. finding the services they want) and effectively taking part in the economy. The Alexandria Project [2] also addresses the issue of communication between users, collections, and mediators, but it does not use an economic framework for making resource allocation decisions.

2   The Service Market Society

The UMDL SMS implements a market-based multi-agent system where agents buy and sell services from each other. Agents can be added to or removed from the system at any time. Instead of having to rely solely on internally designed agents, the UMDL SMS is designed to attract outside agents to provide new services. These agents in turn are motivated by the long-term profit they might accrue by participating in the system.[4]

The raw resources of a digital library consist of collections of information, where a collection might be a database of journal articles or it might be a collection of related web pages. Collection Interface Agents (CIAs) provide access and search services for these collections. Various middlemen, or *mediator* agents

---

[2] For example, the current SMS does not address issues of privacy, security, and even payment. In the description of "buying and selling" in SMS that follows, our current simple model assumes that buyers and sellers are each keeping track of their "balances" and honestly incrementing (decrementing) as services are sold (bought). We have attempted to make our system compatible with the various payment mechanisms being developed elsewhere.

[3] Both projects use the ILU CORBA implementation. Some degree of interoperability between the two projects has been achieved.

[4] While designed to encourage third-party agent/service development, to date the third-party services in the UMDL have been introduced by the project team. Bootstrapping the process to the point where third-parties have sufficient incentive to join is, not surprisingly, hard!

(such as QPAs, see below), transform the raw information resources into finished products or services which the end-user desires. Each user, or library patron, has a User Interface Agent (UIA) which interacts with the UMDL on his or her behalf to acquire these services. Finally, within the system are *facilitator* agents (such as the Registry, SCA, auctions, etc. as described below) which facilitate the process of agents classifying, locating, and connecting agents to provide more comprehensive services.

Figure 1 shows a simple scenario which we will be using throughout this paper. In this scenario, users want to find sources of information for various topics (e.g. history, science or mathematics) and various audience levels (e.g. middle school, high school, or professional). Query Planning Agents (QPAs) [10], act as middlemen, accepting queries from users and returning collections related to those queries. Initially, the user sends a query, via a web-based Java interface, to the UIA. The UIA must then find an agent that can service this query. In order to allow agents to find the services they need, we have implemented an ontology of services. Every agent must be able to describe the services it wishes to buy or sell using terms from the UMDL ontology.

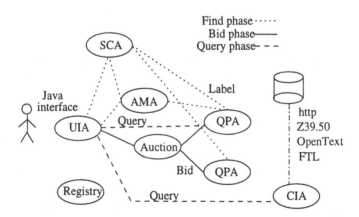

Fig. 1. The UMDL Service Market Society. The User Interface Agent (UIA) describes its needs to the Service Classifier Agent (SCA) and is told the appropriate service label. The UIA asks the Auction Manager Agent (AMA) for an auction where the service is sold, and goes to that auction. The Auction matches the UIA with an agent providing the service (in this case, a Query Planning Agent (QPA), which returns the name of a Collection Interface Agent (CIA)). The SMS supports any number of UIA, CIA, QPA, and Auction agents.

In order to join the UMDL, every agent must register its unique agent-id with the Registry. An agent can then advertise by sending[5] its service description to

---

[5] Agent communications use KQML primitives implemented using CORBA objects, see [1] for details.

the Service Classifier Agent, as shown by the dotted lines, and receiving a service-label. The SCA automatically classifies the advertised service descriptions into a subsumption-based taxonomy. This organization enables the SCA to match requests for services to "semantically close" descriptions, to recommend the most appropriate services out of those that are currently available. We encourage agents to describe their needs with as much detail as possible. The SCA can then recommend the available services with the least general subsuming descriptions.

Once an agent has acquired the appropriate service-label from the SCA, and is ready to buy/sell that service, it sends the desired label to the Auction Manager Agent (AMA) (as shown by dotted lines) which returns a list of auctions which sell matching services. The agent then sends buy or sell bids to a particular Auction agent (solid lines). UMDL *auctions* operate by collecting offers from participating agents and determining agreements consistent with those offers, matching individual buyers and sellers.

In our scenario, UIAs want to buy query planning services while QPAs want to sell this service. Once a match is found for the UIA, it will send its query to the matching QPA. The QPA returns the appropriate CIAs and the UIA then forwards its query to them. The CIAs can translate UMDL queries to a variety of protocols (e.g. http, Z39.50, FTL, etc.) and return the appropriate documents.

The agents in our system are free to return services of differing qualities and to disagree on the exact quality of a given service. We, therefore, expect that some agents might try to take advantage of other agents in the system by manipulating either their buy/sell bids, or the quality (and, therefore, the production cost) of the service they provide. We call such agents *strategic* agents. These strategic agents will need to be able to assess the quality and value of a service received, or to determine the exact price to charge. They can make these determinations by either using knowledge about the expected arrival of buyers/sellers, or by learning models of the other agents. In this paper, we investigate how the addition of these strategic agents changes the dynamics of the UMDL SMS. We find that strategic agents increase the robustness of the system. We also find that the SMS market works to minimize the amount of strategic thinking that the agents can gainfully engage in, but does not completely eliminate the need for having some agents with strategic abilities, even if these abilities are not always used.

3   The UMDL Ontology

We use ontologies to encode declarative descriptions of complex agent services. Declarative descriptions are required to establish a space of services independent of the implementation of the current set of agents.

Representing complexity in a digital library, and any other "real-world" domain, demands expressiveness that is substantially more powerful than that of relational databases. Services have many descriptive dimensions (attributes), may be partially described at any level of granularity (with any combination of dimensions), and may be viewed from many perspectives (accessed by different sequences of attribute values). For example, an agent might seek a service to recommend a collection of articles on volcanoes, for high-school audiences, to be contracted for via auction. Alternatively, the agent might seek an auction that sells a service to recommend collections. (In Figure 2, follow links either from "recommend-dlcollection" at the top, or "auction" at the bottom of the figure). In an ontology, both perspectives can be represented simultaneously, and retrieval supports queries on any level of granularity. Declarative formalisms with less expressiveness than ontologies, such as relational databases, force a commitment to particular levels of granularity and particular perspectives.

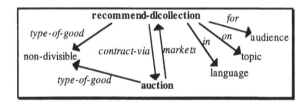

Fig. 2. Multi-dimensional, multi-perspective complexity

To promote reuse, the UMDL ontology is divided into nested modules (each of which is itself called an ontology) [12]. The most general includes library content and services that we consider to be part of a "generic" digital library. The second module adds concepts specific to the UMDL implementation, such as auctions. The third module describes agent services. We call this last ontology "dynamic" because agents define new service concepts at runtime. In contrast, "static" ontologies are either fixed, or are changed slowly over time by committees of persons.

3.1 The Service Classifier Agent

In the current SMS, UIAs, QPAs and Auction agents use the same SCA, and thus subscribe to the same ontologies. Figure 3 illustrates these agents' interactions with the SCA. Agents are in ovals, ontologies in rectangles, and the arrows connecting agents represent messages, paraphrased in natural language. These messages are expressed in Loom, a description logic in the KL-ONE family [5]. To communicate with the SCA, agents use terminology from the nested ontologies. In the figure, the thin line around the SCA is jagged to show that the set of available terms is dynamic; both QPAs and the AMA add concepts to the agent services ontology. The messages are shown with font styles that correspond to the ontology labels (plain, italics, and upper-case), to highlight the source of their terminology.

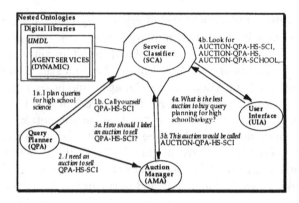

Fig. 3. Agent interaction with the SCA in the SMS

Figure 3 illustrates the ability of the SCA to construct new terminology from existing terms at runtime.[6] Concepts in the SCA's dynamic ontology hide knowledge, just as words chunk meaning in natural language. Auctions sell some service, but they don't need to know anything about that service. The AMA asks the SCA for a service label for an auction, using the QPA's service label, but it does not know anything about that service. The SCA classifies the auction service using characteristics inferred from the QPA's service label. Thus, the SCA can respond to the UIA's request for an auction, which is phrased in terms from the static ontologies, rather than phrased in terms of the label which the AMA used to define the auction service. This appropriate hiding of knowledge reduces overall system complexity, and increases reusability and maintainability.

The most dramatic contribution of the SCA to the SMS derives from its declarative description of services, and its ability to rank available services given a target and search strategy. For example, when a new QPA provides a service that better meets a UIA's needs, this fact is captured by the service description. The UIAs can then automatically switch to buying services from the new QPA.

4 Market-Based Negotiations– Auctions

Since UMDL cannot know at design-time what services will be available in the future or what the best negotiation mechanisms are for any given situation, its languages and protocols have been designed for flexibility and extensibility. In the

---

[6] Note that by "new terminology" we mean new, meaningful combinations of the core terms in the ontology. There are a huge number of ways that the core terms in the ontology can be composed into descriptions, only a small number of which will be meaningful. New terms are those that are dynamically created because they are useful. If the primitive terms in the nested ontologies cannot express a concept in any combination, then the static ontologies must be extended; we assume that at this level the growth of the ontologies requires human intervention.

case of negotiation mechanisms, UMDL uses a generalized auction specification to allow goods and services to be offered under a wide variety of terms [6].

While generalized auctions are not the only possible kinds of negotiation mechanisms, they offer many advantages. They provide a structured, yet flexible market infrastructure promoting automated negotiation due to the following characteristics:

1. **Mediated** (vs. Unmediated): Buyers do not have to separately find and contact every seller; a useful property in a large-scale and dynamic environment. Information about current status can be easily and uniformly disseminated.

2. **Price** (vs. Barter): Under certain circumstances, price minimizes communication between agents.

3. **Formal** (vs. Informal): Standardized offers simplify communication between agents.

Auction specifications consist of parameters which can be tuned to reflect the type of good being sold, timing requirements, or mechanism properties desired. For example, a query planning service might be sold differently depending on how it is bundled (e.g., per-query, subscription), its characteristics (topic, audience, timeliness), its terms (redistribute, read-only), or to whom it is sold (individual, library, group). Different kinds of auctions will have advantages and disadvantages for different types of information goods and services.

Although evaluating tradeoffs between desirable properties of different auction types is important, the role of the UMDL is not to require that a particular auction be used in a given circumstance, but rather to provide an open framework whereby the use of these market facilitator agents is supported. To automate the creation and management of auctions as much as possible, we use the Auction Manager Agent (AMA).

4.1 The Auction Manager Agent

The purpose of the AMA is both to generate and track auctions as well as to serve as a tool for exploring alternative market configurations. Currently the AMA is used to automate the process of creating a well-specified market. Agents request auctions for the services they sell/buy from the AMA. Using the SCA, the AMA determines which auctions sell these services. If one or more such auctions exist, then the agent is notified of their agent-ids. Otherwise, the AMA creates an auction and then informs the requesting agent of its location. Since the AMA uses the SCA to generalize service descriptions, the description sent by the agent does not have to exactly match the auction's service description.

5 Simple Market Scenario– Price Takers

In this section, we discuss two simple scenarios implemented in UMDL and the design process and mechanisms used. The scenarios use the same agents and services as shown in Figure 1. We make the assumption that the agents have been designed within UMDL to fulfill certain system-level objectives. In particular, we assume the QPAs have been designed to behave competitively. Competitive agents take prices as given– ignoring any market power they might possess, thereby eliminating the need to reason strategically about other agents' bidding behavior and simplifying the QPA design.

5.1 Load Balancing

This scenario shows how, under certain conditions, a price mechanism can be used to distribute service load between multiple providers of the same service. Specifically, consider the case where we want to balance the service load between several high-school science QPAs running on separate machines. Each QPA provides the same service, in this case, *exactly* the same service since each one is just a spawned copy of the same code. We simplified this scenario in a number of ways, assuming that all sites provide free access, and all queries are the same.

In designing the QPAs, we assume they are competitive, and bid their marginal costs, namely what it would cost them to provide another unit of their product. This pricing policy directly reflects the cost to the system of using the input resources to provide this service. QPAs use computational and network resources to produce query planning service. Since these resources get congested as the load on a machine or network gets heavier, the marginal cost of adding another query will increase with the number of queries currently being processed. We modeled this technology in the QPAs using a quadratic cost function:

$$\text{Cost(query)} = A * \text{load}^2 + B * \text{load}$$
$$\text{Marginal Cost(query)} = 2 * A * \text{load} + B$$

Each additional query the QPA processes is priced at its marginal cost. Note that this cost function does not represent any real computer load model, but it does capture the basic notion of using a congested resource. The parameters A and B can be set to reflect relative differences between QPA technologies. For example, a QPA with $A, B = 1$ could be thought of as running on a faster machine than a QPA with $A, B = 2$.

All sellers (QPAs) make offers based on their current marginal cost. Buyers (UIAs) are assumed to want to purchase the query planning service immediately upon bidding. Query planning services are traded in an auction which matches the current lowest price seller with an incoming buyer, as long as the buyer's bid is above that price. Note that because of the way the agents have been designed, we know that this auction is incentive compatible for buyers, i.e., their best bidding strategy is to bid their true value for query planning services. This is because the QPAs, who would normally have an incentive to try and strategize about bid amounts, have been engineered to be competitive[7]. Once

---

[7] If the QPAs had not been engineered, a better solution would have been to use a second price auction.

a transaction occurs between a given seller and buyer, both offers are removed from the standing offer list. The QPA recomputes its marginal cost based on having an additional query to process and submits a new, higher, sell offer to the auction.

To see how this results in query load balancing, let's consider what happens where there are two QPAs, (QPA-1 and QPA-2). Given the same initial query load, the sell offers for each agent will be the same, and the first buyer will be matched up arbitrarily with one of them, say QPA-1. At this point, the query load for QPA-1 will rise, causing its marginal cost to rise, and it will submit a new offer at a higher price than before. The next incoming buyer will be matched with the current lowest price seller, QPA-2. QPA-2 now makes its new higher sell offer to reflect its increased load. Assuming that QPA-1 and QPA-2's previous queries are still being processed, both agents are again offering query planning service at the same, although higher, price. If one of QPA-1's queries finishes, then it sends in a new lower offer, and will be matched up to the next incoming buyer. Given a steady load of user queries, this system appears to settle down to an equilibrium price, although we have not done any formal analysis of these results. Notice that the dynamic addition or deletion of an agent does not affect the long-term running of the load balancing mechanism. For example, if any one of the agents were to die, it would only affect the queries that they were processing at that time. Future query planning requests would be matched with the remaining QPAs still participating in the auction. Similarly, spawning a new QPA means that it can start making offers to the query planning auction immediately.

Similar situations where this mechanism would be useful are in the provision of basic library services, which outside agents may not be interested in supplying. By making the agents competitive, UMDL can assure that the system costs are accounted for, that users get a low price, and agent designs are kept simple. Another example is distributing the access load to collections for which the library has a site license. Even though the site license may allow unlimited access, there are still associated network and compute costs, and for popular collections we may want to create mirror sites and distribute the load across them. A consistently high price of access may indicate when a given collection should be mirrored.

The point in the preceding is that the SMS economic foundation provides a flexible means for making decentralized resource allocation decisions. When we consider specifically the problem of load balancing, there are clearly many other load-balancing algorithms that have been developed in fields such as distributed computing and operations research. For many problems, such as when the available resources are fixed, the task needs well-defined, the performance criteria are globally determined, and the control centralized, alternative algorithms can provide optimal or near-optimal (within well-defined bounds) allocations. What we have illustrated in our work is that the economic principles of supply and demand provides an alternative load balancing mechanism which appears to be particularly useful in domains where resources come and go, tasks may have uncertain resource requirements, the participants can have different performance criteria (the costs and values they ascribe to activities and outcomes can differ), and the control is decentralized. More work remains in determining exactly the circumstances in which an approach like ours will outperform more traditional "command and control" methods.

5.2 Price Monitor Agent

In a large-scale, dynamic system, information about the current status of the system can serve as feedback to different kinds of control mechanisms. In this section, we describe a simple monitor agent, called a Price Monitor Agent (PMA), which collects information about an auction's prices over time and uses that information to decide whether to spawn more service providers.

In our scenario, the PMA monitors the price of query planning services. The price in this auction reflects the load on the QPAs— a consistently high price means that the QPAs are heavily loaded. One way to reduce the load is to replicate QPAs (assuming that there are other less heavily loaded machines on the network). When the load is reduced, the price should come down.

The PMA is initially set with a given minimum and maximum price bounds, although they can be changed later. When the price exceeds the upper bound, i.e., the load on each QPA is getting high, it spawns additional QPAs. This effectively distributes the load from future queries.[8] When the price goes below the lower bound, i.e., the QPAs load has fallen, the PMA has a choice of either removing or just inactivating one of the extra QPA, depending on whether it expects the load to increase again in the near term. The effect of this behavior is to keep the load across QPAs (and therefore the response time to users) within specified bounds even though the user demand is dynamic.

Figure 4 shows an overview of how the PMA operates. Below is a description of what is occurring at each step:

1. A heavily loaded QPA sells its services for $0.13.

2. The PMA checks the current price at the Auction.

3. Since the price is above it's upper bound ($0.10), the PMA spawns another QPA.

4. The new QPA sells its services for $0.08.

5. The user is matched with the lowest priced (least loaded) QPA.

---

[8] In fact, there is nothing to prevent a QPA from itself attempting to find another QPA to service a query. That is, an overloaded QPA, which has been awarded a query because it is the least overloaded of all the QPAs, might periodically check the auction and attempt to pass off one or more of its assigned queries. Thus, new QPAs can in principle reduce the current load, although in our current implementation the QPAs do not do this.

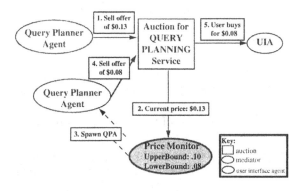

Fig. 4. Price Monitoring Scenario

6. (not shown) When/if the price goes below $0.08, the PMA inactivates one or more of its spawned QPAs.

In our experiments, the PMA, given reasonable bounds for the prices and activity of the agents, was successfully able to keep the price within the given price bounds. However when the price bounds were too tight or the activity on the system was too dynamic, the PMA would oscillate. For example, if too many agents get added, the price may fall too low, causing too many agents to get removed, which causes the price to go too high, and so forth. Providing the monitoring agent with knowledge about usage patterns, or having it collect statistics about usage, is one way to address this problem.

Finally, let us briefly address the question about where to set the upper price bound. Since price reflects load, which in turn reflects response time, we might determine the maximum desired response time and from that compute the maximum price. However, if this is done for all potentially replicable services, then we risk overtaxing the available computational and network resources with too many copies of too many agents. Ultimately, any policy for replication needs to determine whether the resources that will be devoted to a new agent could be more usefully applied elsewhere. While right now the PMA simply uses user-specified bounds (and indeed, only replicates QPAs so that there isn't any competition between requests for spawning different agent types), ultimately the resources available for replicated agents should themselves be auctioned off, such that PMAs for different classes of agents will compete for the resources and those resources will be allocated based on the same economic principles as other UMDL services.

5.3 Conclusions from simple market scenarios

We showed how UMDL agents which use system resources to provide query planning services to library users can be designed to distribute system load efficiently and to respond to dynamic changes in the number and frequency of users' requests. A less obvious benefit to designing the seller agents to be competitive is that the software design is straightforward and modular and requires no information about the behavior of the other agents in the system.

Also, the task of choosing an auction mechanism is vastly simplified when dealing with competitive sellers, especially for issues such as how to achieve incentive compatibility (having bidders bid their true evaluation, so that resources can be allocated efficiently) or deciding what kinds of information the auction should release (clearing price, bid quotes, bids) and how that affects agent behavior and system properties. In this case, sellers are designed to bid what it costs the system to provide the service. The auction used was a type of double auction, where each buyer's bid is cleared immediately and is priced at the lowest seller's price. Thus, library users can bid their true value for the service and be assured that, as long as their value for the service is greater than the cost to the system to provide it, they will acquire the service at system cost. Neither buyer nor seller agents need any information when bidding about other agents or even, in this simplified scenario, auction prices.

Additionally, if library users *were* to bid strategically, i.e., not their true value for the service, all that would happen is that they might bid too low and not acquire a service they would be willing to pay for, or they might bid too high and acquire one for more than they value it, both inefficient system outcomes. Of course, there are still strategic opportunities for buyers. For example, they might try to strategically time when to make a bid, e.g., if prices are lower at midnight than at 9am, then a user's agent might want to store up non-rush queries to be processed later. In this scenario, we assumed that these were live users, actively waiting for queries to be processed and, additionally, that the price for query processing was small enough not to make it worthwhile to try and exploit small jumps in prices. The Price Monitor was developed to support this immediate processing of on-line queries by using the information that price conveys about system costs to smooth the load across the system at a particular time.

This section has focused on the case where all services are offered by the library itself. We showed a mechanism that provides for the efficient allocation of library services between users. If the services are instead commercial services offered by third parties, then strategic behavior on the parts of the buyers and sellers and careful consideration of the properties of the auction mechanism will become important.

6 Strategic Agents

A real economic system provides monetary incentives to its participants and dynamically allocates the available system resources in part because the human beings and corporations that take part in it are smart. They can recognize when they are charging too little or too much, or when they are not getting the quality they expected. They also do not spend all their time thinking about the economy, but only do as much strategic thinking as is needed.

If we want our agent economy to be as robust as the real economy, we will need to have at least marginally intelligent agents. These agents will need to know what to bid— both when price has reached an equilibrium (which is easy), and when the price is fluctuating. For example, if an agent has knowledge about an expected increase in the number of buyers/sellers, it should be able to use this knowledge to its advantage. Also, if an agent is the only seller of a service then it should be able to take advantage of its monopoly, while if the buyers find that a seller's prices are too high for the service it sells, they should be able to avoid buying from him. Agents should, in effect, be strategic. One drawback of this, however, is the possibility that agents will spend all their time thinking strategically rather than carrying out their domain tasks. Fortunately, as we will show, our economy discourages agents from engaging in ever-increasing amounts of strategic thinking.

6.1 P-strategy Agents

In this section, we relax the assumption that agents behave competitively, and investigate how strategic agents affect the UMDL in terms of market and allocation efficiency.

A Strategy based on stochastic modeling (p-strategy) We have developed an agent's bidding strategy based on stochastic modeling (called p-strategy) for the UMDL SMS, the details of which are given in [7]. The main idea behind the p-strategy is to capture the factors which influence the expected utility for the agent, using Markov chains. For instance, a seller is likely to raise its offer price when there are many buyers or when it expects more buyers to come. The number of buyers and sellers at the auction, the arrival rates of future buyers and sellers, and the distribution of buy and sell prices are among the identified factors. The p-strategy is able to take those factors into account in its stochastic model.

In our previous research [7], we have shown that an agent possessing the p-strategy has an advantage over agents that do not possess it when they compete in multi-agent auctions. Given that the p-strategy is effective in the UMDL auction, nothing prohibits any self-interested agent from adopting the p-strategy. We expect many p-strategy agents to coexist in the UMDL, and thus are interested in the collective behavior of such agents. In what follows, we briefly summarize our observations which are more completely detailed elsewhere [8].

Experimental results In our experiments, the p-strategy agents have models of how the auctions in the SMS evolve as buyers and sellers enter and are (sometimes) matched. Thus, these experiments should be considered illustrative

Session	Description	Bidding strategy						
		Seller1	Seller2	Seller3	Seller4	Seller5	Seller6	Seller7
(1)	All competitive	C	C	C	C	C	C	C
(2)	1 p-strategy	C	C	C	C	C	C	P
(3)	2 p-strategy	C	C	C	C	C	P	P
(4)	3 p-strategy	C	C	C	C	P	P	P
(5)	5 p-strategy	C	C	P	P	P	P	P
(6)	All p-strategy	P	P	P	P	P	P	P

Fig. 5. Experiment setting. C is Competitive. P is for p-strategy agents.

of performance for the current SMS economic framework; under different assumptions about, for example, auction parameterizations, different observations might hold. But for the SMS, we are interested in the effects of p-strategy agents on the efficiency. We measure the efficiency of the system in two ways. First, we measure the efficiency of allocation, by comparing a p-strategy agent's absolute and relative performance. Second, we measure the efficiency of the market, using the total profit generated.

Figure 5 shows the six experimental settings with 7 buyers and 7 sellers. The buyers bid their true valuations, while the sellers bid their sell prices depending on their strategies. In Session 1, all seven sellers are type C (Competitive) and bid their true costs. From Session 2 through Session 6, we introduce more type P (p-strategy) agents into the auction.

A p-strategy agent has an upper hand over other-strategy agents, but this may not hold in the presence of other p-strategy agents. To test this we compare the profits of Seller 7 (p-strategy agent) across Sessions 2 to 6. As shown in Figure 6, the marginal profit of the p-strategy (smart) agent decreases as the number of p-strategy agents increases.

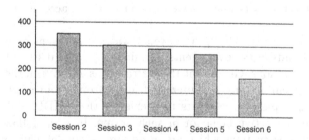

Fig. 6. The profit of the p-strategy agent (seller 7)

By replacing Seller 1 with a fixed-markup agent (who bids its cost plus some fixed markup), we also measure the relative performance of the fixed-markup agent (Seller 1) and the p-strategy agent (Seller 7). In Figure 7, we find that the simpler strategy agent (fixed markup agent) generally gets less profit than the p-strategy agent, but the difference decreases with the increase of p-strategy agents. That is, the disadvantage of being less smart decreases as the number of smart agents increases.

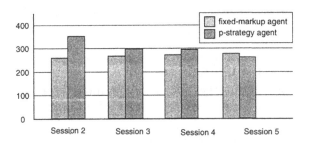

Fig. 7. The profit comparison between the fixed-markup agent and the p-strategy agent.

This result indicates that an agent may want to switch between using p-strategy and using a simpler strategy depending on what the other agents are doing. By dynamically switching to a simpler strategy, an agent can achieve a similar profit (to that of using the p-strategy) while exerting less effort on computing bids.[9]

We measure the market efficiency using the total profit generated from the buyers and sellers (see Figure 8). The total profit eventually decreases with more p-strategy agents, as the market becomes inefficient due to strategic misrepresentation of p-strategy agents (and therefore missed opportunities of matches). Note that the total profit does not decrease as sharply as one might expect (it in fact increases slightly up to Session 4) due to the efficiency of the UMDL auction mechanism.

We conjecture that having strategic sellers poses interesting tradeoffs between strategic inefficiency and surplus extraction. By misrepresenting their true costs, the p-strategy agents miss out on possible transactions. By anticipating the future arrival of buyers, on the other hand, they are able to seize more surplus.

---

[9] While the chances are that the computational effort in computing bids is small compared to the costs of providing the service, it is still important to consider this cost. Specifically, because the UMDL auctions match buyers and sellers as bids are received, higher-cost bidding strategies can delay the submission of bids such that an agent consistently arrives at the auction "too late." The overhead is worthwhile, however, if the agent makes up for missed opportunities by extracting more profit in the cases where it does succeed in making a match.

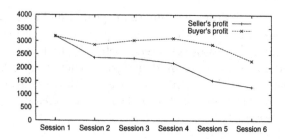

Fig. 8. The efficiency measured by the total profit.

Conclusions from experiments with strategic agents Although a self-interested agent in the UMDL has the capability of strategic reasoning, our experiments show that strategic thinking is not always beneficial. As previously shown, the advantage of being smart decreases with the arrival of equally smart agents.

We expect the UMDL is likely to evolve to a point where some agents are being strategic some of the time. An agent may want to switch between being strategic and not depending on the behavior of other agents: if enough other agents behave strategically, and agent can achieve additional profit even if it stays non-strategic.

Finally, the market efficiency of the UMDL will not decrease as sharply as one might expect. The profit-seeking behavior of self-interested agents will keep the UMDL agent population mixed with some strategic and some non-strategic agents. Thus, even though the market efficiency decreases with the increase in the number of strategic agents, the UMDL will not suffer the market inefficiency in the worst case.

6.2 Learning Agents

In this section, we use the scenario from Figure 1, but now we give sellers the freedom to return a service of any quality. The only thing that will prevent them from doing this is that we also give the buyers the ability to learn, which they use for determining which seller to buy from and at what price. To increase the information available for learning, we also allow the auctions to reveal all information (i.e. bids) they have to all interested agents. The agents are free to ignore any of this added information. By learning from this information, agents can avoid miscreant agents, and the performance of the information economy thus will not be compromised (or at least not for long) by such agents.

Learning in a market system While the UMDL ontology provides a way for agents to characterize the services they sell, there is no guarantee that all the goods sold at an auction for service x are indeed instances of service x. Agents could intentionally misrepresent their services. More frequently, agents might not entirely agree on precisely what constitutes service x. Indeed, subjective preferences might mean that some agents are quite satisfied with service x from a particular provider, while other agents are dissatisfied with that same provider's service. For example, while all agents might agree that QPA1 does sell service x, one agent might think that QPA1's service is faster, better, or more thorough than the same service x as provided by QPA2. This being the agent's subjective opinion, it is unlikely to be in agreement with all the other agents, but the agent might still be willing to pay more for service x from QPA1 than from QPA2.

Learning provides a means for agents to discriminate between services (or providers of services) when they have found sufficient grounds to make the discrimination useful. By learning, an agent can avoid being disappointed in its interactions by learning which agents to not interact with. If agents can learn from others' interactions (by observing others' experiences or sharing their experiences), they can as a society quickly ostracize rogue agents. Indeed, some agents might provide "recommendation services" by sampling and rating agents, and sharing (perhaps for a price) what they have learned with other agents. When agents learn, therefore, they increase the robustness of the system by partitioning away (what they see as) faulty agents.

In essence, learning provides a way for agents to develop expectations about others, and exploit these expectations to their mutual benefit. We can consider this as a rudimentary form of *trust* among agents. For a market-system to work well, an agent needs to be able to trust that its partners' view of good x is the same as its view of x. Similarly, an agent that uses recommender agents needs to trust their recommendations. This trust can be acquired by repeated iterations with the agents in question. Once the trust is acquired the learning is no longer needed, that is, until the trust is broken. This is why we argue that agents need the *ability* to learn, even if this ability is not always exercised.

Lastly, we propose that learning agents are not only useful, they are inevitable. In a society of selfish agents, we can expect that the designers will use every technology available to enhance the profits of their agents. Learning is one such technique. By implementing learning agents ourselves, we can determine how much of an advantage they will have and how they will affect the system.

Experimental Results To demonstrate the viability of the SMS with learning agents and under real-world heavy usage conditions, we ran several tests on the scenario shown in Figure 1. We implemented UIAs that periodically (every 16 seconds) buy a query from some QPA using the protocol described earlier. We also used one Auction, AMA, and SCA, along with several UIAs and QPAs. All the agents were deployed in machines all over our network. The UIAs kept track of how long it took for the QPA's reply to arrive and used this value in their learning. In general, the UIAs preferred fast and cheap service, and they were willing to pay more for faster service. A QPA's only preference was to increase its immediate profit, i.e. place its bid in order to maximize its expected profit (remember that failing to get a sale means the QPA gets zero profit).

We gave the agents different learning abilities (see [11]). 0-level agents used reinforcement learning on the prices/values received. 1-level agents actually tried to model the other agents as 0-level agents. That is, they remembered what other agents had bid in the past and made probabilistic predictions based on the assumption that they will behave in the future as they behaved in the recent past. The 1-level agents then took actions based on these predictions.

0-level agents For our first test we used 0-level UIAs and QPAs. They all began with no knowledge about what prices to bid or accept. UIAs quickly learned that they can expect to get higher value if they pick lower prices, while QPAs learned what price they can charge that will maximize their expected profit. As predicted by economic theory, this price was their marginal cost, i.e. the lowest price they can charge without losing money. This equilibrium was reached even while all the agents acted purely selfishly.

However, this equilibrium is not completely stable. Network and machine delays, along with the agents' occasional explorative actions[10], add noise to the system preventing the price from staying fixed at the marginal cost.

Even with only 0-level agents (i.e. no 1-level agents) we can see how the system behaves in a robust manner. Figure 9 shows the clearing price for an auction which starts with only one seller QPA. This QPA quickly "realizes" that it has a monopoly and starts to raise its prices. A second QPA is then added (as marked by the first vertical line), and we can see how its addition makes the price drop, but eventually it gets overloaded and the price rises again. A third QPA is added (at the second vertical line), affecting the price, and more QPAs are added at regular intervals (one at each vertical line).[11] The equilibrium price gets fairly close to the QPAs' marginal cost of 0. Towards the end the QPAs start to leave the system so the price starts to rise accordingly. This type of experiment gives us confidence that the agents will behave in a reasonable way even under boundary conditions, e.g. when a lot of the agents die, or when new services are added. If the agents were to determine their bid prices based on a fixed utility function, we might expect to find periodic or chaotic behavior [3], which we wish to avoid.

1-level Agents 1-level QPAs take advantage of price fluctuations by keeping models of the QPAs and UIAs and using these to make better predictions as to what they should bid. The 1-level models, while computationally expensive, allow QPAs to track the individual agents more closely, thereby identifying when a UIA is willing to pay more than the going rate. Previous research has shown that the advantages of 1-level models can be correlated to the price volatility (see [11]).

---

[10] The agents were set to take a random action with probability of .05. This keeps them from converging on a local maxima.

[11] Note that these QPAs are *not* added because of some price bounds as with the Price Monitor Agent (Section 5 but rather are simply added at fixed intervals.

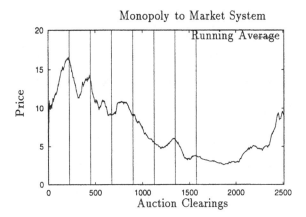

Fig. 9. Clearing price for successive auctions. Initially there is only one seller QPA, and an additional one is added at each of the vertical lines. The QPAs' marginal cost is zero.

However, this strategic thinking is only successful against 0-level UIAs. When we tested the 1-level QPAs against the 1-level UIAs, as seen in Figure 10, we found the QPA's performance on par with other similar 0-level QPAs. In fact, the sellers that made more were the ones that could answer the query faster, not the 1-level seller. In other experiments we also found that 1-level sellers' extra profit is reduced as other 0-level sellers become 1-level. In both cases, the 1-level sellers incentive to be 1-level (instead of 0-level) disappears with increased competition.

Conclusions from Learning Experiments The results on learning deeper agent models show that the UMDL SMS benefits from the existence of agents that have the *ability* to keep deeper models and look out for their best interests, even if they *do not always use this ability*. Agents are encouraged to model others because this can bring them higher profit. However, there is a computational cost associated with modeling, and a decreasing return for the agent as other agents also start to build models. This means that that the SMS will likely evolve to a point where some agents build models, some of the time, in the same manner as we expect some agents to use p-strategy some of the time. This is a great scenario because it gives us a very robust system (i.e. one that can not be sabotaged by deviant agents), while using few resources for this purpose and distributing the resources it uses among the agents.

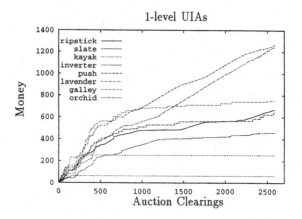

Fig. 10. Total revenue accrued by seller QPAs. Ripstick is the 1-level seller, the rest are 0-level. As time goes on the faster sellers accrue more wealth, not the 1-level seller. Because the different machines have different loads (other users), over time some of the machines are avoided because they respond too slowly, and their accumulated profits level off.

7 Summary

We have given a condensed overview of the UMDL SMS and the agents, protocols, and languages that it encompasses. Through this description, we hope that we have conveyed how our SMS infrastructure supports our desiderata:

- **Flexibility**: In our SMS work, we have already explored several policies for designing an information economy, ranging from a more "public" flavor where agents that are assumed truthful and interested in providing services for the lowest possible price, to a more commercial flavor where agents might misrepresent themselves and will try to maximize their individual profits.

- **Extensibility**: We have described how agents with new services (as described by composing new descriptions in the shared ontology) can join the UMDL, and why they would have incentive to join.

- **Scalability**: We have described how decentralized resource allocation decisions are made through the market mechanisms coupled with agent reasoning methods for computing bids, and how services in high demand can be replicated. Note that, typically, new agents bring their own resources into the system with them; thus, when agent developers have incentive to introduce their agents, they are also introducing resources for managing the larger system (at a minimum, their agents have to decide for themselves on bids to make).

– **Robustness:** We have illustrated how the system can still perform well despite the potentially conflicting desires of the participating agents and the possibility of misrepresentation in the system.

Collectively, the mechanisms we have described can automate much of the administration of a digital library, including organizing information and services using ontological relationships, selecting, evaluating, and remembering useful services using machine learning, and deciding how to allocate (finite) resources to meet the evolving demands of a user community.

These results were achieved via the merging of different technologies which include: ontology design, market oriented design, and nested agent modeling and learning. The agents and protocols that we have described have all been implemented and integrated into the UMDL SMS. Some of these, such as the auctions and the Price Monitor Agent, are also used by agents in the deployed UMDL system. For example, these agents can automatically spawn more QPAs during high demand periods by the students using UMDL simultaneously from many schools. Thus, our SMS "information economy" model is already being used by UMDL patrons; while they are unaware of the economic foundations of the system, those foundations are already being used in a rudimentary way to improve the system performance for the users.

Of course, given the specific needs of the current UMDL user community, and the rights we currently have over the UMDL content, other possible means for controlling resources and providing services would work for the UMDL. Specifically, we could develop management algorithms tailored specifically to the UMDL. While it could be the case that, for the short term, such an alternative might be more effective, we are not convinced of its long-term viability when the system is truly open, dynamic, and large. While much remains to be done within the SMS strategy for addressing these long-term issues (many open issues have been raised throughout this paper), we believe that the SMS has already demonstrated promise in being able to meet the needs of the open, evolving, information economy of the future.

Acknowledgments The rest of the members of the UMDL SMS group all contributed to its design and development. They are: Anil Arora, Bill Birmingham, Eric Glover, Dan Kiskis, Anisoara Nica, and Bill Walsh.

References

1. Edmund H. Durfee, Daniel L. Kiskis, and William P. Birmingham. The agent architecture of the University of Michigan Digital Library. *IEE Proceedings on Software Engineering*, 144(1):61–71, 1997.
2. James Frew, Michael Freeston, Randall B. Kemp, Jason Simpson, Terence Smith, Alex Wells, and Qi Zheng. The Alexandria digital library testbed. *D-Lib Magazine*, July/August 1996.
3. Tad Hogg and Bernardo A. Huberman. Controlling chaos in distributed systems. *IEEE Transactions on Systems, Man, and Cybernetics*, 21(6):1325–1332, December 1991. (Special Issue on Distributed AI).

4. Steven P. Ketchpel, Hector Garcia-Molina, and Andreas Paepcke. Shopping models: A flexible architecture for information commerce. In *Proceedings of the ACM Digital Libraries Conference*, 1997.
5. Robert M. MacGregor. The evolving technology of classification-based knowledge representation systems. In John. F. Sowa, editor, *Principles of Semantic Networks*, pages 385–400. Morgan Kaufmann.
6. Tracy Mullen and Michael P. Wellman. Market-based negotiation for digital library services. In *Second USENIX Workshop on Electronic Commerce*, 1996.
7. Sunju Park, Edmund H. Durfee, and William P. Birmingham. Advantages of Strategic Thinking in Multiagent Contracts (A Mechanism and Analysis). In *Proceedings of the Second International Conference on Multi-Agent Systems (ICMAS-96)*, pages 259–266, 1996.
8. Sunju Park, Edmund H. Durfee, and William P. Birmingham. Emergent properties of a market-based digital library with strategic agents. In *Proceedings of the Third International Conference on Multi-Agent Systems (ICMAS98)*, 1998.
9. Marting Röscheisen, Michelle Baldonado, Kevin Chang, Luis Gravano, Steven Ketchpel, and Andreas Paepcke. The Stanford InfoBus and its service layers. In *MeDoc Dagstuhl Workshop: Electronic Publishing and Digital Libraries in Computer Science*. To appear.
10. José M. Vidal and Edmund H. Durfee. Task planning agents in the UMDL. In *Proceedings of the Fourth International Conference on Information and Knowledge Managment (CIKM) Workshop on Intelligent Information Agents.*, 1995.
11. José M. Vidal and Edmund H. Durfee. The impact of nested agent models in an information economy. In *Proceedings of the Second International Conference on Multi-Agent Systems*, pages 377–384, 1996.
12. Peter Weinstein and Gene Alloway. Seed ontologies: growing digital libraries as distributed, intelligent systems. In *Proceedings of the Second ACM International Conference on Digital Libraries*, June 1997.

Multiagent Systems in Information-Rich Environments

Michael N. Huhns[1]* and Munindar P. Singh[2]**

[1] Department of Electrical and Computer Engineering
University of South Carolina
Columbia, SC 29208, USA
huhns@sc.edu
[2] Department of Computer Science
North Carolina State University
Raleigh, NC 27695-7534, USA
singh@ncsu.edu

Abstract. Information-rich environments are the open environments that characterize most of the modern applications of computing technology. The applications include ubiquitous information access, electronic commerce, virtual enterprises, logistics, and sensor integration, to name but a few. These applications differ from conventional database applications not only in the nature and variety of information they involve, but also in including a significant component that is beyond the information system *per se*: the creation, transformation, use, and ultimate fate of information. The environments are typified only by the large amounts and varieties of information they include, and whose effective and efficient management is key to the above applications. Multiagent systems (MAS) are an important paradigm for building complex information systems, especially cooperative ones. We describe how cooperative information system architectures have evolved a set of common types of computational agents. We also describe two approaches that address complementary aspects of MAS construction.

1 Introduction

Information-rich environments are the modern, open, large-scale environments with autonomous heterogeneous information resources. They are a major target for systems based on agents and multiagent systems (MAS) technologies [6].

Numerous definitions of agents are known in the literature [3, 5, 10]. Indeed, the only agreement seems to be that there is a range of definitions! Some of the important properties of agents include autonomy, adaptability, and interactiveness, but exceptions reveal that an agent need not have these properties. However, we believe that agents *must* be capable of interacting with other agents at

---

* Supported by the Defense Advanced Research Projects Agency.
** Supported by the NCSU College of Engineering, the National Science Foundation under grants IRI-9529179 and IRI-9624425 (Career Award), and IBM corporation.

the social or communicative level [4, 5]. We distinguish social or communicative interactions from incidental interactions that agents may have as a consequence of existing in a shared environment. Independently, Wegner has also argued that interaction is a key extension beyond traditional computer science [14].

1.1 Information-Rich Environments

Information-rich environments have been around for a long time. We previously defined them in broad terms as environments consisting of a large number and variety of distributed and heterogeneous information sources [5]. The associated applications are varied. They involve the purely informational ones, such as database access, information malls, workflow management, electronic commerce, and virtual enterprises. They also include the information component of physical applications, such as distributed sensing, manufacturing, transportation, energy distribution, and telecommunications. Information-rich environments have the following properties. They

- Span enterprise boundaries
- Include heterogeneous components
- Comprise information resources that can be added or removed in a loosely structured manner
- Lack global control of the accuracy of the contents of those resources
- Incorporate intricate interdependencies among their components.

Information-rich environments may often involve a significant physical or social component. However, they are amenable to specialized multiagent systems. *Cooperative Information Systems* are multiagent systems with organizational and database abstractions geared to open environments. Typically, a CIS includes an environment consisting of a variety of information resources, coupled with some kind of a semantic directory or ontology for the domain of interest. The semantic directory contains information about the resources, including any constraints that apply to their joint behavior. Each component of the environment, as well as its human user(s), is modeled as associated with an agent. The agents capture and enforce the requirements of their associated parties. They interact with one another appropriately, and help achieve the necessary robustness and flexibility.

Information access involves finding, retrieving, and fusing information from a number of heterogeneous sources. At the level of abstraction that concerns CIS, we are not concerned with network connectivity or the formatting variations of data access languages. Rather, our concern is with the meaning of the information stored. It is possible, and indeed common, that when different databases store information on related topics, each provides a different model of it. The databases might use different terms, e.g., employee or staff to refer to the same concept. Worse still, they might use the same term to have different meanings. For example, one database may use employee to mean anyone currently on the payroll, whereas another may use employee to mean anyone currently receiving benefits. The former will include assigned contractors; the latter will include retirees. Consequently, merging information meaningfully is nontrivial. The problem is exacerbated by advances in communications infrastructure and competitive pressures, because different companies or divisions of a large company, which previously proceeded independently of one another, are now expected to have some linkage with each other.

The linkages can be thought of as semantic mappings between the application (which consumes or produces information), and the various databases. If the application somehow knows that employee from one database has a certain meaning, it can insert appropriate tests to eliminate the records it does not need. Clearly, this approach would be a nightmare to maintain: the slightest changes in a database would require modifying all the applications that consume its results!

1.2 Carnot

In order to best understand the work described below, it is useful to review the Carnot project, in which the authors participated. Some of the following ideas had their genesis in the experience gained with Carnot.

A number of innovations were introduced in the Carnot project—these are discussed in [13, 17]. What is most relevant here are the *semantic* and the *distribution* services. The semantic services included tools for enterprise modeling and model integration. These tools were used to generate mappings among different resources, modeled in terms of their schemas and terminologies. The mappings were based on a shared ontology for the given domain of interest [16]. The semantic services provided the basis for agent interoperation, letting the agents use models of each other's resources in interacting in a desirable manner. This is similar in some respects to the concept of mediators [15].

The distribution services managed logical data access for both retrieval and updates. They included tools such a common interpretive execution environment as well as a distributed communicating agent facility. The distribution services handled the functionality of workflow management, in a low-level distributed computing fashion and in a high-level agent-based fashion.

Thus, Carnot used agents to provide support for relaxed, distributed, concurrent transactions across heterogeneous databases. Carnot was, however, focused on the problems of enterprise integration within a closed environment, where the component databases were known in advance and fixed.

Of the experiences gained with Carnot, two main observations apply to the enhancements needed to apply cooperative information systems in more general settings. First, although the task of semantic integration was greatly facilitated by the tools developed during Carnot, enhanced integration tools were needed to handle greater varieties of information resources made available by the web. Second, semantic integration was mostly restricted to the static aspects of the information resources, i.e., their schemas and data values, but not for their dynamic aspects, such as their processes and interactions among them. A better understanding of processes, especially as they apply in open environments, is a prerequisite for the integration of the dynamic aspects. There has been some related work in software engineering [2], but it is mostly geared to single processes, not their interaction. This paper discusses the results we have obtained along the above two lines of thought.

1.3 Organization

Section 2 describes some components of an architecture of a multiagent system for information-rich environments. Section 3 describes the enhancements necessary to apply semantic integration to an open environment. Section 4 introduces a form of commitments that is suited to multiagent systems, shows how they can be operated on, and used to specify social policies. Section 5 applies these notions to formalize applications in electronic commerce and virtual enterprises. Section 6 concludes with a discussion of future directions.

2 Architecture

A promising approach is to the challenges of interoperability is to use mediators [15]. A mediator is a simplified agent that acts on behalf of a set of information resources or applications. Figure 1 shows a mediator architecture. The basic idea is that the mediator is responsible for mapping the resources or applications to the rest of the world. Mediators thus shield the different components of the system from each other. To construct mediators effectively requires some common representation of the meanings of the resources and applications they connect. Such a representation is called an ontology [9], and it is often managed by its own specialized agent.

It is a sign of their maturity that cooperative information systems are beginning to evolve a standard set of agent types. The resultant architecture renders development and deployment of CISs much easier, and essentially raises the abstraction level at which CISs can be described. Some of these are

User agents, which have the following characteristics:
  − Contain mechanisms to select an ontology
  − Support a variety of interchangeable user interfaces, such as query forms, graphical query tools, menu-driven query builders, and query languages
  − Support a variety of interchangeable result browsers and visualization tools
  − Maintain models of other agents
  − Provide access to other information resources, such as data analysis tools, workflows, and concept learning tools.
Broker agents implement a "yellow pages" and "white pages" directory service for locating appropriate agents with appropriate capabilities. Brokers manage a namespace service, and may have the ability to store and forward messages, and locate message recipients. Broker agents also function as communication aides, by managing communications among the various agents, databases, and application programs in the environment.

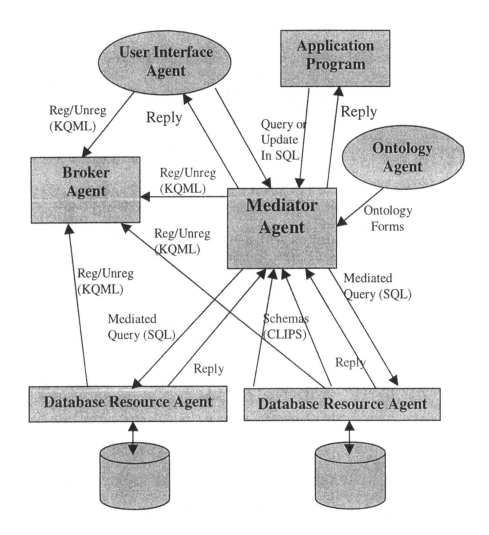

Fig. 1. Typical agent architecture for a cooperative information system

Resource agents come in a variety of common types, depending on which resource they are representing, and provide the following capabilities:
  - Wrappers implement common communication protocols and translate into and from local access languages. For example, a local data-manipulation language might be SQL for relational databases or OSQL for object-oriented databases.
  - SQL database agents manage specific information resources
  - Data analysis agents apply machine learning techniques to form logical concepts from data or use statistical techniques to perform data mining
  - Resource agents apply the mappings that relate each information resource to a common context to perform a translation of message semantics. At most n sets of mappings and n resource agents are needed for

interoperation among n resources and applications, as opposed to n(n-1) mappings that would be needed for direct pairwise interactions among n resources without agents (see Figure 3).

Execution agents, which might be implemented as rule-based knowledge systems, e.g., in CLIPS, are employed to
- Supervise query execution
- Operate as script-based agents to support scenario-based analyses
- Execute workflows, which might extend over the web and might be expressed in a format such as the one specified by the Workflow Management Coalition.

Mediators are specialized execution agents, which
- Determine which resources might have relevant information using help from brokers
- Decompose queries to be handled by multiple agents
- Combine the partial responses obtained from multiple resources
- Translate between ontologies.

Ontology agents are essential for interoperation. They
- Provide a common context as a semantic grounding, which agents can then use to relate their individual terminologies
- Provide (remote) access to multiple ontologies
- Manage the distributed evolution and growth of ontologies. A common context in the form of an ontology or model of the domain can provide such semantic grounding.

Most agent-based information systems incorporate one or more agents of the above types.

3 Semantic Integration and Processing in the Large

A major task for the agents in a cooperative information system is to reconcile the varied semantics of the mostly autonomous resources in the CIS. A focus of our research in CIS is the development of tools for constructing and browsing the ontologies that serve as a basis for semantic reconciliation.

Information-rich environments include not just text and relational data, but varieties of multimedia, forms, and executable code—it has become much more complex than before. As a result, old methods for manipulating information sources are no longer efficient or even appropriate. Surprisingly, structured data has become more difficult to find and retrieve than unstructured text, because keyword searches over previously indexed documents, which can be attempted for text, are unsuitable for data. Data retrieval requires schemas, which are often unavailable, incomplete, or incomprehensible. Mechanisms are needed that allow efficient querying on diverse information sources that support structured as well as unstructured information.

Ontologies appear to be well suited for not only organizing new information, but also managing the storage and retrieval of existing information. An ontology is a model of some portion of the world and is described by defining a set of representational terms. In an ontology, definitions associate the names of entities in a universe of discourse (e.g., classes, relations, functions, or other objects) with human-readable text describing what the names mean, and formal axioms that constrain the interpretation and well-formed use of these terms. For information systems, or for the Internet, ontologies can be used to organize keywords and database concepts by capturing the semantic relationships among the keywords or among the tables and fields in a database. The semantic relationships provide users with an abstract view of an information space for their domain of interest. Ontologies are suitable for graphical representation, and can be scaled and viewed at various levels of abstraction, thereby making them suitable for large information spaces.

As an example of the tools we have been developing for exploiting the benefits of ontologies is the Java Ontology Editor, JOE [8]. JOE provides a graphical user interface for users to (1) browse and edit ontologies, or (2) construct queries based on the ontologies. By being written as a collection of Java applets, JOE can be accessed from any Java-compatible browser, and an ontology can be simultaneously viewed and edited by more than one user. This group-editing feature has the advantage that only one correct version is saved. At the same time, experts from different fields can jointly build an ontology over a length of time or, if desired, merge various small ontologies to create a single encompassing ontology. This feature is desirable in large enterprises. Examples 1 and 2 show how to browse (and edit) an ontology, and how to use it to make queries.

Example 1. Figure 2 shows JOE in its ontology browsing mode, where it is applying one of its abstraction mechanisms (a magnifier) to help users view a large ontology. The entire ontology is displayed within its main window and a magnified view of the selected area in the window on the right. JOE also an editor mode to help users modify an ontology. ∎

Example 2. Figure 3 shows the query mode, in which users can construct queries by setting constraints on displayed attributes. The constructed query "Get the social security numbers (ssn) and the ages of all the Patients whose lastname is 'Johnson' and who were diagnosed-with a Diagnosis named 'cancer' and who live

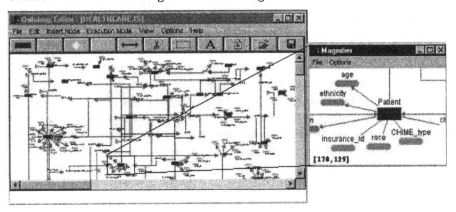

Fig. 2. JOE displaying an ontology

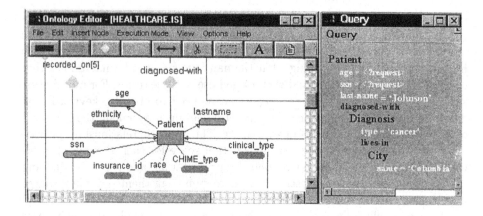

Fig. 3. JOE executing in the query mode

in a City named 'Columbia"' will be shown on a separate window to the right of
the main window. JOE will internally translate the graphical query to an SQL
statement as the user builds the query. The user can simply submit the query
by choosing the "submit" option in the "Query" menu and the results will be
displayed in a third window. JOE also provides an editor where the user, if he
or she is an expert in SQL, can directly modify or type in a new SQL statement
for execution. ∎

4 Interaction-Oriented Programming: Commitments

We hinted above that the notion of process in information-rich environments is
much richer and flexible than in conventional settings. Indeed, traditional abstractions such as database transactions are notoriously unsuited for representing
and managing flexible processes. Agents are a useful metaphor, but merely call-
ing a program an agent doesn't help! We also need corresponding sophisticated
abstractions for programming the agents.

We have been pursuing a research program on *Interaction-Oriented Programming (IOP)* to develop and study primitives for the specification of systems of
agents and constraints on their behavior. These primitives include societies, the
roles agents may play in them, what capabilities and commitments they require,
and what authorities they grant. Agents can autonomously instantiate abstract
societies by adopting roles in them. The creation, operation, and dissolution of
societies are achieved by agents acting autonomously, but satisfying their commitments. A commitment can be canceled, provided the agent then satisfies the
metacommitments applying to its cancelation.

The representations for IOP must support several functionalities, which typically exist informally, and are either effected by humans in some unprincipled way, are hard-coded in applications, or are buried in operating procedures and manuals. Information typically exists in data stores, in the environment, or with interacting entities. The IOP contribution is that it

- enhances and formalizes ideas from different disciplines
- separates them out in an explicit conceptual metamodel to use as a basis for programming and for programming methodologies
- makes them programmable.

The notion of commitments may be familiar from databases. However, in databases, commitments correspond to a value being declared and are identified with the successful termination of a transaction. When a transaction terminates successfully, it commits, but it is not around any more to modify its commitments. Thus the commitments are rigid and irrevocable. If the data value committed by one transaction must be modified a separate, logically independent transaction must be executed to commit the modified value. Traditional commitments presuppose that different computations are fully isolated and that locks can be held long enough that the atomicity of distributed computations can be assured. Although suitable for traditional data processing, for the above reasons, traditional commitments are highly undesirable for information-rich environments, where autonomous entities must carry out prolonged interactions with one another [11].

Commitments reflect an inherent tension between predictability and flexibility. Agents who can commit are easier to deal with. Also, the desired commitments serve as a sort of requirements on the construction of the agents who meet those commitments. However, commitments reduce the options available to an agent.

4.1 Commitments

We propose an alternative characterization of commitments that is better suited to agents and multiagent systems. In our formulation the commitments are directed to specific parties in a specific context. Thus an agent may not offer the same commitments to every other agent. The context is the multiagent system within which the given agents interact. An agent or multiagent system with jurisdiction over some resources and agents is called a *sphere of commitment (SoCom)*.

A commitment is a four-place relation. The *debtor* refers to the agent who makes the commitment, and the *creditor* to the agent who receives the commitment. Commitments are formed in a *context*, which is given by the enclosing SoCom (or, ultimately, by society at large). Based on the above intuitions, we motivate the following logical form for commitments.

Definition 1. A commitment $C(x, y, p, G)$ relates a debtor x, a creditor y, a context G, and a discharge condition p.

4.2 Operations on Commitments

We define the following operations on commitments.

O1. *Create* instantiates a commitment; it is typically performed as a consequence of an agent adopting a role or by exercising a social policy (explained below).

O2. *Discharge* satisfies the commitment; it is performed by the debtor concurrently with the actions that lead to the given condition being satisfied.

O3. *Cancel* revokes the commitment. It can be performed by the debtor.

O4. *Release* essentially eliminates the commitment. This is distinguished from both *discharge* and *cancel*, because *release* does not mean success or failure of the given commitment, although it lets the debtor off the hook. The *release* action may be performed by the context or the creditor of the given commitment.

O5. *Delegate* shifts the role of debtor to another agent within the same context, and can be performed by the new debtor or the context.

O6. *Assign* transfers a commitment to another creditor within the same context, and can be performed by the present creditor or the context.

Through an abuse of notation, we write the above operations also as propositions, indicating their successful execution. We define some additional operations and propositions corresponding to important speech acts. These include $notify$ and $authorize$. $notify(x, y, q)$ mean that x notifies y of q, and $authorize(x, y, p)$ means that x authorizes y to allow condition p.

4.3 Policies

Social policies are conditional expressions involving commitments and operations on commitments. Policies have a computational significance, which is that they can help control the execution of operations on commitments, even without explicit reference to the context. It is their locality that makes policies useful in practice. Agents can commit to social policies just as to other expressions; in this case, the agents' commitments are higher order, and are termed *metacommitments*. An example metacommitment is $cancel(x, \mathsf{C}(x, y, p, G)) \Rightarrow create(x, \mathsf{C}(x, y, q, G))$, which means that x can cancel his commitment for p if instead he adopts a commitment for q (for suitable p and q).

4.4 Applying Commitments

Commitments are computationally applied in the following manner. Initially, abstract SoComs are defined in terms of their *roles*. Each role is associated with the capabilities it requires, the commitments it engenders, and the authorities it creates. The capabilities are the tasks the agent *can* do, the commitments are what the agent *must* do, and the authorities are what the agent *may* do. The commitments, in particular, may be metacommitments. Indeed, they usually are metacommitments, e.g., that the agent will adopt a base commitment upon receiving a request.

At some point, possibly during execution, an agent may decide to enter into a SoCom as a particular role or roles. To do so, he would have to cause the SoCom to be instantiated from the abstract specification. To adopt a role, the agent must have the necessary capabilities, and accept the associated commitments. In doing so, he also obtains the authorities to properly play the role. The agent must then behave according to the commitments. Agents can join a SoCom when configured by humans or during execution: this requires publishing the definition of the abstract SoCom.

5 Designing Commitments

We consider an example in two parts. The first deals with electronic commerce; the second combines in aspects of virtual enterprises [7]. The commitments are designed based on the corresponding roles in human society.

5.1 Electronic Commerce

We first define an abstract SoCom consisting of two roles: *buyer* and *seller*, which require capabilities and commitments about, e.g., the requests they will honor, and the validity of price quotes. To adopt these roles, agents must have the capabilities and acquire the commitments. Example 3 involves two individual agents who adopt the roles of *Buyer* and *Seller* to carry out a simple deal.

Example 3. Consider a situation involving two agents, *Customer* and *Vendor*, with authority over their respective databases. The SoCom manager has an abstract SoCom for buy-sell deals with the roles of *Buyer* and *Seller*. *Buyer*'s capabilities include asking for a price quote and placing an order. *Seller*'s capabilities include responding to price quotes and accepting orders based on checking the inventory locally. *Buyer*'s commitments include paying the quoted price for anything she orders. *Seller*'s commitments include (a) giving price quotes in response to requests and (b) fulfilling orders that he has accepted.

Customer asks the manager to instantiate a deal between her (*Customer*) as *Buyer* and *Vendor* as *Seller*. The manager asks *Vendor* if he would like to join as *Seller*. When *Vendor* agrees, and since both agents have the requisite capabilities, capacities, and resources, the deal is set up.

Customer now wishes to check the price of a valve with a diameter of 21mm. Upon the receipt of the query from *Customer*, *Vendor*—based on its role as *Seller*—offers an appropriate answer. ∎

5.2 Virtual Enterprises

Example 4 considers a more general situation where the role of *Seller* is adopted by an agent who happens to be a Valvano-cum-Hoosier VE—i.e., a SoCom consisting of the hose and valve vendors. Example 5 considers the situation where the Valvano-cum-Hoosier VE detects a problem in the supply of valves for which an order has been placed. The VE automatically meets its commitments by revising the order and notifying the customer.

Now we consider the situation where one or more agents may form a cooperative SoCom or team. For simplicity, we assume that teams have a distinguished agent who handles their external interactions. We refer to this agent as the VE.

Example 4. We now consider two agents with authority over the Valvano and Hoosier databases, respectively. These agents have similar capabilities to the *Seller* of Example 3. They form a VE, called Valvano-cum-Hoosier VE, which can adopt the role of *Seller*. *Buyer* behaves as before and expects *Seller* to behave according to the buy-sell deal. However, *Seller* is implemented differently, with commitments among its members, which we do not elaborate here. The possible commitments of the Valvano-cum-Hoosier VE include the following.

- The VE will give price quotes to anyone who requests them.
- The VE will refund the purchase price if an order with matching valves and hoses cannot be fulfilled. There are still no refunds if an order for matching valves and hoses can be fulfilled.
- If the VE cannot fulfill an order, it will try to find an alternative order that will satisfy *Customer*'s requirements.

Recall that *val* or *hos* would not take refunds individually. Thus a customer might be saddled with valves for which matching hoses could not be found. However, when dealing with the VE, a customer can get a refund in those situations. ∎

In the above examples, the actions are performed by the constituents of the SoCom. Sometimes, however, it is useful to perform actions at a higher level SoCom. Such actions are necessary when the actions of the member agents must be atomically performed or undone. Example 5 is related to this situation.

Example 5. Continuing with Example 4, suppose an order for matching valves and hoses is successfully placed. It turns out later that the valve manufacturer discontinued the model that was ordered, but recommends a substitute. The substitute valve fits different diameter hoses than the original choice. The VE knows that the original order could be satisfied using the new valve and a different set of hoses. The VE can handle this replacement itself and, based on its prior commitment, not charge the customer any extra. The customer does not need to know of the internal exchanges among the members of the VE SoCom. Figure 4 illustrates the execution. ∎

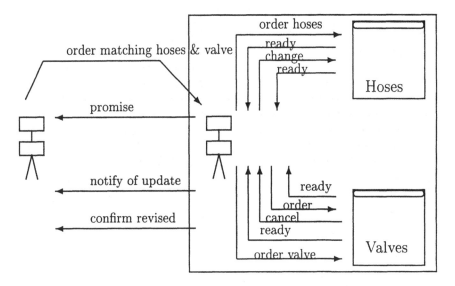

Fig. 4. Commitment-based recovery

In the above example, the discontinuation of a valve after an order for it was accepted is a kind of failure that arises after the original interaction had ended. Traditional approaches would be inapplicable in such a situation.

6 Conclusions and Future Work

Although multiagent systems have been known for a number of years and practical applications of them are spreading, they are still being built in a more or less *ad hoc* manner. Just as for other systems, engineering a multiagent system presupposes the existence of tools and methodologies, which in turn presuppose the existence of suitable representational frameworks and clean theories. As one would expect with MAS being a new area, the state of the art is mixed. Some problems are well-studied or there are clearer inputs from other disciplines—for these, we are seeing useful and practical tools emerging. Other problems are not as well-studied, and the inputs from related disciplines are not applicable to MAS needs, and for these the theories are still begin explored. The approaches described here can be seen as one of each kind.

The ontology tools are the culmination of several years of research and practice. They are achieving the state where they can be easily used, and by people with only minimal training in information management.

The IOP approach, of which we discussed only the aspects relating to commitments, provides a set of high-level abstractions for building systems of autonomous agents. The autonomy is essential when the underlying environment includes autonomous and heterogeneous resources. By separating out the considerations of the infrastructure, IOP promises to be a more effective and portable way of designing multiagent systems for applications such as electronic commerce and virtual enterprises.

There are some important directions for future research. Of special interest to conceptual modeling is the development of richer metamodels than we have at present. A potentially important theme is to identify useful patterns corresponding to the "best practices" in key areas, and incorporating them in our metamodels. An example area would be contracting among autonomous entities, which seems to underlie several of the upcoming open applications. Along with richer metamodels, there is need for a corresponding intuitive semantics. We have made some progress along this direction [12]. One of the themes that should be more intensively addressed is the compositionality of conceptual models. For example, one would like to build separate models for electronic commerce and virtual enterprises, and dynamically compose them to produce a model for a commercially engaged virtual enterprise. Lastly, there is great need for expressive formal tools that support the conceptual models and their semantics.

References

1. Omran A. Bukhres and Ahmed K. Elmagarmid, editors. *Object-Oriented Multidatabase Systems: A Solution for Advanced Applications*. Prentice-Hall, 1996.
2. Bill Curtis, Marc I. Kellner, and Jim Over. Process modeling. *Communications of the ACM*, 35(9):75–90, September 1992.
3. Stan Franklin and Art Graesser. Is it an agent or just a program?: A taxonomy for autonomous agents. In *Intelligent Agents III: Agent Theories, Architectures, and Languages*, pages 21–35, 1997.
4. Michael N. Huhns and Munindar P. Singh. The agent test. *IEEE Internet Computing*, 1(5):78–79, October 1997. Instance of the column *Agents on the Web*.
5. Michael N. Huhns and Munindar P. Singh. Agents and multiagent systems: Themes, approaches, and challenges. In *[6]*, chapter 1, pages 1–23. 1997.
6. Michael N. Huhns and Munindar P. Singh, editors. *Readings in Agents*. Morgan Kaufmann, San Francisco, 1997.
7. Anuj K. Jain and Munindar P. Singh. Using spheres of commitment to support virtual enterprises. In *Proceedings of the 4th ISPE International Conference on Concurrent Engineering: Research and Applications (CE)*, pages 469–476. International Society for Productivity Enhancements (ISPE), August 1997.
8. Kuhanandha Mahalingam and Michael N. Huhns. An ontology tool for distributed information environments. *IEEE Computer*, 30(6):80–83, June 1997.
9. Ramesh S. Patil, Richard E. Fikes, Peter F. Patel-Schneider, Don McKay, Tim Finin, Thomas Gruber, and Robert Neches. The DARPA knowledge sharing effort: Progress report. In *[6]*, pages 243–254. 1997. (Reprinted from *Proceedings of the Third International Conference on Principles of Knowledge Representation and Reasoning, 1992*).
10. Charles J. Petrie, Jr. Agent-based engineering, the web, and intelligence. *IEEE Expert*, 11(6), December 1996.
11. Munindar P. Singh. Commitments among autonomous agents in information-rich environments. In *Proceedings of the 8th European Workshop on Modelling Autonomous Agents in a Multi-Agent World (MAAMAW)*, pages 141–155, May 1997.
12. Munindar P. Singh. An ontology for commitments in multiagent systems: Toward a unification of normative concepts. *Artificial Intelligence and Law*, 1998. In press.

13. Munindar P. Singh, Philip E. Cannata, Michael N. Huhns, Nigel Jacobs, Tomasz Ksiezyk, Kayliang Ong, Amit P. Sheth, Christine Tomlinson, and Darrell Woelk. The Carnot heterogeneous database project: Implemented applications. *Distributed and Parallel Databases: An International Journal*, 5(2):207–225, April 1997.

14. Peter Wegner. Why interaction is more powerful than algorithms. *Communications of the ACM*, 40(5):80–91, May 1997.

15. Gio Wiederhold. Mediators in the architecture of future information systems. In *[6]*, pages 185–196. 1997. (Reprinted from *IEEE Computer, 1992*).

16. Gio Wiederhold and Michael Genesereth. The conceptual basis for mediation services. *IEEE Expert*, 12(5):38–47, September 1997.

17. Darrell Woelk, Philip Cannata, Michael Huhns, Nigel Jacobs, Tomasz Ksiezyk, Greg Lavender, Greg Meredith, Kayliang Ong, Wei-Min Shen, Munindar Singh, and Christine Tomlinson. Carnot prototype. In *[1]*, chapter 18, pages 621–648. 1996.

Strategies for Querying Information Agents

PRASAD CHALASANI, SOMESH JHA, ONN SHEHORY and KATIA SYCARA

Robotics Institute, Carnegie Mellon University, Pittsburgh PA 15213-3890, USA

Abstract. In a simple cooperative MAS model where a collection of "querying agents" can send queries to a collection of "information agents", we formalize the problem of designing strategies so that the expected completion time of the queries is minimized, when every querying agent uses the same strategy. We devise a provably optimal strategy for the static case with no query arrivals, and show via simulations that the same strategy performs well when queries arrive with a certain probability. We also consider issues such as whether or not the expected completion time can be reduced by sending multiple copies of queries, or by aborting copies of answered queries.

1 Introduction

As the internet grows relentlessly, and multi-agent systems (MAS) proliferate, it becomes increasingly important to design algorithms for agents to use limited resources (such as time, memory, bandwidth, etc) efficiently. A badly designed scheme can easily lead to congestion and poor response times. A first step toward the design of good strategies is to consider simple models of agent interactions. Even though these models may be abstract, they can help identify important issues that will arise in realistic models. Morever, strategies devised under simple models can perform well in realistic settings.

With this viewpoint, in this paper we introduce a simple MAS model where there is a collection of *querying agents* (QA) and a collection of *information agents* (IA). The querying agents receive queries (from humans or other agents), which they must send to IAs to obtain an answer. We want to design a strategy for a QA to send queries to IAs so that the expected completion time of the queries is minimized. To see what kinds of issues arise in designing such strategies, suppose the loads of the IAs were observable, and that all IAs are capable of answering any query. Should the QA send its query to the least-loaded information agent? If this were the *only* QA in the system, this is obviously a good strategy. However in an MAS there are a large number of QAs, possibly much larger than the number of IAs. If *every* QA uses the above strategy, then it is no longer clear that this is the best one. For instance if the loads of the information agents are roughly the same, this would be a bad strategy, since the least-loaded information agent would tend to receive a disproportionately large number of queries, and all these queries would take longer to complete, on the average. However if one IA has a much lower load than every other IA, this could be a good strategy.

In this paper we examine the following type of question:

If every QA were to use the *same* querying strategy, which strategy minimizes the expected completion time of the queries?

Since every QA uses the same strategy, we refer to it as a *symmetric* strategy. A natural symmetric strategy is the following *randomized* one: every query agent sends its query to an information agent chosen uniformly at random. This would be a good strategy if the information agents are more or less equally loaded, but what if they aren't? In this paper we examine this problem and design an optimal randomized symmetric strategy for this case of arbitrary loads, and assuming a static situation where each QA has one query and no new queries arrive. Our strategy has the appealing feature that IAs with higher load are less likely to receive queries. We also show by simulations that even in a dynamic model with new query arrivals, ours is a good strategy to follow.

Another important issue we examine is:

If QAs send multiple copies of their queries to different IAs, does this reduce the expected completion time? Is there an optimal number of copies to send?

There is a tradeoff here between two opposing effects on the query completion time. The first is the *load effect*: multiple copies increase the load on the IAs, and every *individual* query copy takes longer on average to be answered. The second is the *multiplicity effect*: since each query has multiple copies at different IAs, it has a greater chance of being answered sooner. It seems intuitive that as more copies are sent, the benefit of multiplicity will be outweighed by the load effect. In this paper we show simulations that show the optimal number of query copies to send, for specific situations.

1.1 Related work

Problems related to ours have been studied extensively in the area of *stochastic scheduling* of parallel systems (for a good introduction, see [2, 5, 6] and the references therein). In all such work, the goal has been to design a *centralized* scheduling algorithm so that job completion times are reduced. By contrast in our MAS model, we emphatically want to design *decentralized* algorithms that different querying agents can use, with as little communication as possible between each other. Decentralized algorithms are easy to implement, more robust in the face of failures, and scale up better than centralized ones. Such algorithms are therefore likely to play an important role in a MAS context. Despite this important difference, some of the techniques in stochastic scheduling research are useful for our purposes. For instance, we have used the concepts of *majorization* and *Schur convexity* [1, 3, 9] to design our optimal randomized algorithm in Section 4.

Several researchers in MAS have approached the problem of designing decentralized strategies from an *economics* viewpoint. For instance, Huberman and Lukose [11] have observed that since most people who access the internet are not charged in proportion to their use, this has lead to the well-known *tragedy of the commons* [8], which is a special kind of *social dilemma*: each individual tends to greedily consume bandwith, leading to a degradation of performance for everyone. This conflict between an individual's myopic strategy and global performance is similar to the one discussed above in the introduction: when every QA sends a query to the least-loaded IA, everyone's performance suffers. Researchers taking the economic viewpoint have proposed that *pricing* internet access can lead to a resolution of this dilemma [12, 14, 17, 18]. Some researchers [10, 15, 19, 20] are pursuing the design of decentralized strategies using models based on *market equilibrium* [7]. In this paper we are formulating the decentralized strategy-design problem purely from a performance viewpoint: if each agent uses a strategy that leads to degraded performance for every agent, then that strategy is perhaps not an optimal one.

Querying strategies for *individual agents* have been considered by, among others, Chalasani et. al. [4] Etzioni et. al. [16], and Lukose and Huberman [13]. These authors have not considered the effect of several agents using the same strategies.

1.2 Organization of the paper

In Section 2 we introduce the basic model assumed throughout the paper. In Section 3 we consider the case where the IAs initially have zero load. For this case we show a lower bound on the expected completion time of *any* strategy. We also design a randomized algorithm that comes close to the lower bound. In Section 4 we consider the case where IAs have arbitrary initial loads and design an optimal symmetric randomized querying strategy. We also show via simulations (subsection 4.1) that this strategy performs better than two other natural ones. Section 5 examines the effect of sending multiple query-copies to different IAs. We show analytical results for some cases, and simulations for others. Section 6 concludes with a discussion of future work.

2 The model

We assume there are m **querying agents** (QA) $A_1, A_2, \ldots, A_m$, and n **information agents** (IA) $I_1, I_2, \ldots, I_n$. Initially, each IA I_i has a **load** ℓ_i, that is, it has ℓ_i queries pending, and, without loss of generality,

$$\ell_1 \leq \ell_2 \leq \ldots \leq \ell_n.$$

Time is measured in **cycles**, and the initial cycle represents time 0. In general, the QAs receive queries that they need to send to IAs for an answer. Every IA is capable of answering every query. In the **static** version of the model, each QA has just one query at time 0. In the **dynamic** version, queries arrive at each QA in each cycle with a certain **arrival probability** α. Each QA can send up to k **copies** (or instances) of the query to different IAs. The query is said to be **completed** as soon as any copy of the query is answered by an IA. Queries never fail, i.e., when an IA chooses to answer a certain query, it successfully does so. Each query takes exactly one cycle to answer. Each IA uses the following **randomized scheduling** policy: Among the queries that are pending, it picks one uniformly at random and answers it, and deletes it from its pending list. Note that under this policy, if the number of pending queries at an IA is large, then *every* query at this IA experiences a longer *expected* completion time. When a QA's query has been answered, the QA may choose to **abort** all (unanswered) copies of its query. We ignore all communication costs and assume that queries and answers are sent instantaneously.

Our goal is to design a good **symmetric** strategy for the QAs to send queries (with possibly multiple copies) to the IAs. By a symmetric strategy we mean that every QA uses exactly the same strategy. In addition to being easy to analyze, such strategies are also easy to implement in a cooperative multi-agent system (MAS) setting. In this paper we will only consider the design of strategies for the static model, and experimentally study the behavior of the dynamic model when each QA uses this static strategy in each cycle.

Consider then the static model, where each QA has just one query at time 0, that it wants to obtain an answer for. For brevity we refer to QA A_i's query simply as "query i". For any (possibly randomized) symmetric strategy, we define the following random variables. We let X_{ij} be the random variable defined as

$$X_{ij} = \begin{cases} 1 & \text{if a copy of query } i \text{ is sent to IA } I_j, \\ 0 & \text{otherwise.} \end{cases}$$

If A_i sends a total of k copies of its query, then clearly

$$\sum_{j=1}^{n} X_{ij} = k.$$

Y_{ij} is the time at which a copy of query i is answered by IA I_j, if it received such a copy, and is ∞ otherwise. The **completion time** of query i is the random variable Z_i defined as

$$Z_i = \min\{X_{i1}Y_{i1}, X_{i2}Y_{i2}, \dots, X_{in}Y_{in}\}.$$

In case only $k = 1$ copy of query is i is sent, to I_j, then of course $Z_i = Y_{ij}$.

3   Single query-copy, unloaded case

We consider first the simplest case of the static model where the initial loads ℓ_i of the IAs are all 0, and each QA sends exactly *one* copy of its query to some information agent (so $k = 1$). What symmetric strategy should the QAs use in order to minimize the expected completion time of their query? We first show a lower bound on the expected completion time, for *any* strategy (symmetric or not).

Lemma 1. *For the static model where each QA sends exactly one copy of its query to an IA, regardless of the strategy used, there is some query whose expected completion time is at least*

$$\left(\lfloor \frac{m}{n} \rfloor + 1\right) \left(1 - \frac{n}{2m}\lfloor \frac{m}{n} \rfloor\right).$$

If m is a multiple of n, this simplifies to

$$\frac{1}{2}\left(1 + \frac{m}{n}\right).$$

Proof: Following the notation introduced above, we write Z_i for the completion time of the query sent by A_i. Consider the *sum* of the completion times of the m queries $Z = Z_1 + Z_2 + \dots + Z_m$. This sum depends on the actual allocation of the m queries among the n IAs. What is the smallest possible value of this sum? Clearly Z is minimized if, for as many cycles as possible, *every* IA is busy answering some query. If m is an integer multiple of n, this is easily achieved by allocating exactly m/n of the queries to each IA. In general, the minimum Z is achieved by allocating $\lfloor m/n \rfloor$ queries to each IA, and allocating each of the remaining $m - n\lfloor m/n \rfloor$ queries to distinct IAs. With this allocation, in cycles 1 to $\lfloor m/n \rfloor$, n different queries are answered in each cycle, and in last cycle number $\lfloor m/n \rfloor + 1$, the remaining $m - n\lfloor m/n \rfloor$ queries are answered. Thus for any querying strategy

$$
\sum_{i=1}^{m} Z_i \geq \sum_{i=1}^{\lfloor \frac{m}{n} \rfloor} (ni) + \left(m - n\lfloor \frac{m}{n} \rfloor\right)\left(\lfloor \frac{m}{n} \rfloor + 1\right)
$$
$$
= \frac{n}{2}\lfloor \frac{m}{n} \rfloor \left(\lfloor \frac{m}{n} \rfloor + 1\right) + \left(m - n\lfloor \frac{m}{n} \rfloor\right)\left(\lfloor \frac{m}{n} \rfloor + 1\right)
$$
$$
= \left(\lfloor \frac{m}{n} \rfloor + 1\right)\left(m - \frac{n}{2}\lfloor \frac{m}{n} \rfloor\right).
$$

By linearity of expectations, $\sum_{i=1}^{m} \mathbf{E}Z_i$ is also lower bounded by the last expression above. By the pigeonhole principle, this implies there is some i such that $\mathbf{E}Z_i$ is at least $1/m$ times that expression, which is the desired lower bound. ■

A simple and natural strategy that comes to mind is the following randomized one: Each QA sends its query to an IA chosen *uniformly at random*. It is clear that every query has the same expected completion time, and we show that this comes very close to the above lower bound.

Lemma 2. *If each QA sends its query to a uniformly randomly chosen IA, the expected completion time for each query is*

$$
1 + (m-1)/(2n).
$$

Proof: Since every query has the same expected completion time, without loss of generality we can focus on A_1's query. We let V be the random variable denoting the index of the information agent to which A_1 sends its query. The completion time Z_1 of A_1's query at I_V depends on the number of *other* queries I_V receives, which we denote by N_V. In particular, the query could be answered at times $1, 2, \ldots, N_V + 1$, each being equally likely. Therefore the conditional expectation of Z_1 given V is

$$
\mathbf{E}(Z_1|V) = \frac{1}{N_V + 1} \sum_{i=1}^{N_V+1} i = (N_V + 2)/2 = 1 + N_V/2,
$$

Note that, regardless of the value of the index V, $\mathbf{E}N_V = (m-1)/n$ since each of the $m - 1$ other QAs independently sends a query to I_V with probability $1/n$. So the expectation of Z_1 is

$$
\mathbf{E}(Z_1) = \mathbf{E}[\,\mathbf{E}(Z_1|V)\,]
$$
$$
= 1 + \frac{1}{2}\mathbf{E}(N_V)
$$
$$
= 1 + (m-1)/(2n).
$$

■

Example. Suppose there are $m = 17$ QAs and $n = 4$ IAs. With the above uniform-random strategy, the expected completion time of any query is, from Lemma 2,

$$1 + (m - 1)/2n = 1 + 16/8 = 3.$$

The lower bound on the expected completion time is, from Lemma 1,

$$(1 + 4)(1 - 4 \times 4/34) = 2.64,$$

so our strategy comes close to the theoretical lower bound. In fact we conjecture that there is no *symmetric* strategy that can do better than the above uniform-random strategy.

4 Single query-copy, pre-loaded case

We continue to assume each QA sends a single copy of its query to some IA, but drop the assumption that the current loads ℓ_i of the IAs are 0. For this case we design an optimal randomized symmetric querying strategy that has an intuitive feature: IAs with a larger load are less likely to receive a query. Specifically, we want to design the following type of strategy for the QAs: The QA sends its query to an I_i with probability p_i. Our goal is to specify the p_i values in such a way that the expected completion time of any query is minimized.

We first derive an expression for the expected completion time of a query, in terms of the probabilities p_i. Since every query will have the same expected completion time, it suffices to consider the completion time of QA A_1's query. However, unlike the unloaded situation, the expected completion of this query *does* depend on which IA it is sent to. As before we let the random variable V denote the IA index to which A_1's query is sent, so that V takes values in $\{1, 2, \ldots, n\}$. We also let N_V denote the number of *other* queries, i.e., from $A_2, \ldots, A_m$, that land at I_V. Given that A_1's query lands at I_V, the completion time of A_1's query is one of $1, 2, \ldots, \ell_V + N_V + 1$, each being equally likely, and the expected completion time is

$$\mathbf{E}(Z_1|V) = \frac{1}{1 + \ell_V + N_V} \sum_{j=1}^{\ell_V + N_V + 1} = 1 + (\ell_V + N_V)/2,$$

Therefore the expected completion time of A_1's query is

$$\mathbf{E}(Z_1) = \mathbf{E}[\mathbf{E}(Z_1|V)] \tag{1}$$

$$= 1 + \frac{1}{2}\mathbf{E}(\ell_V + N_V)$$

$$= 1 + \frac{1}{2}\left(\sum_{i=1}^{n} p_i\ell_i + \mathbf{E}(N_V)\right)$$

$$= 1 + \frac{1}{2}\left(\sum_{i=1}^{n} p_i\ell_i + \mathbf{E}[\mathbf{E}(N_V|V)]\right)$$

$$= 1 + \frac{1}{2}\left(\sum_{i=1}^{n} p_i\ell_i + \mathbf{E}[(m-1)p_V]\right)$$

$$= 1 + \frac{1}{2}\left(\sum_{i=1}^{n} p_i\ell_i + \sum_{i=1}^{n} p_i^2(m-1)\right)$$

$$= 1 + \frac{1}{2}\left(\sum_{i=1}^{n} p_i[\ell_i + (m-1)p_i]\right). \tag{2}$$

From this expression it follows that:

Lemma 3. *The optimal choice of probabilities p_i satisfies*

$$p_1 \geq p_2 \geq \ldots \geq p_n, \tag{3}$$

and in particular there is some k such that $p_i > 0$ for all $i \leq k$ and $p_i = 0$ for all $i > k$.

Proof: The proof is by contradiction. Suppose $p_1, \ldots, p_n$ is an optimal assignment of probabilities. If $p_i < p_{i+1}$ for some $i < n$, we can interchange p_i and p_{i+1} in the expression (2) and the expectation would decrease (since $\ell_i \leq \ell_{i+1}$), which contradicts our assumption that the probabilities were optimal. ∎

How do we find the number k of positive probabilities in the optimal assignment? This turns out to be a non-trivial problem. We have the following result, whose proof appears in the appendix. First we introduce the symbols

$$L(k) = \sum_{i=1}^{k} \ell_k,$$

$$A(k) = (L(k)/2 + m - 1)/k. \tag{4}$$

Theorem 4. *The number of positive probabilities in the optimal assignment is the smallest value of $k < n$ for which $A(k) \leq \ell_{k+1}/2$ if such a k exists, and equals n otherwise. For this k, the optimal probabilities p_i are such that for all $i \leq k$,*

$$\ell_i/2 + (m-1)p_i = A(k),$$

so that

$$p_i = \frac{1}{(m-1)}(A(k) - \ell_i/2). \tag{5}$$

Note that the optimal probabilities have a nice intuitive feature: *IAs with larger loads have a lower probability of receiving a query.*

Example. We illustrate the computations of this section with a simple example. Suppose there are $m = 20$ QAs, and $n = 9$ IAs, with initial loads ℓ_i as follows:

$$\{\ell_1, \ell_2, \ldots, \ell_9\} = \{1, 3, 4, 7, 11, 12, 16, 24, 32\}.$$

The values of $A(k), k = 1, 2, \ldots, 9$ are, from (4),

$$\{19.5, 10.5, 7.67, 6.63, 6.4, 6.33, 6.57, 7.25, 8.22\},$$

and we see that the smallest k for which $A_k \leq \ell_{k+1}/2$ is $k = 6$. Therefore in the optimal solution, probabilities p_1 through p_6 are positive, and $\ell_i/2 + (m-1)p_i$ has has the same value for $i = 1, 2, \ldots, 6$. The corresponding optimal probabilities are, from (5),

$$\{p_1, p_2, \ldots, p_6\} = \{0.307, 0.254, 0.228, 0.149, 0.0438, 0.0175\},$$

and the expected completion time $\mathbf{E}(Z_1)$ is 5.096 cycles. By contrast, if we had used the uniform-random strategy of the previous section (all $p_i = 1/n$), the expected completion time would be 8.167.

4.1 Simulation in the dynamic model

So far we have worked in the static model, i.e., each QA has just one query that needs to be answered. Now we consider the dynamic model, where in each cycle, at each QA, a new query arrives with probability α. To be realistic we also assume a bound M on the **buffer** at each QA, that is, each QA may have no more than M unanswered queries at any time.

For this model we consider what happens if each QA follows a specific static strategy in each cycle. In particular we consider the following three strategies:

- OPT: Each QA sends its query according the optimal static strategy of section 4, with the loads ℓ_i equal to the current loads of the IAs. Note that we
- MIN: Each QA sends its query to the *least-loaded* IA.
- UNIF: Each QA sends its query to an IA chosen uniformly at random.

Note that the first two strategies assume that the IA loads can be observed by the QAs, whereas the UNIF strategy does not require this capability. Figure 1 is a plot showing how these strategies compare with each other. We find that for the most part, our strategy OPT dominates the others.

5 Multiple query copies, unloaded case

Returning to the static model, let us examine strategies where each QA sends k copies of its query to a set of k distinct IAs, where the k-subset is chosen uniformly at random over all possible k-subsets. Note that since we are only considering symmetric strategies, the parameter k is the same for all QAs. The analytic computation of the expected query completion time in this case is somewhat complicated, and we will only consider

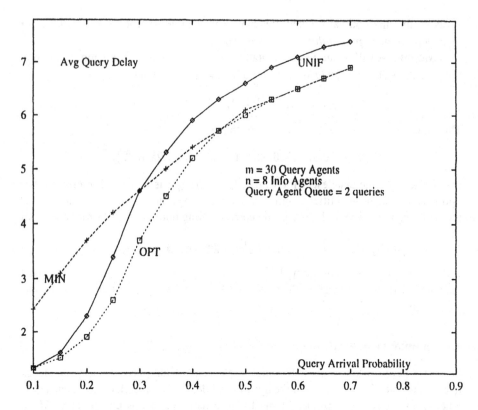

Fig. 1. *Expected completion time of a query in the dynamic model under three different strategies, as a function of the query arrival probability α. The model has $m = 30$ Query Agents, $n = 8$ Information Agents, and the buffer at each QA is limited to 2 unanswered queries. The average completion time is computed over all queries that have completed by 5000 runs.*

the special case $k = n$, i.e., an instance of *each* query is sent to *every* IA. For other k, we will only present simulation results.

For $k = n$, we consider two cases. First we will consider the case where *copies of answered queries are not aborted.* We show the following:

Theorem 5. *In the static model, if each of the m QAs sends a copy of its query to each of the n IAs, and copies of answered queries are not aborted, the expected completion time of any query approaches (for large m and n)*

$$\frac{1 - e^{-n}}{1 - e^{-n/m}}.$$

Proof: As before we focus on query 1 (i.e. QA A_1's query) and consider its completion time. We let Y_i denote the time at which the copy of query 1 sent to IA I_i is answered. Then clearly the completion time of query 1 is

$$Z_1 = \min\{Y_1, Y_2, \ldots, Y_n\}.$$

Therefore the expected completion time of query 1 is

$$\mathbf{E}(Z_1) = \sum_{i=1}^{m} P(Z_1 \geq i)$$

$$= \sum_{i=1}^{m} P(Y_1 \geq i, \ Y_2 \geq i, \ldots, Y_n \geq i),$$

and since the random variables Y_i are independent, this is

$$= \sum_{i=1}^{m} P(Y_1 \geq i)^n$$

$$= \sum_{i=1}^{m} \left(1 - \frac{i-1}{m}\right) \tag{6}$$

$$= \sum_{i=1}^{m} \left[\left(1 - \frac{i-1}{m}\right)^{m/(i-1)}\right]^{(i-1)n/m}$$

$$\simeq \sum_{i=1}^{m} e^{-(i-1)n/m} \quad \text{(for large } m, n\text{)}$$

$$= \frac{1 - e^{-n}}{1 - e^{-n/m}}. \tag{7}$$

■

Now let us consider the case where *all copies of answered queries are aborted.* This case is more complicated to analyze because we have to carefully keep track of how many *distinct* queries are answered in each cycle. We assume a *synchronous* mode of operation, i.e., in each cycle, *first* each IA answers a randomly chosen query from its pending list, and *then* all copies of answered queries are removed from the lists. We then have the following result, whose proof is in the appendix.

Theorem 6. *In the static model, if each of the m QAs sends a copy of its query to each of the n IAs, and copies of answered queries are aborted, the expected completion time E_m of any query is given by the recursion: $E_j = 1$ for $j = 1$, and for $j > 1$,*

$$E_j = 1 - (1 - 1/k)^n + \sum_{i=1}^{\min\{j-1,n\}} \sum_{r=0}^{i} (-1)^r \binom{j-1}{i} \binom{i}{r} \left(\frac{i-r}{j}\right)^n (E_{j-i} + 1).$$

Simulations. In Fig. 2 we show how the average query delay changes as the number of query-copies k is increased. Interestingly, for many cases it is found that the query first decreases as k is increased, and then increases, indicating that there is a certain optimum number k of query-copies. As noted in the introduction, there are two opposing effects on the expected query completion time: the multiplicity effect, and the load effect. Clearly the initial decrease in expected completion time can be explained by the fact that the multiplicity effect dominates, and the subsequent increase occurs because the load effect starts to dominate.

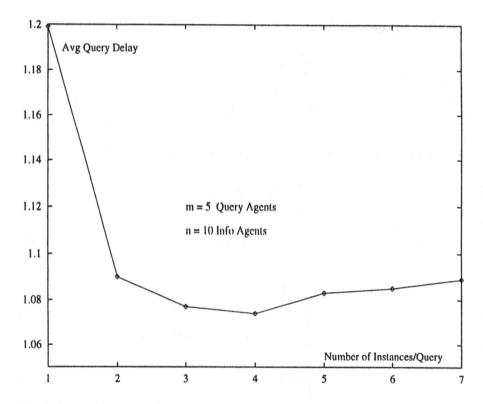

Fig. 2. *Expected completion time of a query, as a function of the number k of copies of the query that are sent. The plot is based on a simulation of the static model with m = 5 Query Agents, n = 10 Information Agents, and the average completion is computed over 5000 runs.*

6 Conclusion

In this paper we introduced a simple cooperative MAS model where there is a collection of information agents (IA) and a collection of querying agents (QA) that can send queries to the IAs. We designed a provably optimal randomized symmetric strategy for the static case where each QA has one query and each IA has an arbitrary initial load. We considered the issue of when it helps to send multiple query copies to different IAs. This paper only represents an initial step in a potentially fruitful and important research area, namely the design of decentralized algorithms for multi-agent systems. In the future we plan to study the use of economics-based approaches and also explore connections with the area of stochastic scheduling.

References

1. A.W.Marshall and I.Olkin. *Inequalities: theory of majorization and its applications.* Academic Press, 1979.

2. F. Baccelli, Z. Liu, and D. Towsley. Extremal scheduling of parallel processing systems with and without real-time constraints. *Journal of the ACM*, 40:1209–1237, 1993.

3. E. Beckenbach. *Inequalities*. Springer-Verlag, 1965.

4. P. Chalasani, S. Jha, O. Shehory, and K. Sycara. Query restart strategies for web agents. In *Autonomous Agents*, 1997. Submitted.

5. C. Chang and D. Yao. Rearrangement, majorization and stochastic scheduling. Technical Report IBM RC 16250 (#72136), IBM, Nov 1990.

6. E. Coffman and Z. Liu. On the optimal stochastic scheduling of out-forests. *Operations Research*, 40:S67–S75, 1992.

7. D. Duffie. *Security Markets: Stochastic Models*. Academic Press, 1988.

8. G. Hardin. The tragey of the commons. *Science*, 162:1243–1248, 1968.

9. G. Hardy, J. Littlewood, and G. Polya. *Inequalities*. Cambridge University Press, 1934.

10. B. Huberman, R. Lukose, and T. Hogg. An economics approach to hard computational problems. *Science*, 275:51–54, 1997.

11. B. A. Huberman and R. M. Lukose. Social dilemmas and internet congestion. *Science*, 277:535–537, July 25 1997.

12. J.K.MacKie-Mason and H. R. Varian. Some economics of the internet. In *Proc. 10th Michigan Public Utility Conf.*, 1993.

13. R. Lukose and B. Huberman. A methodology for managing risk in electronic transactions over the internet. In *3rd Int. conf. computational economics*, 1997.

14. J. MacKie-Mason and H. Varian. Pricing the internet. In B. Kahin and J. Keller, editors, *Public access to the internet*. MIT Press, 1995.

15. T. Mullen and M. Wellman. A simple computational market for network information services. In *Proc. first Int. Conf. on Multiagent Systems (ICMAS)*, 1995.

16. O.Etzioni, S. Hanks, T. Jiang, R. Kark, O. Madani, and O. Waarts. Efficient information gathering on the internet. In *Proc. Foundations of Comp. Sc.*, 1996.

17. D. Stahl, A. Gupta, and A. Whinston. Pricing of services in the internet. Technical report, University of Texas at Austin, 1995.

18. H. Varian. Economic mechanism design for computerized agents. In *USENIX Workshop on Electronic Conference*, New York, July 1995.

19. M. Wellman. A market-oriented programming environment and its application to distributed multicommodity flow problems. *J. Artificial Intelligence*, 1:1–23, 1993.

20. M. Wellman. The economic approach to artificial intelligence. *ACM Computing Surveys Symp. on Artif. Intell.*, 27(3), 1995.

A   Proof of Theorem 4

Let us first introduce the variables

$$e_i = \ell_i/2 + (m-1)p_i, \quad i = 1, 2, \ldots, n,$$

and rewrite the expression (2) for $\mathbf{E}(Z_1)$ as

$$\mathbf{E}(Z_1) = \frac{1}{m-1} \sum_{i=1}^{n} (e_i + \ell_i/2)(e_i - \ell_i/2)$$

$$= \frac{1}{m-1} \sum_{i=1}^{n} (e_i^2 - \ell_i^2/4). \tag{8}$$

Since the p_i are probabilities that add up to 1, we must have

$$\ell_i/2 \leq e_i \leq \ell_i/2 + (m-1), \quad i = 1, 2, \ldots, n \tag{9}$$

$$\sum_{i=1}^{n} e_i = L(n)/2 + m - 1 \tag{10}$$

Thus our original problem of choosing the optimal probabilities can be recast as one choosing the $\{e_i\}$ so that the expectation (8) is minimized subject to the constraints (9) and (10). Suppose there are two distinct indices i, j such that (a) p_i and $p_j > 0$ are strictly positive in the optimal solution, and (b) $e_i < e_j$. Clearly this means e_i and e_j lie strictly within the range defined by (9). Therefore there is some sufficiently small $\epsilon > 0$ such that if we increase e_i by ϵ and decrease e_j by ϵ, we still satisfy the constraints (9) and (10). However the value of $e_i^2 + e_j^2$ is smaller, since, in general for any positive x, y,

When $x + y$ is fixed, $x^2 + y^2$ is smaller when x and y are "closer" to each other, i.e., when $|x - y|$ is smaller.

(This type of argument is a special case of a *majorization* argument for *Schur-convex* functions (see, for example [1, 9]).) This means the expectation (8) is smaller, a contradiction. Therefore we conclude that for all positive p_i in the optimal solution, the value of e_i must be the same. A similar argument shows that if $i < j$ and $p_i = 0$ in the optimal solution, then $p_j = 0$ as well. Therefore if k is the number of positive probabilities in the optimal solution, for each $i \leq k$ the value of e_i is the same, and for $i > k$, $e_i = \ell_i/2$. Since $\sum_{i=1}^{k} e_i = L(k)/2 + m - 1$, it follows that for $i \leq k$, $e_i = A(k)$.

Suppose k is the number of positive probabilities in the optimal solution. Clearly if $A(k) > \ell_{k+1}/2$, this means $e_k > e_{k+1} = \ell_{k+1}/2$. As before this means we can decrease e_k by a small $\epsilon > 0$ and increase e_{k+1} by ϵ and reduce the sum $e_k^2 + e_{k+1}^2$ while still satisfying the constraints (9) and (10). This is a contradiction, so $A_k \leq \ell_{k+1}/2$. Now we claim that if

$$A_j \leq \ell_{j+1}/2$$

for some j, then this continues to hold for all larger j. To see this, note that

$$\begin{aligned}
A(j+1) &= \frac{L(j+1)}{2(j+1)} + \frac{m-1}{j+1} \\
&= \frac{1}{j+1} \left(j \left(L(j)/(2j) + (m-1)/j \right) + \ell_{j+1}/2 \right) \\
&= \frac{1}{j+1} \left(j A(j) + \ell_{j+1}/2 \right) \\
&\leq \frac{1}{j+1} \left(j \ell_{j+1}/2 + \ell_{j+1}/2 \right) \\
&= \ell_{j+1}/2 \\
&\leq \ell_{j+2}/2.
\end{aligned}$$

Therefore the number k of positive probabilities in the optimal solution is the *smallest* $k < n$ such that $A(k) \leq \ell_{k+1}/2$ is such a k exists, or equals n otherwise. ∎

B Proof of Theorem 6

Again we fix our attention on the completion time of query 1. Let E_j denote the expected completion time of query 1 when there are j distinct queries remaining. Initially, we of course have $j = m$. Clearly if $j = 1$ we have $E_1 = 1$. For $j > 1$, we have the following mutually exclusive and exhaustive events: Event A_0: Query 1 is answered in the current cycle, in which case the expected time is 1,a and the probability of event A is one minus the probability that none of the IAs answer query 1, i.e.,

$$P(A) = 1 - (1 - 1/k)^n .$$

The remaining events are A_i for $i = 1, 2, \min\{j - 1, n\}$, where A_i is the event that exactly i distinct queries are answered in the current cycle, all different from query 1. If event E_i occurs, all copies of the i answered queries will be removed, so we are left with $j - i$ distinct queries. Thus the expectation given that event A_i occurs is $(1 + E_{j-i})$. So we can write, for $j > 1$,

$$E_j = P(A_0) + \sum_{i=1}^{\min\{j-1,n\}} P(A_i)(1 + E_{j-i}).$$

We only need to show how to compute the probabilities $P(A_i)$. We can write this as

$P(A_i) =$ (Number of ways of choosing i special queries out of $j - 1$)

$\times\ P$(each IA picks only among the i special queries)

$\times\ P$(each of the i special queries is picked by some IA),   (11)

which is

$$P(A_i) = \binom{j - 1}{i} \left(\frac{i}{j}\right)^n P_i,$$

where P_i is the last probability in (11). We compute this probability by considering the complementary event: the event that at least one of the i special queries is *not* picked by any IA. For $r \le i$ the probability that a particular r-subset of the i special queries are not picked by any IA is $(1 - r/i)^n$. By inclusion-exclusion, we then have

$$P_i = \sum_{r=0}^{i} (-1)^r \binom{i}{r} (1 - r/i)^n .$$

Thus finally the recursive formula for our expectation E_j is: if $j = 1$ then $E_j = 1$, and if $j > 1$,

$$E_j = 1 - (1 - 1/k)^n + \sum_{i=1}^{\min\{j-1,n\}} \binom{j - 1}{i} \left(\frac{i}{j}\right)^n P_i(1 + E_{j-i}),$$

which simplifies to

$$E_j = 1 - (1 - 1/k)^n + \sum_{i=1}^{\min\{j-1,n\}} \sum_{r=0}^{i} (-1)^r \binom{j - 1}{i} \binom{i}{r} \left(\frac{i - r}{j}\right)^n (E_{j-i} + 1).$$

■

Grand Challenge Problems on Cross Cultural Communication
–Toward Socially Intelligent Agents–

Takashi Kido[1]

NTT MSC SDN BHD, 18th Floor, UBN Tower, No. 10, Jalan P. Ramlee , 50250
Kuala Lumpur, Malaysia

Abstract. The stage is set for studying cultural influences on human-human, human-agent and agent-agent communications. So far much attention has been paid to create adaptive agents which have adaptive user interface or flexible capability to communicate with another software agents. However little effort has been made for examining cultural influence in communications. I believe that as in the human-human communication, the cultural issues are unavoidable even in the communications conducted by software agents. "Socially intelligent agent", which can adapt itself to fill such cultural gaps between the parties involved in the communication, needs to identify the difference in forms of social interactions. This paper raises six grand challenge problems on cross cultural communication that CIA community should jointly tackle in creating such socially intelligent agents.

1   Introduction

In order to communicate with the foreigner effectively, it is important to understand their cultural background. In this paper, the word "culture" includes every social aspects which affect individuals decision making and communication styles. The word "individual" here means not only human but also includes robot or software agent.

The purposes of this paper are (1) to show the importance of cross cultural communication for AI and Agent studies and (2) to provide grand challenge problems that CIA community should jointly find answers.

2   Why Cross Cultural Communication Now?

There are several reasons why studies on cross cultural communication are important in CIA community. (1) The opportunity to meet with different cultures has been increasing due to the improvement of information technology and transportation. Therefore, there are great demands for mutual understanding of human-human cross cultural communication. (2) Applying AI and Agent technologies would potentially benefit international business or international group activities. (3) The study of user interface or software agent has been confronting cultural issues. In order to improve human-machine interaction, it is essential to understand the cultural influences. In fact, newly introduced human-machine interface can be rated differently based on the user's cultural background. (4) Future robots and software agents will need to interact with each other and humans, in respect of established social protocols or cultural differences.

We believe that the "socially intelligent agent" study meets the cultural problems. The term "socially intelligent agent" was introduced in AAAI97 Fall Symposium series held in MIT. [5] [2] This symposium was focused on studies in human-like social behavior and expertise and also on approaches to design and evaluate artificial systems to interact socially with humans in an acceptable manner. Although current robots or software agents are still far from humans or natural social creatures, new forms of social interaction need to be developed in the future.

We are now starting new projects in Malaysia under the initiative of MSC (Multimedia Super Corridor) project which is lead by Malaysian government to develop multimedia utopia in the down of 21st century. This national project tries to create an environment where multi-national, multi-cultural entities come and produce various kind of software and multimedia products. These projects provide us a good environment for research on cross cultural communication.

3 GrandChallenge Problems

We propose the following 6 projects as challenge problems which AI and Agent communities should tackle.

3.1 What is the cross cultural communication? Case-study

Culture underlines every aspect of social behavior and influence individual communication style, personality, character, motivation, knowledge, and cognitive mechanisms. [3] Actually, there are cross-cultural differences, in both verbal and non-verbal forms, in expression of emotion. For example, in the American culture, looking directly into the eyes of the person to whom you are talking with is seen as a positive trait; a sign of confidence. The Japanese culture, on the other hand, sometimes considered this negative, rude and improper. In order to (1) mutually understand different values, communication styles all over the world and (2) create new technology to support cross cultural activities, we propose to organize a place where we can share several case studies for cross cultural communication.

3.2 Linguistic studies for cross cultural communication

Cross-cultural differences in communication styles have been explored extensively in the field of linguistics and cultural anthropology. How difference in languages affects the human's mind and social behavior is an interesting question. Such kind of work should be the basis for designing intelligent software agents.

3.3 User Interface and new media for cross cultural communication

It is important for software developers to understand cultural differences in human-human communication and to apply them for user interface design. Because, in many cases, the rating for new design and interface greatly depends on the cultural background of the users. [4] For instance, there is a report that U.S. users do not tend to favor anthropomorphic agents while Japanese users prefer them. [3] This report says that Microsoft's "Bob" did not stimulate to much interest in the U.S. marketplace, while Japanese users seem to openly embrace human-like agents. Although further surveys and analysis are necessary to conclude this issue, it is true that cultural differences have great influence on human-computer interaction. It is a great issue to be discussed on how new media and design can affect the human mind and the culture.

3.4 Negotiation strategy among different cultural agents

History shows that understanding cultural differences is very important for successful negotiations on international business and diplomatic affairs. In order to obtain best results through negotiation, the negotiators should understand the background and the cultures of their counterpart. In cyber age, a software agent may negotiate with other agents in order to resolve some conflicts or maximize their own utility by negotiating with other agents. Some effective strategies on negotiation by rational agents are proposed based on the game theory. [7] If the agent has its own personality and behaves like a human, non-rational and culture dependent negotiation may be required to success in the negotiation. This story is realistic when many service agents and information agents emerge on the internet world.

3.5 Internet technology and its impact for cross cultural communication

The rapidly expanding global infrastructure of the Internet has given great impacts on the world wide communications and it also provides several opportunities for application, to validate and to shape the new technology for cross cultural communication. [9][1] For example, virtual meeting place, where people from all over the world meet on Internet, provides cross-cultural environment for various information exchanges. In designing a way to locate people with similar interests and also to introduce them to each other, intelligent matchmaking system should be developed. [8] Another possibility is adaptive web sites: sites that record user access logs and automatically improve their organization and presentation based on user access data. [11] Culturally adaptive web sites requires the function in detecting different forms of communicative behaviors and responding to them appropriately by using user access data. Machine learning technology will play a prominent role for this purposes.

3.6 The origin and evolution of communication, social norms and culture

To understand the origin of language and meaning is a long term vision of communication science. [6] All living creatures have their own communication styles each of which is different from one based on the another species. This communication style is formed by natural evolution. Axelrod shows how cooperative behavior emerges from the competitive and selfish agent's world. [13] One of the assumption is that a culture is a by-product of natural evolution. If this assumption is true, we can simulate future possible cultures under various conditions. The interesting question is "how do team work or culture depended behavior evolve in social dynamics?" or "how do social relationships develop?" For this purpose, one of the possibilities is to provide a common simulation environments for evaluation of various theories, algorithms, etc. (RoboCup is one of the good examples for this common task [12]) Further discussions are expected in this workshop.

4 Conclusion

In this paper, we emphasized the importance of cross cultural communication studies for AI and Agent communities and provided grand challenge problems that CIA community should jointly tackle. These challenge problems on cross cultural communication include (1) The case study of several cross cultural communications (2) Linguistic approaches (3) The effect on Human-Computer Interaction (4) Negotiation strategy (5) Internet Application (6) Evolution of communication, social norms and culture. Further discussion is expected in the following workshop and also on other activities.

References

1. Takashi Kido: A Vision of AL-Spider: -Toward Adaptive Information Gathering-. IJCAI97 Workshop on The Future of AI and the Internet. (1997)
2. Takashi Kido: Is Social Intelligence necessary for Agent-Agent Interaction? -Toward Socially Intelligent Software Agents-. 1997 AAAI Fall Symposium on Socially Intelligent Agents. (1997) 73-74
3. Patricia O'Neill-Brown: Setting the Stage for the Culturally Adaptive Agent. 1997 AAAI Fall Symposium on Socially Intelligent Agents. (1997) 93-97
4. Chisato Numaoka: Innate Sociability: Sympathetic Coupling. 1997 AAAI Fall Symposium on Socially Intelligent Agents. (1997) 98-102
5. Kerstin Dautenhahn: Ants Don't Have Friends -Thoughts on Socially Intelligent Agents. 1997 AAAI Fall Symposium on Socially Intelligent Agents. (1997) 22-27
6. Luc Steels: Perceptually grounded meaning creation. Second International Conference on Multi-Agent Systems (ICMAS96). (1996) 338-343
7. Matthias Klusch: A Polynomial Kernel-Oriented Coalition Algorithm for Rational Information Agents. Second International Conference on Multi-Agent Systems (ICMAS96). (1996) 157-164

8. Leonard N. Foner: Yenta: A Multi-Agent, Referral-Based Matchmaking System. Second International Conference on Multi-Agent Systems (ICMAS96). (1996) 436
9. Alexander Franz and Hiroaki Kitano: Internet-Based Information Systems: Papers from the 1996 AAAI Workshop. AAAI Press. (1996)
10. Todd Siler: Think Like A Genius. Bantam Books. (1997)
11. Mike Perkowitz and Oren Etzioni: Adaptive Web Sites: an AI Challenge. Proceedings of Fifteenth International Joint Conference on Artificial Intelligence (IJ-CAI97). (1997) 16–21.
12. Hiroaki Kitano, et al.: The RoboCup Synthetic Agent Challenge 97 Proceedings of Fifteenth International Joint Conference on Artificial Intelligence (IJCAI97). (1997) 24–29.
13. R. Axelrod: The Evolution of Cooperation. Basic Books. (1984)

Agents in Electronic Commerce: Component Technologies for Automated Negotiation and Coalition Formation

Tuomas Sandholm*

sandholm@cs.wustl.edu
Washington University
Computer Science Department
One Brookings Drive
St. Louis, MO 63130-4899

Abstract. Automated negotiation and coalition formation among self-interested agents are playing an increasingly important role in electronic commerce. Such agents cannot be coordinated by externally imposing their strategies. Instead the interaction protocols have to be designed so that each agent really is motivated to follow the strategies that the protocol designer wants it to follow. This paper reviews six component technologies that we have developed for making such interactions less manipulable and more efficient in terms of the computational processes and the outcomes:

1. OCSM-contracts in marginal cost based contracting,
2. leveled commitment contracts,
3. anytime coalition structure generation with worst case guarantees,
4. trading off computation cost against optimization quality within each coalition,
5. distributing search among insincere agents, and
6. unenforced contract execution.

Each of these technologies represents a different way of battling self-interest and combinatorial complexity simultaneously. This is a key battle when multiagent systems move into large scale open settings.

1 Introduction

Automated negotiation systems with self-interested agents are becoming increasingly important. One reason for this is the *technology push* of a growing standardized communication infrastructure—Internet, WWW, NII, EDI, KQML, FIPA, Concordia, Voyager, Odyssey, Telescript, Java, *etc*—over which separately designed agents belonging to different organizations can interact in an open environment in real-time and safely carry out transactions. The second reason is strong *application pull* for computer support for negotiation at the operative

---

* This material is based upon work supported by the National Science Foundation under CAREER Award IRI-9703122 and Grant No. IRI-9610122.

decision making level. For example, we are witnessing the advent of small transaction electronic commerce on the Internet for purchasing goods, information, and communication bandwidth. There is also an industrial trend toward virtual enterprises: dynamic alliances of small, agile enterprises which together can take advantage of economies of scale when available (e.g., respond to more diverse orders than individual agents can), but do not suffer from diseconomies of scale.

Multiagent technology facilitates such negotiation at the operative decision making level. This automation can save labor time of human negotiators, but in addition, other savings are possible because computational agents can be more effective at finding beneficial short-term contracts than humans are in strategically and combinatorially complex settings.

This paper discusses multiagent negotiation in situations where agents may have different goals, and each agent is trying to maximize its own good without concern for the global good. Such self-interest naturally prevails in negotiations among independent businesses or individuals. In building computer support for negotiation in such settings, the issue of self-interest has to be dealt with. In *cooperative distributed problem solving* [7, 5], the system designer imposes an interaction *protocol*[2] and a *strategy* (a mapping from state history to action; a way to use the protocol) for each agent. The main question is what social outcomes follow given the protocol and *assuming that the agents use the imposed strategies.* On the other hand, in *multiagent systems* [30, 25, 23, 16, 12], the agents are provided with an interaction protocol, but each agent will choose its own strategy. A self-interested agent will choose the best strategy for itself, which cannot be explicitly imposed from outside. Therefore, the protocols need to be designed using a *noncooperative, strategic* perspective: the main question is what social outcomes follow given a protocol which *guarantees that each agent's desired local strategy is best for that agent—and thus the agent will use it.* This approach is required in designing robust non-manipulable multiagent systems where the agents may be constructed by separate designers and/or may represent different real world parties.

The rest of this paper overviews six component technologies which we have developed for such negotiations:

1. OCSM-contracts in marginal cost based contracting,
2. leveled commitment contracts,
3. anytime coalition structure generation with worst case guarantees,
4. trading off computation cost against optimization quality within each coalition,
5. distributing search among insincere agents, and
6. unenforced contract execution.

---

[2] Here a protocol does not mean a low level communication protocol, but a negotiation protocol which determines the possible actions that agents can take at different points of the interaction. The *sealed-bid first-price auction* is an example protocol where each bidder is free to submit one bid for the item, which is awarded to the highest bidder at the price of his bid.

Each of these technologies is discussed at a high level, and pointers to the detailed technical papers on these topics are provided.

2 Technology 1: OCSM-contracts in marginal cost based contracting

The capability of (re)allocating tasks among agents is a key feature in automated negotiation systems. In many domains, significant savings can be achieved by reallocating tasks among agents. Some tasks are inherently synergic, and should therefore be handled by the same agent. On the other hand, some tasks have negative interactions, in which case it is better to allocate them to different agents. Furthermore, different agents may have different resources which leads to different capabilities and costs for handling tasks. This section discusses task allocation among self-interested agents in the following model which captures the above considerations. While we use the term "task", the items to be allocated can be anything else as well—financial securities, collectibles, resources, *etc.*—as long as the following model captures the setting. [3]

Definition 1. Our *task allocation problem* is defined by a set of tasks T, a set of agents A, a cost function $c_i : 2^T \to \Re \cup \{\infty\}$ (which states the cost that agent i incurs by handling a particular subset of tasks), and the initial allocation of tasks among agents $\langle T_1^{init}, ..., T_{|A|}^{init} \rangle$, where $\bigcup_{i \in A} T_i^{init} = T$, and $T_i^{init} \cap T_j^{init} = \emptyset$ for all $i \neq j$. [4] [5]

The original contract net and many of its later variants lacked a formal model for making bidding and awarding decisions. More recently, such a formal model was introduced which gives rise to a negotiation protocol that provably leads to desirable task allocations among agents [22, 24, 26]. In that model, contracting decisions are based on marginal cost calculations, i.e. that model invokes the concept of *individual rationality* on a per contract basis (which implies individual rationality of sequences of contracts). A contract is individually rational (IR) to an agent if that agent is better off with the contract than without it.

Specifically, a contractee q accepts a contract if it gets paid more than its marginal cost

$$MC^{add}(T^{contract}|T_q) = c_q(T^{contract} \cup T_q) - c_q(T_q)$$

---

[3] In settings such as securities reallocation where the items have positive value to each agent—unlike in task reallocation—the cost functions take on negative values.

[4] This definition generalizes what are called "Task Oriented Domains" [16]. Specifically, we allow asymmetric cost functions among agents (e.g. due to different resources). We also allow for the possibility that some agent may be unable to handle some sets of tasks. This is represented by a cost of infinity.

[5] Although a static version of the problem is discussed, the contracting scheme works even if tasks and resources (resources affect the cost functions) are added and removed dynamically.

of handling the tasks $T^{contract}$ of the contract. The marginal cost is dynamic in the sense that it depends on the other tasks T_q that the contractee already has. [6]

Similarly, a contractor r is willing to allocate the tasks $T^{contract}$ from its current task set T_r to the contractee if it has to pay the contractee less than it saves by not handling the tasks $T^{contract}$ itself:

$$MC^{remove}(T^{contract}|T_r) = c_r(T_r) - c_r(T_r - T^{contract}).$$

In the protocol, agents then suggest contracts to each other, and make their accepting/rejecting decisions based on these marginal cost calculations. An agent can take on both contractor and contractee roles. It can also recontract out tasks that it received earlier via another contract. The scheme does not assume that agents know the tasks or cost functions of others.

With this domain independent contracting scheme, the task allocation can only improve at each step. This corresponds to hill-climbing in the space of task allocations where the height-metric of the hill is social welfare $(-\sum_{i \in A} c_i(T_i))$. The fact that the contractor pays the contractee some amount between their marginal costs (e.g. half way between) causes the benefit from the improved task allocation to be divided so that no agent is worse off with a contract than without it.

The scheme is an *anytime algorithm*: contracting can be terminated at any time, and the worth (payments received from others minus cost of handling tasks) of each agent's solution increases monotonically. It follows that social welfare increases monotonically.

Details on an asynchronous distributed implementation based on marginal costs can be found in [22, 24, 29]. To our knowledge, this TRACONET (TRAnsportation COoperation NETwork) system was the first implementation of the contract net that used actual real-world marginal costs as the basis of contracting [18, 21, 19, 20, 22]. Its scaling up was verified on large scale real-world data from five independent dispatch centers.

2.1 Convergence to the globally optimal task allocation

In most contract net implementations, each contract regards only one task , i.e. one task is moved from one agent to another against a payment [37, 33, 9]. Such an *original (O) contract* can be understood as a particular search operator in the global hill-climbing contracting algorithm that is used for task reallocation. When the contracting protocol is equipped with O-contracts only, it may get stuck in a local optimum where no contract is individually rational but the task allocation is not globally optimal.

---

[6] Sometimes computing the value of the cost function for even a single task set is hard. For example, if the tasks are cities for a traveling salesman to visit, the computation is $\mathcal{NP}$-complete. Therefore, the marginal costs cannot actually be computed by subtracting two cost function values from each other in practice. Instead they need to be approximated [22, 24, 29].

To solve this problem, we have recently introduced several new contract types: *cluster (C) contracts* [22, 18] where a set of tasks is atomically contracted from one agent to another, *swap (S) contracts* where a pair of agents swaps a pair of tasks, and *multiagent (M) contracts* where more than two agents are involved in an atomic exchange of tasks [26, 29, 24]. Each of the four contract types avoids some of the local optima that the other three do not:

Theorem 2. *For each of the four contract types (O, C, S, and M), there exist task allocations where no IR contract with the other three contract types is possible, but an IR contract with the fourth type is [26].*

Unfortunately, even if the contracting protocol is equipped with all four of the contract types, the globally optimal task allocation may not be reached via IR contracts—even if there were an oracle for choosing the sequence of contracts:

Theorem 3. *There are instances of the task allocation problem where no IR sequence from the initial task allocation to the optimal one exists using O-, C-, S- and M-contracts [26].*

Clearly, no subset of the contract types suffices either. Another problem is that without an oracle, contracting may get stuck in a local optimum even if some IR sequence exists because the agents may choose some other IR sequence.

To address this shortcoming, a new contract type, *OCSM-contract*, has been defined, which combines the characteristics of O-, C-, S-, and M-contracts into one contract type—where the ideas of the four earlier contract types can be applied simultaneously (atomically):

Definition 4 [26, 24]. An *OCSM-contract* is defined by a pair $\langle \mathbf{T}, \rho \rangle$ of $|A| \times |A|$ matrices. An element $T_{i,j}$ is the set of tasks that agent i gives to agent j, and an element $\rho_{i,j}$ is the amount that i pays to j.

So OCSM contracts allow moving from a task allocation to any other task allocation with a single contract.

It could be shown that an IR sequence always exists from any task allocation to the optimal one if the contracting protocol incorporates OCSM-contracts. However, a stronger claim is now made. The following theorem states that OCSM-contracts are sufficient for reaching the global task allocation optimum in a finite number of contracts. The result holds for any sequence of IR OCSM-contracts, i.e. for any hill-climbing algorithm that uses OCSM-contracts: an oracle is not needed for choosing the sequence. This means that from the perspectives of social welfare maximization and of individual rationality, agents can accept IR contracts as they are offered. They need not wait for more profitable ones, and they need not worry that a current contract may make a more profitable future contract unprofitable. Neither do they need to accept contracts that are not IR in anticipation of future contracts that make the combination beneficial. Furthermore, these hill-climbing algorithms do not need to backtrack.

Theorem 5. *Let $|A|$ and $|T|$ be finite. If the contracting protocol allows OCSM-contracts, any hill-climbing algorithm (i.e. any sequence of IR contracts) finds* *the globally optimal task allocation in a finite number of steps (without back-tracking) [26, 24].*

Proof. With OCSM-contracts there are no local optima (that are not global optima) since the global optimum can be reached from any task allocation in a single contract. This last contract will be IR because moving to the optimum from some suboptimal allocation improves welfare, and this gain can be arbitrarily divided among the contract parties. Thus the algorithm will not run out of IR contracts before the optimum has been reached. With finite $|A|$ and $|T|$, there are only a finite number of task allocations. Since the algorithm hill-climbs, no task allocation will be repeated. Therefore, the optimum is reached in a finite number of contracts.

OCSM-contracts are also necessary: no weaker set of contract types suffices—even if there were an oracle to choose the order in which to apply them:

Theorem 6. *If there is some OCSM-contract that the protocol does not allow, there are instances of the task allocation problem where no IR sequence exists from the initial allocation to the optimal one [26].*

While OCSM-contracts are necessary in the general case, there may well be cost functions $c_i(\cdot)$ with special structure that guarantees that the global optimum is reached even with less powerful contract types [26].

Theorem 5 gives a powerful tool for problem instances where the number of possible task allocations is relatively small. On the other hand, for large problem instances, the number of contracts made before the optimal task allocation is reached may be impractically large—albeit finite. For example on a large-scale real-world distributed vehicle routing problem instance, the TRACONET [22] contracting system never reached even a local optimum even with just O-contracts—with multiple hours of negotiation on five Unix machines. Another problem is that although any OCSM-contract can be represented in $O(|A|^2 + |T|)$ space, the identification of welfare increasing contracts may be complex—especially in a distributed setting—because there are $\frac{v^2-v}{2} = \frac{|A|^{2|T|}-|A|^{|T|}}{2}$ possible OCSM-contracts, and the evaluation of just one contract requires each contract party to compute the cost of handling its current tasks and the tasks allocated to it via the contract. With such large problem instances, one cannot expect to reach the global optimum in practice. Instead, the contracting should occur as long as there is time, and then have a solution ready: the anytime character of this contracting scheme becomes more important.

3 Technology 2: Leveled commitment contracts

In traditional multiagent negotiation protocols among self-interested agents, once a contract is made, it is binding, i.e. neither party can back out [16, 22, 26, 1, 8, 12, 32, 6, 39]. Once an agent agrees to a contract, it has to follow through with it no matter how future events unravel. Although a contract may be profitable to an agent when viewed *ex ante*, it need not be profitable when viewed after some future events have occurred, i.e. *ex post*. Similarly, a contract may have too low expected payoff *ex ante*, but in some realizations of the future events, the same contract may be desirable when viewed *ex post*. Normal full commitment contracts are unable to efficiently take advantage of the possibilities that such—probabilistically known—future events provide.

On the other hand, many multiagent systems consisting of cooperative agents incorporate some form of decommitment possibility in order to allow the agents to accommodate new events. For example, in the original contract net protocol, the agent that had contracted out a task could send a termination message to cancel the contract even when the contractee had already partially fulfilled the contract [37]. This was possible because the agents were not self-interested: the contractee did not mind losing part of its effort without a monetary compensation. Similarly, the role of decommitment possibilities among cooperative agents has been studied in meeting scheduling using a contracting approach [34]. Again, the agents did not require a monetary compensation for their efforts: an agent agreed to cancel a contract merely based on the fact that some other agent wanted to decommit. In such multiagent systems consisting of cooperative agents, each agent can be trusted to use such an externally imposed strategy even though using that strategy might not be in the agent's self-interest.

Some research in game theory has focused on utilizing the potential provided by probabilistically known future events by *contingency contracts* among self-interested agents. The obligations of the contract are made contingent on future events. There are games in which this method provides an expected payoff increase to both parties of the contract compared to any full commitment contract [15]. Also, some deals are enabled by contingency contracts in the sense that there is no full commitment contract that both agents prefer over their fallback positions, but there is a contingency contract that each agent prefers over its fallback.

There are at least three problems regarding the use of contingency contracts in automated negotiation among self-interested agents. First, the agents might not know the entire space of possible future events. Second, contingency contracts get cumbersome as the number of relevant events to monitor from the future increases. In the limit, all domain events (changes in the domain problem, e.g. new tasks arriving or resources breaking down) and all negotiation events—contracts from other negotiations—can affect the value of the obligations of the original contract, and should therefore be conditioned on. Furthermore, these future events may not only affect the value of the original contract independently: the value of the original contract may depend on combinations of future events [29, 22, 16]. Thus there is a potential combinatorial explosion of items to be conditioned on. Third, verification of the unraveling of the events may not be viable. Sometimes an event is only observable by one of the agents. This agent may have an incentive to lie to the other party of the contract about the event in case the event is associated with a disadvantageous contingency to the directly observing agent. Thus, to be viable, contingency contracts would require an event verification mechanism that is not manipulable and not prohibitively complicated or costly.

We have devised *leveled commitment contracts* as another method for taking advantage of the possibilities provided by probabilistically known future events [30, 24]. Instead of conditioning the contract on future events, a mechanism is built into the contract that allows unilateral decommitting at any point in time. This is achieved by specifying in the contract decommitment penalties, one for each agent. If an agent wants to decommit—i.e. to be freed from the obligations of the contract—it can do so simply by paying the decommitment penalty to the other party. Such contracts are called leveled commitment contracts because the decommitment penalties can be used to choose a level of commitment. The method requires no explicit conditioning on future events: each agent can do its own conditioning dynamically. Therefore no event verification mechanism is required either.

While the leveled commitment contracting protocol has intuitive appeal and several practical advantages [24], it is not obvious that it is beneficial. First, the breacher's gain may be smaller than the breach victim's loss. Second, agents might decommit insincerely. A truthful agent will decommit whenever its best outside offer plus the decommitting penalty is better than the current contract. However, a rational self-interested agent will be more reluctant in decommitting. It will take into account the chance that the other party will decommit, in which case the former agent gets freed from the contract obligations, does not have to pay a decommitting penalty, and will collect a decommitting penalty from the other party. Due to such reluctant decommitting, contracts may end up being kept even though breaking them would be best from the social welfare perspective.

We analyzed this issue formally [30, 24]. A Nash equilibrium analysis was carried out where both contract parties' decommitting strategies (characterized by how good an agent's outside offer has to be to induce the agent to decommit) were best responses to each other. Both agents were decommitting insincerely but neither was motivated to change the extent of his lie given that the other did not change. It was shown that even under such insincere decommitting, the leveled commitment protocol outperforms the full commitment protocol. First, it enables contracts by making them IR in settings where no full commitment contract is IR (the reverse cannot happen). Second, leveled commitment contracts increase both contract parties' expected payoffs over any full commitment contracts.

Making multiple contracts sequentially introduces additional complications because a decommitment may motivate the victims to decommit from some of their other contracts. We have studied methods of increasing the decommitment penalties over time so as to reduce such cascade effects to an efficient level [2]. One of the key results is that infinite decommit-recommit loops cannot be avoided via any schedule of increasing the penalties if the timing is done locally from the time the contract was made. Instead, an element of global time (e.g. from the beginning of the entire negotiation) needs to be used to avoid such loops. Finally, we have experimented with leveled commitment among agents that do lookahead into the future contracts vs. myopic agents that do not [3].

4 Technology 3: Anytime coalition structure generation with worst case guarantees

Coalition formation is another important issue in multiagent systems. By forming coalitions, i.e. coordinating their activities within each coalition, the agents can often reach considerable cost savings. As is often done [10, 41, 36, 11], this section discusses coalition formation in *characteristic function games (CFGs)*. In such games, each coalition S is associated with its value v_S. Coalition formation in CFGs includes three activities:

1. *Coalition structure generation*: formation of coalitions by the agents such that agents within each coalition coordinate their activities, but agents do not coordinate between coalitions. Precisely this means partitioning the set of agents into exhaustive and disjoint coalitions. This partition is called a *coalition structure (CS)*. For example, in a game with three agents, there are seven possible coalitions: $\{1\}, \{2\}, \{3\}, \{1,2\}, \{2,3\}, \{3,1\}, \{1,2,3\}$ and five possible coalition structures: $\{\{1\}, \{2\}, \{3\}\}, \{\{1\}, \{2,3\}\}, \{\{2\}, \{1,3\}\}, \{\{3\}, \{1,2\}\}, \{\{1,2,3\}\}$.
2. *Solving the optimization problem* of each coalition. This means pooling the tasks and resources of the agents in the coalition, and solving this joint problem. The coalition's objective is to maximize monetary value: money received from outside the system for accomplishing tasks minus the cost of using resources. (In some problems, not all tasks have to be handled. This can be incorporated by associating a cost with each omitted task.)
3. *Dividing the value* of the generated solution among agents. This value may be negative because agents incur costs for using their resources.

These activities may be interleaved, and they are not independent. For example, the coalition that an agent wants to join depends on the portion of the value that the agent would be allocated in each potential coalition.

4.1 Coalition structure generation

Classically, coalition formation research has mostly focused on the payoff division activity. Coalition structure generation and optimization within a coalition have not previously received as much attention. Research has focused [10, 41] on superadditive games, i.e. games where $v_{S \cup T} \geq v_S + v_T$ for all disjoint coalitions $S, T \subseteq A$. In such games, coalition structure generation is trivial because the agents are best off by forming the grand coalition where all agents operate together.

Superadditivity means that any pair of coalitions is best off by merging into one. Classically it is argued that almost all games are superadditive because, at worst, the agents in a composite coalition can use solutions that they had when they were in separate coalitions.

However, many games are not superadditive because there is some cost to the coalition formation process itself. For example, there might be coordination overhead like communication costs, or possible anti-trust penalties. Similarly, solving the optimization problem of a composite coalition may be more complex than solving the optimization problems of component coalitions. Therefore, under costly computation, component coalitions may be better off by not forming the composite coalition [31]. Also, if time is limited, the agents may not have time to carry out the communications and computations required to coordinate effectively within a composite coalition, so component coalitions may be more advantageous.

In games that are not superadditive, some coalitions are best off merging while others are not. In such settings, the social welfare maximizing coalition structure varies, and coalition structure generation becomes highly nontrivial. The goal is to maximize the social welfare of the agents A by finding a coalition structure

$$CS^* = \arg \max_{CS \in \text{partitions of A}} V(CS),$$

where

$$V(CS) = \sum_{S \in CS} v_S$$

The problem is that the number of coalition structures is large ($\Omega(|A|^{|A|/2})$), so not all coalition structures can be enumerated unless the number of agents is extremely small—in practice about 15 or fewer. Instead, one would like to search through a subset ($N \subset$ partitions of A) of coalition structures, and pick the best coalition structure seen so far:

$$CS_N^* = \arg \max_{CS \in N} V(CS)$$

Taking an outsider's view, the coalition structure generation process can be viewed as search in a *coalition structure graph*, Figure 1. Now, how should such a graph be searched if there are too many nodes to search it completely?

One desideratum is to be able to guarantee that this coalition structure is within a worst case bound from optimal, i.e. that

$$k \geq \frac{V(CS^*)}{V(CS_N^*)}$$

is finite, and as small as possible. Let us define n_{min} to be the smallest size of N that allows us to establish such a bound k.

4.2 Minimal search to establish a bound

Theorem 7. *To bound k, it suffices to search the lowest two levels of the coalition structure graph (Figure 1). With this search, the bound $k = |A|$, this bound is tight, and the number of nodes searched is $n = 2^{|A|-1}$. No other search algorithm (than the one that searches the bottom two levels) can establish a bound k while searching only $n = 2^{|A|-1}$ nodes or fewer [27].*

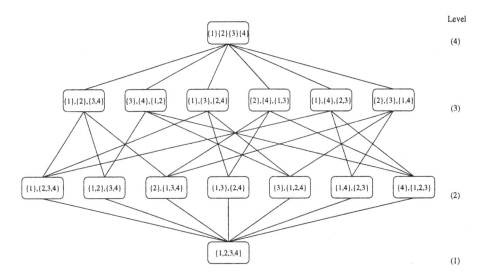

Fig. 1. Coalition structure graph for a 4-agent game. The nodes represent coalition structures. The arcs represent mergers of two coalition when followed downward, and splits of a coalition into two coalitions when followed upward.

Interpreted positively, this means that—somewhat unintuitively—a worst case bound from optimum can be guaranteed without seeing all CSs. Moreover, as the number of agents grows, the fraction of coalition structures needed to be searched approaches zero, i.e. $\frac{n_{min}}{|\text{partitions of } A|} \to 0$ as $|A| \to \infty$. This is because the algorithm needs to see only $2^{|A|-1}$ coalition structures while the total number of coalition structures is $\Omega(|A|^{|A|/2})$.

Interpreted negatively, the theorem shows that exponentially many coalition structures have to be searched before a bound can be established. This may be prohibitively complex if the number of agents is large—albeit significantly better than attempting to enumerate all coalition structures. Viewed as a general impossibility result, the theorem states that no algorithm for coalition structure generation can establish a bound in general characteristic function games without trying at least $2^{|A|-1}$ coalition structures. [7] This sheds light on earlier algorithms. Specifically, all prior coalition structure generation algorithms for general characteristic function games [36, 11]—which we know of—fail to establish such a bound. In other words, the coalition structure that they find may be **arbitrarily far from optimal.**

---

[7] In restricted domains where the v_S values have special structure, it may be possible to establish a bound k with less search. Shehory and Kraus have analyzed coalition structure generation in one such setting [35]. However, the bound that they compute is not a bound from optimum, but from a benchmark (best that is achievable given a preset limit on the size of coalitions) which itself may be arbitrarily far from optimum.

4.3   Lowering the bound via further search

The following algorithm will establish a bound in the minimal amount of search, and then rapidly reduce the bound further if there is time for more search. If the domain happens to be superadditive, the algorithm finds the optimal coalition structure immediately.

Algorithm. COALITION-STRUCTURE-SEARCH-1 [27]

1. Search the **bottom** two levels of the coalition structure graph.
2. Continue with a breadth-first search from the **top** of the graph as long as there is time left, or until the entire graph has been searched.
3. Return the coalition structure that has the highest welfare among those seen so far.

The next theorem shows how this algorithm reduces the worst case bound, k, as more of the graph is searched. For convenience, we introduce the notation $h = \lfloor \frac{|A|-l}{2} \rfloor + 2$.

Theorem 8. *After searching level l with COALITION-STRUCTURE-SEARCH-1, the bound k is $\lceil \frac{|A|}{h} \rceil$ if $|A| \equiv h - 1 \pmod h$ and $|A| \equiv l \pmod 2$. Otherwise the bound is $\lfloor \frac{|A|}{h} \rfloor$. The bound is tight [27].*

As was discussed earlier, before $2^{|A|-1}$ nodes have been searched, no bound can be established, and at $n = 2^{|A|-1}$ the bound $k = |A|$. The surprising fact is that by seeing just one additional node, i.e. the top node, the bound drops in half ($k = \frac{|A|}{2}$). Then, to drop k to about $\frac{|A|}{3}$, two more levels need to be searched. Roughly speaking, the divisor in the bound increases by one every time two more levels are searched. So, the anytime phase (step 2) of COALITION-STRUCTURE-SEARCH-1 has the desirable feature that the bound drops rapidly early on, and there are overall diminishing returns to further search, Figure 2.

4.4   Comparison to other algorithms

All previous coalition structure generation algorithms for general CFGs [36, 11]—that we know of—fail to establish any worst case bound because they search fewer than 2^{a-1} coalition structures. Therefore, we compare COALITION-STRUCTURE-SEARCH-1 to two other obvious candidates:

- **Merging algorithm**, i.e. breadth first search from the top of the coalition structure graph. This algorithm cannot establish any bound before it has searched the entire graph. This is because, to establish a bound, the algorithm needs to see every coalition, and the grand coalition only occurs in the

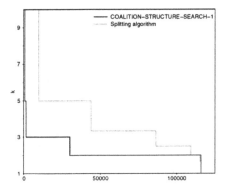

Fig. 2. Ratio bound k as a function of search size in a 10-agent game.

bottom node. Visiting the grand coalition as a special case would not help much since at least part of level 2 needs to be searched as well: coalitions of size $a - 2$ only occur there.

- **Splitting algorithm**, i.e. breadth first search from the bottom of the graph. This is identical to COALITION-STRUCTURE-SEARCH-1 up to the point where 2^{a-1} nodes have been searched, and a bound $k = a$ has been established. After that, the splitting algorithm reduces the bound much slower than COALITION-STRUCTURE-SEARCH-1. This can be shown by constructing bad cases for the splitting algorithm: the worst case may be even worse. To construct a bad case, set $v_S = 1$ if $|S| = 1$, and $v_S = 0$ otherwise. Now, $CS^* = \{\{1\}, ..., \{a\}\}$, $V(CS^*) = a$, and $V(CS_N^*) = l - 1$, where l is the level that the algorithm has completed (because the number of unit coalitions in a CS never exceeds $l - 1$). So, $\frac{V(CS^*)}{V(CS_N^*)} = \frac{a}{l-1}$,[8] Figure 2. In other words the divisor drops by one every time a level is searched. However, the levels that this algorithm searches first have many more nodes than the levels that COALITION-STRUCTURE-SEARCH-1 searches first.

4.5 Variants of the coalition structure generation problem

One would like to construct an anytime algorithm that establishes a lower k for any amount of search n, compared to any other anytime algorithm. However, such an algorithm might not exist. It is conceivable that the search which establishes the minimal k while searching n' nodes ($n' > n$) does not include all nodes of the search which establishes the minimal k while searching n nodes. This hypothesis is supported by the fact that the curves in Figure 2 cross in the end. However, this is not conclusive because COALITION-STRUCTURE-

---

[8] The only exception comes when the algorithm completes the last (top) level, i.e $l = a$. Then $\frac{V(CS^*)}{V(CS_N^*)} = 1$.

SEARCH-1 might not be the optimal anytime algorithm, and because the bad cases for the splitting algorithm might not be the worst cases.

If it turns out that no anytime algorithm is best for all n, one could use information (e.g. exact, probabilistic, or bounds) about the termination time to construct a *design-to-time algorithm* which establishes the lowest possible k for the specified amount of search.

So far we have discussed algorithms that have an *off-line search control* policy, i.e. the nodes to be searched have to be selected without using information accrued from the search so far. With *on-line search control*, one could perhaps establish a lower k with less search because the search can be redirected based on the values observed in the nodes so far. With on-line search control, it might make a difference whether the search observes only values of coalition structures, $V(CS)$, or values of individual coalitions, v_S, in those structures. The latter gives more information.

None of these variants (anytime vs. design-to-time, and off-line vs. on-line search control) would affect the result that searching the bottom two levels of the coalition structure graph is the unique minimal way to establish a worst case bound, and that the bound is tight. However, the results on searching further might vary in these different settings.

5 Technology 4: Trading off computation cost against optimization quality within each coalition

Under unlimited and costless computation, each coalition would solve its optimization problem exactly, which would define the value, v_S, of that coalition. However, in practice, in many domains it is too complex from a combinatorial viewpoint to solve the problem exactly. Instead, only an approximate solution can be found. In such settings, self-interested agents would want to strike the optimal tradeoff between solution quality and the cost of the associated computation.

We address this issue [31] by adopting a specific model of bounded rationality where each agent has to pay for the computational resources that it uses for deliberation. A fixed computation cost $c_{comp} \geq 0$ per CPU time unit is assumed. The domain cost associated with coalition S is denoted by $c_S(r_S) \geq 0$, i.e., it depends on (decreases with) the allocated computation resources r_S, Fig. 3 left. For example in a vehicle routing problem, the domain cost is the sum of the lengths of the routes of the coalition's vehicles. [9] The functions $c_S(r_S)$ can be viewed as *performance profiles* [4, 40] of the problem solving algorithm. They are used to decide how much CPU time to allocate to each computation. With this model of bounded rationality, the value of a coalition with bounded-rational agents can be defined. Each coalition minimizes the sum of solution cost (i.e.,

---

[9] In games where the agents receive revenue from outside—e.g., for handling tasks— this revenue can be incorporated into $c_S(r_S)$ by subtracting the coalition members' revenues from the coalition's domain cost.

domain cost, which decreases as more computation is allocated) and computation cost (which increases as more computation is allocated):

$$v_S(c_{comp}) = -\min_{r_S}[c_S(r_S) + c_{comp} \cdot r_S]. \tag{1}$$

This coalition value decreases as the CPU time unit cost c_{comp} increases, Fig. 3 right. Intuitively, as the unit cost of computation increases, agents need to pay

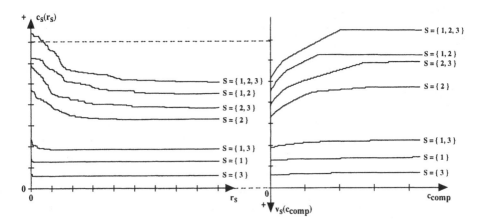

Fig. 3. Example experiment from a vehicle routing domain with agents 1, 2, and 3. Left: performance profiles, i.e., solution cost as a function of allocated computation resources. The curves become flat when the algorithm has reached a local optimum. Right: bounded-rational coalition value as a function of computation unit cost. The value of each coalition is negative because the cost is positive. The curves become flat at a computation unit cost c_{comp} that is so high that it is not worthwhile to take any iterative refinement steps: the initial solutions are used (their computation requirements are assumed negligible).

more for the computation or they have to use less computation and acquire worse solutions accordingly. Our model also incorporates a second form of bounded rationality: the base algorithm may be incomplete, i.e., it might never find the optimal solution. If the base algorithm is complete, the bounded-rational value of a coalition when $c_{comp} = 0$ equals the rational value ($v_S(0) = v_S^R$). In all, the bounded-rational value of a coalition is determined by three factors:

- The *domain problem*: tasks and resources of the agents (e.g. trucks and delivery orders in a vehicle routing problem). Among rational agents this is the only determining factor.
- The *execution architecture* on which the problem solving algorithm is run. Specifically, the architecture determines the unit cost of computation, c_{comp}.
- The *problem solving algorithm*. Once the coalition formation game begins, the algorithm's performance profiles are considered fixed. This model incorporates the possibility that agents design different algorithms for different

possible allocations of computation resources. We make no assumptions as to how effectively the algorithm uses the execution architecture. This is realistic because in practice it is often hard to construct algorithms that optimally use the architecture. For example, Russell and Subramanian have devised algorithms that are optimal for the architecture in simple settings, but in more complex settings they had to resort to an asymptotic criterion of optimality [17].

From our model of bounded rationality, the social welfare maximizing coalition structure can be determined. Similarly, the stability of the coalition structure can be determined: can the payoff be divided so that no group of agents gets higher payoff by moving out of the coalition structure by forming their won coalition? To avoid studying coalition games on a case by case basis, we have theoretically shown classes of performance profiles for which the welfare maximizing coalition structure and its stability can be determined directly without using Equation 1 and enumerating all possible coalition structures [31].

We have also experimented with our model of bounded rationality in a real-world vehicle routing problem. The main findings were the following. First, computational cost often does away with superadditivity, so it is no longer the case that every pair of coalitions is best off merging—which would imply optimality of the grand coalition. This is because the optimization problem of the composite coalition is significantly harder than the optimization problems of the component coalitions. Second, stability of the coalition structure is very sensitive to the problem instance, and varies in practice. Third, the coalition structure that our normative theory of bounded rational agents prescribes is closer to what human agents would choose based on domain specific considerations (such as adjacency of the dispatch centers and combinability of their loads) than is the classical normative prescription for agents whose rationality is unlimited [31].

This work on coalition formation under costly optimization within each coalition can be tied together with the nonexhaustive search for a welfare maximizing coalition structure (Section 4). The coalition structure generation algorithm can be used to search for a coalition structure, and only afterwards would the coalitions in the chosen coalition structure actually attack their optimization problems. If the performance profiles include uncertainty, this separation of coalition structure generation and optimization does not work e.g. because an agent may want to redecide its membership if its original coalition receives a worse optimization solution than expected.

Recently we have also studied coalition formation in conjunction with belief revision among bounded rational agents [38].

6 Technology 5: Distributing search among insincere agents

This section discusses a method of distributing any given search algorithm among self-interested agents. Distribution of search may be desirable because the search can be done more efficiently in parallel, and the agents will share the burden of computation. The method assumes that each agent has the information required to search the part of the space allocated to it.

As an example, this method can be used to distribute the algorithm COALI-TION-STRUCTURE-SEARCH-1. Self-interested agents prefer greater personal payoffs, so they will search for coalition structures that maximize personal payoffs, ignoring the ratio bound, k. The following algorithm can be used to motivate self-interested agents to exactly follow the socially desirable search. The randomizations in that algorithm can be done without a trusted third party by using a distributed nonmanipulable protocol for randomly permuting the agents [41].

Algorithm. DISTRIBUTED SEARCH FOR SELF-INTERESTED AGENTS

1. **Deciding what part of the coalition structure graph to search**. This can be decided in advance, or be dictated by a central authority or a randomly chosen agent, or be decided using some form of negotiation.

2. **Partitioning the search space among agents**. Each agent is assigned some part of the coalition structure graph to search. The enforcement mechanism in step 4 will motivate the agents to search exactly what they are assigned, no matter how unfairly the assignment is done. One way of achieving *ex ante* fairness is to randomly allocate the set search space portions to the agents. In this way, each agent searches equally on an expected value basis, although *ex post*, some may search more than others. Another option is to distribute the space equally among agents, or have some agents pay others to compensate for unequal amounts of search.

3. **Actual search**. Each agent searches its part of the search space, and tells the others which CS maximized $V(CS)$ in its search space.

4. **Enforcement**. Two agents, i and j, will be selected at random. Agent i will re-search the search space of j to verify that j has performed its search. Agent j gets caught of mis-searching (or misrepresenting) if i finds a better CS in j's space than j reported (or i sees that the CS that j reported does not belong to j's space at all). If j gets caught, it has to pay a penalty P. To motivate i to conduct this additional search, we make i the claimant of P. There is no pure strategy Nash equilibrium in this protocol. (If i searches and the penalty is high enough, then j is motivated to search sincerely. But then i is not motivated to search since it cannot receive P.) Instead, there will be a mixed strategy Nash equilibrium where i and j search truthfully with some probabilities. By increasing P, the probability that j searches can be made arbitrarily close to one. The probability that i searches approaches zero, which minimizes enforcement overhead.

5. **Additional search**. The previous steps can be repeated if more time to search remains. For example, the agents could first do step 1 of COALITION-STRUCTURE-SEARCH-1. Then, they could repeatedly search more and more as time allows.

6. **Payoff division**. Many alternative methods for payoff division among agents could be used here. The only concern is that the division of $V(CS)$ may affect what CS an agent wants to report as a result of its search since different CSs may give the agent different payoffs—depending on the payoff division scheme. However, by making P high enough compared to $V(CS)$s, this consideration can be made negligible compared to the risk of getting caught.

---

7   Technology 6: Unenforced contract execution

After negotiation, the deals need to be executed. In conventional commerce, deals are usually enforced by law. For example, if a car dealership does not deliver the automobile after the customer has paid for it, the customer can resort to litigation. However, such enforced protocols are problematic in electronic commerce, e.g. over the Internet. First, adequate laws for ecommerce may be lacking, or the transacting agents (human or computational) may be governed by different laws, e.g. they may be sited in different countries. Also, the laws might not be strictly enforced, or enforcing them—e.g. by litigation—might be impractically expensive. We would like the agents' ecommerce transactions to work properly independent of such fluctuations in enforcement. Secondly, an ecommerce party may vanish at any point in time, e.g. by logging out. Thus the laws cannot be enforced unless the vanished agent represented some real world party and the connection between the agent and the accountable real world party can be traced.

Current ecommerce technology is based on such enforced transactions. The problems of traceability and trust are being tackled for example by establishing trusted third parties like banks and credit card companies for electronic commerce, as well as by attempting to build cybercommunities of trust. The developing infrastructure for ecommerce among computational agents is also following the approach of enforced traceable transactions. For example, Telescript technology strived to strictly and accountably tie each computational agent to the real world party that it represents.

Instead, we present a method that allows transactions to be carried out without enforcement. This enables transactions in settings where the parties cannot identify each other, or where litigation is not viable. From the perspective of computational agents, it allows the agents to be more autonomous because they do not have to be strictly tied to the real world parties that they represent. In cases where this type of unenforced exchange is possible, it is preferable to the strictly enforced mode of exchange due to savings in enforcement costs (e.g. litigation costs, or operation costs of trusted third party intermediaries) and insensitivity to enforcement uncertainty.

The fulfillment of a mutual contract can be viewed as one agent delivering and the other agent paying, in money or some commodity. We propose a method for carrying out such an exchange without enforcement. The exchange is managed so that for both agents—supplier and demander—at any point in the exchange, the future gains from carrying out the rest of the exchange (*cooperating* according to the contract) are larger than the gains from *defecting*. Defection means terminating the exchange prematurely by vanishing. For example, defection may be beneficial to a demander agent if the supplier agent has delivered much more than what the demander has yet paid for.

By intelligently splitting the exchange into smaller chunks, the agents can avoid situations where at least one of them is motivated to defect. In other words, each agent only delivers a portion of its deliverables at a time. At the next step, the agents deliver some more, *etc.* We will call a sequence of deliveries and payments *safe* if neither agent is motivated to defect at any point in the exchange. Game theoretically speaking, the exchange is safe if it can be carried to completion in subgame perfect Nash equilibrium.

Some chunkings allow safe exchange while others do not. We have devised algorithms that find a safe chunking if one exists for any given exchange. The sequence of delivering the chunks matters as well: some sequences are safe while others are not. The obvious candidate algorithms for sequencing fail to guarantee safety of the sequence. We have devised a nontrivial sequencing algorithm that provably finds a safe sequence if one exists, and always terminates in quadratic time in the number of chunks. The algorithm works for settings where agents value each chunk independently. If the chunks are interdependent in value, the sequencing cannot be done in polynomial time in general [25, 24, 28].

8 Conclusions

Multiagent systems consisting of self-interested agents are becoming ubiquitous; automated negotiation and coalition formation are playing an increasingly important role in electronic commerce. Such agents cannot be coordinated by externally imposing the agent's strategies. Instead the interaction protocols have to be designed so that each agent really is motivated to follow the strategies that the protocol designer wants it to follow.

This paper reviewed six component technologies that we have developed for making such interactions less manipulable and more efficient in terms of the computational processes and the outcomes:

1. OCSM-contracts in marginal cost based contracting,
2. leveled commitment contracts,
3. anytime coalition structure generation with worst case guarantees,
4. trading off computation cost against optimization quality within each coalition,
5. distributing search among insincere agents, and
6. unenforced contract execution.

In microeconomics and game theory, substantial knowledge exists of impossibility results and of constructive possibility demonstrations of interaction protocols and strategies for self-interested agents [14, 13]. However, the computational limitations of the agents deserve more attention. It is clear that such limitations have fundamental impact on what strategies agents want to use, and therefore also on what protocols are desirable, and what is (im)possible. This is one area where microeconomics and computer science fruitfully blend.

In the future, systems will increasingly be designed, built, and operated in a distributed manner. A larger number of systems will be used by multiple real-world parties. The problem of coordinating these parties and avoiding manipulation cannot be tackled by technological or economic methods alone. Instead, the successful solutions are likely to emerge from a deep understanding and careful hybridization of both.

Acknowledgments

This paper is an overview of several more detailed articles. Some of them are joint work with co-authors: Martin Andersson, Kate Larson, Victor Lesser, Onn Shehory, and Fernando Tohmé.

References

1. Martin R Andersson and Tuomas W Sandholm. Contract types for satisficing task allocation: II experimental results. In *AAAI Spring Symposium Series: Satisficing Models*, pages 1–7, Stanford University, CA, March 1998.
2. Martin R Andersson and Tuomas W Sandholm. Leveled commitment contracting among myopic individually rational agents. In *Proceedings of the Third International Conference on Multi-Agent Systems (ICMAS)*, Paris, France, July 1998.
3. Martin R Andersson and Tuomas W Sandholm. Leveled commitment contracts with myopic and strategic agents. In *Proceedings of the National Conference on Artificial Intelligence*, Madison, WI, July 1998.
4. Mark Boddy and Thomas Dean. Deliberation scheduling for problem solving in time-constrained environments. *Artificial Intelligence*, 67:245–285, 1994.
5. Alan H. Bond and Les Gasser. *Readings in Distributed Artificial Intelligence*. Morgan Kaufmann Publishers, San Mateo, CA, 1988.
6. John Q. Cheng and Michael P. Wellman. The WALRAS algorithm: A convergent distributed implementation of general equilibrium outcomes. *Computational Economics*, 1997.
7. E Durfee, V Lesser, and D Corkill. Cooperative distributed problem solving. In A Barr, P Cohen, and E Feigenbaum, editors, *The Handbook of Artificial Intelligence*, volume IV, pages 83–147. Addison Wesley, 1989.
8. Eithan Ephrati and Jeffrey S Rosenschein. The Clarke tax as a consensus mechanism among automated agents. In *Proceedings of the National Conference on Artificial Intelligence*, pages 173–178, Anaheim, CA, 1991.
9. Cheng Gu and Toru Ishida. A quantitative analysis of the contract net protocol. In *Proceedings of the First International Conference on Multi-Agent Systems (ICMAS)*, page 449, San Francisco, CA, June 1995. In the poster collection.
10. James P Kahan and Amnon Rapoport. *Theories of Coalition Formation*. Lawrence Erlbaum Associates Publishers, 1984.

11. Steven Ketchpel. Forming coalitions in the face of uncertain rewards. In *Proceedings of the National Conference on Artificial Intelligence*, pages 414–419, Seattle, WA, July 1994.

12. Sarit Kraus, Jonathan Wilkenfeld, and Gilad Zlotkin. Multiagent negotiation under time constraints. *Artificial Intelligence*, 75:297–345, 1995.

13. David M Kreps. *A Course in Microeconomic Theory*. Princeton University Press, 1990.

14. Andreu Mas-Colell, Michael Whinston, and Jerry R. Green. *Microeconomic Theory*. Oxford University Press, 1995.

15. H. Raiffa. *The Art and Science of Negotiation*. Harvard Univ. Press, Cambridge, Mass., 1982.

16. Jeffrey S Rosenschein and Gilad Zlotkin. *Rules of Encounter*. MIT Press, 1994.

17. Stuart Russell and Devika Subramanian. Provably bounded-optimal agents. *Journal of Artificial Intelligence Research*, 1:1–36, 1995.

18. Tuomas W Sandholm. A strategy for decreasing the total transportation costs among area-distributed transportation centers. In *Nordic Operations Analysis in Cooperation (NOAS): OR in Business*, Turku School of Economics, Finland, 1991.

19. Tuomas W Sandholm. Automatic cooperation of area-distributed dispatch centers in vehicle routing. In *International Conference on Artificial Intelligence Applications in Transportation Engineering*, pages 449–467, San Buenaventura, CA, 1992.

20. Tuomas W Sandholm. Automatic cooperation of factorially distributed dispatch centers in vehicle routing. In *abstract collection of the Joint International Conference on Operational Research / Management Science (EURO / TIMS)*, page 51, Helsinki, Finland, 1992.

21. Tuomas W Sandholm. A bargaining network for intelligent agents. In *Finnish Artificial Intelligence Conference (STeP-92), New Directions in Artificial Intelligence*, volume 3, pages 173–181, Espoo, Finland, 1992.

22. Tuomas W Sandholm. An implementation of the contract net protocol based on marginal cost calculations. In *Proceedings of the National Conference on Artificial Intelligence*, pages 256–262, Washington, D.C., July 1993.

23. Tuomas W Sandholm. Limitations of the Vickrey auction in computational multiagent systems. In *Proceedings of the Second International Conference on Multi-Agent Systems (ICMAS)*, pages 299–306, Keihanna Plaza, Kyoto, Japan, December 1996.

24. Tuomas W Sandholm. *Negotiation among Self-Interested Computationally Limited Agents*. PhD thesis, University of Massachusetts, Amherst, 1996. Available at http://www.cs.wustl.edu/~sandholm/dissertation.ps.

25. Tuomas W Sandholm. Unenforced E-commerce transactions. *IEEE Internet Computing*, 1(6):47–54, Nov–Dec 1997. Special issue on Electronic Commerce.

26. Tuomas W. Sandholm. Contract types for satisficing task allocation: I theoretical results. In *AAAI Spring Symposium Series: Satisficing Models*, pages 68–75, Stanford University, CA, March 1998.

27. Tuomas W Sandholm, Kate S Larson, Martin R Andersson, Onn Shehory, and Fernando Tohmé. Anytime coalition structure generation with worst case guarantees. In *Proceedings of the National Conference on Artificial Intelligence*, Madison, WI, July 1998.

28. Tuomas W Sandholm and Victor R Lesser. Equilibrium analysis of the possibilities of unenforced exchange in multiagent systems. In *Proceedings of the Fourteenth International Joint Conference on Artificial Intelligence*, pages 694–701, Montreal, Canada, August 1995.

29. Tuomas W Sandholm and Victor R Lesser. Issues in automated negotiation and electronic commerce: Extending the contract net framework. In *Proceedings of the First International Conference on Multi-Agent Systems (ICMAS)*, pages 328–335, San Francisco, CA, June 1995. Reprinted in *Readings in Agents*, Huhns and Singh, eds., pp. 66–73, 1997.

30. Tuomas W Sandholm and Victor R Lesser. Advantages of a leveled commitment contracting protocol. In *Proceedings of the National Conference on Artificial Intelligence*, pages 126–133, Portland, OR, August 1996.

31. Tuomas W Sandholm and Victor R Lesser. Coalitions among computationally bounded agents. *Artificial Intelligence*, 94(1):99–137, 1997. Special issue on Economic Principles of Multiagent Systems. Early version appeared at the International Joint Conference on Artificial Intelligence, pages 662–669, 1995.

32. Tuomas W Sandholm and Fredrik Ygge. On the gains and losses of speculation in equilibrium markets. In *Proceedings of the Fifteenth International Joint Conference on Artificial Intelligence*, pages 632–638, Nagoya, Japan, August 1997.

33. Sandip Sen. *Tradeoffs in Contract-Based Distributed Scheduling*. PhD thesis, Univ. of Michigan, 1993.

34. Sandip Sen and Edmund Durfee. The role of commitment in cooperative negotiation. *International Journal on Intelligent Cooperative Information Systems*, 3(1):67–81, 1994.

35. Onn Shehory and Sarit Kraus. Task allocation via coalition formation among autonomous agents. In *Proceedings of the Fourteenth International Joint Conference on Artificial Intelligence*, pages 655–661, Montreal, Canada, August 1995.

36. Onn Shehory and Sarit Kraus. A kernel-oriented model for coalition-formation in general environments: Implemetation and results. In *Proceedings of the National Conference on Artificial Intelligence*, pages 134–140, Portland, OR, August 1996.

37. Reid G. Smith. The contract net protocol: High-level communication and control in a distributed problem solver. *IEEE Transactions on Computers*, C-29(12):1104–1113, December 1980.

38. Fernando Tohmé and Tuomas W Sandholm. Coalition formation processes with belief revision among bounded rational self-interested agents. In *IJCAI Workshop on Social Interaction and Communityware*, pages 43–51, Nagoya, Japan, August 1997.

39. Michael Wellman. A market-oriented programming environment and its application to distributed multicommodity flow problems. *Journal of Artificial Intelligence Research*, 1:1–23, 1993.

40. Shlomo Zilberstein and Stuart Russell. Optimal composition of real-time systems. *Artificial Intelligence*, 82(1–2):181–213, 1996.

41. Gilad Zlotkin and Jeffrey S Rosenschein. Coalition, cryptography and stability: Mechanisms for coalition formation in task oriented domains. In *Proceedings of the National Conference on Artificial Intelligence*, pages 432–437, Seattle, WA, July 1994.

Cooperative vs. Competitive Multi-Agent Negotiations in Retail Electronic Commerce

Robert H. Guttman and **Pattie Maes**
MIT Media Laboratory
20 Ames Street, E15-301
Cambridge, MA 02139
{guttman,pattie}@media.mit.edu
http://ecommerce.media.mit.edu

Abstract

A key lesson learned from economic and game theory research is that negotiation protocols have substantial, rippling effects on the overall nature of the system. online auctions are increasingly popular negotiation protocols for software agents (and humans) to compete on the prices of goods and services. This paper takes a critical look at these competitive protocols in retail markets from economic, game theoretic, and business perspectives. Our analysis suggests that online auction protocols are, in fact, less efficient and more hostile than would be expected (or desired) in retail markets. Furthermore, we identify the importance of customer satisfaction and propose more cooperative multi-agent decision analysis tools (e..g, Multi-Attribute Utility Theory) and negotiation protocols (e.g., Distributed Constraint Satisfaction) as promising techniques to support it.

1. Retail Market Negotiations

Today's mass market retail is largely defined as *monopolistic competition* [1]. Whenever improved or unique products (e.g., faster computers or Tamagotchis) create a significant demand, similar products will eventually come to market that are very close (but not perfect) substitutes for the original. This new supply dismantles the monopoly and dissipates the demand. Thus, today's retail can be described as a competition amongst merchants for consumers' patronage.

The relationship that a merchant wishes to have with its customers, however, is not competitive. On the contrary, today's retail merchants desire highly cooperative, long-term relationships with their customers to maximize *customer satisfaction* [2]. This goal of maximizing customer satisfaction is to increase the probability of repeat purchases and new customers through positive reputation. The relationship among today's merchants and a given consumer is depicted in Figure 1.

But what will the landscape of retail look like in the future? Will tomorrow's online retail look anything like today's physical-world retail? We are already seeing online businesses that challenge the status quo (e.g., Amazon.com) and technologies that are dramatically changing the face of retail commerce – e.g., agent systems that reduce transaction costs for both merchants and consumers and create personalized and community-based experiences to help merchants increase sales [3].

However, certain fundamental economic characteristics of retail will likely *not* change. For example, future online retail markets will still have consumers who wish to satisfy their individual needs with well-matched merchant offerings. It is also likely that monopolistic competition will remain a defining characteristic of most online retail markets.[1] As such, merchants will still strive for highly cooperative, long-term relationships with their customers to maximize customer satisfaction.

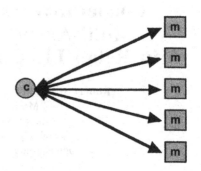

Figure 1 - Traditional retail markets. Merchants compete with one another for consumers' patronage. However, merchants desire a cooperative relationship with each of their customers.

As we have learned from economic and game theory research, a system's protocols have substantial, rippling effects on the overall nature of the system. Therefore, as designers of agent systems for mediating online transactions, we need to seriously consider which protocols we choose to employ. Although we have (and should exploit) the opportunity to prescribe new solutions to old problems, we may find that accurately modeling the competitive and cooperative levels among retailers and consumers will lead to more effective and efficient retail marketplaces as well as the long-term adoption and validation of our agent technologies for electronic commerce.

In this vain, this paper analyzes several electronic markets and their corresponding negotiation protocols. In particular, we take a critical look at competitive negotiation protocols for their appropriateness in online retail markets from economic, game theoretic, and business perspectives. Finally, we explore cooperative negotiation protocols that show more promise in accurately modeling the economic relationships in retail electronic commerce.

2.   Competitive Negotiations

Negotiation is a form of decision-making where two or more parties jointly search a space of possible solutions with the goal of reaching a consensus [4]. Economics and Game Theory describe such an interaction in terms of protocols and strategies. The protocols of a negotiation comprise the rules (i.e., legitimate actions) of the game. An example of a simple negotiation protocol is the non-discriminatory English auction where (in one form) the only legal action is to (publicly) bid higher than the current highest bid by at least the minimum bid amount before the auction closes.

For a given protocol, a bidder uses a rational strategy (i.e., a plan of action) to maximize his or her *utility*. Decision analysis tools help identify optimal strategies given a bidder's preferences and knowledge (e.g., motivation, valuation, risk, information asymmetry, etc.) and is captured by a *utility function*. *Expected utilities* are utilities that

[1] There has been much speculation on the role of intermediaries in online markets. Many believe that intermediaries (e.g., retailers) will be decreasingly relevant as technologies begin to take over their roles and as manufacturers bypass their current distribution channels for direct sales. However, even if this will be our future, the resulting marketplaces will be more competitive (not less) forcing merchants to compete ever more fiercely for consumers' patronage.

consider probabilistic outcomes and events such as an opponent's future reaction to a player's action. Oftentimes, a utility function only reflects a player's self-interest. In other cases, it encompasses desirable social welfare or global performance goals such as system-wide equilibria [5, 6].

Competitive negotiations can be described as the decision-making process of resolving a conflict involving two or more parties over a single mutually exclusive goal. The Economics literature describes this more specifically as the effects on market price of a limited resource given its supply and demand among self-interested parties [1]. The Game Theory literature describes this situation as a zero-sum game where as the value along a single dimension shifts in either direction, one side is better off and the other is worse off [4].

The benefit of dynamically negotiating a price for a product instead of fixing it is that it relieves the seller from needing to determine the value of the good a priori. Rather, this burden is pushed into the marketplace itself. A resulting benefit of this is that limited resources are allocated fairly -- i.e., to those buyers who value them most. As such, competitive negotiation mechanisms are common in a variety of markets including stock markets (e.g., NYSE and NASDAQ), fine art auction houses (e.g., Sotheby's and Christie's), flower auctions (e.g., Aalsmeer, Holland), and various ad hoc haggling (e.g., automobile dealerships and commission-based electronics stores). More recently, software agents have been taught competitive negotiation skills (e.g., auctioneering and auction bidding skills) to help automate consumer-to-consumer, business-to-business, and retail shopping over the Internet [3].

2.1. Classified Ad Negotiations

Kasbah [7, 8] is a Web-based multi-agent classified ad system where users create buying agents and selling agents to help transact goods. These agents automate much of the buyers' and sellers' brokering and negotiations. A user wanting to buy or sell a good creates an agent, gives it some strategic direction, and sends it off into a centralized agent marketplace. Kasbah agents proactively seek out potential buyers or sellers and negotiate with them on behalf of their owners. Each agent's goal is to complete an acceptable deal, subject to a set of user-specified constraints such as a desired price, a highest (or lowest) acceptable price, and a date by which to complete the transaction.

Negotiation between Kasbah buying and selling agents is bilateral, competitive, and straightforward as shown in Figure 2. After buying agents and selling agents are matched, the only valid action in the negotiation protocol is for buying agents to offer a bid to sellers. Selling agents respond with either a binding "yes" or "no".

Given this protocol, Kasbah provides buyers with one of three negotiation "strategies": anxious, cool-headed, and frugal

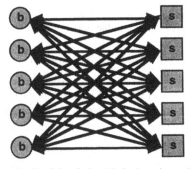

Figure 2 - Traditional classified ad markets. Buyers and sellers are in ad hoc, bilateral, competitive negotiations with one another respectively for unique (but potentially similar) limited resources.

– corresponding to a linear, quadratic, or exponential function respectively for increasing its bid for a product over time. The simplicity of these negotiation heuristics makes it intuitive for users to understand what their agents are doing in the marketplace.[2] This was important for user acceptance as observed in a recent Media Lab experiment [7]. A larger Kasbah experiment is now underway at MIT allowing students to transact books and music [8].

2.2. Stock Market Negotiations (CDAs)

AuctionBot [10, 11] is a general purpose Internet auction server at the University of Michigan. AuctionBot users create new auctions to buy or sell products by choosing from a selection of auction types and specifying its parameters (e.g., clearing times, method for resolving bidding ties, the number of sellers permitted, etc.). Buyers and sellers can then bid according to the multilateral, competitive negotiation protocols of the created auction.

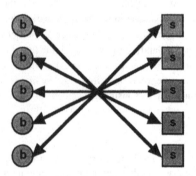

Figure 3 - Traditional stock markets. Within an unbiased, centralized marketplace, buyers and sellers are in multilateral, competitive negotiations with one another for limited resources.

One auction type that AuctionBot offers is the Continuous Double Auction (CDA). An example CDA market is the NASDAQ stock market. Kasbah's current protocols and negotiation strategies also resemble a CDA[3] ; however, whereas Kasbah agents negotiate bilaterally, AuctionBot agents participating in a true and more efficient CDA negotiate multilaterally as shown in Figure 3.

Of the last two negotiation models discussed, the classified ad model (Figure 2) more closely resembles the retail market model (Figure 1). However, an important distinction is that there is no competition among consumers (i.e., buyers) in retail markets. This is because retailers typically sell production goods, not limited resources.[4] This lack of consumer competition in retail markets means that the actions of other consumers have negligible impact on retailers' current prices of the goods in question.

2.3. Retail Auction Negotiations

Two of the original (non-academic) auction Web sites are OnSale [12] and eBay's AuctionWeb [13] and are still very popular. Likely reasons for their popularly include their novelty and entertainment value in negotiating the price of everyday goods, as well as the potential of getting a great deal on a wanted product. In any case, the popularity of OnSale and eBay's AuctionWeb has quickly spawned an already competitive and growing

---

[2] Unlike other multi-agent marketplaces [9], Kasbah does not concern itself with optimal strategies or convergence properties. Rather, Kasbah provides more descriptive strategies that model typical haggling behavior found in classified ad markets.
[3] For more on this perspective, see [7].
[4] The pricing of production goods is based on marginal costs – a very different economic model than auctioning limited resources. (More on this later.)

industry. Yahoo! lists more than 90 active online auctions today [14]. Forrester Research reports that auctions will be core to making business-to-business transactions more dynamic, open and efficient [15]. online auctions like FastParts [16] and FairMarket [17] are already making this happen in the semiconductor and computer industries.

What's most relevant here is that many online auctions are augmentations to *retail* sites with retailers playing the roles of both auctioneer and seller (i.e., a sales agent). For example, First Auction [18] is a service of Internet Shopping Network, one of the first online retailers. Cendant's membership-driven retail site, netMarket [19], has also recently added auctions to its repertoire of online services. New auction intermediaries such as Z Auction [20] offer their auction services to multiple manufactures and resellers as a new sales channel.

With this much "auction fever," you would think that auctions are a panacea for retail shopping and selling. On the contrary, upon closer look we see that auctions have rather hostile characteristics. For example, although the protocols for the two most prevalent types of online auctions, first-price open-cry English and Yankee [21], are simple to understand and bid, determining the optimal bidding *strategy* is non-trivial[s] and, more importantly, can be financially adverse. In fact, in first-price open-cry auctions (i.e., highest bid wins the good for that price), the winning bid is always greater than the product's market valuation. This is commonly known as "winner's curse" as depicted in Figure 4. This problem is exacerbated in retail auctions where buyers' valuations are largely private[6]. Buyers with private valuations tend to (irrationally) skew bids even further above the product's true value.

Figure 4 - "Winner's curse" is the paradox that the winning bid in an auction is greater than the product's market valuation. This occurs in all first-price open-cry auctions, the most prevalent type on the Internet.

Although winner's curse is a short-term financial benefit to retailers, it can be a long-term detriment due to the eventual customer dissatisfaction of paying more than the value of a product. Two universal auction rules that compound this problem are: (1) bids are non-retractable and, worse yet, (2) products are non-returnable. This means that customers could get stuck with products that they're unhappy with and paid too much for. In short, online auctions are less lucrative and far less forgiving than would be expected in retail shopping.

---

[s] Factors to be considered include information asymmetry, risk aversion, motivation and valuation.

[6] The motivation of a buyer with private-valuation is to acquire goods for personal consumption (or for gifts). This is in contrast to a buyer with common-valuation (e.g., in stock) where the motivation is to make money through the buying (and later reselling) of goods which have no other intrinsic value to the buyer.

Another customer dissatisfaction problem owing to online auctions is the long delay between starting negotiations and purchasing the product. For example, due to communication latency issues and wanting a critical mass of bidders, the English and Yankee auction protocols as implemented over the Internet extend over several days. This means that after a customer starts bidding on a product, she/he must continuously bid for the product (or have a shopping agent do it as provided by AuctionWeb) up until the auction closes several days later. This does not cater to impatient or time-constrained consumers.[7] To make matters worse, only the highest bidder(s) of an auction can purchase the auctioned good meaning that the other customers need to wait until the good is auctioned again and then restart negotiations.[8] Additionally, since bids are non-retractable and binding, consumers are unable to reconsider earlier buying decisions during this delayed negotiation stage.

There are other buyer concerns with English and Yankee style auctions such as *shills*. Shills are bidders who are planted by sellers to unfairly manipulate the market valuation of the auctioned good by raising the bid to stimulate the market. Although deemed illegal in all auctions, shills can be hard to detect especially in the virtual world where it is relatively inexpensive to create virtual identities (and thus virtual shills). Also, there is usually no negative consequence to the seller if one of his/her shills (accidentally) wins the auction.

Competitive negotiation auctions in retail markets also pose problems for *merchants*. Although auctions can relieve merchants of the burden of establishing prices for limited resources (e.g., fine art and stocks), this benefit is less realizable for *production goods* as in retail markets. Unlike fine art, for example, it is relatively easy to determine the marginal costs of production goods.[9] If auctioning these goods, however, it is non-trivial for the merchant to determine the optimal size of the auctioned lots and the frequency of their auction [22]. Such a determination requires an understanding of the demand for the good since it directly affects inventory management and indirectly effects production schedule.[10] Therefore, retailers are still burdened with determining the value of their goods a priori.

In addition, where sellers may have shills, buyers may collude by forming *coalitions*. A buyer coalition is a group of buyers who agree not to outbid one another. In a discriminatory (i.e., multi-good) auction, the result of this is that the coalition can buy goods for less than if they competed against one another thus unfairly cheating the seller. The coalition can then distribute the spoils amongst themselves (e.g., evenly, by holding a second private auction, etc.). As with shills, collusion through buyer coalitions is also considered illegal. However, as with shills, it can be hard to detect buyer collusion, especially in online markets where bidders are virtual. In fact, Multi-Agent Systems research has developed technologies that can efficiently form coalitions even among previously unknown parties [24] — posing an additional threat to online retail auctions.

As explained, online auctions are unnecessarily hostile to customers and offer no

---

[7] In fact, such delays are the antithesis to *impulse buying*.

[8] Even in traditional static catalog retail (as well as CDAs), consumers can purchase products immediately.

[9] Granted, the pricing of retail products can get involved. This is where marketing tactics come into play such as branding, market segmentation, price discrimination, etc.

[10] This relates directly to the just-in-time (JIT) concept for manufacturing, inventory, and retailing [23]. However, it is not yet clear how best to gauge demand in JIT inventory and retailing (e.g., via negotiation or sales).

long-term benefits to merchants. Essentially, they pit merchant against customer in price tug-of-wars. This is not the type of relationship merchants prefer to have with their customers [2]. Unlike most classified ad and commodity markets (e.g., stock markets), merchants often care less about profit on any given transaction and care more about long-term profitability. This ties directly to customer satisfaction and long-term customer relationships. The more satisfied the customer and intimate the customer-merchant relationship, the greater the opportunity for repeat customer purchases and additional purchases through direct referrals and indirectly through positive reputation.

Furthermore, consumers are much more in the driver's seat in online markets than in physical-world markets largely due to the dramatic reduction in search costs [25]. This increases the competition among retailers and forces them to positively differentiate themselves online in value dimensions other than price.

Looking at Figure 5, we see more clearly why first-price, open-cry auctions are particularly poor negotiation protocols for retail markets. Comparing traditional retail markets (Figure 1) with online retail auctions (Figure 5), we see that these online auctions invert the relationships among retailers and consumers. Instead of merchants competing for consumer patronage, online retail auctions force consumers to compete with one another for a specific merchant offering. Also, rather than supporting

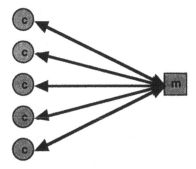

Figure 5 - online retail auctions. Consumers compete with one another for merchant offerings. Also, the relationship between the merchant and each of its customers is highly competitive.

cooperative negotiations between merchants and customers, the relationships in retail auctions are highly competitive. Furthermore, since online retail auctions are time-consuming and bids are non-retractable and binding, bidding in one auction (generally) precludes the consumer from bidding for the same (or similar) product in another merchant's auction. This means that other merchants' prices have no direct impact on consumers' bids during the extended auction bidding period (which contrasts with stock markets as shown in Figure 4).

3. Cooperative Negotiations

The degree of cooperation among negotiators falls within a continuum. After all, even in competitive negotiations, all parties need to cooperate sufficiently to engage in negotiation as well as agree on the semantics of the negotiation protocols.

However, one clear distinction that can be made between competitive and cooperative negotiations concerns the number of dimensions that can be negotiated across. For example, all of the competitive negotiation protocols discussed in the previous section allow for negotiation only within the price dimension. The cooperative negotiation protocols that we discuss in this section, on the other hand, allow agents (and humans) to negotiate over multiple dimensions.

Therefore, cooperative negotiations can be described as the decision-making process of resolving a conflict involving two or more parties over multiple interdependent, but *non*-mutually exclusive goals [26]. The study of how to analyze multi-objective decisions comes from economics research and is called multi-attribute utility theory (MAUT) [27]. The game theory literature describes cooperative negotiation as a non-zero-sum game where as the values along multiple dimensions shift in different directions, it is possible for *all* parties to be better off [4].

In essence, cooperative negotiation is a win-win type of negotiation. This is in stark contrast to competitive negotiation which is a win-lose type of negotiation.

Desired retail merchant-customer relationships and interactions can be described in terms of cooperative negotiation — the cooperative process of resolving multiple interdependent, but non-mutually exclusive goals. A merchant's primary goals are long-term profitability through selling as many products as possible to as many customers as possible for as much money as possible with as low transaction costs as possible. A customer's primary goals are to have their personal needs satisfied through the purchase of well-suited products from appropriate merchants for as little money and hassle (i.e., transaction costs) as possible. A cooperative negotiation through the space of merchant offerings can help maximize both of these sets of goals.

From a merchant's perspective, cooperative negotiation is about tailoring its offerings to each customer's individual needs resulting in greater customer satisfaction. From a customer's perspective, cooperative negotiation is about conversing with retailers to help compare their offerings across their full range of value resulting in mutually rewarding and hassle-free shopping experiences.

3.1. Multi-Attribute Utility Theory

Multi-objective decision analysis prescribes theories for quantitatively analyzing important decisions involving multiple, interdependent objectives from the perspective of a single decision-maker [27]. This analysis involves two distinctive features: an uncertainty analysis and a utility (i.e., preference) analysis. Techniques such as bayesian network modeling aid uncertainty analysis. Multi-attribute utility theory (MAUT) analyzes preferences with multiple attributes.

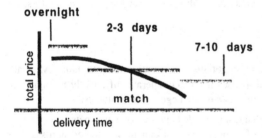

Examples of uncertainty in retail shopping are "will she like this product as a gift?" and "how much do I trust this merchant?" Such uncertainties weighed against other factors play a part in consumers' buying decisions. From a merchant's perspective, analyzing an uncertainty like "what will be the demand for this product?" is vital for pricing products and managing inventory.

Figure 6 - This graph plots a consumer's and a merchant's multi-attribute utilities for a product's total price vs. delivery time (in days). In this example, the merchant offers three delivery options at different price points of which the "2-3 days" option best matches the consumer's utility profile.

Often, decisions have multiple attributes that need to be considered. For example, in retail shopping, the price of a product could be important, but so could its delivery time. What is the

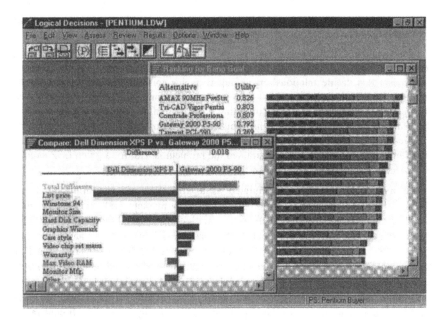

Figure 7 - A screenshot of Logical Decisions for Windows (LDW). This screenshot shows the results of a computer buying decision after LDW captured the decision-maker's utilities across multiple product attributes and value add. One results window shows the product rankings and the other a side-by-side comparison of two product

relationship and tradeoff between these two? Figure 6 gives a simple example of this.

Multi-objective decision analysis and MAUT can (and have) been used to tackle many different types of decision problems including electrical power vs. air quality, airport location, heroin addiction treatment, medical diagnostic and treatment, business problems, political problems, etc. These theories have also been instantiated in computer systems. The PERSUADER system at Carnegie Mellon University, for example, integrates Case-Based Reasoning and MAUT to resolve conflicts through negotiation in group problem solving settings [28]. Logical Decisions for Windows (LDW) by Logical Decisions, Inc. [29] is a general-purpose decision analysis tool for helping people think about and analyze their problems. Figure 7 shows LDW at work on a computer buying decision problem.

MAUT can help consumers make retail buying decisions. Likewise, MAUT techniques can help retailers create pricing policies for their added value – e.g., delivery options, extended warranty options, loan options, payment options, restocking fees, gift services, etc. However, MAUT alone does not constitute a cooperative negotiation protocol. Rather, MAUT is a decision analysis tool that can help capture and execute a strategy for an existing protocol. One such promising protocol is distributed constraint satisfaction.

3.2. Distributed Constraint Satisfaction

MAUT analyzes decision problems *quantitatively* through utilities. Constraint Satisfaction Problems (CSPs) analyze decision problems more *qualitatively* through constraints. A CSP is formulated in terms of variables, domains, and constraints. Once a decision problem is formulated in this way, a number of general purpose (and powerful) CSP techniques can analyze the problem and find a solution [30].

Finite-domain CSPs are one type of CSP and are composed of three main parts: a finite set of *variables*, each of which is associated with a finite *domain*, and a set of *constraints* that define relationships among variables and restricts the values that the variables can simultaneously take. The task of a CSP engine is to assign a value to each variable while satisfying all of the constraints. A variation of these "hard" constraints is the ability to also define "soft" constraints (of varied importance) which need not be satisfied. The number, scope, and nature of the CSP's variables, domains, and constraints will determine how constrained the problem is and, for a given CSP engine, how quickly a solution (if any) will be found.

Many problems can be formulated as a CSP such as scheduling, planning, configuration, and machine vision problems. In retail markets, CSP techniques can be used to encode hard constraints such as "I'm not willing to spend more than $2,000 for this product," and soft constraints such as "availability is more important to me than price." Even constraints such as "I prefer the Gateway 2000 P5-90 over the Dell Dimension XPS P (but I don't know why)" are legitimate. PersonaLogic (see Figure 8) uses CSP techniques to help shoppers evaluate product alternatives. Given a set of constraints on product features, PersonaLogic filters products that don't meet the given hard constraints and prioritizes the remaining products using the given soft constraints. This approach can also be applied to sales configuration systems such as Dell's "Build Your Own System" [31] and Trilogy's Selling Chain™ [32].

An important side-feature of CSPs is that they can clearly explain why they made certain decisions such as removing a product from the results list (e.g., "Product X is not

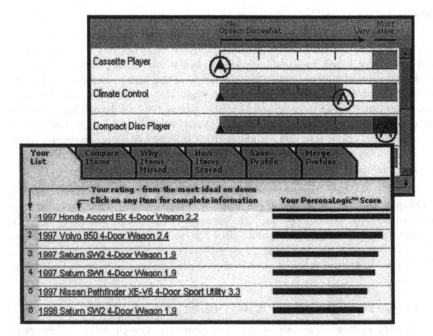

Figure 8 - Screenshots of PersonaLogic assisting a customer select automobile features with results.

an option because it has only 16 MB of RAM and you specified that the product should have at least 32 MB of RAM."). This feature is important because it relates to consumer trust (and ultimately, customer satisfaction). Trust is partially achieved by the shopping agent exhibiting somewhat predictable behavior and being able to explain its actions and decisions.

Most relevant to this paper, it should be possible to extend PersonaLogic to perform bilateral, cooperative negotiations between a merchant and a customer as shown in Figure 1 by using Distributed Constraint Satisfaction Problem (DCSP) protocols. DCSPs are similar to CSPs except that variables and constraints are distributed among two or more loosely-coupled agents [33]. This maps well to retail markets where consumers and merchants each have their respective set of constraints on merchant offerings. Furthermore, the loosely-coupled agents in a DCSP communicate to jointly solve a problem through established cooperative protocols [33]. This supports the desired cooperative relationship between a merchant and each of its customers.

However, DCSPs have been designed for fully cooperative group problem solving. Do DCSP techniques require more cooperation than is appropriate for merchant-customer interactions? For example, a customer may not be willing to divulge her reservation value (e.g., a willingness to pay up to $2,000 for a computer) to a merchant for fear of first-degree price discrimination with the merchant (unfairly) capturing all of the surplus in the market. However, first-degree price discrimination is tenuous in markets with monopolistic competition [1]. This suggests that DCSP techniques are not overly cooperative for bilateral, cooperative negotiations in retail markets.

4. Conclusion and Future Work

This paper analyzed several electronic markets and their corresponding negotiation protocols from economic, game theoretic, and business perspectives. We discussed how competitive negotiation protocols, and online auctions in particular, are inappropriate for online retail markets. Fundamentally, merchants strive for highly cooperative, long-term relationships with their customers to maximize customer satisfaction. This helps increase the probability of repeat purchases and new customers through positive reputation. Not surprisingly, none of the competitive negotiation protocols we discussed satisfied this need. Rather, they pitted merchant against customer in price tug-of-wars.

Cooperative multi-agent decision analysis tools and negotiation protocols, on the hand, appear to map much better to the retail market model depicted in Figure 1. For example, multi-attribute utility theory (MAUT) can help consumers make complex buying decisions (see Figure 7) taking into account multiple factors including merchants' unique added value (e.g., extended warranty options, delivery options, etc.). Constraint satisfaction techniques can also help consumers make complex buying decisions (see Figure 8) and this paper explored using cooperative distributed constraint satisfaction problem (DCSP) protocols to best support today's (and likely tomorrow's) retail market model (see Figure 1).

This analysis has guided the design of our new multi-agent system called Tete-a-Tete (T@T). T@T employs a combination of MAUT and DCSP techniques to mediate negotiations among consumer-owned shopping agents and retailer-owned sales agents. Once completed, we hope to show in our subsequent analysis of T@T that a bilateral, cooperative negotiation approach to retail electronic commerce allows merchants to tailor their offerings to each customer's individual needs resulting in more efficient markets and greater customer satisfaction than possible with competitive online auctions.

5. Acknowledgements

We would like to thank Peter Wurman and Michael Wellman for their help in refining our understanding of their AuctionBot system.

6. References

[1] R.H. Frank. *Microeconomics and Behavior, 3rd ed.* McGraw-Hill, Inc., 1996.

[2] Forrester Research Report. "Affordable Intimacy Strengthens online Stores." September, 1997.

[3] R. Guttman, A. Moukas, and P. Maes. "Agent-mediated Electronic Commerce: A Survey." To appear, *Knowledge Engineering Review*, June 1998.

[4] J. Rosenschein and G. Zlotkin. *Rules of Encounter: Designing Conventions for Automated Negotiation among Computers.* MIT Press, 1994.

[5] J. Cheng and M. Wellman. "The WALRAS algorithm: A Convergent Distributed Implementation of General Equilibrium Outcomes." To appear, *Computational Economics*.

[6] T. Sandholm and V. Lesser. "Equilibrium Analysis of the Possibilities of Unenforced Exchange in Multiagent Systems." *14th International Joint Conference on Artificial Intelligence (IJCAI'95)*. Montreal, Canada, 1995.

[7] A. Chavez, D. Dreilinger, R. Guttman, and P. Maes. "A Real-Life Experiment in Creating an Agent Marketplace." *Proceedings of the Second International Conference on the Practical Application of Intelligent Agents and Multi-Agent Technology (PAAM'97)*. London, UK, April 1997.

[8] Kasbah URL: <http://kasbah.media.mit.edu/>

[9] C. Sierra, P. Faratin, and N. Jennings. "A Service-Oriented Negotiation Model Between Autonomous Agents." *Proceedings of the Eighth European Workshop on Modeling Autonomous Agents in a Multi-Agent World (MAAMAW'97)*. Ronneby, Sweden, May 1997.

[10] P. Wurman, M. Wellman, and W. Walsh. "The Michigan Internet AuctionBot: A Configurable Auction Server for Human and Software Agents." In the *Proceedings of the Second International Conference on Autonomous Agents*. May, 1998.

[11] AuctionBot URL: <http://auction.eecs.umich.edu/>

[12] OnSale URL: <http://www.onsale.com/>

[13] eBay's AuctionWeb URL: <http://www.ebay.com/aw>

[14] Yahoo! online Auction URL: <http://www.yahoo.com/Business_and_Economy/Companies/Auctions/online_Auctions/>

[15] Forrester Research Report, *Business Trade and Technology Strategies: Sizing Intercompany Commerce, vol. 1, no. 1.* July 1997.

[16] FastParts URL: <http://www.fastparts.com/>

[17] FairMarket URL: <http://www.fairmarket.com/>

[18] First Auction URL: <http://www.firstauction.com/>

[19] netMarket URL: <http://www.netmarket.com/>

[20] Z Auction URL: <http://www.zauction.com/>

[21] P. Milgrom. "Auctions and Bidding: A Primer." *Journal of Economic Perspectives*, pp. 3-22. Summer 1989.

[22] C. Beam, A. Segev, and J. G. Shanthikumar. "Electronic Negotiation through Internet-based Auctions." CITM Working Paper 96-WP-1019, December 1996.

[23] G. Morgenson. "The Fall of the Mall." Forbes, May 24, 1993.

[24] T. Sandholm and V. Lesser. "Coalition Formation among Bounded Rational Agents." *14th International Joint Conference on Artificial Intelligence (IJCAI'95)*, Montreal, Canada, 1995.

[25] E. Schwartz. *Webonomics : Nine Essential Principles for Growing Your Business on the World Wide Web*. Broadway Books, 1997.

[26] R. Lewicki, D. Saunders, and J. Minton. *Essentials of Negotiation*. Irwin, 1997.

[27] R. Keeney and H. Raiffa. *Decisions with Multiple Objectives: Preferences and Value Tradeoffs*. John Wiley & Sons, 1976.

[28] K. Sycara. "The PERSUADER." In *The Encyclopedia of Artificial Intelligence*. D. Shapiro (ed.), John Wiley and Sons, January, 1992.

[29] Logical Decisions URL: <http://www.logicaldecisions.com/>

[30] E. Tsang. *Foundations of Constraint Satisfaction*. Academic Press, 1993.

[31] Dell "Build Your Own System" URL: <http://www.dell.com/store/index.htm>

[32] Trilogy's Selling Chain™ URL: <http://www.trilogy.com/prodserv/products/main.html>

[33] M. Yokoo and E. Durfee. "Distributed Constraint Satisfaction for Formalizing Distributed Problem Solving." *Proceedings of the 12th IEEE International Conference on Distributed Computing Systems*, 1992.

Enhancing Mobile Agents with
Electronic Commerce Capabilities

Hartmut Vogler, Marie-Luise Moschgath, Thomas Kunkelmann

Darmstadt University of Technology
Information Technology Transfer Office
Wilhelminenstr. 7
D-64283 Darmstadt, Germany
{vogler, malu, kunkel}@ito.tu-darmstadt.de

Abstract. *The paradigm of mobile agents offers a powerful and flexible opportunity to develop distributed applications on a high-level of abstraction. One of the most interesting tasks for mobile agents is an active search for relevant information in non-local domains on behalf of their users. A mobile agent will be sent out on behalf of an user to various host servers in the Internet and to find information. In the future this information might not be freely accessible, so the agent may have to pay for them. Thus the mobile agent has to be equipped with electronic commerce capabilities. This implies a fault tolerant and secure infrastructure for the mobile agent. In this paper we present a system which offers electronic commerce capabilities for mobile agents. These capabilities a part of an architecture which guarantees different security issues and fault tolerance for mobile agents. Security for the partners involved is handled by encryption methods based on a public key authentication mechanism and by secret key encryption of the communication. To achieve fault tolerance for the agent system, especially for the agent transfer to a new host, we use Distributed Transaction Processing (DTP). This architecture can be used on top of existing mobile agent systems, e.g. as an enhancement of the "GO-Statement", and offers a high reliability because the implementation is based on standardized components.*

Keywords: mobile agents, electronic commerce, security, fault tolerance, distributed transactions

1 Introduction

Mobile agents [HCK95] offer a new possibility for the development of applications in distributed systems. The paradigm of mobile agents is based on various sections of computer science. The term *agent* was originally coined by the artificial intelligence community, where agents are defined as autonomous, reactive and pro-active entities which have a social ability [WoJe95]. From the operating system point of view, mobile agents are an evolution of codeshipping and object and process migration. In the research field of networking and distributed systems, mobile agents are an extension of client/server-computing [ZLU95] and of the World Wide Web capabilities using *Java* [ArGo96] as well as an emerging technology for the next generation of telecommunications [MRK96]. Encompassing these three areas of computer science, the paradigm of mobile agents has become one of the most interesting topics of the today's research work.

Mobile agents are no longer a theoretical issue as different architectures for their implementations have been proposed. Research institutes as well as companies develop high-quality prototype systems for mobile agents, e.g. *ARA* [PeSt97], *Mole* [SBH96] or *Telescript* [Whi94]. Yet, these agent systems typically do not satisfy all requirements that mobile agents need for a full environment. However, these systems are open for further extensions to include additional characteristics.

One of the most interesting tasks for mobile agents is an active search for relevant information in non-local domains on behalf of their users. This includes retrieving, analyzing, manipulating and integrating information available form different sources. For example, a mobile agent will be sent out on behalf of an user to various servers to retrieve the latest version of a technical paper concerning "Electronic Commerce". On its itinerary, a mobile agent can interact on an ask/receive paradigm with a static agent residing on the host that offers the information. Thus, the mobile agent can find out only the relevant information or data and avoid unnecessary network traffic. In this scenario of information gathering in the Internet, commercial aspects [KaWh96] has become more and more relevant, e.g. the mobile agent has to pay for information, or in other possible application scenarios will be paid for a service it offers. As a consequence, mobile agents have to be equipped with electronic commerce capabilities to be an autonomous entity in the electronic market place. This unfortunately demands a high level of security and fault tolerance for the mobile agent either is not robbed, or does get lost or duplicated on its itinerary.

In this paper we describe an enhancement of mobile agent systems for electronic commerce based on the concept of a bank service for the Internet introduced by *First Virtual* [FV96] with special extensions for mobile agents, which offer additional control within the payment. This enhancement is part of an architecture for mobile agent systems that offers fault tolerance as well as security and can be used on top of existing systems.

In section 2 we describe our extension for mobile agent systems with the embedded electronic commerce capabilities for the agent. The core of our system builds an instance called *trust service* and a special protocol for agent migration, which is a combination of data logging, encryption mechanisms and distributed transactions. In section 3 we discuss various realization and implementation aspects. We conclude our paper in section 4 with a summary and an outlook on our future work.

2 A Mobile Agent System with Electronic Commerce Capabilities

In a scenario where a mobile agent is equipped with electronic commerce capabilities it necessary to guarantee that an agent does not get lost or duplicated during its itinerary. Thus, the main objective for the design of our architecture was to achieve a reliable, fault tolerant and secure agent transfer which guarantees the *exactly-once-semantic* (only-once-type-2-semantic) [MüSc92].

The problem of a reliable and fault tolerant agent transfer is an application level topic. We can guarantee a reliable transfer on the transport protocol level by using TCP/IP, but after this transfer, an agent has to be initiated at the new host. This offers various fault situations, which can easily cause an inconsistent state for the whole agent system by the loss or duplication of an agent. Thus, other classes of fault semantics (may-be, at-most-once, at-least-once) are not acceptable for mobile agents. In our system we guarantee the exactly-once-semantic by ensuring the agent migration with distributed transactions [BeNe96] and the 2-phase-committ (2PC) protocol.

However, the usage of distributed transactions and the 2PC protocol contains some drawbacks such as the bad performance of the 2PC protocol due to its blocking characteristics. *Distributed transaction processing (DTP)* also introduces implementation overhead and additional software components. In analyzing these pros and cons of DTP in the context of mobile agents, we came to the conclusion that the benefit of distributed transactions should be used for additional valuable features of an agent system. Therefore we built a DTP-based enhancement of existing systems for host security as well as agent security, which additionally allows agent management and control. From the application point of view, the most interesting enhancements of our systems are the electronic commerce capabilities for mobile agents.

2.1 Trust Service

In analyzing the security problems in the mobile agent paradigm [FGS96], we came to the conclusion that it is not possible to achieve full security with complete functionality for the agent without trust between the agent and the host. By aid of a third party, which has information about all instances of the agent system, a kind of trusted situation or contract can be achieved. In our architecture we call this instance *trust service*. This trust service is the core of our architecture for agent security and fault tolerance. On the one hand, our concept of a trust service is based on the concepts of *Kerberos* [NeTs94] in the way that we also use a trusted third party for session key generation and distribution. On the other hand it is important to see the difference between our trust service and well-known security services like the security service of the *Distributed Computing Environment* (DCE) [Hu95]. Our trust service extends these concepts to handle the specific problems of mobile agents and is based on common security concepts and services.

The trust service in our architecture is responsible for a special security protocol, which is explained in section 2.3, and for the logging of data about the agents and the host. These data include a record with the agent's identity, the host ID and the time interval of the visit. The trust service and the protocol additionally guarantee the correctness and consistency of these data. With these data we have enough information about the agent and the host so that in case of a breach of trust we can ascertain the originator and call him to account. Our system also offers the basis for agent control and management.

We assume that every instance of the system, hosts as well as users of the agent system, are registered at the trust service. This registration must be associated with a legally binding contract in order to achieve a trusted starting point. To use PGP [Gar94] in our system we also assume that every participant in the agent system possesses a certified public key [Kal93].

The concept of a trusted host is an abstraction for an entire machine or only an agent environment on a host. Therefore, it is not possible to use only a host based authentication mechanism like the *Secure Socket Layer* (SSL) [FKK96].

2.2 Virtual Bank Service (VBS)

In conjunction with registration, a user of the agent system announces to the Virtual Bank Service (VBS) that he will participate with his agents in the electronic cash system as a buyer and/or as a seller. Therefore, the user needs a private e-mail account and a regular bank account. In Figure 1 we see the registration of a user at the VBS.

The user sends his application including his full name and his PIN choice, encrypted with the public key P_v of VBS via e-mail to the bank. The VBS confirms the application by returning a reference number, which is used in the next step for authentication. The reference number is encrypted with the public key P_u of the buyer and the private key S_v of the VBS. Now the user sends his sensitive financial data (credit card number or bank account), encrypted with his private key S_u and the public key P_v to VBS.

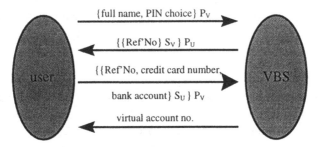

Fig. 1. Registration at the VBS

The VBS establishes a virtual account and notifies the user about the virtual account number (VAN), generated from the user's PIN. All sales effected with this virtual account number have to be confirmed by the owner before the credit card will be charged. The VAN can be used for all agents a user announces to the system. Furthermore, the VAN can be used only in conjunction with a valid agent ID in our payment protocol, which we explain later.

This concept, introduced by First Virtual [FV96], with freely accessible data for the payment, seems to be the suitable mechanism for mobile agents because this concept needs no authentication of the participants and supposes no secure transmission of information. This concept abstains from encryption mechanisms and avoids technical hurdles (e.g. export restrictions of the USA for encryption mechanisms) and additional costs.

Other popular electronic cash systems are based either on secret information (credit card number), like the *iKP* (Internet Keyed Payment Protocol) of IBM [IBM96] or on electronic proxies for money (electronic coins or coupons), like *DigiCash* [Dig96] or *Millicent* [DEC96]. In either case the agent has to keep secret information which should not be visible to a third party. Even if an agent migrates on a chain of trusted hosts, it is against the intention of those electronic cash systems to make the payment data freely accessible to other instances than the transaction partners. So, only solutions with freely accessible data are suitable for mobile agents.

2.3 Life-Cycle of an agent

The following items describe the life-cycle of an agent in our architecture and its integration in an electronic market place.

Registration

The originator announces a new agent to the trust service. The trust service generates a unique ID for the agent, which is used in conjunction with the registered user and which is sent back. This communication is protected by public key encryption. With the agent-ID and the VAN of the agent owner, the agent is equipped to perform money transactions.

When the agent is initiated at the host of its originator, it looks for a new target host by aid of special traders for agents as suggested in [PKL97]. To find a suitable new host the trader must possess agent-specific information concerning the resources, environment conditions and services offered at the host.

Agent transfer

After a successful negotiation between the target host and the agent, a copy of the agent will be transferred to the new host. To achieve security we use two different mechanisms. Distributed transaction processing guarantees a consistent state of the whole agent system during transport. With encryption we achieve protection against modification during the transfer and authentication of the agent in an unreliable network.

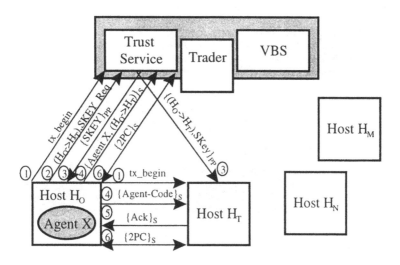

Fig. 2. Protocol steps of an agent transfer

Figure 2 illustrates the different protocol steps of an agent transfer:

1. The originator host (H_o) demarcates the begin of a distributed transaction (*tx_begin*), in which the trust service and the target host (H_r) will be involved. This implies that all following action and commands will be executed in a transactional context.

2. The originator host requests a *session key* (S) [Sch96] for secure communication and a secure transfer of the agent to the target host.

3. The trust service generates a session key and propagates it to the originator and the target host by using public key protocol (PP).

4. The originator host transfers a copy of the agent, encrypted with the session key, to the target host. The open design of our architecture allows the use of various mechanisms or protocols for the agent transfer.

5. After decrypting the agent, the target host initializes the copy of the agent and acknowledges the receipt.

6. The originator host initiates the 2PC protocol to conclude the transaction. A successful conclusion of the transaction implies that the results, i.e. deletion of the old agent, start of the new agent and update of data at the trust service, are made permanently visible. With the end of the transaction the session key is invalidated.

Money transactions

Once it is successfully transferred, the agent can process its tasks on the residing host, e.g. information retrieval on the local database. Therefore it can cooperate with a static agent on the host. In the future, the mobile agent may have to pay for information or, in other possible application scenarios, it will be paid for a service it offers. Figure 3 illustrates our protocol for the money transaction between a buyer agent and a seller agent.

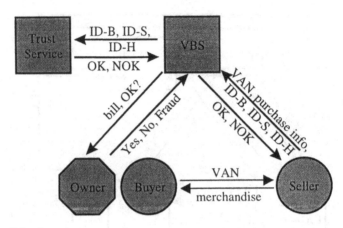

Fig. 3. Protocol for the money transaction

After a successful agreement is arranged between the local agent and the mobile agent, the buyer gives its virtual account number to the seller, which contacts the VBS to confirm the payment. Therefore the seller transmits the virtual account number together with information concerning the business, the identifiers of both parties (ID-B: identification of the buyer; ID-S: identification of the seller) and the host (ID-H: identification of the host) to the VBS. The VBS verifies by the aid of the trust service the consistency of the information (e.g. the mobile resides actually resides on this host), and acknowledges the validity to the seller. If the seller chooses the first payment sequence, he hands over the ordered article or information to the buyer after receiving an acknowledge. Later on, the VBS sends a bill (including the description and the price of the item, information about the seller, and the request for confirmation) to the owner of the agent. The owner now has the opportunity to confirm or to reject the sale or to shout 'fraud'. Only in the first case does the seller receive the payment. If the seller selects the second payment sequence, it has to wait for an acknowledgment. Therefore the VBS sends forthwith a request to the owner of the agent, waits for its answer and informs the seller. Only if the seller receives 'OK' does it hand over the article. The first payment sequence is designed for sales with low amounts, the second for sales with high amounts.

Our architecture offers an agent the ability to cope with money transactions based on the First Virtual concept of freely accessible data. It is important to realize that the VAN is only valid in combination with a correct agent ID. Additionally, the bank service can check the consistency of a money transaction by aid of the logging information at the trust service. It can be validated that an agent involved in the business actually resides at the right host, from where the money transaction was announced to the bank. In case of an error or cheating by one party, this can be traced back and the money transaction will be refused. It is then up to the seller and the trust service to initiate further action.

This protocol for money transactions can be modified or enhanced for the special requirements of an application scenario. Therefore we propose a modification to keep the costs for a single transaction in an adequate range in a way that the bank does not check all money transactions for consistency. Instead, the bank only checks transactions with a high amount and take random samples for small business transactions.

To achieve a better control of the agent, the system can be enhanced with limits concerning the agent's money transactions. With our architecture, the owner is able to define a maximal amount of money the agent can spend in one transaction or during the whole itinerary. These limits are stored and managed at the trust service.

Termination of the agent

There exist various methods to eliminate a mobile agent in our system. If an agent has finished its tasks it will either return to its owner or terminate at the current host. In both cases an appropriate message must be sent to the trust service, which logs this information. From this moment the agent is invalid.

An agent can also be eliminated anytime on behalf of its owner or the trust service. Therefore the trust service sends a message to the current host, which deletes the agent. Similar to the first case the agent is now invalid and cannot perform any further actions. Also the virtual account number in conjunction with the agent ID is invalidated.

With our system we can eliminate a leakage in existing agent systems which have to use special protocols for orphan detection and termination [Bau97]. Furthermore, our architecture offers the facility to define deadlines for mobile agents and to control them by the trust service.

3 Realization and Implementation Aspects

One of our design goals is to demonstrate the platform independence of our concepts. To do this, we evaluated the realization of our architecture using various platforms for DTP. We also examined performance aspects and how to scale our system for large distributed systems.

3.1 TIP based realization

In [VKM97a] we proposed a realization of the transactional migration in our system based on the recently published *Transaction Internet Protocol* (TIP) [LEK97] by Microsoft and Tandem. The *Internet Engineering Task Force* (IETF) is currently standardizing TIP for the Internet. There exists also a publicly accessible reference implementation of TIP in JAVA [TIP97]. TIP includes one- and two-phase commit protocols developed for the Internet. TIP is rather easy to handle but offers less routines for transaction management and control. To use TIP in our system we proposed an enhancement for encryption and for the exchange of our specific data like the agent ID. We layered this extension between the TIP protocol and the TCP/IP stack.

3.2 OTS-CORBA based realization

Another very promising approach is the realization of the transactional migration in
our system using the Common Object Broker Request Architecture (CORBA)
[OMG95] with its *Object Transaction Service* (OTS) [OMG94]. In [VKM97b] the
assignment of the OTS components to the instances of our system is described. The
whole communication for our protocol is based on object calls using CORBA, so only
interface specifications are necessary.

3.3 Performance Aspects

One drawback of distributed transaction processing results in a loss of performance.
However, for most applications there are no real-time requirements for the transport of
a mobile agent, so this problem is less important for our protocol. If no error occurs,
the loss of performance in relation to a normal agent transfer without transactions is
not significant. Exact performance data will be available with the first benchmarks of
different mobile agent systems.

If one of the hosts crashes or the network connection breaks down, the transmission
of the agent will be blocked. After a time-out the transaction will be aborted and the
agent on the old host remains valid, and after a reconnection a new migration of the
agent can be initiated. The protocol is non-blocking with respect to the overall agent
system; only the actions of a specific agent will be delayed by an error in its migration
phase.

3.4 Scaling for large distributed systems

The design of our architecture is suitable for scaling in large distributed systems like
the Internet. Our trust service is responsible for a specific *agent domain*, which can
cooperate with other domains. This concept is similar to CORBA or OTS where all
instances, servers as well as clients, pertain to one domain. It is important to see that
for instance, an OTS domain is absolutely independent of a CORBA domain. If
several CORBA domains can interoperate, this enables one OTS domain to span the
various CORBA domains [KVT96].

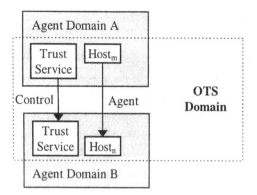

Fig. 4. Agent and OTS Domain

When an agent moves to a new agent domain, the control of this agent will be given to the new trust service. To preserve a consistence state of the agent system, the new trust service must to be involved in the agent transfer and the corresponding distributed transaction. Figure 4 illustrates the relationship between an agent and an OTS domain.

4 Conclusion and Future Work

We presented how mobile agents can be equipped with electronic commerce capabilities. These capabilities are part of an architecture for mobile agent security and fault tolerance which can be set up on top of existing mobile agent systems, e.g. as an enhancement of the "GO-Statement". Our architecture is highly secure against external attacks and offers a high reliability because the implementation is based on standardized components.

As future work we see the development of mechanisms for agent control and management. With the data at the trust service about the agent and its itinerary we have the basis to implement suitable control and management functions. Another interesting topic for further work may be the evaluation of the specification for *Mobile Agent Facilities* (MAF) [MAF97] to conform our system to this standard.

Literature

[ArGo96]   K. Arnold, J. Gosling: *The Java Programming Language*, Addison-Wesley, ISBN 0201-63455-4, 1996

[Bau97]   J. Baumann: A Protocol for Orphan Detection and Termination in Mobile Agent Systems, Technical Report, TR-1997-09, University of Stuttgart, 1997

[BeNe96]   P. Bernstein, E. Newcomer: *Principles of Transaction Processing*, ISBN 1-55860-415-4, Morgan Kaufmann Publisher, 1996

[DEC96]   Digital Equipment Corporation: *MILLICENT Digital's Microcommerce System* http://www.research.digital.com/SRC/millicent/, 1996

[Dig96]   DigiCash Home Page: http://www.digicash.com/

[FGS96]   W. Farmer, J. Guttman, V. Swarup: *Security for mobile agents: Issues and requirements*, In Proc. of the 19th National Information Systems Security Conference, Baltimore, MD, 1996

[FKK96]   A. O. Freier, P. Karlton, P.C. Kocher: *The SSL Protocol Version 3.0*, ftp://ietf.org/internet-draft/draft-ietf-tls-ssl-version3-00.txt, 1996

[FV96]   First Virtual Home page: http://www.fv.com

[Gar94]   S. Garfinkel: *PGP: Pretty Good Privacy*. ISBN 1-56592-098-8, O'Reilly & Associates, 1994

[HCK95]   C.D. Harrison, D.M. Chess, A. Kershenbaum: *Mobile Agents: Are they a good idea?*; IBM Research Report #RC 19887, IBM Research Division, 1995

[Hu95]   W. Hu: *DCE Securtity Programming*, ISBN 1-56592-134-8, O'Reilly & Accociates, 1995

[IBM96]   IBM Research Hawthorne and Zürich: *Internet Keyed Payment Protocols (iKP)*, http://www.zurich.ibm.com/Technology/Security/extern/ecommerce/iKP.html, 1996

[Kal93]   B. Kaliski: *Privacy Enhancement for Internet Mail: Part IV: Key Certification and Related Services*, RFC 1424, RSA, February 1993

[KaWh96]   R. Kalakota, A. B. Whinston: *Frontiers of Electronic Commerce*, ISBN 0-201-84520-2, Addison-Wesley Publishing Company, Inc., 1996

[KVT96]   T. Kunkelmann, H. Vogler, S. Thomas: *Interoperability of Distributed Transaction Processing Systems*, Proc. Int'l Workshop on Trends in Distributed Systems (TREDS'96), Aachen, Germany, Springer Verlag LNCS 1161, 1996

[LEK97]   J. Lyon, K. Evans, J. Klein: *Transaction Internet Protocol*, Version 2.0, Internet-Draft, ftp://ds.internic.net/internet-drafts/draft-lyon-itp-nodes-04.txt, 1997

[MAF97]   Joint Submission by General Magic Inc., GMD FOCUS, IBM Corp.: *Mobile Agent Facilities*, http://genmagic.com/agents/MAF/, 1997

[MRK96]   T. Magedanz, K. Rothermel, S. Krause: *Intelligent Agents: An Emerging technology for next generation telecommunication*, Proc. of INFOCOM'96, 1996

[MüSc92]   M. Mühlhäuser, A. Schill: *Software Engeneering für verteilte Anwendungen*, ISBN 3-540-55412-2, Springer Verlag, 1992

[NeTs94]   B. C. Neuman and T. Ts'o: *Kerberos: An Authentication Service for Computer Networks*, IEEE Communications Magazine, Volume 32, Number 9, 1994

[OMG95]   Object Management Group: *The Object Request Broker: Architecture and Specification*, Revision 2.0, 1995

[OMG94]   Object Management Group: *Object Transaction Service*, 1994

[PeSt97]   H. Peine and T. Stolpmann: *The Architecture of the Ara Platform for Mobile Agents*, Proc. of the First International Workshop on Mobile Agents MA'97 Berlin, LNCS No. 1219, Springer Verlag, 1997

[PKL97]   A. Park, A. Küpper, S. Leuker: *JAE: A Multi-Agent System with Internet Services Access*, Proc. of the 4th Int. Conference on Intelligence in Services and Networks IS&N'97, Cernobbio, Italy, Springer Verlag, LNCS 1238, 1997

[SBH96]   M. Straßer, J. Baumann, F. Hohl: *Mole - A Java based Mobile Agent System*, Proc. of the ECOOP '96 Workshop on Mobile Object Systems, 1996

[Sch96]   B. Schneier: *Applied Cryptography*, ISBN 0-471-11709-9, J. Wiley & Sons, Inc., 1996

[TIP97]   Transaction Internet Protocol, Reference Implementation, http://204.203.124.10/pdc/docs/TIP.zip

[VKM97a]   H. Vogler, T. Kunkelmann, M.-L. Moschgath: *Distributed Transaction Processing as a Reliability Concept for Mobile Agents*, Proc. 6th IEEE Workshop on Future Trends of Distributed Computing Systems (FTDCS'97), Tunis, Tunisia, IEEE Computer Society 1997

[VKM97b]   H. Vogler, T. Kunkelmann, M.-L. Moschgath: *An Approach for Mobile Agent Security and Fault Tolerance using Distributed Transactions*, 1997 Int'l Conference on Parallel and Distributed Systems (ICPADS'97), Seoul, Korea, IEEE Computer Society 1997

[WoJe95]   M. Woolbridge, N.R. Jennings: *Intelligent Agents: Theory and Practice*, Knowledge Engineering Review 10(2), 1995

[Whi94]   J. E. White: *Telescript Technology: The foundation for the electronic Marketplace*, White Paper. General Magic Inc., 1994

[ZLU95]   K. Zielinski, A. Laurentowski, A. Uszok: *Multi-Agent Model As an Extension to the Client/Server Processing Paradigm*, Proceedings of the Distributed Intelligent and Multi Agent Systems Workshop'95, November 1995

Dynamics of an Information-Filtering Economy

Jeffrey O. Kephart, James E. Hanson, David W. Levine, Benjamin N. Grosof,
Jakka Sairamesh, Richard B. Segal, and Steve R. White

IBM Thomas J. Watson Research Center
P.O. Box 704, Yorktown Heights, NY 10598, USA
{kephart,hanson,dwl,grosof,jramesh,rsegal,srwhite}@watson.ibm.com

Abstract. Our overall goal is to characterize and understand the dynamic behavior of information economies: very large open economies of automated information agents that are likely to come into existence on the Internet. Here we model a simple information-filtering economy in which broker agents sell selected articles to a subscribed set of consumers. Analysis and simulation of this model reveal the existence of both desirable and undesirable phenomena, and give some insight into their nature and the conditions under which they occur. In particular, efficient self-organization of the broker population into specialized niches can occur when communication and processing costs are neither too high nor too low, but endless price wars can undermine this desirable state of affairs.

1   Introduction

Today, we are witnessing the first steps in the evolution of the Internet towards an open, free-market *information economy* of automated agents buying and selling a rich variety of information goods and services[2, 4, 6, 16, 19, 22]. We envision the Internet some years hence as a seething milieu in which billions of economically-motivated agents find and process information and disseminate it to humans and, increasingly, to other agents. Over time, agents will progress naturally from being mere facilitators of electronic commerce transactions to being financial decision-makers, at first directly controlled by humans and later with increasing autonomy and responsibility. Ultimately, inter-agent economic transactions may become an inseparable and perhaps dominant portion of the world economy.

The evolution of the Internet into an information economy seems as desirable as it does inevitable. After all, economic mechanisms are arguably the best known way to adjudicate and satisfy the conflicting needs of billions of *human* agents. It is tempting to wave the Invisible Hand and assume that the same mechanisms will automatically carry over to *software* agents. However, automated agents are *not* people! They make decisions and act on them at a vastly greater speed, they are immeasurably less sophisticated, less flexible, less able to learn, and notoriously lacking in "common sense". How might these differences affect the efficiency and stability of future information economies?

Previous research in automated economies is equivocal. Under certain assumptions, large systems of interacting self-motivated software agents can be susceptible to the emergence of wild, unpredictable, disastrous collective behavior[13,

14]. On the other hand, a large body of work on market mechanisms in distributed multi-agent environments suggests that efficient resource allocation or other desirable global properties may emerge from the collective interactions of individual agents[1, 3, 5, 8, 10, 11, 15, 17, 21].

Our goal is to understand the dynamic, emergent behaviors — both good and bad — of information economies from an *agent's*-eye view, and from this to formulate basic design principles that will foster efficient electronic commerce. We pursue this goal by combining analysis and simulation of information economies with concurrent development of an information economy prototype.

In this paper, we focus on a simple model of an information filtering economy, such as might be embedded in a larger information economy. The model is inspired by information dissemination services that can be found on the Internet today, and sets them in an economic context. After introducing the model in section 2, we analyze and simulate its dynamical behavior in section 3, illustrating as we go the promise and the pitfalls inherent in this and similar economies. We conclude with a brief summary of our findings in section 4.

2 Model of the news filtering economy

Fig. 1 represents our information filtering model economy, consisting of a *source* agent that publishes news articles, C *consumer* agents that want to buy articles they are interested in, B *broker* agents that buy selected articles from the source and resell them to consumers, and a *market* infrastructure that provides communication and computation services to all agents. Each agent's internal parameters (defined below) are printed inside its ellipse. Solid lines represent the propagation of a sample article through broker 1. Broken lines indicate payment, and are labeled with symbols (explained below) for the amount paid.

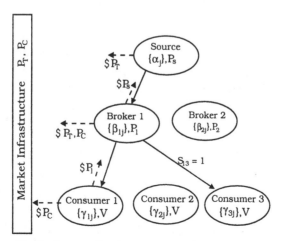

Fig. 1. Part of an idealized news filtering economy. Only a subset of agents is shown. See text for interpretation of symbols.

The source agent publishes one article at each time step t. It classifies articles according to its own internal categorization scheme, assigning each a *category index* j. The nature of the categories, and the number J of them, do not change. We represent this (hidden) classification scheme by a random process in which an article is assigned category j with fixed probability α_j. The set of all α_j is the source's *category prevalence* vector α. Each article is labeled with its category index and offered for sale to all brokers at a fixed price P_S. For each article sold to each broker, the source pays a fixed *transport cost* P_T.

Upon receiving an offer, each broker b decides whether or not to buy the article using its own evaluation method, which may be *uncorrelated* with the source's categorization scheme. For each evaluation that it makes, the broker pays the system a fixed *computation cost* P_C. The broker's evaluation method is approximated by a random process parametrized by its *interest vector* β_b: it buys an article labeled (by the source) with category j with probability β_{bj}. When broker b purchases an article, it immediately sends it to a set of *subscribing* consumers, paying tranportation cost P_T for each. Subscribers examine the article, and pay the broker P_b if they want the right to use ("consume") it. The broker's internal parameters β_b and P_b are under its direct control.

Subscriptions are represented by a *subscription matrix* S, where $S_{bc} = 1$ if consumer c subscribes to broker b, and $S_{bc} = 0$ if not. Subscriptions are maintained only with the consent of both parties, and may be cancelled by either. For example, a broker b might reject a consumer c if the cost of sending articles exceeds the expected payment from c, or c might reject b if the cost of sifting through lots of junk outweighs the benefit of receiving the rare interesting article. The bilateral nature of the agreement is represented by setting $S_{bc} = \sigma_{bc}^{(b)}\sigma_{bc}^{(c)}$, where $\sigma_{bc}^{(b)} = 1$ if broker b wants consumer c as a subscriber and 0 if not; analogously, $\sigma_{bc}^{(c)}$ represents consumer c's wishes.

When a consumer receives one or more copies of an article from brokers to which it subscribes, it pays the computation cost P_C to determine whether it is *interested* in the article, then decides whether (and from whom) to buy it. Like the brokers, the consumers' evaluation function is approximated by a stochastic process parametrized by an interest vector γ_c: consumer c will be interested in an article labeled with category j with fixed probability γ_{cj}. The consumer then determines whether the *anticipated value* V for interesting articles warrants paying the price P_{b^*} demanded by the chosen broker b^*, and if so purchases the usage rights to the article.

An alternative formulation replaces the consumer's computational cost P_C with a negative value or cost P_J incurred when "junk" is received. The transformation $V \to V + P_J$, $P_C \to P_J$ renders these two views equivalent.

3 Behavior of the news filtering economy

In this section we illustrate desirable and undesirable phenomena that can occur in our news filtering economy. First, we define the *state* of the system, from which any desired aspect of behavior can be derived. Then, we derive the state and behavior of simple systems with a few well-informed brokers and an infinite number of consumers. Finally, we simulate a system of many brokers and consumers with limited knowledge of the system state, and show that it can self-organize into a configuration that is beneficial to brokers and consumers alike.

We define the *state* of the system at time t, $\mathcal{Z}(t)$, as the collection of broker prices P_b, broker interest vectors β_b, and the subscription topology matrix S. Our goal is to understand the evolution of $\mathcal{Z}(t)$, given (i) an initial configuration $\mathcal{Z}(0)$; (ii) the values of the various extrinsic (possibly time-varying) variables: the category prevalences α_j, the costs P_S, P_T, and P_C, the consumer value V, and the consumer interest vectors γ_c; and (iii) the algorithms used by each agent to dynamically modify those variables over which it has control, including specification of a) the state information accessible to the agent and b) the times at which the modifications are made.

Any desired individual or aggregate aspect of behavior can be extracted from the history of $\mathcal{Z}(t)$ and the extrinsic variables. Two particularly important quantities are the expected utility per article for consumers and brokers. It can be shown that the expected utility per article U_c for consumer c is given by:

$$U_c = \sum_{b=1}^{B} \sum_{j=1}^{J} \alpha_j S_{bc} \beta_{bj} \left(\prod_{b'=1}^{B} (1 - S_{b'c} \beta_{b'j} \Theta(P_b - P_{b'})) \right) [(V - P_b)\gamma_{cj} - P_C] \quad (1)$$

where $\Theta(x)$ is the step function: $\Theta(x) = 1$ for $x > 0$, and 0 otherwise. The product term in large parentheses is the probability that an article in category j is not offered by any broker for a price less than P_b. The term in square brackets is the expected value of an article in category j: it always costs the consumer P_C to process it, regardless of its worth, and with probability γ_c consumer c will pay P_b to receive information worth V.

The appropriate utility function for the broker is its expected profit per article, given by:

$$W_b = \sum_{c=1}^{C} \sum_{j=1}^{J} \alpha_j S_{bc} \beta_{bj} \left[P_b \gamma_{cj} \left(\prod_{b'=1}^{B} (1 - S_{b'c} \beta_{b'j} \Theta(P_b - P_{b'})) \right) - P_T \right] \quad (2)$$
$$- \sum_{j=1}^{J} \alpha_j (\beta_{bj} P_S + P_C)$$

3.1 Single broker case

Given that effective monopolies can occur even in multi-broker systems, it is useful and instructive to establish a few simple results for systems with a single broker. First, suppose the broker offers a single category, and that the number of consumers is arbitrarily large, i.e. $B = 1$, $J = 1$, and $C \to \infty$. The broker tries to maximize its utility by choosing a set of preferred consumers (those c for which $\sigma_c^{(b)} = 1$), setting a price P, and setting its interest level β. The consumers try to maximize their utility simply by declaring whether they wish to subscribe to the broker (in which case $\sigma_c^{(c)} = 1$).

Analysis of Eqs. 1 and 2 shows that, for a wide range of parameters, the equilibrium state is $\{\beta = 1, P = P^*, S_c = \Theta(P^*\gamma_c - P_T)\Theta((V - P^*)\gamma_c - P_C)$. The subscription matrix element S_c, which defines whether or not consumer c has subscribed to the broker, is the product of two step functions, which can be understood intuitively as follows. The first step function, $\Theta(P^*\gamma_c - P_T)$, represents the veto power of the broker: it only wishes to serve consumers that are interested enough (and the price is high enough) so that the expected revenue from an article will exceed the cost of sending it. The second step function, $\Theta((V - P^*)\gamma_c - P_C)$, represents the consumer's veto power: it only wishes to subscribe to the broker if it is interested enough (and the price is low enough) so that the expected net benefit of receiving an article exceeds the cost of processing it. The monopolistic equilibrium price P^* is constrained by the step functions and the restriction $\gamma_c < 1$ to be in the range $P_T < P^* < V - P_C$; its exact value depends in detail upon P_C, P_T, V, and the distribution of consumer interest probabilities $\Gamma(\gamma_c)$ in the population. For example, when Γ is a uniform distribution, P^* is the solution to a cubic equation involving P_C, P_T, and V.

Now suppose that the number of categories J offered by the broker is arbitrary [7]. Assuming that the category prevalences are all equal ($\alpha_j = 1/J$) and the distribution of consumer interests within a given category is given by Γ, one can derive analytic expressions for the monopolistic equilibrium price as a function of the number of categories. Substituting this function $P^*(J)$ back into Eq. 2, one can derive the broker's optimal utility as a function of the number of categories, and then from this the optimal number of categories. Illustrative results for two very different distributions Γ are shown in Fig. 2.

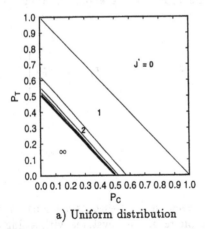
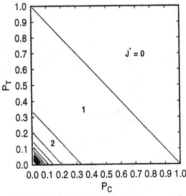

a) Uniform distribution   b) All-or-nothing distribution, $\nu = 0.03$.

Fig. 2. The optimal number of categories J^* for the broker to offer as a function of P_C and P_T (with $V = 1$). a) Γ is a uniform distribution in the interval $(0,1)$, so $\nu = 0.5$. b) Γ is an all-or-nothing distribution: $\gamma_j = 1$ with probability $\nu = 0.03$, else $\gamma_j = 0$.

For a wide class of distributions, three behavioral regimes are observed. When the combined cost of transport and processing is sufficiently high $(P_C + P_T > V)$, the optimal number of categories J^* is 0. In this "dead" regime, an article costs more to send and process than it is worth, even if the consumer is guaranteed to be interested in it, and so no articles will be bought or sold. At the other extreme, when the costs are sufficiently low $(P_C + P_T < \nu V$, where ν is the mean of the distribution $\Gamma)$, the broker is motivated to offer *all* categories that exist $(J^* \to \infty)$. In real information filtering applications, one expects ν to be quite small, since each consumer regards most information as junk. It is useful to think of $J^* \to \infty$ as a (presumably tiny) **spam regime**, in which it costs so little to send information, and the financial impact on a consumer of receiving junk is so minimal, that it makes economic sense to send all articles to all consumers. In between these two regimes, the optimal number of categories is finite.[1]

3.2 Two broker case: price competition and warfare

To explore some effects of price competition, we begin by considering a simple two-broker system with a single information category. We assume that brokers and consumers are fully knowledgeable about the state of the system (in particular, they know the prices and interest vectors of all of the brokers). Furthermore, they instantly adjust their desired subscription vectors $\sigma_{bc}^{(b)}$ and $\sigma_{bc}^{(c)}$ to maximize their utility given the current set of prices and interest vectors. This last assumption removes the degrees of freedom associated with the subscription matrix by expressing it in terms of the other state parameters (prices and interest vectors) — a tremendous simplification.

We assume that the brokers update their prices asynchronously. One plausible strategy is for a broker to set its price to the value that maximizes its profit, assuming all other prices remain fixed. Such an update strategy is guaranteed to produce the optimal profit up until the moment when the next broker updates *its* parameters. We call such a strategy "myopically optimal", or **myoptimal**.

A useful construct for understanding the resulting dynamics is the *profit landscape*. We define a broker's profit landscape as its utility (given in Eq. 2) as a function of the prices offered by all brokers in the system, itself included. A contour map of the profit landscape for broker 1 in a system with $P_C = P_T = 0.3$, $V = 1$, and a uniform distribution of consumer interests is shown in Fig. 3a.

The landscape shown in Fig. 3a has two distinct humps. The "cheap" hump on the right corresponds to the case where broker 1 is cheaper $(p_1 < p_2)$. Here, its profit is completely independent of p_2, and it can charge the monopolistic price derived previously. The "expensive" hump on the left corresponds to the case in which broker 1 is more expensive than broker 2, but still able to find customers. This comes about when broker 2 is charging so little that it cannot afford to keep marginal customers — i.e., customers with low interest levels γ_c — as subscribers. (Recall from the discussion of the single-broker case that a broker

---

[1] Closed-form expressions for the finite $J^* > 1$ contours appear impossible; these contours have been computed numerically in Fig. 2.

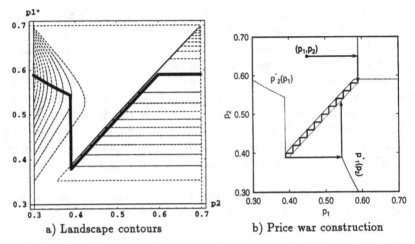

a) Landscape contours   b) Price war construction

Fig. 3. a) Contour map of profit landscape for broker 1 for $P_T = P_C = 0.3, V = 1$, with overlaid optimal price function $p_1^*(p_2)$. Profit is higher in dark regions. b) Graphical construction of price-war time series, using functions $p_1^*(p_2)$ and $p_2^*(p_1)$.

will veto a subscription from an insufficiently interested prospective customer.) For these marginal customers, the only alternative is to subscribe to broker 1. In other words, broker 2's rejects constitute broker 1's market.

If broker 1 is myoptimal, it can derive from its profit landscape a function $p_1^*(p_2)$ that gives the value of p_1 that maximizes the profit when broker 2 charges price p_2. This function is represented as a heavy solid line in Fig. 3a. For $0.3 < p_2 < 0.389$, $p_1^*(p_2)$ is given by the solution to a cubic equation involving cube roots of square roots of p_2; in this region it looks fairly linear. The "vertical" segment at $p_2 = 0.389$ is a discontinuity as the optimal price jumps from the "expensive" hump to the "cheap" hump. When $0.389 < p_2 < 0.590$, $p_1^* = p_2 - \epsilon$, where ϵ is a price quantum — the minimal amount by which one price can exceed another. For $0.590 < p_2 < 0.7$, $p_1^* = 0.590$, the monopolistic price.

If broker 2 also uses a myoptimal strategy, then by symmetry its landscape and price-setting function $p_2^*(p_1)$ are identical under an interchange of p_1 and p_2. Then the evolution of both p_1 and p_2 can be obtained simply by alternate application of the two price optimization functions: broker 1 sets its price $p_1(t+1) = p_1^*(p_2(t))$, then broker 2 sets its price $p_2(t+2) = p_2^*(p_1(t+1))$, and so forth. The time series may be traced graphically on a plot of both $p_1^*(p_2)$ and $p_2^*(p_1)$ together, as shown in Fig. 3b. Assume *any* initial price vector (p_1, p_2), and suppose broker 1 is the first to move. Then the graphical construction starts by holding p_2 constant while moving horizontally to the curve for $p_1^*(p_2)$. Then, p_1 is held constant while moving vertically to the curve $p_2^*(p_1)$. Alternate horizontal moves to $p_1^*(p_2)$ and vertical moves to $p_2^*(p_1)$ always lead to a **price war** during which the brokers successively undercut each other, corresponding to zig-zagging between the diagonal segments of the curves. Eventually, the price gets driven down to 0.389, at which point the undercut broker (say broker 1) opts out of the price war, switching to the expensive hump in its profit landscape by setting $p_1^*(0.389) = 0.543$. This breaks the price war, but unfortunately it triggers a new one. The brokers are caught in a never-ending, disastrous limit cycle of price wars punctuated by abrupt resets, during which their time-averaged utility is half what they expected, and less than half of the monopolistic value.

3.3   General myoptimal case; discussion

Generalizing to an arbitrary number of brokers and categories, and permitting each broker to myoptimally update both its price *and* its interest vector, we observe more complex analogs of price wars, in which both prices and interest vectors are drawn into limit cycles. In the spam regime, the system tends to behave very wildly. When J^* is finite, the interest vectors can display some metastability, but price wars can develop even among brokers with different interest vectors (if they overlap sufficiently).

Price wars are even a problem when $J^* = 1$. Consider a system in this regime with n brokers and n categories. Such a system can accommodate each broker's wish to be a monopolist in a single category. If all categories are preferred equally by the users, each broker will ultimately specialize in a single unique category (even when J^* is somewhat more than 1) [7]. However, if the consumer population slightly favors one category, a system of niche monopolists is unstable, because each broker will cut its price in an effort to own the favored category. Simulations reveal that slightly less favored categories tend to be available much less often than the consumer population would like. Consequently, the total consumer utility is often reduced during a price war, despite the low prices [12].

Intuitively, any sort of economy consisting of myoptimal agents is likely to be plagued with price-war limit cycles. Geometrically, this behavior can be traced to the multi-peaked, discontinuous topology of the profit landscape, which in turn arises from the consumers' preference for the cheapest brokers. Of course, this does not imply that agent economies are doomed to failure. The assumption of myoptimality is unrealistic in several respects, and the fact that price wars occur relatively infrequently in human economies offers some hope.

The economics literature describes several possible mitigating effects that may explain why price wars are not rampant in human economies [18]. Expressed in terms of our model, these include explicit collusion among brokers, or tacit collusion — using foresight to avoid triggering price wars. Other factors thought to hinder price wars include frictional effects (consumers may find it too costly or bothersome to shop around, and brokers may find it costly to update prices or change products too often) or spatial or informational differentiation (i.e. different consumers might value the same good differently, depending on their physical location or knowledge).

These mitigating factors are likely to be weaker in agent-based economies than they are in human economies. Explicit collusion might require fairly sophisticated languages and protocols (and might be declared illegal!) In large decentralized systems, efforts to employ foresight may be hampered by imperfect knowledge of the system state and the strategies of the other agents. Even if these are known perfectly, it may be computationally infeasible to predict the future. [2] Consumer inertia may be greatly reduced when agents rather than people are doing the shopping, and price updates may be cheaper to compute and advertise. Localization effects are likely to be much smaller for information goods and services than they are for carrots and carwashes. Given these considerations, it is very possible that real agent economies will experience price wars much more frequently than do human economies.

3.4 Limited competitive knowledge; niches and prices

In order to understand the behavior of more realistic economies in which brokers and consumers are less informed about the system state, and less immediately responsive to environmental changes, we have built an agent simulation environment that allows us to experiment with a wide range of utility maximization strategies for consumers and brokers. In particular, we do not assume that brokers know each other's prices (or interest vectors), nor that the brokers know the consumers' interest vectors. Instead, they must make do with historical data based on their own parameters (e.g. prices and interest vectors) and experience (e.g. consumer demand and profits).

Here we describe a simulation run involving 10,000 consumers, 500 brokers, and 100 categories. In this run, a typical consumer was completely interested ($\gamma_{cj} = 1$) in roughly 3 out of the 100 categories and completely uninterested ($\gamma_{cj} = 0$) in all other categories. The computation and transport costs were $P_C = 30$ and $P_T = 30$; the information value was $V = 150$. Under these circumstances, $J^* = 1$. To set prices, the brokers use an extremely simple-minded strategy: they randomly shift their price by a small amount up or down. If (after a suitable period of time), the broker finds that its profit per unit time has increased, it keeps moving the price in the same direction; otherwise it reverses direction. We call this a *derivative-following* algorithm. Brokers adjust their interest vectors in a similar way, increasing or decreasing β_j by an amount depending upon the profit or loss recently experienced when selling an article in category j. The brokers and consumers estimate the utility of adding or cancelling subscriptions using a matchmaker that periodically gauges agents' interests by issuing questionnaires about a given set of articles.

Each consumer initially establishes a subscription with a single randomly chosen broker. From time to time, agents make asynchronous, independent decisions about adjusting prices, interest vectors, or subscriptions. Figure 4 shows the distribution of consumers' utilities at three different moments in their evolution. Starting from a state in which virtually all of the consumers have negative utilities, the economy adapts itself such that most consumers have positive utilities, and at worst a few have zero.

---

[2] In a simulation of just 4 brokers, 4 categories, and 10,000 consumers, computing a single *myoptimal* decision requires a few hours on a high-end workstation. Other researchers have shown that agents *can* learn to predict one another's actions, but the experiments have involved societies of fewer than ten agents [9, 20].

Of the original 500 brokers, only 122 remain active at time $t = 200,000$ (i.e., after 200,000 articles have flowed through the system). The others have either gone broke or are not participating in the market because they are buying no articles from the news source. Many brokers die out within the first few thousand time steps, while others thrive at first but then suddenly start losing to competition. *All* of the 122 that remain at $t = 200,000$ have chosen just a single category in which to specialize, and among them cover 86 distinct categories.

At $t = 0$, almost all of the consumers have negative utility because the random initial conditions typically do not give them a large enough ratio of interesting articles to junk. Rapid improvements are soon made as the agents mutually sort out the subscription topology. During this phase, many consumers temporarily drop out of the economy, while the remaining ones eke some positive utility out of the brokers. Once a broker has a semi-coherent following, positive feedback sets in: the broker is encouraged by its clientele to provide articles that they will find interesting. Once the broker specializes to a small number of categories, other consumers are now attracted. By $t = 100,000$, all of the brokers have specialized into a single category, and no consumers receive any junk.

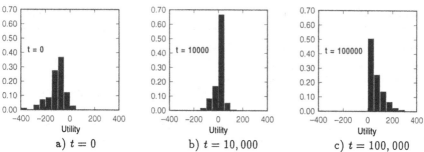

| a) $t = 0$ | b) $t = 10,000$ | c) $t = 100,000$ |

Fig. 4. Evolution of the consumer utility distribution.

In this run, dramatic cyclical price wars were not observed, although more benign short-lived price wars played a role in driving superfluous brokers out of the market. Because the derivative-following price-setting algorithm forbids large discontinuous changes in prices, it appears unlikely to support dramatic cyclical price wars of the sort we found in the myoptimal case. Unfortunately, since the profit landscape typically contains several distinct humps separated by discontinuities, the derivative-following algorithm can often cause the economy to become stuck in highly suboptimal states. In other simulation runs in which the brokers initially offered an excessive number of categories, the system consistently evolved to a state in which no articles were sold. Making the system more robust to unfavorable initial conditions (or more responsive to environmental changes) requires permitting discontinuous jumps in price or interest vectors, but these capabilities also put the system at greater risk for cyclical price wars.

4 Conclusion

Our investigation of the dynamic behavior of an information filtering economy revealed at least two important effects: spontaneous specialization, which is generally desirable, and cyclical price wars, which are by and large undesirable even to consumers that may on the surface seem to benefit from lowered prices.

We found that specialization is driven by two distinct mechanisms working together. First, if the extrinsic transport and processing costs P_T and P_C are intermediate between the low-cost "spam" regime and the high-cost "dead" regime, a monopolist broker prefers to offer a small number of categories. Second, competition among multiple brokers encourages them to become monopolists in largely non-overlapping sets of one or a few categories. Niche specialization is typically desirable from the perspective of both the brokers and the consumers.

Standard models of price wars [18] typically lead to a *stable* point at which no one makes a profit. The news filtering economy is extremely prone to *unstable* limit-cycle price wars, behavior that can be traced to the multi-humped, discontinuous topography of the profit landscape. Price wars undermine the tendency of the system to efficiently self-organize itself. We found that cyclic price wars could be eliminated in a system of brokers and consumers that had little knowledge of the system state and very simplistic algorithms for updating prices and interests, permitting useful specialization to occur. However, one cannot conclude that individual ignorance leads to societal bliss. The conservative price-setting strategy makes the system less nimble, and more susceptible to failure. Furthermore, even if ignorance led to good collective behavior, it would hardly be a stable strategy: there would be a strong incentive to use a better informed or more intelligent agent that could outperform its weaker opponents. Other effects that may hinder price wars in human economies, such as explicit and tacit collusion, frictional effects, and spatial or informational differentiation are likely to be weaker in agent economies. Price wars may indeed prove to be a serious problem to contend with in large agent economies of any sort, and merit our continued attempts to understand and control them.

Acknowledgments

We thank Bill Schneider, Wenke Lee, Anastasia Anastasiadi, and Hoi Chan for their contributions to the information economy simulator and prototype.

References

1. W. P. Birmingham, E. H. Durfee, T. Mullen, and M. P. Wellman. The distributed agent architecture of the University of Michigan Digital Library. In *AAAI Spring Symposium on Information Gathering in Heterogeneous, Distributed Environments*. AAAI Press, 1996.

2. A. Chavez and P. Maes. Kasbah: an agent marketplace for buying and selling goods. In *Proceedings of 1st International Conference on the Practical Application of Intelligent Agents and Multi-Agent Technology*, London, April 1996.

3. S. Clearwater, editor. *Market based control: a paradigm for distributed resource allocation.* World Scientific, Singapore, 1995.

4. J. Eriksson, N. Finne, and S. Janson. Information and interaction in MarketSpace — towards an open agent-based market infrastructure. In *Proceedings of the Second USENIX Workshop on Electronic Commerce*, November 1996.

5. D. F. Ferguson. *The Application of Microeconomics to the design of resource allocation and control algorithms in Distributed Systems.* PhD thesis, Columbia University, 1989.

6. R. H. Guttman, A. Moukas, and P. Maes. Agent-mediated electronic commerce: A survey. *Knowledge Engineering Review*, June 1998.

7. J. E. Hanson and J. O. Kephart. Spontaneous specialization in a free-market economy of agents. In *Proceedings of Workshop on Artificial Societies and Computational Markets at the Second International Conference on Autonomous Agents*, May 1998.

8. T. Hogg and B. A. Huberman. Controlling chaos in distributed systems. *IEEE Transactions on Systems, Man, and Cybernetics*, 21:1325, 1991.

9. J. Hu and M. P. Wellman. Learning about other agents in a dynamic multi-agent system. In *Proceedings of the Second International Conference on Autonomous Agents*, 1998.

10. B. A. Huberman, editor. *The Ecology of Computation*, Amsterdam, 1988. North-Holland.

11. B. A. Huberman, R. M. Lokose, and T. Hogg. An economics approach to hard computational problems. *Science*, 1996.

12. J. O. Kephart, J. E. Hanson, and J. Sairamesh. Price-war dynamics in a free-market economy of software agents. In *Proceedings of Alife VI*, June 1998.

13. J. O. Kephart, T. Hogg, and B. A. Huberman. Dynamics of computational ecosystems. *Physical Review A*, 40:404–421, 1989.

14. J. O. Kephart, T. Hogg, and B. A. Huberman. Collective behavior of predictive agents. *Physica D*, 42:48–65, 1990.

15. J. F. Kurose, M. Schwartz, and Y. Yemini. A microeconomic approach to optimization of channel access policies in multiaccess networks. In *Proc. of 5th Int. Conf. Distrib. Comput. Syst.*, 1985.

16. M. S. Miller and K. E. Drexler. Markets and computation: agoric open systems. In B. A. Huberman, editor, *The Ecology of Computation.* North-Holland, Amsterdam, 1988.

17. M. Stonebraker et al. An economic paradigm for query processing and data migration in Mariposa. In *Proc. of Parallel and Distributed Information Systems*, pages 58–67, 1994.

18. J. Tirole. *The Theory of Industrial Organization.* The MIT Press, Cambridge, MA, 1988.

19. M. Tsvetovatyy, M. Gini, B. Mobasher, and Z. Wieckowski. MAGMA: an agent-based virtual market for electronic commerce. *Applied Artificial Intelligence*, 1997.

20. J. M. Vidal and E. H. Durfee. The impact of nested agent models in an information economy. In *Proceedings of the Second International Conference on Multi-agent Systems (ICMAS96).* MIT Press, December 1996.

21. M. P. Wellman. A market-oriented programming environment and its application to distributed multicommodity flow problems. *Journal of Artificial Intelligence Research*, 1:1, 1993.

22. J. White. Mobile agents white paper. General Magic, Inc., 1996.

Levels of Adaptivity in Systems of Coordinating Information Agents

Katia P. Sycara

The Robotics Institute, Carnegie Mellon University
5000 Forbes Avenue, Pittsburgh, PA 15213
katia@cs.cmu.edu

Abstract. Complex information environments, e.g. the Internet, are open systems. An open system is one in which the system components are not known in advance, can change over time, and may be highly heterogeneous. For example, the Internet can be viewed as a large, distributed information resource with heterogeneous nodes and communication links that could appear and disappear unpredictably. To face the challenges that open environments present, agent-based information systems must be *multiagent* and *adaptive*. We are developing a multiagent, reusable system infrastructure, RETSINA[1], that enables development of adaptive information systems. In this paper, we describe the different types and levels of adaptation in RETSINA, such as adaptation within an individual agent as well as inter-agent organization and coordination. We have used RETSINA to develop a variety of Internet-based applications.

1 Introduction

The World Wide Web is a vast and mostly unorganized repository of information that changes over time. The Web is a heterogeneous collection of knowledge nodes and links whose topology and content is unstructured and changing. This open environment makes it very difficult for a person or machine system to collect, filter, and evaluate information that is needed to support problem solving tasks. The notion of Intelligent Software Agents (e.g., [6, 31, 16, 26, 17, 18, 12]), has been proposed to address this challenge. Although a precise definition of an intelligent agent is still forthcoming, the current working notion is that Intelligent Software Agents are programs that act on behalf of their human users in order to perform laborious tasks, such as locating and accessing information from various on-line information sources, resolving inconsistencies in the retrieved information, filtering away irrelevant or unwanted information, integrating information from heterogeneous information sources and adapting over time to their human users' information needs and the shape of the Infosphere. The most commonly agreed on characteristics of software agents are that they are *autonomous, collaborative*, and *adaptive*.

The current state of the art in agent development is that mostly (1) a single user interacts with a single agent, and (2) each agent must be developed from

---

[1] The URL for RETSINA is http://www.cs.cmu.edu/~softagents/.

scratch for each particular application. In contrast, our research goal is more ambitious and long term. We are developing a multi-agent system reusable infrastructure, called RETSINA (Reusable Environment of Task-Structured Intelligent Networked Agents) [24] where multiple agents compartmentalize specialized task knowledge and coordinate among themselves to gather and filter information in response to user-initiated problem solving. We have developed applications in different domains (e.g. financial portfolio management [25], organizational decision making [23]and crisis response) using the RETSINA framework.

In RETSINA, there are three types of agents: *interface agents* tied closely to an individual human's goals, *task agents* involved in the processes associated with arbitrary problem-solving tasks, and *information agents* that are closely tied to a source or sources of data. In this paper, we will focus specifically on the behavior and coordination of *information agents* and we will use the functioning of information agents in our implemented applications (e.g. the WARREN system) to illustrate our points.

To operate effectively in open environments agent systems must be *adaptive*. Adaptivity in the control literature means that a system has the capability to modify its own behavior to achieve the best possible mode of operation. A general definition of adaptive control implies that an adaptive system must be capable of performing the following functions: providing continuous information about the present state of the system or identifying the process; comparing present system performance to the desired or optimum performance and making a decision to change the system to achieve the defined optimum performance; and initiating a proper modification to drive the control system to the optimum. These three principles—*identification, decision,* and *modification*—are inherent in any adaptive system.

The RETSINA agents have been designed explicitly to be adaptive. Adaptation is behavior of an agent in response to unexpected (i.e., low probability) events or dynamic environments. Examples of unexpected events include the unscheduled failure of an agent, an agent's computational platform, or underlying information sources. Examples of dynamic environments include the occurrence of events that are expected but it is not known *when* (e.g., an information agent may reasonably expect to become at some point overloaded with information requests), events whose importance fluctuates widely (e.g., price information on a stock is much more important while a transaction is in progress, and even more so if certain types of news become available), the appearance of new information sources and agents, and finally underlying environmental uncertainty (e.g., not knowing beforehand precisely how long it will take to answer a particular query).

In RETSINA, adaptivity is exhibited at multiple levels, from the application level of interacting agents down to selecting different individual method executions based on changing conditions. Thus, in RETSINA, the following types and levels of adaptivity have been implemented:

- Adaptivity of an individual agent. An individual agent can exhibit adaptivity relative to a variety of internal reasoning processes:

- • agent communication
- • agent coordination
- • agent planning
- • agent scheduling
- • agent execution monitoring
- – Adaptivity regarding learning from interactions with a user or another agent.
- – Adaptivity at the organizational level of the multi-agent system.
- – Adaptivity with respect to multi-agent system performance.

Software adaptivity at all these levels results in: (a) agent systems that support runtime selection of agents for collaborative performance of a task, thus reconfiguring themselves to improve system performance and robustness, (b) agent systems that have a model of their own specifications and behavior and can alter their behavior based on changes in the environment, and (c) agent systems that introspect, diagnosing anomalies at runtime and repairing them.

In this paper, we present the various levels of adaptivity of the RETSINA agents. We will present an overview of the individual agent architecture, agent organization scheme and give specific examples of adaptation. The paper is organized as follows. In the next section we will discuss the individual architecture of a RETSINA agent. In section 3, we will discuss the organization of the agents in the RETSINA system. In section 5 we will present the internal adaptation schemes of some components internal to an agent. Adaptation between agents at the organizational level will be presented in section 6. In section 7, we will present adaptivity for performance requirements and constraints. In section 8, we present agent adaptation to changing user interests. Finally, conclusions and future work will be presented in section 9.

2 The RETSINA Agent Model

An agent is a *software unit of design* that can operate autonomously and interact with other similar units to build complex systems. This approach has the advantage of more objectively distinguishing agents from other types of software (e.g. Objects [3], Actors [1], OMG CORBA distributed objects [27]). An agent corresponds to an application component.

Typically, a single information agent will serve the information needs of many other agents (humans or intelligent software agents). An information agent is also quite different from a typical World Wide Web (WWW) service that provides data to multiple users. Besides the obvious interface differences, an information agent can reason about the way it will handle external requests and the order in which it will carry them out (WWW services are typically blindly concurrent). Moreover, information agents not only perform information gathering in response to queries but also can carry out long-term interactions that involve *monitoring* the Infosphere for particular conditions, as well as information updating. The RETSINA agents communicate through message passing using the KQML [13] communication language.

The dominant domain level behaviors of an information agent are: retrieving information from external information sources in response to one shot queries (e.g. "retrieve the current price of IBM stock"); requests for periodic information (e.g. "give me the price of IBM every 30 minutes"); monitoring external information sources for the occurrence of given information patterns, called change-monitoring requests, (e.g. "notify me when IBM's price increases by 10% over $80"). Information originates from external sources. Because an information agent does not have control over these external information sources, it must extract, possibly integrate, and store relevant pieces of information in a database local to the agent. The agent's information processing mechanisms then process the information in the local database to service information requests received from other agents or human users. Other simple behaviors that are used by all information agents include advertising their capabilities, managing and rebuilding the local database when necessary, and checking for KQML messages from other agents.

Currently the RETSINA framework provides an abstract basic agent architecture consisting of and integrating reusable modules, as depicted in Figure 2, and a concrete implementation of each module. Each agent is multithreaded Java code, and each module of an agent operates asynchronously. This enables the agent to be responsive to changing requirements and events. Each RETSINA agent consists of the following reusable modules:

- *communication and coordination* module that accepts and interprets messages from other agents, and sends replies.
- *planner* module that produces a plan that satisfies the agent's goals and tasks.
- *scheduler* module that schedules plan actions.
- *execution monitoring* module that initiates and monitors action execution.

The modules use well defined interfaces to interact with data structures that are used for keeping process information and for control purposes. In addition, each agent has the following knowledge components:

- *a library that contains both domain independent and domain dependent plan fragments (Task Schemas)* indexed by goals. These plan fragments are retrieved and incrementally instantiated according to the current input parameters.
- *Belief Database* that contains facts, constraints and other knowledge reflecting the agent's current model of the environment and the state of execution.
- *Schedule* that depicts the sequence of actions that have been scheduled for execution.

We have provided an implementation of each of these modules and the associated data structures. Since we characterize agents from the structural point of view we are not committed to particular implementations of the planner, scheduler or any other module. The interfaces between the modules and the control flow paths are well defined. Different modules for planning or scheduling, for example can be "plugged-in" as long as they provide specific interface functionality. For a more extensive description of the agent architecture, see [24].

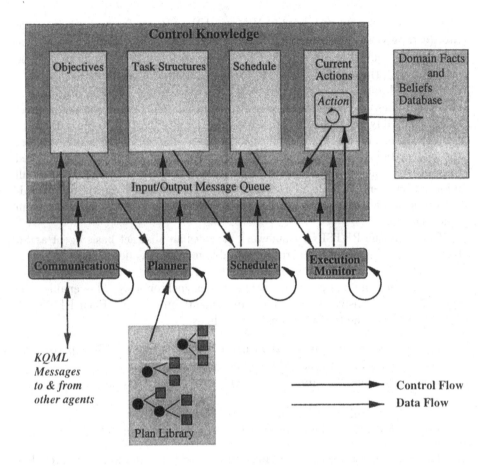

Fig. 1. The RETSINA Architecture

Below, we give a short description of each of the modules of a RETSINA agent.

Communication and Coordination: this module accepts and interprets messages from other agents. It encapsulates a parser, which is specific for the communication language used by the agent. Whenever the Communicator receives a message, the *Parser* creates a new *Objective*, which is inserted in the *ObjectiveDB* queue. In our current implementation the Communicator encapsulates a parser for KQML messages.

Planner: this module retrieves *Objectives* from the *ObjectiveDB* and produces plans that transform the *Objectives* to sets of executable *Actions*. Besides the objectives that are communicated to an agent by others, an agent also has internally generated objectives, e.g., to periodically check for incoming messages, or to sense the environment. In our current implementation, the planner's behavior is represented in an explicit representation formalism, a hierarchical task network (HTN). For more details on HTN planning in RETSINA, see [30].

Each agent has a library of domain dependent *Task Schemas* (elemental plan instances), which are used to identify the set of runtime *Actions* that have to be executed to satisfy the *Objectives* and constraints (see Fig. 2). The library also includes a set of domain-independent *Task Schemas* that can be typically found in several agents with similar functionalities. For example, two information agents will share the "run-query" task structure which runs a query on an Internet information source. Each agent has a library of *Task Reductions* (see Fig. 2), which represent alternative ways of carrying out a task by specifying a set of decompositions of high level tasks to sub-tasks and executable actions. *Actions* are the final result of a task reduction.

Task schemas and task reductions also have notations of whether the task can be performed by the agent or it requires the services (capabilities) of another agent. If another agent is required, then the agent with the subtask must attempt to find such an agent and interact with it. This will be further explained in section 3.

Scheduler: this module retrieves the agent's current set of all *enabled* actions from the *TaskDB*, and decides which action, if any, is to be scheduled for execution next. Constraints on the scheduler's processing include (a) periodic actions must be scheduled at least once during their period, (b) actions must be scheduled so as to complete execution before their deadlines, (c) actions that miss their period or deadline are considered to have failed. In our current implementation, we use a simple earliest-deadline-first scheduling heuristic. However, it would be easy to plug-in any other scheduling policy.

Execution Monitor: this module takes as input the agent's next scheduled action and prepares, initiates, and monitors its execution. In our system, the execution monitor module initiates action execution by directly invoking and monitoring a code object attached to the action. Action execution can have external effects on the state of the world, and internal effects on an agent's state of knowledge. If an action produces information, that information may need to be routed to other actions that utilize the information. Thus, the execution monitor is responsible for carrying out information flow within the plan. It also monitors the action with respect to resource usage and completion progress. For example, the action may have a completion deadline which, if not met, results in the action being interrupted, the action marked as failed, and this failure outcome recorded in the Beliefs Database from which the planner reads it and decides whether to replan.

Belief Database: it contains the agent's beliefs about the environment, such as facts, rules, and constraints. It also contains assertions, such as name, address and capability descriptions of the agent's collaborators, if the agent has decided to cache such information. In addition, it records results of action execution. The Beliefs Database is dynamically updated at run-time based on the occurrence of environmental events and interactions with other agents.

We are developing the RETSINA infrastructure so it can include agents designed by different designers that do not necessarily use the RETSINA agent architecture. Such "legacy" components can be accommodated as follows: Since actions are associated with procedural code, a legacy component can be wrapped by the agent architectural modules and can be treated as procedural code that is invoked by the execution monitor.

3 RETSINA Agent Organization and Interactions

The RETSINA organization of agents has the following main features:

- The agents can be distributed across different machines.
- Agents *advertise* their functionality to others via *middle agents*. This allows for flexible agent interactions.
- Interoperability between heterogeneous agents is achieved at *agent level*, not at system infrastructure level. Agents can cooperate because they share the same communication language and a common vocabulary, which contains words appropriate to common application areas and whose meaning is described by shared ontologies.

RETSINA agents are designed to function in a completely distributed manner. RETSINA agents are not tied to hosts. Since much of their state and functionality is based on declarative specifications and these specifications are compact, transporting them across networks is not resource intensive. Due to their well defined interfaces and the state information saved by the agents, starting them again on another host is easily possible. In the RETSINA view, an application can be built using component agents from a *virtual networked repository* (e.g. the Internet).

In an open multi-agent system, agents are free to appear and disappear. Each agent specializes in some task, for example getting stock price information from a Web page, collecting news associated with a particular stock, or getting information about a company's annual earnings from the Edgar database. These are some of the functions that different information agents specialize in the Warren portfolio management application. The information agents collaborate to integrate this information to help the user make stock buy or sell decisions.

Any agent that enters the system and intends to let other agents use its services, must clearly declare this intention by making a commitment to taking on a well-defined class of future requests. This declaration is called an *advertisement* and contains both a specification of the agent's *capability* with respect to the type of request it can accept (as defined in its interface), and both general and service-specific constraints on those future requests. An advertisement can include not only a description of agent capability, but also meta level information such as how much this service costs (these costs can indicate resource scarcity, not necessarily monetary costs), how responsive the service agent usually is, etc. Knowing these parameters allows a requesting agent to:

- know which agent can provide a needed service.

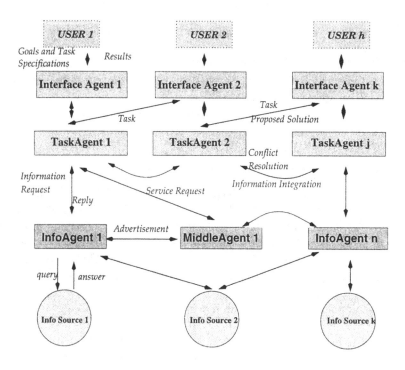

Fig. 2. The RETSINA Organization

- rationally select a particular provider to service a request [9]. For example, under situation X, a less precise but more timely reply might be the most desirable, whereas in situation Y, precision cannot be sacrificed at any cost (monetary or time cost).

In our current implementation agents are truthful and cooperative, thus their advertisement corresponds to an agent's best knowledge of its current capabilities.

Since it is obviously infeasible for an agent to advertise its capabilities to all the agents in the system (in an open system, an agent does not know which other agents are present in the virtual repository), specific agents in the organization play the role of *Middle Agents*[8]. Middle-Agents are agents that know the name of many other agents and their corresponding capabilities. Middle-Agents have a well-known name, i.e., all agents have a predefined, static procedure for contacting them. We have identified and implemented different types of middle agents [8]. These include *matchmakers* or *yellow page* agents that match advertisements to requests for advertised capabilities, *blackboard* agents that collect requests, and *brokers* that process both. In preliminary experiments [8] we have seen that the behaviors of each type of middle-agent have certain performance characteristics— for example, while brokered systems are more vulnerable to certain failures, they are also able to cope more quickly with a rapidly fluctuating agent workforce.

The RETSINA framework allows both agent names and capabilities to be communicated at run-time. This mechanism allows the run-time selection of agents based on specification of capability.

4 Levels of Adaptivity

The RETSINA architecture allows for adaptability at multiple levels making the system robust in the face of many types of disruption. The architecture models many different aspects of the world which are handled in a modular fashion.

If applications are organized as collections of cooperating agents that share information on capabilities, then these applications can *organize to adapt* according to the requirements of application functionality. This means an *emergent organization* uses specifications of the tasks that need to be performed to select agents that interact with each other. Adaptation at the organizational level allows applications great flexibility in selecting agents to achieve specified goals.

However to fit into this organization, agents must be able to share information about themselves, their inputs and outputs. In addition, performance measures of each agent need to be explicit and transparent to the entire application. Each agent also needs to dynamically monitor itself and inform other parts of the system of changes. This implies that each component of an adaptive system also needs to be adaptive requiring *agent adaptivity*.

RETSINA supports adaptivity both at the component level and the organizational level.

5 Individual Agent Adaptivity

An individual agent can exhibit various types of adaptive behavior pertaining to the different types of reasoning it is capable of. In this section, we provide a brief description of adaptation of the different RETSINA agent reasoning modules. For more details, see [10].

Planning Adaptation The planning module of a RETSINA agent uses a planning approach based on hierarchical task networks (HTN) and a plan formalism that admits sophisticated control structures such as looping and periodic tasks [30]. Final action selection, sequencing, and timing are left up to the agent's local scheduler. A task typically has alternative task reductions, that is alternative execution paths that can satisfy it. In addition, TaskReduction schemas specify preconditions and postconditions for task reductions, and different types of constraints (state, temporal and resource constraints). These prescribe task interdependencies and dictate static control flow. In addition to these static relations, there are also runtime relations. Runtime information flow is expressed by *provisions* whose variables are bound during runtime reflecting information coming in from the environment (e.g. sensors) or supplied by other agents. Actions have different types of *outcomes* to indicate different results of action execution (e.g., completion, different types of failures). Such outcomes of one subtask reduction can be propagated at runtime to match provisions of another subtask. If the value(s) of the outcome(s) matches the value(s) of the provision, then the subtask is *enabled* and can be scheduled for execution.

This mechanism supports the representation and efficient execution of plans *with periodic actions, externally triggered actions and loops* [30]. Task schemas and alternative task reductions are blueprints for representing agent requirements, specification information and processing structure. This representation enables an agent to understand its requirements and reason about how its behavior can satisfy the requirements.

Some types of adaptivity expressed by an agent at this level include:

- **Adapting to failures:** At any time, any agent in the system might be unavailable or might go off-line. Our planner's task reductions handle these situations so that such failures are dealt with smoothly. If alternate agents are available, they will be contacted and the subproblem restarted. If no alternate agent is available, the planner will replan.
- **Multiple reductions:** Each task can potentially be reduced in several different ways, depending on the current situation. Thus even simple tasks such as answering a query may result in very different sequences of actions (asking a middle agent, using an already known agent, using a cached previous answer).
- **Interleaved planning, information gathering, and execution:** The reduction of some tasks can be delayed until other, "information gathering" tasks, are completed.

Previous work has focussed on coordination mechanisms alone. In particular, the Generalized Partial Global Planning family of coordination mechanisms is a domain-independent approach to multi-agent scheduling- and planning-level coordination that works in conjunction with an agent's existing local scheduler to adapt a plan by adding certain constraints [11]. These include commitments to do a task with a minimum level of quality, or commitments to do a task by a certain deadline. If the resulting plan can be successfully scheduled, these local commitments can be communicated to other agents where they become non-local commitments to those agent's local schedulers [21].

Scheduling Adaptation Once a plan is formulated, the plan steps (actions) must be scheduled and executed. Scheduling of actions is based on runtime information. Reasoning about optimal utilization of resources can also alter the schedule of actions, for instance if a group of actions can be executed at once with performance gains, then some actions can be delayed and some advanced in the schedule. Having an explicit schedule also presents a natural opportunity to pinpoint the loads on the agent system during various conditions of execution, allowing for adaptation to those conditions. For example, a record of missed deadlines is kept. It can be utilized to reason about potential solutions to agent overload (e.g., agent cloning, see section 7).

Execution Adaptation A RETSINA agent has two general types of flexibility at the action execution level: (a) monitoring of action execution that may lead to replanning and alternative action selection, and (b) monitoring of conformance to temporal and resource constraints so that constraint violations can be fixed.

The execution monitor monitors the action by optionally providing the associated computation limited resources—for example, the action may be allowed only a certain amount of time and if the action does not complete before that time is up, the computation is interrupted and the action is marked as having failed.

When an action is marked as failed, the exception handling process takes over to replan from the current execution point to help the agent recover from the failure. The process informs the other agent modules of the failure and adapts by either explicitly following failure links or by informing the planner. The information about the failure is propagated to the agent's planner to enable repair of the plan at the component level. For example, if a needed agent is unavailable, the requestor can try contacting a middle agent that could indicate someone else with the same capability.

6 Organizational Adaptation

Using middle agents [8] allows service requesters to find and select service providers at run time. This runtime adaptation to availability, capability and performance of agents (which are in essence components of an application system) is designed into RETSINA. In this way, RETSINA organizational flexibility provides basic abilities for runtime management, selection and scheduling of agents that are required at different points during execution. In addition, agents with same or similar capabilities can be part of the agent society. If, at run time, an agent providing some capability is unavailable, another agent with the same capability can be found (if one exists) and dynamically inserted into the system. Thus, middle agents allow a system to operate robustly in the face of agent appearance and disappearance, and intermittent communications, characteristics that are present in most real world environments.

Middle agents are significant in another respect: they lay the foundation for *evolutionary system design*. Since specification based services do not require explicit addressing of procedures, new and improved methods for performing the same task can be introduced into the agent system without having an effect on the other parts of the agent system. This allows for components with enhanced capabilities, i.e. component upgrades, to be added dynamically at runtime. This can be done by "unadvertising" the old agent and advertising the upgraded agent under the same name. Thus, if agents have cached the name of the agent, they need not resort to middle agents when they need to interact with it in the future.

Using the capability-based adaptive coordination provided by the middle agents, RETSINA can support the runtime formation of different types of multiagent organizations:

- **Uncoordinated Team:** agents use a basic shared behavior for asking questions that first queries the matchmaker as to who might answer the query, and then chooses an agent randomly for the target query. Such organizations provide very low overhead, but potentially unbalanced loads. System reliability is limited by individual data sources, and there might exist problems linking queries across multiple ontologies.
- **Economic Markets:** (e.g., [28]) agents use price, reliability, and other utility characteristics with which to choose another agent. The matchmaker can supply to each agent the appropriate updated pricing information as new agents enter and exit the system, or alter their advertisements. Agents can dynamically adjust their organization as often as necessary, limited by transaction costs. Potentially such organizations provide efficient load balancing and the ability to provide truly expensive services (expensive in terms of the resources required).
- **Federations:** (e.g., [29, 15, 13]) agents give up individual autonomy over choosing who they will do business with to a locally centralized "facilitator" (an extension of the matchmaker concept) that "brokers" requests. Centralization of message traffic potentially allows greater load balancing and the provision of automatic translation and mediation services.
- **Bureaucratic Functional Units:** Traditional manager/employee groups of a single multi-source information agent (manager) and several simple information agent (employees). By organizing into functional units, i.e., related information sources, such organizations concentrate on providing higher reliability (by using multiple underlying sources), simple information integration (from partially overlapping information), and load balancing.

7 Adaptivity to Performance: Agent Cloning

Assume a multiagent system (MAS) that receives a stream of tasks. Besides the *capabilities* which indicate the types of tasks the agents can perform, they also have associated *capacities* which indicate the amounts of resources that the agents can access and use for task execution. Tasks are categorized by types that can be handled by agents with appropriate capabilities. Some times, the tasks that must be processed by an agent overload it. Such overloads are of two different general categories:

1. An agent in a MAS is overloaded, but the MAS as a whole has the required capabilities and capacities.
2. The MAS as a whole is overloaded, i.e., the agents that comprise the MAS do not have the necessary capacities (however there may be idle resources in the computational system where the agents are situated).

As a result of such overloads, the MAS will not perform all of the tasks in time, although the required resources may be available to it. The following solutions suggest themselves:

1. overloaded agents should pass tasks to others agents which have the capabilities and capacities to perform them.
2. overloaded agents create new agents to perform excess tasks and utilize unused resources or migrate to other hosts.

Cloning is a possible response of an agent to overloads. Agent overloads are due, in general, either to the agent's limited capacity to process current tasks or to machine overloads. Other approaches to overloads include task transfer and agent migration. Task transfer, where overloaded agents locate other agents which are lightly loaded and transfer tasks to them, is similar to processor load balancing. Agent migration, which requires that overloaded agents, or agents that run on overloaded machines, migrate to less loaded ones, is similar to process migration and mobile agents [5]. Agent migration can be implemented by creating its clone on a remote machine, transferring its tasks to it and dying. Thus, agent mobility is an instance of agent cloning.

To perform cloning, an agent must reason about its own load (current and future), its host load as well as capabilities and loads of other machines and agents. Accordingly, it may decide to: create a clone; pass tasks to a clone; merge with other agents; or die. Merging of two agents, or self-extinction of underutilized agents is an important mechanism to control agent proliferation.

Since the agent's own load and the loads of other agents vary over time in a non-deterministic way, the decision of *whether and when* to clone is non-trivial. Prior work [7] has presented a model of cloning based on prediction of missed task deadlines and idle times on the agent's schedule in the RETSINA multi-agent infrastructure [24]. We have also implements a stochastic model of decision making based on dynamic programming to determine the optimal timing for cloning [22].

The necessary information used by an agent to decide whether and when to initiate cloning comprises parameters that describe both local and remote resources. To acquire the above information an agent must be able to read the operating system variables. In addition, the agent must have self awareness on two levels—an agent internal level and a MAS level. The internal self awareness should allow the agent to realize what part of the operating system retrieved values are its own properties (that is, agent internal parameters). The system-wise self awareness should allow the agent to find, possibly via middle agents [8], information regarding available resources on remote machines.

To examine the properties of the cloning mechanism and its advantages, a simulation was performed. To simulate the RETSINA agents, we have measured their resource consumption. We simulated the agent system with and without cloning, with the following settings: 10 to 20 agents; 10 clones allowed; up to 1000 tasks dynamically arriving at the system; normal distribution of tasks with respect to the required capabilities and resources for execution (10% of the tasks beyond the ability of the agents to perform them within their particular deadlines); an agent can perform 20 average tasks simultaneously.

The simulation results show that cloning increases (on average) the performance of the multi-agent system. In more detail, the additional performance as a result of cloning (if any) outweighs the efforts put into cloning. The simulation results show that for small numbers of tasks (0 to 100) a system which practices cloning performs (almost) as well as a system with no cloning. However, when the number of tasks increases, the cloning system performs much better. Nonetheless, beyond some threshold, (around 350 tasks) even the cloning cannot help. For more details on the cloning method, see [22].

8   Adaptivity to User Information Needs

Through interactions with a user, an agent can learn user interests, user intent, and user plans. Currently, RETSINA agents can learn user interests for judging whether a WWW document is of interest to the user. A RETSINA agent that filters documents based on learned user profile is WebMate [4]. There are several machine learning approaches that can be used to learn a user profile, such as Bayesian classifier, Nearest Neighbor, PEBLS, Decision Trees, TF-IDF, Neural Nets [20, 19]. In order for a particular technique to be effective, it should match the characteristics of the task and the user.

The filtering task for WebMate involves judging whether an article is relevant or irrelevant to the user based on the user profile, in an environment where the prior probability of encountering a relevant document is very low compared to the probability of encountering an irrelevant document. In such an environment, it would be very frustrating and time consuming for a user to interact with an agent that starts with no knowledge but must obtain a set of positive and negative examples from user feedback. When a user browses, he does not want to evaluate all web pages that might contain potentially interesting information. To reduce the user evaluation burden, WebMate collects only examples that are interesting to the user (only positive training examples). This kind of interaction presents potential problems since the documents that a user might label as "I like It" might fall into many distinct domains (e.g fishing, computer science, soccer). Those subclasses correspond to the different interests a user has. There have been two methods to address the problem of multiple user interests. The first is to keep a single user profile where the keywords might come from different domains but are "averaged'. This method has the disadvantage that averaging the vectors from the different documents might decrease too much the weights of words that are important for only a few of the interest categories. The second method is to ask the user to explicitly provide labels for the sub-categories of interest. WebMate does not ask the user to label the category that the interesting document is in, but learns the categories automatically.

In contrast to other systems that learn a user profile and use it statically to determine relevant documents, WebMate learns the user profile incrementally and continuously. When a new positive example is known, the system updates the profile. In order to save on storage space, the system doesn't keep any of the previous positive example documents. It only keeps the profile learned from those positive examples. In this way, the system will adapt to the user's evolving and recent interests.

WebMate utilizes TF-IDF method with multiple vectors representation. The basic idea of the algorithm is to represent each document as a vector in a vector space so that documents with similar content have similar vectors. Each dimension of the vector space represents a word and its weight. The values of the vector elements for a document are calculated as a combination of the statistics term frequency $TF(w, d)$ (the number of times word w occurs in document d) and document frequency $DF(w)$ (the number of documents the word w occurs in at least once). From the document frequency the inverse document frequency $IDF(w)$ can be calculated.

$$IDF(w) = \log \frac{|D|}{DF(w)}$$

$|D|$ is the total number of documents. The value $d^{(i)}$ of an element in the vector is then calculated as the product

$$d^{(i)} = TF(w_i, d) \times IDF(w_i)$$

WebMate learns and tracks multiple user interests using an algorithm we have developed for *multi TF-IDF* vector learning [4]. The algorithm is run whenever a user marks a document as "I like it". Thus, the user profile is incrementally, unobtrusively and continuously updated.

We utilize the approach of learning user profile to compile a personal newspaper [2, 14]. We do this in two ways.

One way is to automatically spide a list of URLs that the user wants monitored. An example of such a URL is one that consists of many news headlines like the home page of the NewsLinx Company[2]. WebMate (1) parses the html page, (2) extracts the links of each headline, (3) fetches those pages, (4) constructs the TF-IDF vector for each of those pages (using as additional heuristics that words in title and headings are given additional weights), and (5) calculates the similarity with the current profile. If the similarity is greater than some threshold, it recommends the page to the user, and sorts all the recommended pages in decreasing order of similarity to form the personal newspaper. All operations are often performed in the middle of the night when the network traffic is low. In the morning, the user can read the recommended personal newspaper.

If the user does not provide any URLs that he would like to be the information sources, WebMate constructs a query[20] using the top several words in the current user profile and sends it to popular search engines (e.g. Altavista, Yahoo). If the result is needed immediately, the results returned by the search engines are directly used as the recommended web pages. Otherwise, the system fetches the pages corresponding to each and every URL in the results. It then

---

[2] http://www.newslinx.com/

calculates the similarity of the profile and these web pages and recommends the pages whose similarity is greater than some threshold presenting the results in descending order of relevance. For more details on WebMate, see [4] and URL: http://www.cs.cmu.edu/~softagents/Webmate/.

9 Current & Future Work

This paper has discussed adaptivity in the RETSINA system of multiple intelligent agents that collaborate to find and filter information from the Web. We have discussed adaptivity at different levels: organizational, planning, scheduling, execution, learning user interests and adaptivity to performance concerns. Work under way includes agent adaptivity with respect to user intent and plans not only for single user but also for a collaborating team of users. An area of active research is learning through agent interactions as well as adaptivity in agent coordination. We have already done work in learning from agent interactions in the domain of negotiation where the agents update models of each other through Bayesian belief update [32]. An area of future work is adaptive function allocation and task delegation in collaborative situations between user(s) and agent(s) where the agent(s) adaptively expand their role and acquire increasing autonomy.

Acknowledgements

This research has been sponsored in part by NSF grant IRI-9612131 and ONR grant N-00014-96-1-1222. We would like to thank the members of the Intelligent Software Agents research group at Carnegie Mellon University for implementation of the RETSINA multiagent infrastructure.

References

1. G. Agha, I. Mason, S Smith, and C. Talcott. Towards a theory of actor computation. In *Proc. Third Int. Conf. on Concurrency Theory (CONCURR 92)*, LNCS 630, pages 565–579. Springer-Verlag, 1992.
2. Marbo Balabonovic and Yoav Shoham. Combining content-based and collaborative recommendation. *Communications of the ACM*, March 1997.
3. G. Booch. *Object Oriented Design With Applications*. The Benjamin-Cummings Publishing Company, 1991.
4. Liren Chen and K. Sycara. Webmate : A personal agent for browsing and searching. In *Proceedings of the Second International Conference on Autonomous Agents (Agents 98)*, 1998.
5. D. Chess, B. Grosof, and C. Harrison. Itinerant agents for mobile computing. Technical Report RC 20010, IBM Research Division, 1995.
6. P. R. Cohen and H. J. Levesque. Intention=choice + commitment. In *Proceedings of AAAI-87*, pages 410–415, Seattle, WA., 1987. AAAI.

7. K. Decker, Pannu A., K. Sycara, and Williamson M. Designing behaviors for information agents. In *Proceedings of the First International Conference on Autonomous Agents (Agents-97)*, Los Angeles, February 1997.

8. K. Decker, K. Sycara, and M. Williamson. Middle-agents for the internet. In *Proceedings of IJCAI-97*, 1997.

9. K. Decker, M. Williamson, and K. Sycara. Modeling information agents: Advertisements, organizational roles, and dynamic behavior. In *Proceedings of the AAAI-96 Workshop on Agent Modeling*, 1996.

10. Keith Decker and Katia Sycara. Intelligent adaptive information agents. *Journal of Intelligent Information Systems*, 9:239–260, 1997.

11. Keith S. Decker and Victor R. Lesser. Designing a family of coordination algorithms. In *Proceedings of the First International Conference on Multi-Agent Systems*, pages 73–80, San Francisco, June 1995. AAAI Press. Longer version available as UMass CS-TR 94-14.

12. O. Etzioni and D. Weld. A softbot-based interface to the internet. *Comm. of the ACM*, 37(7), July 1994.

13. T. Finin, R. Fritzson, D. McKay, and R. McEntire. Kqml as an agent communication language. In *Proceedings of the Third Int. Conference on Information and Knowledge Management (CIKM94)*, 1994.

14. Peter W. Foltz and Susan T. Dumais. Personalized information delivery: An analysis of information filtering methods. *Communications of the ACM*, 35(12):51–60, 1992.

15. Michael R. Genesereth and Steven P. Ketchpel. Software agents. *Communications of the ACM*, 37(7), July 1994.

16. Kan Lang. Newsweeder: Learning to filter netnews. In *Proceedings of Machine Learning Conference*, 1995.

17. Pattie Maes. Agents that reduce work and information overload. *Communications of the ACM*, 37(7), July 1994.

18. Tom Mitchell, Rich Caruana, Dayne Freitag, John McDermott, and David Zabowski. Experience with a learning personal assistant. *Communications of the ACM*, 37(7), July 1994.

19. Anandeep Pannu and Katia Sycara. Learning text filtering preferences. In *1996 AAAI Symposium on Machine Learning and Information Access*, 1996.

20. M. Pazzani, J. Muramatsu, and D. Billsus. Syskill & webert: Identifying interesting web sites. In *Proceedings of AAAI-96*, Portland, 1996. AAAI.

21. M.V. Nagendra Prasad and V.R. Lesser. Learning situation-specific coordination in generalized partial global planning. In *AAAI Spring Symposium on Adaptation, Co-evolution and Learning in Multiagent Systems*, Stanford, March 1996.

22. O. Shehory, K. Sycara, P. Chalasani, and S. Jha. Agent cloning. In *ICMAS-98*, Paris, France, July, 1998.

23. K. Sycara and D. Zeng. Coordination of multiple intelligent software agents. *International Journal of Intelligent and Cooperative Information Systems*, 5(2 & 3):181–211, 1996.

24. Katia Sycara, Keith Decker, Anandeep Pannu, Mike Williamson, and Dajun Zeng. Distributed intelligent agents. *IEEE Expert*, 11(6), December 1996.

25. Katia Sycara, Keith Decker, and Dajun Zeng. Intelligent agents in portfolio management. In N. Jennings and M. Woolridge, editors, *Agent Technology: Foundations, Applications, and Markets*, chapter 14, pages 267–283. Springer, 1998.

26. Katia Sycara and Dajun Zeng. Visitor-hoster: Towards an intelligent electronic secretary. In *Proceedings of the CIKM-94 (International Conference on Informa-*

tion and Knowledge Management) Workshop on Intelligent Information Agents, National Institute of Standards and Technology, Gaithersburg, Maryland, December 1994.

27. Steve Vinoski. Corba: Integrating diverse applications within distributed heterogeneous environments. *IEEE Communications Society magazine*, 35(2):46, 1997.

28. Michael Wellman. A market-oriented programming environment and its application to distributed multicommodity flow problems. *Journal of Artificial Intelligence Research*, 1:1–23, 1993.

29. G. Wiederhold, P. Wegner, and S. Cefi. Toward megaprogramming. *Communications of the ACM*, 33(11):89–99, 1992.

30. M. Williamson, K. Decker, and K. Sycara. Unified information and control flow in hierarchical task networks. In *Proceedings of the AAAI-96 workshop on Theories of Planning, Action, and Control*, 1996.

31. M. Wooldridge and N. R. Jennings. Intelligent agents: Theory and practice. *The Knowledge Engineering Review*, 10(2):115–152, 1995.

32. Dajun Zeng and Katia Sycara. Benefits of learning in negotiation. In *Proceedings of AAAI-97*, Providence, Rhode Island, U.S.A., July 27-31 1997.

Adaptive Choice of Information Sources
(Extended Abstract)

Sandip Sen[1]

Department of Mathematical & Computer Sciences, University of Tulsa,
600 South College Avenue,
Tulsa, OK 74104-3189.
URL: http://euler.mcs.utulsa.edu/ sandip/

Abstract. We present a number of learning approaches by which agents can adapt to select information sources that satisfy performance requirements. Performance can be interpreted both in terms of the quality of information provided by the sources, as well as the response time to process information requests. We first present a couple of approaches by which self-motivated agents can learn to choose lightly-loaded resources. The resultant load balancing effect results in increasing throughput for the entire system as well as faster response times for individual agents. We also present an expected utility maximization approach to selecting information sources that are likely to deliver better quality information to different classes of queries.

1 Restricting resource status information to aid group stability

We have studied one particular aspect of distributed decision-making in some detail: the effect of limited local knowledge on group behavior. Whereas intuition suggests that agents are equipped to make better local decisions with more complete and correct information, self-interested choices can at times lead to group instabilities with complete global information. We believe that reducing the amount of information available to such rational decision makers can be an effective mechanism for achieving system stability. The research question that we are asking is the following: Can limited local knowledge be a boon rather than a bane in an information system consisting of multiple agents?

To investigate this issue, we use a resource utilization problem where a number of agents are distributed between several identical resources. We assume that the cost of using any resource is directly proportional to its usage. This cost can be due to a delay in processing of the task in hand, or a reduction in the quality of the resource due to congestion. Hence, there is a justified need for agents to seek out and move to resources with lesser usage. Other researchers have shown that such systems can exhibit oscillatory or chaotic behavior where agents continually move between resources resulting in lack of system stability and ineffective utilization of system resources. The case has also been made that the introduction of asynchronous decision making or heterogeneous decision-making schemes can improve system convergence. We see our current work as providing a natural, complimentary mechanism for enabling agents in similar situations to quickly converge to the optimal system state.

We assume that there are m agents and n identical resources (in general, $m > n$). Moreover, resources are neither introduced nor eliminated during the life time of the agents. All agents remain active and they make their decisions synchronously. At any time instant, an agent use only one resource, and over time tries to move to a resource that is less used by other agents. In this study, we show that when an agent has less knowledge about the utilization of each resource in the resource set, the contention for resources decreases and results in quicker convergence to stable resource usage.

At present we model the knowledge of an agent about the resources by using an *r-window*. An r-window is a window through which an agent can observe the load on some of its neighboring resources. At each time step, each agent has to make the following decision: whether it should continue to use the present resource or should it move to another resource in its r-window with less utilization.

It can be shown that a deterministic and greedy decision procedure of choosing the resource with the lowest utilization in the r-window will lead to system oscillations. Hence, we are motivated to use a probabilistic decision procedure. The probability that an agent will shift from the current resource to another resource is inversely proportional to the difference of the usage of these two resource. The particular procedure that we use first calculates the probability of moving to each of the resources in the r-window, and then normalizes theses values by the corresponding sum. The probability of an agent that decides to continue to use the same resource i is given by:

$$f_{ii} = \frac{1}{1 + \tau \exp^{\frac{r_i - \alpha}{\beta}}}, \tag{1}$$

where r_i is the number of agents currently using resource i (this is also the utilization of or load on that resource), and τ, α, and β are control parameters. On the other hand, the probability of moving to another resource $j \neq i$ is given by:

$$f_{ij} = \begin{cases} 1 - \frac{1}{1 + \tau \exp^{\frac{r_i - r_j - \alpha}{\beta}}} & \text{if } j \in W_i \ \& \ r_i > r_j, \\ 0 & \text{otherwise,} \end{cases} \tag{2}$$

where W_i are the resources within the r-window of an agent using resource i. Now, the probability that an agent a_k occupying a resource i will occupy a resource j in the next time step is given by normalizing the above terms:

$$Pr(i, j) = \frac{f_{ij}}{\sum_j f_{ij}}. \tag{3}$$

Using a series of experiments we have reached the following conclusions:

- If agents are allowed access to the status of smaller number of resources, the loads on different resources are balanced in less time.
- Convergence rate to stable configurations can be significantly enhanced if local groups make their decisions sequentially.

2 Application of agent modeling to system load balancing

Agents in a multiagent system (MAS) can benefit by modeling other agents in their environment. In particular, being able to predict decisions to be taken by other agents enables an agent to improve its own utility. We have developed a learning mechanism by which an agent can approximately model the decision function used by another agent given a collection of decisions made by that agent. We consider the case of binary decisions based on a single decision variable. A polynomial time, incremental algorithm to adjust the coefficients of a family of orthogonal functions, Chebychev polynomials, is presented which can be used to develop a model of other agent's decision function. We have proved that, in the limit, this algorithm is guaranteed to produce an accurate model.

We applied this modeling approach to the problem of balancing the loads on processors in a distributed system. In this domain, each of a set of A agents receive JR jobs to process per unit time. There are P processors, each of which can process jobs at the rate of SR jobs per unit time. Each processor also has an unbounded input queue on which jobs can be placed. When an agent receives a job to process, it visits the processors in some random order. For each processor, it looks at the input queue length of waiting jobs, and then samples a probability function, P, with this queue length to decide whether or not to place the job on this queue. This process is repeated until the job is assigned. This decision time to select a resource is assumed to be negligible. We assume that each agent observes the load on the resource in which another agent places a job as well as the number of previous visits in which it did not place the job. The resources visited or the loads on those resources is not available to other agents. A modeling agent will use the information available about the decisions taken by other agents to find resources which are less likely to be selected by other agents. If only some of the agents in the system are modelers, this approach can produce more equitable distribution of jobs to resources. In our experiments we have used 50 agents, 5 resources, JR=1, and SR=10. The performance metric we want to minimize is the standard deviation of the queue-lengths.

The non-modeling agents are assumed to be using either a greedy strategy of choosing the minimum loaded resource after visiting all resources (these are called G-agents), or choosing the resource based on a probability function of the queue-length (these are called P-agents). The probability function used by P-agents to decide on submission of a job to a resource with current queue length Ql is selected to be

$$P(Ql) = -0.02 * Ql + 0.2.$$

The modeling agents (M-agents) choose the probability for submission from the probability of submission of other agents in that resource. The probability that a modeling agent i is going to submit its job to resource j is given by:

$$P_{ij} = min(1, 10 - \sum_{a \in A - \{i\}} P_{aj}).$$

Given that with equal load distribution, 10 jobs would be submitted per time period per resource, this function means that modeling agents are likely to choose resources that are expected to have lower than average submission of new jobs.

Experiments confirm that whereas a homogeneous group of modeling agents do not perform much better than a homogeneous group of greedy agents, throughput of systems are significantly enhanced when heterogeneous groups containing modeling and G-agents or modeling and P-agents are used.

3   Learning to select information sources

Agents that learn about other agents and can exploit this information possess a distinct advantage in competitive situations. Games provide stylized adversarial environments to study agent learning strategies. We have developed a scheme for learning opponent action probabilities and a utility maximization framework that exploits this learned opponent model. We have shown that the proposed expected utility maximization strategy generalizes the traditional maximin strategy, and allows players to benefit by taking calculated risks that are avoided by the maximin strategy. To show the general applicability of the expected utility maximization framework, we have also developed an agent that learns to select one of several search engines to query depending on the nature of the query posed by the user. Assuming different search engines are good for different kinds of queries, our agent will use its experience to probabilistically model the expected utility to be obtained from these search engines given the category of a query.

Decision theoretic principles can be used by agents to make rational action choices in the face of environmental uncertainty. An agent is rational if and only if it chooses an action that yields the highest expected utility, averaged over all the possible outcomes. This is called the principle of Maximum Expected Utility. If the outcome of an action a at a state E is uncertain and can result in one of several possible outcomes $Result_i(a)$, and the function $U(S)$ measures the utility of state S to the agent, then the expected utility of taking action a in state E can be expressed as

$$EU(a|E) = \sum_i Pr(Result_i(a)|E, Do(a)) \times U(Result_i(a)),$$

where $Pr(.)$ represents probabilities, $Do(a)$ represents the proposition that action a is executed in the current state, and i ranges over different outcomes. Let A be the set of actions available to the agent. The MEU principle prescribes that the agent would choose the action that maximizes expected utility:
$MEU(A, E) = argmax_{a \in A} EU(a|E)$.

We have shown that MEU agents can outperform minimax players in board game situations. To demonstrate the applicability of the MEU principle in non-game situations, we investigated the decision problem of an agent choosing one of several search engines for performing category based search on the internet so as to maximize the quality of information retrieved. The agent has the option of choosing from a finite set of search engines for its search queries on a finite set of categories. The performance of the search engines are modeled probabilistically. We have approximated the utilities of the search engines discretely by assuming the utility to be the number of quality matches returned with a corresponding probability. Our search agent learns these probabilities from experience and calculates the expected utilities for each of the search engines for different categories.

When queried for a particular category of search, the agent chooses the search engine with the maximum expected utility (MEU). We have experimented with a single search category and three simulated search engines. Each search engine is defined by a probability distribution over one of several utility values. The search engine selection agent learns an approximation of these probabilities by repeatedly querying the search engines. Once the probabilities are learned, the expected utilities of each of the search engines are calculated and the MEU strategy chooses the search engine with the maximum expected utility.

To evaluate the performance of the MEU strategy we compare it against the following heuristic strategy. For N queries, each of the three search engine is queried. The search engine that returns the highest utility result in the most number of such cases is then selected for subsequent usage (this strategy is similar to what naive users use to select a search engine based on their initial experience with search engines).

Our experiments show that the MEU strategy outperforms the simple heuristic when the probability distribution for the search engines are skewed such that one search engine returns very high utilities with small probabilities. When all utilities are returned equiprobably, the MEU and simple heuristic returns identical choices. These results are quite preliminary, and we plan to further investigate the applicability of MEU strategies on multiple categories, more search engines, and on more complex queries with disjunctions and conjunctions. Special operators have to be defined for combining results for queries that span multiple categories.

Acknowledgments These research projects have been supported, in part, by the National Science Foundation under a Research Initiation Award IRI-9410180 and a CAREER award IRI-9702672.

Agent Mediated Collaborative Web Page Filtering*

Shaw Green[1], Pádraig Cunningham[1], Fergal Somers[2]

[1]Department of Computer Science, Trinity College Dublin, Ireland.
[2]Broadcom Éireann Research Ltd., Dublin, Ireland
Shaw.Green@cs.tcd.ie, Padraig.Cunningham@tcd.ie, fs@broadcom.ie

Abstract. Intelligent filtering of multimedia documents such as World Wide Web (WWW) pages is an extremely difficult task to automate. However, the determination of a page's relevance to one's interests is a skill that comes with ease to most humans. This paper outlines a system architecture, developed using Agent Oriented Design (AOD), aimed at providing page filtering within a limited domain. This domain is specified via an explicit taxonomy. A prototype system was built using this architecture, which draws upon a user's innate ability to determine the relevance of web pages to their own information needs. It is argued that the resulting system incorporates the best aspects of existing Automated Collaborative Filtering (ACF) systems, whilst still retaining the benefits of the more traditional, feature based approach. In support of this claim and the general success of these systems, initial evaluation of the system is also reported.

1. Introduction

Many systems in recent times have attempted to tackle the difficult problem of selecting pages for presentation from the diverse and ever changing pool of material published on the World Wide Web (WWW). An important requirement of which is to only retrieve material that is of direct relevance to a user's interests and current information requirements.

It can be argued that these systems can be grouped into two major classes. First, there is the traditional feature based approach where the individual web pages are represented in some fashion by appropriate semantic structures or features. These features are then matched against other features that represent the user's interests and current goals. Examples of this type of system include the major search engines [URL1] which represent each of their indexed pages using a number of different feature based representations. These are then matched against the keywords that the user enters. These keywords assume a dual role of representing both the user's interests and their current goals. Another example of this class of system would be the sub-symbolic neural network news-group and web page filtering systems.

This approach contrasts with the featureless approach to the problem. Implementing a family of statistical clustering algorithms, these systems are often termed Automated Collaborative Filtering (ACF) [URL2] systems. Such systems are

---

* This research was sponsored by Broadcom Éireann Research Ltd.

essentially devoid of any form of "feature". Instead users of such systems are required to classify presented pages according to some personal measure of a pages "worth". This information is used to construct clusters of users with similar interests.

Both these approaches have their advantages and disadvantages. Feature based, particularly keyword based systems allow their users to focus the system not just on their interests but also on their current information needs. Any information outside this current subset of their interests will probably not be welcome, as it would be considered interesting but not relevant. ACF systems do not deal in short term requirements at all. Instead they focus on finding "Like Minded Individuals" and thus concentrate solely on interests. On the other hand ACF systems neatly side-step one of the major flaws of feature based systems, namely the poor representational capacity of features. Although keywords and other features are undoubtedly useful, they often fail to adequately represent the true meaning of the underlying text. This is because they lack the context that the full natural language text provides and are therefore often ambiguous.

This paper describes a system architecture designed to provide document filtering based upon a user profile within a specified domain. Details are presented of an implementation of our abstract architecture that allows web page filtering within an Irish context. This filtering system relies heavily on inter user collaboration. We claim that this system successfully combines the important characteristics of both traditional and Automated Collaborative Filtering(ACF) techniques

Section 2 of the paper describes other work relating to this topic. *Section 3* describes the architecture in some detail, whilst *Section 4* gives details of the example implementation of this architecture. *Section 5* gives details of some initial experiments conducted to assess the effectiveness of this system. The paper concludes with *Section 6* that presents the conclusions drawn from this work.

2. Related Work

When considering the existing work within this field, it is worthwhile to first consider the features common to all such systems. We identify an architecture consisting of three components arranged in a hierarchy. The topmost level of this hierarchy is concerned with the presentation of information to the user. There will therefore be information passed upwards from lower levels of the hierarchy as well as feedback from the user to pass to lower levels. The middle component in the architecture is concerned with selecting which material, from that available, to present to an individual user. This contrasts with the bottom-most level that represents those system elements that actually retrieve information from external sources and make it available for retrieval within the system.

The FAB system [Balabanovic 1997] consists of two major types of agent. Firstly, it has the concept of an agent for collecting material to provide to its users. These "Collection" agents obviously correspond to the information collection component of the architecture above. They retrieve material based on an agent profile that is then placed in a central information repository. The other major type of agent is the "selection agent" which corresponds to the information subscription layer of the reference architecture. These agents are responsible for drawing material from the central information repository for presentation to the user. Upon presentation of this information, the user ranks the material. This feedback is then used as the basis for modification of both the user's own personal profile and the profiles maintained by the collection agents.

Another architecture in the same domain is that proposed by Davies [Davies et al. 1996] as instantiated by their Jasper system. Each user in the Jasper Architecture is represented by an agent. When the user identifies a page as being of interest to them this agent is responsible for adding details of this page to that individual's store of interesting pages. These details include the URL of the page, any user annotations and a summary of the page's content, produced using a proprietary text summarisation package. Each agent also maintains an explicit profile entered by the user, which is supposed to adequately capture the user's information needs. The Jasper system as well as allowing a number of different querying styles, more interestingly also allows the communication of pages to other agents with similar interest profiles Jasper is an interesting system as it adopts the use of groups of users in an implicit rather than an explicit fashion. A possible weakness of this system however is its reliance solely on an explicitly entered user profile particularly as this profile again seems to be based on simple keywords.

Amalthaea [Moukas 1997] is another multi-agent system aimed at identifying pages of possible interest to a user based upon a profile of their interests. Again two major classes of agents are used, filtering agents and discovery agents. These agents are evolutionary in nature and are organised into a marketplace. That is the overall behaviour of the system emerges from individual agents in competition with one another based upon locally available information. In the case of Amalthaea the information available is in the form of user feedback on presented links. This information is "credited" between the information filtering agents that presented the link and discovery agent that retrieved it. Positive credit is assigned for pages the user rated highly. Correspondingly, negative credit is assigned for information presented that the user rated poorly. The information filtering agent, acts as a mask on the discovery agent's output, filtering documents based upon weighted keyword vectors.

SAIRE [Odubiyi 1997] is another multi-agent information retrieval engine. SAIRE operates in the space science domain, and adopts a somewhat different approach than those systems previously mentioned. SAIRE utilises legacy information retrieval systems and therefore concentrates on providing a scaleable architecture that is easy to use. SAIRE is organised into three levels. The topmost level contains those agents responsible for accepting input from the user. The system accepts input in a number of different modalities including written and spoken natural language. The middle layer of the architecture acts as a co-ordinator with the information retrieval engines at the bottom most level. One interesting aspect of the SAIRE project is the use of user stereotypes. Based upon previous work from the User Modelling community (e.g. ARCHON [Wittig 1992] and PROTUM[Vergara 1994]). SAIRE users assign themselves to one of a number of stereotypical user groups that are then specialised to fit the individual user. The SAIRE system is of particular interest to us as it makes use of stereotypical user profiles something we are interested in exploring.

To summarise therefore we have identified a three level architectural model within which a number of approaches are possible. We have described a number of recent systems that can be described in terms of this model and identified some of the benefits and weaknesses of these systems. In general, the more successful of these systems adopt some kind of market oriented approach. As with any marketplace it is populated by consumers and producers, the commodity in this case being information and the currency being user feedback. As always the success or failure of these systems lies in the details. In Figure 1 we identify a number of key characteristics that we use to classify and summarise the above systems. These characteristics will be returned to when we come to evaluate our own system. Some explanation of the "Implicitly" entries in the above table is required. Amalthaea does not explicitly maintain a user profile. In Amalthaea it is distributed amongst all the information filtering agents .If this representation is taken to be the user profile, then these are indeed adaptive. Again for Amalthaea the use of information filtering agents implies the existence of groups of users with similar interests otherwise an organisation with one filtering agent per user would make more sense.

Characteristic	FAB	Jasper	Amalthaea	SAIRE
Adaptive User Profile	Yes	No	Implicitly	Yes
Organised Credit Assignment	Yes	No	Yes	No
Support for User Groups	Yes	Partial	Implicitly	Yes
Support for Keyword Search	Yes	Yes	No	Yes
Support for Inter User Collaboration	No	Yes	No	No
Automatic Addition of New Information	Yes	No	Yes	No

Fig. 1. Summary of Key Features.

3. The ARC Architecture

The **A**utomated **R**ecommendation via **C**ollaboration (**ARC**) architecture is an attempt to provide a flexible platform upon which to build a variety of document retrieval solutions. The architecture is based upon an explicit user profile and a taxonomy to limit the scope of the system's domain of discourse.

As can be seen in Figure 2 below, any system based upon the ARC architecture will consist of a number of distinct components each responsible for different parts of the overall systems functionality.

Firstly an overall skeleton for the architecture is provided by a taxonomy agent. It maintains the categories under which documents are held and the inter-relationships between these categories. There is also a set of interest agents, one per category supplied in the taxonomy, which are responsible for managing all the content available within the system relating to the agents assigned category. Functions for this agent would including adding and removing items of content and of course supplying documents upon request matching the personal agent's requirements. Finally there will also be a set of personal agents, one per user. Each personal agent will be a fairly lightweight entity, responsible for allowing communication to, and receiving communication from relevant interest agents. Additionally each personal agent is responsible for maintaining some form of user profile detailing the user's interests.

As already noted above, this architecture describes a class of system that operates within a specified domain partitioned via an explicitly specified taxonomy. Although this is somewhat restrictive, it is not overwhelmingly so, as the categories can be made fairly broad, and the number of categories fairly large. This would result in a system that covers a broad range of possible content. There is also a presumption that some kind of profile will be available detailing the user's interests. Beyond these two presumptions the detail of any implementation of the architecture is undefined. This is a deliberate attempt to allow the widest range of possible systems to be based upon this architecture. Section 4, which follows, gives details of one such implementation of this architecture. The implementation provides a "What's Cool on the Net" service with an Irish flavour.

4. Implementation Details

This section details one such prototypical application. It tackles document filtration in the World Wide Web (WWW) domain. This domain, containing as it does, documents containing elements of many different media types, presents particular challenges when trying to determine overall document semantics. Also such a system has the advantage that it allows access to a large number of potential users via the Internet which would be impossible to obtain any other way. This is particularly important for systems, such as those developed based upon ARC, which depend heavily on inter-user collaboration.

4.1. Prototype Application

The Prototype application is designed to give two distinct views on the same set of information, namely links to web material with an Irish flavour. Which of the two views to be shown to an individual user at any given instance in time depends on the nature of their current goals. As was noted earlier, we distinguish between long term and short-term information needs. We support this distinction by allowing a keyword search style of interaction as well as a featureless view which functions as a kind of "What's cool in Ireland". Both these views share the same underlying data and are supported via the same set of agents. This system makes extensive use of recommendations from its user base rather than trying to use keyword based requests from existing search engines. The system therefore depends on a degree of altruism on the part of its users. As Webhound amongst other systems has demonstrated however, this is usually forthcoming providing the system proves genuinely useful to its user base from the outset. Thus a system such as this requires pump-priming with a number of web page links entered semi-manually by the system developer. The system was primed with around 2000 links spread across the 80 categories. The choice of these links is not of critical importance however, as the system acts to automatically filter out web links which are not found to be relevant. Further details of this implementation on an agent by agent basis are given below. The overall organisation of the implementation can be seen in Figure 2.

Taxonomy Agent

We initially envisaged a simple hierarchical taxonomy, this proved too simplistic however. This is due to a simple hierarchical structure not being rich enough to capture all the associations between interests that are naturally formed. The taxonomy provided in this implementation attempts to capture at least some of these relationships. The taxonomy provided allows the marking of pairs of interests as being related. Whilst maintaining the basic hierarchical structure, the taxonomy allows arbitrary relationships between pairs of interests to be constructed. These relationships between categories are based upon their mutual selection when the user first specifies their interests. The hypothesis in this case is that a user has an interest in both X and

Y. If this is the case then topic X and Y may be of interest to others, who also specify either X or Y as being of interest. Of course one such user is not sufficient to establish this type of linkage and the agent allows for this by using a mechanism similar to that described for the weighting of web pages (See Below).

These linkages are utilised within the system to provide initial users with a stereotypical initial profile. This profile is an expansion of their explicitly stated interests. This profile can subsequently be pruned back automatically based on user feedback on presented pages.

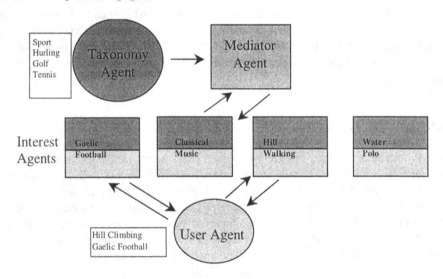

Fig. 2. Instantiation of the ARC Architecture

Interest Agents

These agents, 80 in this case, provide the major functionality of the system. As previously noted the user's interests can be split into long and short-term requirements. Clearly the long term requirements can be given adequate expression via the user profile maintained by the user's personal agent (see below). What about the short term goals however? This system gives the user an ability to communicate these by allowing them to enter a set of keywords, which characterise the web pages they are currently seeking. Note that these keywords are utilised within the context of the user profile, which it is thought should considerably reduce the problems associated with ambiguity of keywords. Consider for example a word with multiple meanings such as "club" which for example could stand for such things as football clubs, dance clubs & golf clubs depending on the context. If a user of our system has flagged an interest only in football and not in golf or dancing then this keyword is no longer ambiguous. This is, it is felt, one of the major advantages of the use of a user profile in this type of system. In order to support this use of keywords, the interest agents are responsible for creating a keyword vector representation of each page entered into the system. When the user presents their list of keywords to the system these are simply matched against the keywords for each page.

As previously mentioned the interest agents also have a mechanism for removing irrelevant or poor quality material, each time a page is presented to a user, they are asked to rate its relevance to them. This information is used to update the page's weight, decreasing it if the page is rated poorly, increasing it for a good rating. A page's weight also decays naturally if it is not presented at all. Any page's weight that falls below a pre-defined threshold is removed from the system. New documents are introduced into the system by means of user recommendations. In this case the user is asked to submit the URL along with a title for the page and a measure of its usefulness, this measure is used to set the documents initial weight.

The featureless style of interaction presents different problems. We make use of this mode of interaction to allow for the adaptation of the user profile as the focused keyword style of interaction is simply too focused for this type of adaptation to take place. When the user interacts with the system in this mode, they are presented with a set of links based loosely on their user profile. In fact the group from which each link is drawn is decided using a Genetic Algorithm(GA) style roulette wheel. Eighty percent of the wheel is allocated to the groups within the user profile according to their allotted strengths. The other twenty percent is split equally between the remaining groups in the taxonomy. Furthermore in order to decide which link from within each interest group to select a further roulette wheel is used. Each link within the group is allocated a slot the size of which is determined by the strength associated with the link. These strengths are updated as indicated in our discussion of the keyword-based view. The total number of links presented is dependent on the user's preference settings.

Personal Agents

The personal agents are fairly lightweight being concerned chiefly with facilitation of communication between each individual user and the rest of the system.

The main function of this agent is to maintain the user profile. This requires the agent to update the strength of each element within the users profile based upon feedback given on items presented drawn from that category. Items presented from outside the profile and ranked highly cause the corresponding category to be added to the profile at an initially low strength.

The results of an initial evaluation of this prototype can be found in Section 5 of this paper.

5. Experimental Evaluation

This section gives details of two experiments conducted in order to empirically demonstrate the effectiveness of the various learning mechanisms used within the prototype system. The first experiment was very tightly controlled and was constructed in order to demonstrate the effectiveness of the filtering mechanism within a single interest category. The second experiment allowed the user to use the system in a less constrained manner and was intended to demonstrate the systems ability to refine a user profile.

5.1. Interest Group Filtering (Experiment 1)

Experimental Procedure

As was previously mentioned this experiment was very strictly controlled and was designed to show the effectiveness of the interest group based filtering of web pages. The subjects, eight in total were drawn from the Computer Science department here in Trinity College Dublin. Each subject was asked to imagine they were planning a short break into a particular area of Ireland (Wicklow) and were planning to engage in a number of outdoor activities in this area. It should be noted that all subjects were native to Dublin and thus had at least some familiarity with the area concerned. Each experimental subject was assigned the same single interest profile for the purposes of the experiment. The experiment itself consisted of each subject carrying out the following three simple tasks :-

- First, each subject was requested to enter a three keyword query which was given to them as part of the experiment. This three keyword query was the same for all subjects. Entering this query resulted in a set of documents being returned which they were requested to rate with respect to relevance.
- Second, each subject was requested to provide to the system two pages which they had not been provided with, but which they felt would be relevant if they were planning such a holiday. Obviously, some subjects would have this material to hand whilst for others this would require some searching.
- Finally, after everyone had completed stage 2 everyone was requested to redo the first stage. This resulted in a new list of material which they were again requested to rate.

Results

The results of this experiment are presented in graphical form as Figure 3. They clearly show a marked and significant difference between the acceptability of the initially presented set of data and that presented after the filtering process has taken place. This is clear, even though the system has only been in operation for one iteration. If we average the results across users and take the mean value and associated standard deviation this result is equally clear. We get a mean of 1.4 with a standard deviation of 4.5 with the initially presented data This indicates a low acceptance rate for the material although the level of acceptance varied markedly as indicated by the standard deviation. After the filtering process has taken place the acceptance value rises to 3.1 and the standard deviation drops to around three. Both these figures are pleasing as they indicate both a rise on average in acceptability along with a convergence across the user group.

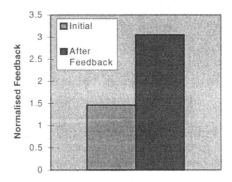

Fig. 3. User feedback before and after learning.

5.2. Adapting to fit an individual user (Experiment 2)

As well as demonstrating the effectiveness of the page filtering, we also hoped to demonstrate the effectiveness of two aspects of the system which concern themselves with user adaptation.

First, one would like to show that the process of modifying the initially entered user profile is useful. That is, that the initially entered user profile isn't the optimal profile for the user concerned. Second, one would also like to show that the system view of the usefulness of a particular document in a given context mirrors that of its user base. It is with these two points in mind that the following experiment was devised.

Experimental Procedure
Twelve subjects were requested to create themselves an initial interest profile from the categories of interest available within the system. They were then requested to download and subsequently rank a set of pages. They were then requested to download and rank a second set of links which would be based upon their updated profile.

Results
Figures 4 and 5present in graphical form the results obtained from the experiment described above. As can be seen from Figure 4 the second ranking of pages was consistently better than the first indicating that the system does indeed learn to better estimate the interests of the user. This effect was however somewhat smaller than we had hoped - a point which is discussed in our conclusions (Section 6).

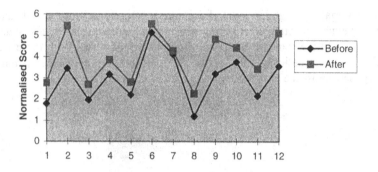

Fig. 4. Analysis of User feedback.

Figure 5 is intended to illustrate the narrowing of the gap between the systems expectations of a users perception of a pages quality, and the reality. Unfortunately the picture is somewhat clouded by a separate process illustrated in Figure 4 i.e. an overall increase in the quality of the pages presented to the user. Even taking this factor into consideration it would seem fair to state that some convergence between system and user is occurring.

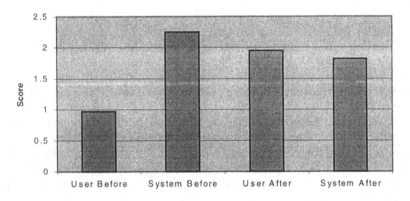

Fig. 5. Comparison of System and User Page Ratings.

6. Discussion of Results and Conclusion

As was mentioned in Section 2 we have identified a number of characteristics, which can be used to distinguish between different agent based information retrieval solutions.

The results presented above provide guidelines as to the direction to take on some of these issues. For instance in a domain such as ours where the topics of interest are simple and clearly defined it could be argued that the effort required in building a system which constructs a dynamic profile is unnecessary. The number of new interests added to a user profile after the user initially specifies their profile is typically very low indicating that the initially selected interests are satisfactory. The explicit nature of our profiles is potentially useful however as the user could be shown their profile at any time and make modifications to it if they are unhappy.

Similarly the facility for users to recommend material to other like minded users is clearly useful. However in the absence of a large user base (as was the case for the system described here) this needs to be augmented with automatic page retrieval facilities.

The use of the user profile and associated interest agents to provide context for a keyword based search is also of interest and warrants further investigation.

In conclusion, it is felt that the prototype system was successful in its goals of bringing together feature and featureless modes of interaction within the one system. Such a system provides an interesting platform for the investigation of issues relating to information retrieval and user modelling. The results of our initial evaluation show that the system was effective in its provision of pages. It would however be interesting to apply the same basic architecture to the problem of sensibly expanding on a keyword search thereby leveraging the power of the pre-existing search engine technology.

7. References

URL 1, Altavista Search Engine Web Page http://www.altavista.digital.com

URL 2, Collaborative Filtering Page http://www.sims.berkeley.edu/resources/collab/

Balabanovic M. An Adaptive Web Page Recommendation Service. In Proceedings of Autonomous Agents, Marina del Rey CA, USA 1997

Davies N.J., Weeks R. & Revett M.C. Information Agents for the World Wide Web in the BT Technical Journal 14:4 pg 105-123. 1996

Moukas A. and G. Zacharia. Evolving a Multi-Agent Information Filtering Solution in Amalthaea. In Proceedings of Autonomous Agents, Marina del Rey CA,USA 1997

Odubiyi J. et al. SAIRE - A Scalable Agent-based Information Retrieval Engine. In Proceedings of Autonomous Agents, Marina del Rey CA, USA. 1997.

Wittig T. (editor) ARCHON: An Architecture for Multi-agent Systems. Ellis Horwood, 1992

Vergara H. PROTUM: A Prolog-based tool for User Modelling . University of Konstanz, D-78434, Konstanz, Germany 1994.

Content-Based Collaborative Information Filtering:

Actively Learning to Classify and Recommend Documents

DELGADO, Joaquin; ISHII, Naohiro and URA, Tomoki
Department of Intelligence & Computer Science
Nagoya Institute of Technology
Gokiso-cho, Showa-ku, Nagoya 466 JAPAN
{jdelgado,ishii,tomkey}@ics.nitech.ac.jp

Abstract. Next generation of intelligent information systems will rely on cooperative agents for playing a fundamental role in actively searching and finding relevant information on behalf of their users in complex and open environments, such as the Internet. Whereas relevant can be defined solely for a specific user, and under the context of a particular domain or topic. On the other hand shared "social" information can be used to improve the task of retrieving relevant information, and for refining each agent's particular knowledge. In this paper, we combine both approaches developing a new content-based filtering technique for learning up-to-date users' profile that serves as basis for a novel collaborative information-filtering algorithm. We demonstrate our approach through a system called *RAAP* (Research Assistant Agent Project) devoted to support collaborative research by classifying domain specific information, retrieved from the Web, and recommending these "bookmarks" to other researcher with similar research interests.

Keywords: Cooperative Information Systems, Software Agents, Collaborative Information Retrieval, Social Filtering, and On-line machine learning algorithms.

1 Introduction

Undoubtedly, in the next generation of intelligent information systems, cooperative information agents will play a fundamental role in actively searching and finding relevant information on behalf of their users in complex and open environments, such as the Internet. Whereas *relevant* can be defined solely for a specific user, and under the context of a particular domain or topic. Because of this, the development of intelligent, personalized, content-based, *document classification* systems is becoming more and more attractive now days. On the other hand, learning profiles that represent the user's interests within a particular domain, later used for *content-based filtering*, has been shown to be a challenging task. Specially because, depending on the user, the relevant attributes for each class *change in time*. This makes the problem even not suitable for traditional, fixed-attribute machine learning algorithms.

Documents, as well as user's profiles, are commonly represented as keyword vectors[1] in order to be compared or learned. With the huge variety words used in natural language, we find ourselves with a noisy space that has extremely high dimensionality (10^4 - 10^7 features). On the other hand, for a particular user, it is reasonable to think that processing a set of correctly classified relevant and irrelevant documents from a certain domain of interest, may lead to identify and isolate the set of relevant keywords for that domain. Later on, these keywords or features can be used for discriminating documents belonging to that category from the others. Thus, these user-domain specific sets of relevant features, that we call *prototypes*, may be used to learn to classify documents. It is interesting enough to say that these prototypes may change over time, as the user develops a *particular view* for each class. This problem of personalized learning of text classification, is in fact, similar to the one of on-line learning, from examples, when the number of relevant attributes is much less than the total number of attributes, and the concept function changes over time, as described in [1].

On the other hand, cooperative multi-agent systems have implicitly shared "social" information, which can be potentially used to improve the task of retrieving relevant information, as well as refining each agent's particular knowledge. Using this fact, a number of "word-of-mouth" *collaborative information filtering*[2] systems, have been implemented as to recommend to the user what is probably to be interesting for him or her. This is done based on the ratings that other *correlated users* have assign to the same object. Usually this idea has been developed for specific domains, like "Music" or "Films"

---

[1] This is called the Vector Model and has been widely used in Information Retrieval (IR) and AI.
[2] Also called Social Filtering [5]

as in Firefly[*] and Movie Critic[*], or for introducing people (matchmaking) as in Yenta[2]. A major drawback of these systems is that some of them completely deny any information that can be extracted from the content. This can be somehow convenient for domains that are hard to analyze in terms of content (such as entertainment), but definitely not suitable for textual content-driven environments such as the World Wide Web (WWW). Besides, these systems usually demand from the user, a direct intervention for both classifying and/or rating information.

In this paper we describe a multi-agent system called *RAAP* (Research Assistant Agent Project) that intends to bring together the best of both worlds – Content-based and Collaborative Information Filtering. In *RAAP*, personal agents both helps the user (a researcher) to classify domain specific information found in the WWW, and also recommends these URLs to other researchers with similar interests. This eventually brings benefits for the users as they are recommended only peer-reviewed documents, especially if they perform information and knowledge intensive collaborative work, such as scientific research. Tested in our research laboratory, this system was developed, not only to prove that content-based and collaborative filtering techniques can be combined, but that they are both necessary to improve the results of the overall learning process. In other words, our agents learn both from local and shared resources. Its strategy includes a *"Classification-Recommendation"* feedback process in which the agent suggests the classification of a saved document, and documents' ratings are extracted from user's actions such as accepting/rejecting a recommendation, or reviewing the agent's suggestion. Thus, the better that it classifies the better that it recommends. In the same way, as more users use the system, either collecting information or receiving recommendations from others, the more is the chance to update the user's prototype for each domain of study, giving the agent a chance for being more accurate in the next classification step.

We introduce a new text classification algorithm, somewhat similar to the version of Rocchio's algorithm adapted to text classification [3]. A major difference is that, due to the active nature of our system, indexing terms are domain specific and can be added or replaced in the prototype. Also, we perform a special type of relevance feedback [4] every time a document is added to the database, instead of learning from training sets with a fix set of indexing terms. This is made possible because the user implicitly rates documents as interesting or not within a certain class, as shown later in the description of the system

We used our classification algorithm, combined with *Expected Information Gain*, to do *relevant feature selection* for creating a positive prototype of indexing terms for each class. In this paper we will be using phrases, words and stemmed words as indexing terms, where the terms can be drawn from a manually build keyword list or from the documents that the user has saved.

As for the collaborative filtering, a combination of document clustering with the traditional Pearson-r algorithm was implemented. The *user vs. category matrix*, needed for calculating the correlation between a pair of users, is automatically constructed by counting, for that user, the number of times a document is successfully classified into a certain class. We also use a *user confidence* factor that serves as feedback for the recommendation process.

Finally, we give some experimental results and analysis. We also discuss about the similarity of our approach with the on-line learning algorithms in a Mistake Bounded model, widely discussed in Computational Learning Theory, and compare these techniques with traditional IR.

2 Description of RAAP

The Research Assistant Agent Project (*RAAP*) is a system developed with the purpose of assisting the user in the task of classifying documents (bookmarks), retrieved from the World Wide Web, and automatically recommending them to other users of the system, with similar interests. In order to evaluate the system, we narrowed our objectives to supporting a specific type of activity, such as *Research and Development (R&D)* for a given domain. In our experiment, tests were conducted using *RAAP* for supporting research in the *Computer Science* domain.

[*] http://www.firefly.net
[*] http://www.moviecritic.com

RAAP consists of a bookmark database with a particular view for each user, as well as a software agent that monitors the user's actions. Once the user has registered an "interesting" page, his agent suggests a classification among some predefined categories, based on the document's content and the user's profiles (Fig. 1). Then the user has the opportunity to reconfirm the suggestion or to change classification into one, that he or she considers best for the given document as shown in Fig.2.

Figure 2 Classification   **Figure 3 Recommendation**

In parallel, the agent checks for newly classified bookmarks, and recommend these to other users that can either accept or reject them when they eventually login the system and are notified of such recommendations, as illustrated in Fig.3.

The first time of registration into the system, the user is asked to select the research areas of interest by he time of registration. This information is used to build the initial profile of that user for each class. The agent updates the user's profile for a specific class every time certain number k of documents are successfully classified into it. In that way, *RAAP*, only uses up-to-date profiles for classification, reflecting always the latest interests of the user. During this process the agent learns how to improve its classification and narrow the scope of the people to whom it recommends in a way we shall explain in the following sections.

A flowchart for *RAAP's* front-end is given in Fig. 4

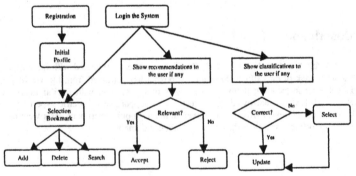

Figure 4 *RAAP's* Front-End Flowchart

3 Learning to Classify

In the flavor of traditional IR, we must state our classification problem as a combination of two: *Text Categorization* and *Relevance Feedback for Retrieval*. Text Categorization can be defined as assigning predefined categories to free text documents. On the other hand, Relevance Feedback is an application of machine learning to raked retrieval systems. Such systems begin with an initial query, usually stated by the user, to construct a classifier used to rank documents, distinguishing the relevant from non-relevant ones. Then the user has the option of labeling some of the top ranked documents, that later are given to a supervised learning procedure, which uses them, along with the original request, to produce a new classifier that usually improves the effectiveness of the retrieval.

Text Categorization and Retrieval, although very related, has been treated by the IR community quite separately. Some authors like T. Tokunaga [6] have the opinion that the categorization is more suitable for evaluating measures than retrieval, because it avoids the problem of defining *relevance* of documents that differs from user to user. In the same line of thought, D. Lewis states in [7] that for text classification, features must be useful across a wide range of classes, since features typically cannot be created for each user of category. To come across these barriers is precisely what we're aiming at.

Perhaps *information routing* or *filtering*, most recently applied in Internet oriented applications (e.g. directing electronic mail the appropriate folder or recipient), is the concept most suited for our task, in the sense of having both, properties for categorization and retrieval.

3.1 Building the Prototypes

In our system, a **document** belonging to a user u_i s as a finite list of terms, resulting of filtering out a stoplist of common English words, from the original document fetched from the WWW using its URL. These documents are either explicitly "bookmarked" or "accepted" by the user. In case of being "rejected", sometimes it can also be "saved" by the user's agent as negative example. Under this notion, and from now on, we will be using the words "document", "page" and "bookmark" without distinction. We will also be using "class", "category" and "topic" in the same way.

Because we are trying to build a document classification system that learns, it is of our interest to keep track of the positive and negative examples among the documents that have been already classified. In *RAAP*, **positive examples** for a specific user u_i and for a class c_j, are the documents *explicitly registered* or *accepted* by u_i and classified into c_j. Note that accepting a recommended bookmark is just a special case of registering it. On the other hand, **negative examples** are either *deleted* bookmarks, *misclassified* bookmarks or *rejected* bookmarks that happens to be classified into c_j. In the case of rejected bookmarks the document is only classified by the agent – we don't ask the user to reconfirm the classification for rejected bookmarks. In this sense, and as measure of precaution, we only take rejected bookmarks that fall into a class in which the user has at least one bookmark correctly classified (a class in which the user has shown some interest).

Let $C_{i,j}^+$ be the set of all documents classified as positive examples for user u_i and class c_j
Let $C_{i,j}^-$ be the set of all documents classified as negative examples for user u_i and class c_j

Now for a given user, we want to build a classifier Q for each category, as a list of terms, in order to apply the dot product similarity measure (Eq. 1), widely used in IR for the purpose of ranking a document D respect a given query. The classifier most similar to the document would indicate candidate class.

(1)
$$sim(Q,D) = \sum_{\tau \in Q} w(\tau,Q)w(\tau,D)$$

For term weighting, we chose TF-IDF (Eq. 1.1), as it is one of the most successful and well-tested term weighting schemes in IR. It consists of the product of $tf_{\tau,d}$, the term-frequency (TF) of term τ in the document d, by $idf_\tau = log_2(N/dt_\tau) + 1$, the inverse document frequency (IDF), where N is the total number of documents of collection and dt_τ is the total number of occurrences of τ in the collection. <u>Note that we maintain a different collection for each user.</u>

$$w(\tau,d) = \frac{tf_{\tau,d}\left[\log_2\left(\dfrac{N}{df_\tau}\right)+1\right]}{\sqrt{\sum_i\left(tf_{\tau_i,d}\left[\log_2\left(\dfrac{N}{df_{\tau_i}}\right)+1\right]\right)^2}}$$

(1.1)

Our problem now consists in learning accurate classifiers that reflects the user's interests both in terms of *relevance feedback* and *feature selection*.

3.1.1 Relevance Feedback

Given the unique terms in Q, $P=\{\tau_1, \tau_2, \tau_3,..., \tau_r\}$, named P as for Prototype, it is it easy to see that both Q and D can be represented as numerical vectors, containing the respective weights of these terms in Q and D, denoted as $\vec{Q}$ and $\vec{D}$ respectively. Their dot product is, in fact, the similarity measure explained before. We can also express Q and D as numerical vectors, containing the term frequency of each elements of P within them, denoted respectively, as:

$$Tf(Q) = <\ tf_{\tau_1,Q}, tf_{\tau_2,Q}, tf_{\tau_3,Q},..., tf_{\tau_r,Q}> \quad \text{and} \quad Tf(D) = <\ tf_{\tau_1,D}, tf_{\tau_2,D}, tf_{\tau_3,D},..., tf_{\tau_r,D}>$$

We can now describe mathematically a very simple approach to the process of relevance feedback as:

(2) $$\boxed{Tf(Q^{i+1}) = Tf(Q^i) + \alpha Tf(D)}$$

Where $\alpha = 1$ if $D \in C_{i,j}^+$

$\alpha = -1$ if $D \in C_{i,j}^-$

And then, recalculate $\vec{Q}^{i+1}$ based on the values of $Tf(Q^{i+1})$.

Another approach found in the literature, is the Rocchio's Algorithm [3]:

(2.1) $$\boxed{\vec{Q} = \frac{\beta}{\left|C_{i,j}^+\right|}\sum_{j \in C_{i,j}^+}\vec{D}_j - \frac{\gamma}{\left|C_{i,j}^+\right|}\sum_{j \in C_{i,j}^+}\vec{D}_j}$$

Note that $\left|C_{i,j}^+\right| \neq C_{i,j}^-$

Usual values are:

$\beta=4$ and $\gamma=4\beta$

The basic problem of these algorithms and the main reason why we couldn't use them for our system is that *they do not take into account the possibility that the dimension of the vectors $\vec{Q}$ and $\vec{D}$ may change in time.* In other words, that unique terms listed in P can be added or deleted in order to reflect the user's current interests (feature selection).

Perhaps Rocchio's algorithm can be adapted to be recalculated each time a unique term is added or deleted to P, but the computational cost would be very high. This is without mentioning the size of the complement of the positive examples, used to calculate the negative part of the formula.

Instead, we propose a new algorithm for incrementally building $\vec{Q}$ in order to reflect effectively the user's current interests. We shall give at first a couple of useful definitions:

Definition 1: *We define positive prototype for a class c, user u_j at time t,*

$$P_{i,j}^{(t)+} = \{\tau_1, \tau_2, \tau_3,..., \tau_r\}$$

as a finite set of unique indexing terms, chosen to be relevant for c_i, up to time t (see feature selection).

Definition 2: *We define negative prototype for a class c, user u_j at time t,*

$$P_{i,j}^{(t)-} \subseteq P_{i,j}^{(t)+} / \forall \tau \in P_{i,j}^{(t)-}, \exists d \in C_{i,j}^- \wedge (tf_{\tau,d} > 0)$$

As a subset of the corresponding positive prototype, whereas each one of its elements can be found at least once in the set of documents classified as negative examples for class c_i

---

The dot product between the numerical vectors of Q and D is denoted as $(\vec{Q} \bullet \vec{D})$.

Now we construct the vector of our positive prototype as follows,

> **At time $t+1$**
>
> if $(P_{i,j}^{(t+1)+} = P_{i,j}^{(t)+})\{$
>
> $\qquad Tf(Q_{i,j}^{(t+1)+}) = Tf(Q_{i,j}^{(t)+}) + Tf(D_{i,j}^{(t)+})$
>
> $\qquad$ Update $\vec{Q}_{i,j}^{(t+1)+}$, based on $Tf(Q_{i,j}^{(t+1)+})$
>
> $\}$ else$\{$
>
> $\qquad$ forall $\tau \in P_{i,j}^{(t+1)+} - P_{i,j}^{(t)+}$ do$\{$
>
> $\qquad\qquad$ calculate $w(\tau,d)$ for the n - most recently processed
>
> $\qquad\qquad$ documents$\in C_{i,j}^{+}$ and update these values in $\vec{Q}_{i,j}^{(t+1)+}$
>
> $\}\}\}$
>
> Where n is the number of documents used as basis for feature selection.

This algorithm is to be applied in the same way for the negative prototype. We can now re-define the similarity measure between a class c_j and a document D as:

(3)
$$sim_i^t(c_j, D) = (\vec{Q}_{i,j}^{(t)+} \circ \vec{D}_{i,j}^{(t)}) - (\vec{Q}_{i,j}^{(t)-} \circ \vec{D}_{i,j}^{(t)})$$

Expressing this equation in words, we should say that for a given user u_p the similarity between a class c_j and an incoming document D at time t, is equal to the similarity of D, with respect of the classifier of the corresponding positive prototype minus the similarity of D, with respect of the classifier of the corresponding negative prototype. This intuitively says that a document is similar to a class if its similar to the class positive prototype and not similar the class negative prototype. It is important to say that the initial positive prototype for each class is a list of selected core keywords from that domain that were integrated into the system to provide at least an initial classification.

Finally, we use a heuristic for *RAAP's* ranking. This heuristics states that *it is more likely that a new document is to be classified into a class in which the user has shown some interest before.* We chose the class with the highest ranking among these.

3.1.2 Feature Selection

Automatic feature selection methods include the removal of non-informative terms according the corpus statistics. In comparative studies on feature selection for text categorization [8], information gain (IG) is shown to be one of the most effective for this task. Information gain is frequently employed as a term-goodness criterion in the field of machine learning [9,10].

Given all these interesting properties we decided to use IG for selecting informative terms from the corpus. We re-define the expected information gain that the presence or absence of a term τ gives toward the classification of a set of pages (S), given a class c_j and for a particular user user u_i as:

(4)
$$E_{i,j}(\tau,S) = I(S) - [P(\tau = present)I(S_{\tau = present}) + P(\tau = absent)I(S_{\tau = absent})$$
$$where,$$
$$I_{i,j}(S) = \sum_{c \in \{C_{i,j}^+, C_{i,j}^-\}} -P(S_c) \log_2(p(S_c))$$

In Eq. 4, $P(\tau = present)$ is the probability that τ is present on a page, and $(S_{\tau = present})$ is the set of pages that contain at least one occurrence of τ and S_c are the pages belonging to class c.

Using this approach, in RAAP, the user's agent finds the k most informative words from the set S of the n most recently classified documents. As in *Syskill & Webert* [11] we chose $k=128$ and arbitrary selected $n=3$ for our experiments.

Out of the selected 128 terms, 28 are to be fixed, as they constitute the core list of keywords or a basic ontology for a topic, given for that class as an initial classifier. Within the rest 100 words, we adopt the following scheme for adding or replacing them in the positive prototype:

1. Perform *stemming* [12] over the most informative in order to create the list of terms.
2. Replace only the terms that are in the prototype but not in the list of the most informative terms.
3. As shown in the algorithm for constructing the classifier, update the weights of the newly added or replaced terms with respect of the n documents processed by the agent for this purpose.

We conclude this section saying that even if IG is a computationally expensive process, in RAAP this is drastically improved both by having n low and only updating the weights for the selected terms only with respect of these documents. We also provide a mechanism in which the "memories" of the terms that repeat in time, are left intact, given that their accumulated weight and information value is high.

4 Learning to Recommend

For the purpose of learning to who recommend a page saved by the user, the agent counts with two matrixes. They are the *user vs. category* matrix M_{mn} and the *user's confidence* factor, where m is the number of users in the system and n the number of categories. The first one is automatically constructed by counting, for a specific user, the number of times a document is successfully classified into a certain class. During the initial registration in *RAAP*, the matrix is initialized to one for the classes that the user has shown interest.

	John	Kato	Ishii	Joacx	Gina
Information Retriev	7	7	3	4	7
Temporal Reasonin	4	3	2	0	4
CBR	1	3	7	2	3
Distributed AI	2	5	3	7	2

Table 1 User-Category Matrix

The first idea was the user-category matrix to calculate the correlation between a user u_x and the rest, using the Pearson-r algorithm (Eq. 5). Then recommend the newly classified bookmarks to those with highest correlation.

(5)

$$correl(u_x, u_r) = \frac{\sum_{i=1}^{n} u_{x,i} - \overline{u}_{x,i})(u_{r,i} - \overline{u}_{r,i})}{\sqrt{\sum_{i=1}^{n} u_{x,i} - \overline{u}_{x,i})^2 \sum_{i=1}^{n} (u_{r,i} - \overline{u}_{r,i})^2}}$$

$$\text{where } \overline{u}_{j,i} = \frac{\sum_{i=1}^{n} u_{j,i}}{n}; j \in \{x, r\}$$

One problem with this approach is that the correlation is only calculated as an average criterion of likeness between two users, regardless of the relations between the topics. That is, if the agent decides to recommend a bookmark classified into a class x, but it happens to be that its user is highly correlated to another user based on the values in the matrix respect other classes, then the bookmark would be recommended to that user anyway. These classes can be presumably unrelated to the class of the bookmark, which is undesirable since we only want the agents to recommend bookmarks to people that have interest in the topics to which it belongs or in related ones. What we really want is to give more weight in the correlation between users to those classes more related to the class of the bookmark that is going to be recommended. For this reason we introduce the concept of similarity between two classes for a user u_i at time t, as the dice coefficient between the positive prototypes of the classes.

(6)

$$rel_i^t(c_m, c_n) = \frac{2 \times \left| P_{i,m}^{(t)+} \cap P_{i,n}^{(t)+} \right|}{\left| P_{i,m}^{(t)+} \right| + \left| P_{i,n}^{(t)+} \right|}$$

Where $|A \cap B|$ is the number of common terms, and $|A|$ is the number of terms in A.

Given the class of the bookmark c_j, the class similarity vector is defined as:

(6.1)
$$\vec{R}_j = < rel_i'(c_j,c_1), rel_i'(c_j,c_2),...,rel_i'(c_j,c_n) >$$
where $n =$ # of classes

Now we multiply this vector by the user-category matrix obtaining a weighted, user-category matrix.

(7)
$$WM = \vec{R}_j \times M$$

Using this new User-Category matrix similar to the one shown in Table 1, but with modified (weighted) values, we proceed to calculate the weight between the subject user u_x (who recommends) and the others u_i (candidates to receive the recommendation) as the correlation between them multiplied by the confidence factor between them.

(8)
$$Weight(u_x,u_i) = correl(u_x,u_i) * confidence(u_x,u_i)$$

In Eq. 8, the confidence factor of user u_x with respect u_i, is a function with a range between 0.1 and 1. It returns 1 for all new users respect others, and it decreased or increased by a factor of 0.01 every time a bookmark recommended by user u_x is accepted or rejected by u_i respectively. Note that $confidence(u_x, u_i) \neq confidence(u_i, u_x)$. This means that the confidence is not bi-directional, but differs for every combination of pair of users.

For deciding to who recommend we used a threshold of 0.5 for the minimum weight, as well as recommending to at most to $f(n) = \lceil 1/(n-264))+5 \rceil$ number of users, where n is the total number of users in the system. We use $f(n)$ to maintain a reasonable proportion of the number of users that are selected as recipients for the recommendation, respect the number of registered users that at some moment of time can be huge.

To avoid circular references in the recommendation chain, the agents verify that the recommended document is not already registered in the target's database.

5 Experimental Results

In order to evaluate the system we set up an experiment with 9 users in our laboratory. They were asked to interact freely with RAAP during a week, registering home pages only with content relevant to their current studies. A number of 70 bookmarks were registered and classified by the agents/users into a total of 9 topics. An overall accuracy of 55.49% was achieved in the process of classification. 73 recommendations occurred, whereas 66.66% were accepted. Only 42 of the 70 bookmarks registered in the database where unique, which suggests that 40% of the registered bookmarks actually came from recommendations.

We must point out that for *RAAP* there was no training data available, other than the bookmarks itself. The learning was performed on-line and incrementally throughout the interaction with the system. In spite of this, our classification algorithm showed to be satisfactory, to the extent that in the majority of the cases the user didn't even need to rectify the agent's suggestion. The relatively high percentage of accepted recommendations indicates that its not only feasible to support collaborated filtering on content-based filtering, but also that with the increase of *relevant* data as product of the recommendations, the classification accuracy is very likely to improve.

6 Discussion

Machine learning for text classification offers a variety of enhancements comparing it with traditional IR. The exponential growth of computing and networking has led to the development of new applications of text classification and retrieval, as well as more demand on its effectiveness. Active (on-line) and passive (of-line) learning are to be combined in order to achieve better results in understanding the complex semantics of natural language.

On the other hand computational agents promise to be the solution for managing, filtering, and sharing information on behalves of their users in open environments such as the Internet. Learning in social structures such as Multi-Agent Systems gives the opportunity to take advantage of common knowledge for cooperative problem solving, ignored some time before in traditional AI.

The combinations of techniques of both areas not only offer us interesting challenges but also introduce new open questions. For instance, how should we evaluate systems like *RAAP*? Are the traditional methods of evaluations in text retrieval such as *precision* and *recall* applicable to personalized and collaborative information retrieval systems? How do we learn when the concept function changes in time? If an agent cannot classify a document, can it ask another agent to do this task (cooperation & coordination)? These were some questions just to mention a few.

There are many types of applications in which we could apply the techniques introduced in this paper. Besides *RAAP*, intended for collaborative information retrieval, we can think now of an application for *collaborative paper review*. In scientific journals and high level conferences, there is always the problem of deciding what experts, in the different sub-fields of the general domain, are going to review a specific paper, based on its content. On the other hand, papers sometimes belong to several of these sub-fields. Having papers semi-automatically classified and sent (as a recommendation) to the corresponding experts, that can, of course, accept or reject a paper for review, is the aim of such application. Note that it should be enough for the experts to register in the system.

Finally, we must point out the recent advances in Computational Learning Theory (COLT), in the Mistake Bounded model, that may represent the key for solving hard problems such as learning target functions that change in time and the selection of relevant features [14]. This is the case of learning users' profiles. Some recent developments in active learning and multiplicative update algorithms [15], as well as in infinite attribute model, are giving some theoretical support to what has been until now just empirical observations.

7 Related Works

There are a several related works that intend to filter and recommend to the user "interesting" Web pages. We can classify them into those using content-based filtering techniques and those using collaborative filtering.

Among the content-based filtering systems we can mention *Syskill & Webert* [11], a system that builds user's profile using Expected Information Gain, and compares the effectiveness of several Machine Learning algorithms for the task of classifying a page as interesting or not for the user. A main difference with our system is that, in *Syskill & Webert*, the domains of the set of web pages used for training and testing the algorithms are previously decided. In other words, this system only recommends to the user pages within a specific topic, extracted from a previously decided online directory, or a list of pages that result from a query to search engine such as LYCOS. It does not perform text categorization of a new document -- at least not among the domains; nor it gives any advice about whether the domain itself is in fact interesting or not for the user! Another difference is that the user's profile is built only once and is not automatically updated afterwards. Learning is performed off-line, with the need of training set with previously rated pages. An another similar system is *WebWatcher* [15], which recommends hyperlinks within a Web page, using the TF-IDF document similarity metrics also used in our system.

Collaborative filtering systems are more rare in the literature and currently oriented more to commercial systems that perform recommendations in the entertainment domain, such as *Movie Critic* and *Firefly*, as we mentioned in the introduction. Some more classical systems are *Ringo* [16], a music recommending system (upon which *Firefly* is based) and *Grouplens* [17], a system that personalized selection of Netnews. Both systems employ Pearson-*r* correlation coefficients to determine similarity between users, regardless of the content of the information being recommended. In any case the user is asked to rate the content, using some predefined scale, in order to calculate this correlation.

Up to the time of the writing of this paper, there have been few reported systems that try to combine both techniques. In the matchmaking domain, that is, recommending people, instead of recommending documents, we can mention *Yenta* [2], and *Referral Web* [18]. These systems somehow perform keyword based textual analysis of private and public documents in order to refine their recommending algorithms that are originally based on collaborative filtering techniques. *RAAP* differs to these systems in several ways, being the objective to filter documents and performing on-line learning of user's profiles. These profiles are later used not only to match similarities among people but also among personal domains of interests.

8 Conclusion and Future Work

The contributions of this paper are threefold:

1) We proposed the combination of content-based information filtering with collaborative filtering as the basis for multi-agent collaborative information retrieval. For such purpose the system RAAP was explained in detail.
2) A new algorithm for active learning of user's profile and text categorization was introduced.
3) We proposed a new algorithm for collaborative information filtering in which not only the correlation between users and also the similarity between topics is taken into account.

Some experimental results that support our approach were also presented. As future work we are looking forward test *RAAP* in broader environments and to compare it with other similar systems, as well as improve the efficiency of both the classification and recommendation processes.

Acknowledgements

This work was supported by the Hori Foundation for the Promotion of Information Science and the Japanese Ministry of Science, Culture and Education (Monbusho).

References

1. Blum, A., "On-line Algorithms in Machine Learning" (a survey). Dagstuhl workshop on On-Line algorithms (June 1996).
2. Foner, L., "A Multi-Agent Referral System for Matchmaking", in *Proceedings of the First International Conference on the Practical Applications of Intelligent Agent Technology (PAAM'96)*, London (April 1996).
3. Buckley, C., Salton,G., et.al.: "The effect of adding relevance information in a relevance feedback environment" . In *Proceedings of the 17th International ACM/SIGIR Conference on Research and Development in Information Retrieval* (1994).
4. Salton,G., Buckley, C., "Improving retrieval performance by relevance feedback", Journal of the American Society for Information Science, 41,288-297 (1990).
5. Maes, P.:,"Agents that Reduce Work and Information Overload", *Comm ACM*, 37, No7 (1994).
6. Tokunaga, T., Iwayama M.: "Text categorization based on weighted inverse document frequency", Technical Report 94-TR0001, Department of Computer Science, Tokyo Institute of Technology (March 1994).
7. Lewis, D.: "Challenges in machine learning for text classification", in *Proceedings of the Ninth Annual Conference on Computational Learning Theory*, P1. New York (1996). ACM
8. Yang, Y., Pedersen, J. "Feature selection in statistical learning of text categorization", *Proceedings of the Fourteenth International Conference on Machine Learning (ICML'97)*, (1997).
9. Quinlan, J.R., "Induction of decision trees". Machine Learning, 1(1):81-106 (1986)
10. Mitchell T., "Machine Learning" McGraw Hill, 1996
11. Pazzani,M.,Muramatsu,J.,and Billsus, D., "Syskill & Webert: Identifying interesting websites", In *Proceedings of the American National Conference on Artificial Intelligence (AAAI'96)*, Portland, OR. (1996)
12. Frakes, W.,Baeza-Yates,R.: "Information Retrieval: Data Structure & Algorithms" Printice Hall, NJ (1992)
13. Blum, A.,Langley, P.: "Selection of Relevant Features and Examples in Machine Learning", Artificial Intelligence, 97:245—277, (1997)
14. Blum, A.: "Empirical support for Winnow and Weighted-Majority based algorithm: results on a calendar scheduling domain", Machine Learning 26:5—23. (1997).
15. Armstrong, R., Frietag, D., Joachims, T. and T.M. Mitchell: "WebWatcher: a learning apprentice for the world wide web" In *Proceedings of the 1995 AAAI Spring Symposium of Information Gathering from Heterogeneous, Distributed Environments*, Stanford, CA, 1995. AAAI Press.
16. Shardanand, U. and Maes P.: "Social Information Filtering: Algorithms for Automation "Word of Mouth"": ACM/CHI'95. http://www.acm.org/sigchi/chi95/Electronic/documnts/papers/us_bdy.htm
17. Resnick, P., Iacovou N., Sushak, M., Bergstrom, P., Riedl, J.: "GroupLens: An Open Architecture for Collaborative Filtering of Netnews", in the *Proceedings of the CSCW 1994 conference*, October 1994.
18. Kautz, H., Selman, B. and Shah, M.: "The Hidden Web", AI Magazine, Summer 1997. AAAI Press.

Domain Experts for Information Retrieval in the World Wide Web

Wolfgang Theilmann, Kurt Rothermel

Institute of Parallel and Distributed High-Performance Systems, University of
Stuttgart, D-70565 Stuttgart, Germany,
[theilmann|rothermel]@informatik.uni-stuttgart.de

Abstract. The World Wide Web is the largest collection of documents
that ever existed. Users of this information space do need tools for simple
and powerful retrieval of the information they are interested in. But the
existing search tools have turned out to be insufficient. They either do
not scale with the large amount of available data or their results are of
low quality.

We present a new concept for information retrieval in the World Wide
Web which satisfies both quality and efficiency. So-called domain experts
acquire knowledge about specific domains. They use mobile agents to
investigate the Web for documents relevant to their domain. By storing
this knowledge, experts can answer future queries directly without any
remote actions.

1 Introduction

With the invention of the World Wide Web the Internet has become a very
popular forum for publishing documents. In summer 1997, there were already
more than 150 million Web pages distributed on around 650,000 sites [4]. The
great challenge for past and current research in information retrieval (IR) is to
help people profit from this immense database. But there is yet no approach
that satisfies this information need in a both effective[1] and efficient[2] way.

In this article we discuss the reasons for this lack of solutions and present a
new approach that has some significant advantages in comparison to the existing
IR-tools.

The Specifics of the World Wide Web. What is so special about the World
Wide Web that information retrieval systems are still unsatisfying? The main
characteristics of the Web making it different from normal databases are:

- Size: The size of the Web (e.g. measured by the number of available documents) is tremendously large, larger by orders of magnitude than any existing
  database.

---

[1] Effectiveness is a measure for the quality of IR-tools. Usually, it is expressed in
terms of *precision* (the ratio of relevant documents retrieved out of the total number
of retrieved documents) and *recall* (the ratio of relevant documents retrieved out of
all relevant documents).

[2] Efficiency is a measure for the use of system resources, e.g. memory usage, network
load etc.

- Dynamic contents: The contents of the Web is very dynamic. Every day thousands of documents come and go. This makes it difficult for any index to keep its information up to date.
- No central authority: There is no authority that supervises publishing in the Web. Anybody that has access to a server can publish anything. This results in "noisy" and unorganized information sources.
- Heterogeneity: The available information is heterogeneous. Text documents, software, images etc. can be published and new formats come up dynamically.

What is the Problem? For each of the characteristics of the Web mentioned above there exist acceptable solutions solving the specific problems "bound to" that one property. The main problem is the combination of these solutions.

A new Approach. In this article, we present a new concept for information retrieval in the World Wide Web. Our concept is based on so-called *domain experts*. In the context of this article a domain is any area of knowledge (or information) in which the contained information is semantically related. A domain expert knows the specifics of its domain enabling it to decide automatically whether or not a document is relevant for it. The expert autonomously investigates the Web for interesting documents and stores the so acquired knowledge in a local database. It uses mobile filter agents that go to specific sites and examine remote documents for their relevance to the expert's domain. These agents are designed to be mobile in order to provide an efficient investigation of the Web. The exploration is triggered either by a user query or proactively to enlarge the knowledge of the expert. To acquire initial knowledge, a domain expert uses existing search engines in order to collect URLs (Uniform Resource Locators) of possibly interesting documents. These documents are further examined by the mobile filter agents. This way an expert builds a knowledge base about Web documents in its domain and it is able to answer user queries directly without any usage of remote servers.

This article is organized as follows: After discussing the related work in Section 2 we present our approach in detail in Section 3. Section 4 describes two potential application areas for a specific domain expert and we finish with some conclusions in Section 5.

2 Related Work

2.1 Centralized Approaches

So far centralized search tools are the only ones that have come to a worldwide usage. Probably the main reason for this fact is that they can be set up without any agreement between the information providers.

Index Based Search Engines (e.g., AltaVista [1], Lycos [8]) try to index the whole Web. So-called robots periodically scan Web pages and list them in an index. Keyword based queries are answered by using this index. While working automatically, index based search engines can cover only a decreasing fraction of the Web [4]. The quality of query results is often unsatisfying for a normal user [3, 5, 7].

Directories (e.g., Yahoo! [13]) organize their index of documents in a prede-fined hierarchy. Users can browse in this hierarchy or perform a search in a certain part of it. Newly registered documents have to be categorized manu-ally. This leads to a high precision of the retrieval results. Obviously, there are more documents in the Web to be categorized manually. Therefore, the recall of directory services depends extremely on the query topic. For very common information needs (where the provider of the directory service spends a lot of effort to gather information) directories are quite useful. A user with a very spe-cific information need will not be satisfied because the directory simply has not registered any document relevant to his query. Directories scale perfectly due to their hierarchical structure that can be distributed easily.

Specialized search engines that gather information only about a special topic are usually constructed as directories, i.e. documents are selected and classified manually.

2.2 Distributed Approaches

To address the scalability problem of information retrieval in the Web a lot of distributed approaches have been followed. The most prominent examples are mentioned below.

Hierarchical, with Server Descriptions. The systems WHOIS++ [11] and Discover [10] are both organizing information in a hierarchy, which is based on descriptions obtained from the different information servers. Queries are routed to the appropriate information servers. The contents of each information server is summarized and forwarded to the next higher level that condenses the set of underlying summaries. The information servers are treated as homogeneous entities, i.e. their description consists of keywords which represent the server's documents but which are not linked with the documents they appear in. For example an information server which contains documents about public domain software and about mobile agents will be described by the keywords *public, domain, software, mobile* and *agents*. Obviously, the conclusion that this server contains software for mobile agents is wrong.

The problem of these approaches is that the contents of ordinary information servers is very widespread. For example, the Web server of a university contains information about the education program, technical reports, staff etc. This re-sults in imprecise collection descriptions (compare with the preceding example) and necessitates queries to be routed to lots of servers (because many servers contain possibly relevant documents).

The system *HyPursuit* [12] improves the former approaches by clustering the contents of collections. Clustered contents of different information servers can be combined on an higher level by restructuring these clusters. This approach alle-viates the problem of imprecise information server descriptions. In the example mentioned above the information server would be described as consisting of two clusters, one about public domain software and the other about mobile agents. The problem with query routing remains the same.

Hierarchical, with Specialized Indexes. To circumvent the problems with query routing and imprecise collection descriptions, some IR-tools try to build up specialized indexes. The system *Harvest* [3] is based on *gatherers* and *brokers*. Gatherers collect index information on local servers. Brokers construct specialized indexes using the information provided by gatherers and other brokers. The links of a broker (which gatherers/brokers shall be queried in order to collect information) have to be defined manually. A special broker (the *Harvest Server Registry*) is used to register information about all brokers. This registry helps people to find the appropriate broker(s) for their information need. While this approach is extremely efficient with respect to index data distribution and broker updating, it suffers from its need to create the broker links manually. For this reason a broker is not able to detect new information resources that belong to its domain.

The search tool *Pharos* [5] realizes an automatic distribution of document metadata to specialized indexes. Documents and indexes can be described by using three different taxonomies (subject, time and place). Documents are automatically categorized on their information server, and their descriptions are forwarded to the appropriate indexes (called mid-level servers) using Harvest technology. Massively replicated high-level servers have knowledge about the domains of mid-level servers and try to propose appropriate mid-level servers to a user, who queries them. The progress achieved with *Pharos* is the automatic integration of new information sources into the specialized indexes. The price for this progress is the necessity of defining a world wide standard for document description (the fixed definition of the taxonomies). This results in a limited precision achievable with this approach and in restrictions for the construction of specialized indexes (only domains that can be expressed with the above taxonomies can be built).

Decentralized. We present two approaches that try to realize information organization and retrieval in a totally decentralized manner. The system *Ingrid* [6] realizes distribution on a document basis. Documents are described by 15 keywords. Every document description includes links to other documents that share at least one of its keywords. The links are inserted in a way that there is a path between two documents iff they have at least one keyword in common. A problem of this approach is the simple description of documents. For example, it is not possible to use exact phrase queries if document descriptions consist of only 15 keywords. Also efficiency is not convincing because many steps are needed in the query routing process.

A distribution based on Web proxies is proposed in [7]. So called *proxy search engines* (PSEs) learn from the user's search behaviour and user's relevance feedback to the search results. This affects the knowledge a PSE gathers. With a predefined list of topics PSEs can specialize themselves and acquire knowledge about the specialization of other PSEs. With this knowledge they can either answer queries themselves or forward a query to another PSE. While this approach is quite interesting in its way of distribution and scaling, the quality of search results is as low as in traditional centralized search engines.

The general problem of totally decentralized IR-systems is that effective IR-algorithms are quite complex and need much knowledge (like dictionaries). It is not efficient (in terms of memory usage) to replicate this data massively in a distributed system. To avoid such inefficiencies decentralized systems use very simple IR-techniques. This is the reason for the inherent lack in effectiveness of these approaches.

3 Domain Experts - A New Approach

3.1 Motivation

Regarding the existing IR-tools and considering their specific advantages and disadvantages we can identify three aspects that are crucial for an effective and efficient IR-system:

1. IR-tools have to work in a distributed way. Regarding the size of the Web (i.e. the number of documents and users) it is obvious that centralized solutions cannot cope effectively and efficiently with this vast information space. While the large number of users can be treated with simple replication, real distribution of document metadata amongst different servers is absolutely necessary for the management of frequently changing documents.
2. Document metadata has to be grouped according to its content. This is necessary to provide a fast and efficient routing of a user's query to the appropriate group(s). Otherwise many document indexes have to be processed for every single query.
3. Strategies have to be different for the various domains. Considering the heterogeneity of the Web it is not realistic to think that one single search algorithm can produce results of high quality for every domain. A search algorithm for personal homepages, for example requires other strategies and knowledge than a search for public domain software.

We will now present our concept of *domain experts* that takes all of these three aspects into account.

3.2 Overview

A domain expert is supplied with domain specific knowledge (strategies, algorithms etc.), which enables it (among other things) to decide on its own if a document belongs to its domain.

Domain experts automatically build up a specialized index. In contrary to traditional indexes, this index is based not only on keywords contained in the indexed documents, but also comprises meta descriptions (meta keywords) of documents that are expressed implicitly, e.g. in the document's structure or environment.

The construction of this index happens in the following way: At the beginning of its life cycle a domain expert has its domain specific knowledge but does not know any document that belongs to its domain. The expert expands its document knowledge by *learning* from a traditional search engine. In this phase the expert is already able to answer user queries. An incoming query is forwarded to a search engine. The resulting URLs are taken as a first hint pointing to interesting documents. The expert sends out mobile filter agents in order to scan the remote documents (described by the URLs) and to decide which documents shall be registered in the expert's document knowledge base. The acquired knowledge is used to answer the query.

Later on, as the document knowledge of the domain expert grows it becomes more and more *autonomous*, i.e. independent of traditional search engines. It is able to answer the majority of user queries directly by inspecting its document knowledge base. A search engine is just queried to check if new documents have been published or if old documents have been updated (new timestamp). Mobile agents are sent out only if new or modified documents have been found by the search engine. This is expected to happen only seldom in the autonomous phase.

Finally, a domain expert tries to discover new documents *proactively* a previous user query. This can be done in several ways:

- The environment of an interesting document (documents on the same Web server) can be examined for other possibly interesting documents.
- Relevant documents already found can be processed for further hints, like URLs, a person's name, names of conferences etc. These can be exploited to find other interesting documents.
- External knowledge bases can be queried to acquire new or additional knowledge.

After acquiring enough hints the domain expert generates a proactive internal query. This query is then processed by the filter agents like an ordinary user query.

3.3 Architecture

An overview of the domain expert's architecture and its basic way of processing queries is given in Figure 1. The order of the different steps to process an incoming query is shown by the numbers aside the arrows. Optional steps are marked with numbers in braces.

The normal processing of an incoming query proceeds as follows: The query arrives at the *query processor* (1) which asks the *knowledge gatherer* (2) to get some initial knowledge from external knowledge bases. The gatherer uses a classical search engine to retrieve some document links (URLs) that might be interesting (3). Note that the resulting documents will satisfy only some of the user's query keywords. Probably, just a small fraction of these documents will belong to the expert's domain and an even smaller fraction will satisfy the user's query. The query processor will then verify if the links delivered by the gatherer are already known in its *document knowledge base* (4). Links that should be examined further (because they have not been scanned before or have been modified) are forwarded to the *agent coordinator* (5). The agent coordinator decides which agent platforms it wants to send mobile *filter agents* to and which documents

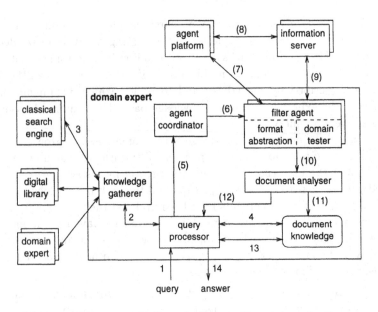

Fig. 1. Architecture of a Domain Expert; Processing of a Query

should be processed by each agent (6). The mobile filter agents migrate to the remote agent platforms they are assigned to (7) and examine their set of documents (8). Other documents are directly examined by a filter agent residing on the domain expert's platform (9). As a result, filter agents deliver the documents that belong to the domain of the domain expert (10). These documents are further analysed (keywords and meta keywords are computed) and the resulting knowledge is inserted into the document knowledge base (11). The query processor is notified (12), then it calculates the answer to the query by using the document knowledge base (13) and delivers the final answer to the user (14).

Notice that the use of the mobile agents (steps 5 to 12) is optional. At the beginning of the learning phase the probability for these steps is nearly 1. When the expert becomes more and more autonomous it becomes almost 0. External domain experts or other digital libraries are only used in the proactive phase.

3.4 Mobile Filter Agents

When a domain expert receives a list of document links (URLs) from an existing search engine it has to examine those links that are not contained in its document knowledge base. We now have the following situation: A lot of data is widely distributed and has to be examined. Only a little fraction of this data is really needed locally. Obviously, it is not possible to install filter agents all over the world because the filter algorithm is different for each domain expert. Therefore, we realize the filter agents as mobile agents that can transfer their code and data to remote places and start remote execution afterwards. The life cycle of these mobile filter agents consists of four steps:

Step 1: Distribution. At the beginning the agent coordinator receives a list of documents (URL and size given) that have to be examined. It has to decide to which agent platforms it shall send a mobile filter agent and which documents shall be processed by which agent. We will not assume that every server in the Internet provides access for mobile agents to allow for the most general approach. So we need an algorithm that computes an optimal distribution of the mobile agents given the locations of existing agent platforms and a list of documents to be examined. This clustering process computes groups of documents, each group processed by one agent resp. from one agent platform. The criteria for the optimization process are the costs needed for agent migration and (remote) document processing. An example for a clustering process is shown in Figure 2.

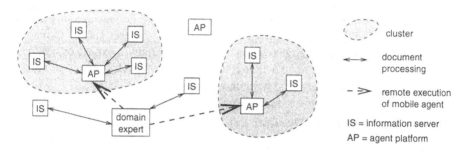

Fig. 2. Example for a clustering process: 2 clusters are built, each contains one agent platform and a set of information servers (which documents are examined from the agent platform); 1 agent platform is unused; 2 information servers are examined directly from the domain expert

Step 2: Analysation. The mobile filter agents migrate to their designated agent platforms and analyse their set of documents.

Step 3: Intermediate Results. The agents can return intermediate knowledge to the agent coordinator. For example, assume that an agent finds interesting hyperlinks that it does not want to process by itself. It sends this information to the coordinator which decides either to forward it to another agent or to set up a new agent. The advantage of analysing these hyperlinks immediately is that the coordinator can possibly profit from the already distributed agents and does not need to set up a new agent.

Step 4: Integration. Finally, the filter agents return their results to the domain expert. This result consists of a fuzzy degree of containment to which each document belongs to the considered domain. The domain expert decides which range of degrees it can accept and integrates the meta description of the accepted documents into its document knowledge base.

3.5 Generic Platform

The crucial point for the feasibility of our approach is to which extent the architecture of a domain expert can be made generic.

Domain Specific Requirements. The only component that requires a domain dependent part is the filter agent. To enable simple construction of specific filter agents we split up a filter agent into two parts: the general *format abstraction* and the domain specific *domain tester*. The format abstraction realizes the abstraction from the actual representation of a document (html, postscript etc.). It converts each document into a unified representation. The format abstraction acts like a lexical analyser that produces a sequence of tokens. Getting these tokens as input, the domain tester can be formulated as an automaton. Its result is a fuzzy value that describes the degree to which the considered document belongs to its domain.

Possible Domain Specific Extensions. Other components that can (but need not!) be extended in a domain specific way are the *document analyser*, the knowledge gatherer and the query processor.

The document analyser calculates other domain specific features of a document (keywords and meta keywords). The knowledge gatherer can be extended to use other external knowledge sources, e.g. another domain expert or a digital library. The query processor can be extended to improve the proactive search facilities of a domain expert in a domain specific way.

3.6 Knowledge of the Domain Expert

The document knowledge comprises both, descriptions of documents belonging to the experts domain (keywords and meta keywords) and descriptions of documents not belonging to the domain (just URL and date of last modification are stored). The latter is necessary to prevent that the filter agents are repeatedly sent out to documents of which the expert already knows that they do not belong to its domain. Note that the expert does not have to store URL and modification date for every document in the Web. Only the links delivered by the external search engine have to be taken into account. This can be expected to be only a small fraction of the Web because these links always satisfy at least some of the keywords contained in the user's queries.

The knowledge a domain expert gathers about documents of its domain is represented in *facets*. Possible facets may be "keyword", "author" etc. Each facet is associated with an automaton (see the previously described domain tester and document analyser) that computes the actual instances of its facet in the processed document. Possible formalisms for formulating these automata are regular expressions, stack automata and Java code.

This way of knowledge representation is extremely flexible. It is easy to extend the domain and document knowledge by a new facet that can be computed for every document. Users can be allowed to extend their queries with code that computes some additional facets. Eventually, the user interface to a domain expert can be constructed automatically just by looking which facets are supported by the expert.

The definition of the expert's domain restricts the range of relevant documents to a manageable set. The expert can regularly check this set in order to detect if a document was modified or became invalid.

3.7 Cooperation between Domain Experts

Cooperation between several domain experts can improve effectiveness and efficiency of the single domain experts. Hierarchical cooperation (expert x can use expert y if x knows y already when x was constructed) is quite simple and can be integrated in the same way as the use of external search engines or digital libraries.

An automatic cooperation protocol between different experts is very desirable. However, it enforces a kind of common semantic (an ontology). Facets have to be formulated according to this semantic. This would restrict the flexibility of facet definition and would abolish a good part of our architecture's flexibility. Therefore, we do not plan to introduce this kind of (real) cooperation into out model.

3.8 Access to Domain Experts

It is necessary for the user to have uniform access to all existing domain experts. Therefore, we need a kind of domain expert white board (similar to the server registry realized in the Harvest system) in which all domain experts have to register themselves (including some additional parameters like a short description of the domain and the supported facets).

Query routing to appropriate domain experts consists of two steps:

1. It has to be determined which broker is appropriate for a query.
2. The general query format has to be mapped to the domain specific interface.

In a simple approach, the user can select the expert to which he wants to address a query from a list or a hierarchical structure. A domain specific form is then presented and the user can fill in his query parameters. Finally, the query is sent to the selected domain expert.

Semi-automatic mapping of general query formats to domain specific interfaces can be done similar to the system *search broker* [9]. This aspect of domain experts is currently under investigation.

4 Potential Application Areas

To illustrate our approach we present two application areas for specific domain experts. The same domains have been used as application areas in the presentation of the Harvest system [3].

An Expert for the Publication Domain. An interesting domain for a domain expert is that of scientific publications. This expert has knowledge about the general structure of a publication: it contains a title, the author's names, an abstract, an introduction, a description of related work, a conclusion and a list of references. The filter agents use this domain specific knowledge in order to decide if a document might be a scientific publication or not. Obviously, the result of this filtering process won't be a boolean value but a fuzzy parameter between 0 and 1.

The domain expert can initiate a proactive search by analysing the references of a publication. The extracted names of the author (resp. conference/workshop names) can be followed in cooperation with an expert in the personal homepage domain (resp. conference/workshop domain) to discover new publications.

The domain expert offers the possibility to formulate precise queries. A user can ask for example for articles of a special group of authors or for articles in which a special reference is cited.

An Expert for Downloadable Public Domain Software. A second example for an interesting domain is that of public domain software that can be downloaded directly from the Web. The knowledge of such a domain expert comprises information about existing programming languages and protocol specific information (e.g. HTTP, ftp) that can be used to download a file. Again this knowledge enables the filter agents to decide if software can be downloaded from a specified Web page.

An advanced query that can be sent to this domain expert may be a search for locations where agent software frameworks written in Java can be downloaded.

5 Conclusion

In this paper we have presented a new approach for information retrieval in the World Wide Web, based on the concept of domain experts.

Domain experts will be efficient for three reasons: First of all, we use an existing search engine that performs as an anchor for our search. This helps us to avoid reindexing the whole Web for every domain expert. Secondly, the use of mobile agents provides a way to filter the sea of remote documents (delivered by a search engine or any other mechanism) more efficiently than downloading all documents and filtering them locally. Thirdly, domain experts restrict the range of documents that are relevant for them in an intelligent way. Therefore, they are able to store knowledge about interesting documents in a local database and to keep this knowledge up to date. This mechanism saves us from remotely reexamining lots of documents for every query.

The main features contributing to the effectiveness of domain experts are:

- Domain experts realize a prefiltering/preclustering of the documents in the Web.
- The computation of domain specific features (facets) provides a possibility for users to formulate more precise queries (in a simple manner) and to get more precise results.
- The approach is quite flexible. This flexibility guarantees that the formulation of domain experts can be done adequately also for situations not foreseen.
- Domain experts collect their knowledge automatically considering the entire Web. In the beginning they depend on traditional search engines. But later on they proactively search for new documents. This mechanism ensures a higher recall than can be achieved by traditional search engines.

Finally, a great strength of our approach is that it can be introduced step by step without any need for an international standard, i.e. already a single domain expert can be set up and work very well.

We will soon finish a first prototype of a domain expert for the domain of scientific publications. This prototype will use the mobile agent system Mole [2].

References

1. AltaVista: http://altavista.digital.com
2. Joachim Baumann, Fritz Hohl, Kurt Rothermel, Markus Straßer: *Mole - Concepts of a Mobile Agent System.* accepted for WWW Journal, Special issue on Distributed World Wide Web Processing: Applications and Techniques of Web Agents, Baltzer Science Publishers, 1998
3. C.Mic Bowman, Peter B. Danzig, Darren R. Hardy, Udi Manber, Michael F. Schwartz, Duane P. Wessels: *Harvest: A Scalable, Customizable Discovery and Access System.* Technical Report CU-CS-732-94, Department of Computer Science, University of Colorado - Boulder, USA, March 1995
4. David Brake: *Lost in Cyberspace.* New Scientist, 28 June 1997,
   URL: http://www.newscientist.com/keysites/networld/lost.html
5. R. Dolin, D. Agrawal, A. El Abbadi, L. Dillon: *Pharos: A Scalable Distributed Architecture for Locating Heterogeneous Information Sources.* Proc. 6th ACM Int. Conference on Information and Knowledge Management, Las Vegas, Nevada, USA, November 10-14, 1997, F. Golshani and K. Makki (Eds.)
6. Paul Francis, Takashi Kambayashi, Shin-ya Sato, Susumu Shimizu: *Ingrid: A Self-Configuring Navigation Infrastructure.* Proc. 4th Int. World Wide Web Conference, Boston, MA, USA, December 11-14, 1995,
   URL: http://www.w3.org/Conferences/WWW4/Program_Full.html
7. Arkadi Kosmynin: *From Bookmark Managers to Distributed Indexing: An Evolutionary Way to the Next Generation of Search Engines.* IEEE Communications Magazine, June 1997
8. Lycos: http://www-english.lycos.com/
9. Udi Manber: *The Search Broker.* University of Arizona, USA, July 5, 1997, URL: http://sb.cs.arizona.edu/sb/paper.html
10. Mark A. Sheldon, Andrzej Duda, Ron Weiss, David K. Gifford: *Discover: A Resource Discovery System based on Content Routing.* Proc. 3rd Int. World Wide Web Conference, Darmstadt, Germany, April 10-14, 1995, Elsevier Science B.V., Journal Computer Networks and ISDN Systems 27:6
11. C. Weider, J. Fullton, S. Spero: *Architecture of the Whois++ Index Service.* Network Working Group, RFC 1913, February 96,
    URL: ftp://ds.internic.net/rfc/rfc1913.txt
12. Ron Weiss, Bienvenido Velez, Mark A. Sheldon, Chanathip Namprempre, Peter Szilagyi, Andrzej Duda, David K. Gifford: *HyPursuit: A Hierarchical Network Search Engine that Exploits Content-Link Hyper text Clustering.* Proc. 7th ACM Conference on Hypertext, Washington, DC, March 1996, ACM Press, 1996, ISBN 0-89791-778-2, URL: http://www.cs.unc.edu/~barman/HT96/
13. Yahoo!: http://www.yahoo.com

Semantic Navigation Maps for Information Agents

Wolfgang Benn and Otmar Görlitz[i]

Chemnitz University of Technology
Department of Computer Science,
09107 Chemnitz, Germany
{wolfgang.benn | otmar.goerlitz}@informatik.tu-chemnitz.de

Abstract: In this paper we propose a new approach to represent entity semantics of loosely coupled systems by maintaining the topological neighborhood of context relations in a particular domain by a self organizing Kohonen map. We discuss how this technique can be applied to a distributed information system in order to find the most promising site to answer a particular query. Moreover, we show the applicability of our approach to any other system whose context can be described by certain semantical features. In general, our representation method can be seen as a kind of semantic distribution schema applicable for loosely coupled systems of various types - i.e., where systems can be information systems as well as databases or Internet-sites.

Introduction

With the ever-increasing availability of knowledge online, the problem arises for the user to find within the enormous amount of information just that data he is looking for. In the WorldWideWeb, one of the largest distributed information systems today, search engines are provided for the user. Unfortunately, it is nearly impossible to retrieve information for a well-defined context. In the communication with human beings it is self-evident to answer a question only in the required context. For WWW-

---
[i] This work has been supported by the Deutsche Forschungsgemeinschaft (contract no. BE 1786/2-1).

search engines this is almost impossible. The lack of understanding semantics, as well in the query as in the data, represents the greatest disadvantage for the search engines. They have to confront the user with a huge amount of possible answers and leave it to him to manually select the answer for his question. So what they achieve is a preselection of information. They simply reduce the search space.

With the development of information agents a more sophisticated method for the preselection of data is available [25,26]. An information agent is a software program that autonomously and target driven visits the information sources to find answers for a user-query. In general, the agents know the locations of the information sources, but not much about the sort of information they will find there. They move to the information source (in the remainder of this article also mentioned as knowledge base) and select data, which seem to them matching the users query. Although endowed with a certain understanding for the semantic of the query, like the search engines the agents know nothing about the semantic schema of the information sources.

Thus, without a priori knowledge about the semantical content of an information source, the agents have to visit all known sites. But it would be desirable to conserve already gained knowledge about the semantic closure of visited sites. This is especially interesting in a system of cooperating agents where the task of knowledge acquisition can be shared as well as the information each agent collects.

Apparently, in a system of distributed knowledge bases it would be most useful to answer the question which systems include which sort of information. For this purpose we designed a semantical distribution map. The map completes the distribution schema for loosely coupled systems as the logical part. It makes the semantics of the involved systems explicit, visible and exploitable so to say. Information retrieval based on the semantical distribution schema is a dramatical improvement on the conventional methods, which could only rely on structural information. Information agents, for instance, can use the map as navigation base to find those information sources, which most likely contain data matching the users query. This prediction is based on the semantical similarity between the searched information and the information stored in the knowledge base. The agent can therefore start its search at the most promising site.

Our approach bases on the representation of ontological system semantics with self-organizing Kohonen maps – so-called SOMs [1]. Such maps transform property vectors, which form the input space of a Kohonen map, into a two-dimensional area of neurons that make up the SOM's output space, by preserving the logical neighborhood of properties. Thus, we define a property vector:

$$V(p_1, p_2, ..., p_n)$$

with the interpretation that p_i stands for a certain semantical property of a system and the values of p_i are in the interval [0,1] in order to express qualitative differences between systems with similar properties. To own a property can mean for a database that it contains a certain data object or a particular schema element. For real time systems a property can express, that the system owns a particular competence. Nevertheless, for an information system it may be interpreted that this system deals with a particular kind of information. A complete feature vector then defines the position of the system within the semantic space of the domain. E.g. the context profile of a knowledge base modelled as a feature vector positions that information source somewhere in the domain of knowledge stored in the distributed information system. The particular partition of the general domain is defined by the semantic of the data in the actual knowledge base.

Generally spoken, our approach can be applied for technical systems as well as for real-world systems because

- it abstracts from special semantic properties of systems to numeric values,

- keeps the spatial relations between the system's properties in the representation

- and thus, explicits knowledge about system semantics in an exploitable format.

The remainder of this paper is organized as follows: In the next section we explain how the representation of information and its context can be performed with property- or feature-vectors. Here we use a simple example from the WWW search and classification engine Yahoo. Section three gives an overview of Kohonen's SOMs and shows what we had to modify there to get better representations. In section four we apply our representation in examples and show how to find promising information sources for queries. Finally we discuss several problems of maintaining semantic distribution maps and conclude.

Description of information and context

In our paper we assume that there exist information agents with the task to extract certain facts from knowledge bases. Often the data has to be filtered, processed or compared. For instance we consider the WWW-service "Bargain Finder". Bargain Finder searches where to obtain a particular music CD at the best price. This implies for the information agent to visit the locations of CD-shops in the WWW, ask if the specific CD is available and how much it would cost. Generally, the agent asks a knowledge base if a certain object or information about the object is available within the domain of the information source.

Realworld-objects however, are used in several different contexts. In each context the semantic of the object may vary. So the Bargain Finder needs to know, the information source is a CD-shop and therefore sells the music CD. A wrong context would be a site which tries itself to purchase CD's or plays them on demand.

Apparently it is important to describe the desired context for a query and also to know the context of the information within a knowledge base.

How can we conceive context? Context seems to emerge with the relations of an object to other objects or the behavior of objects. As example we take a look at the internet searcher Yahoo. Yahoo differs from other websearchers because it maintains a knowledge base about the contents of WWW-sites. For a query it looks first into its knowledge base before it issues the query to other searchers which crawl the web. For this reason Yahoo has a suggestion service where users can announce their sites with a description of the contents to Yahoo's knowledge base. The site then is sorted into Yahoo's appropriate category. Categories in Yahoo form a hierarchy. Beginning with *Top*, which does not specialize the contained information in any way, followed by a number of most general classifications like *Business & Economy*, *Computers & Internet*, *Science*. Subsequent layers stepwise refine the context of the information contained in the category. However, within a category it is possible to have a link to another category, which not necessarily has to have the same supercategory. This means, the tree structure in modelling categories is broken to a directed graph. The following picture shows a small part of Yahoo's category-graph.

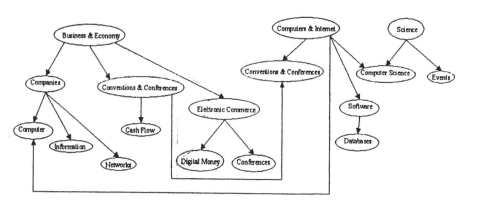

Figure 1 : A subgraph of Yahoo's categories.

The nodes of the graph contain designators of a category and the edges point to a subcategory. We can see that designators can refer to different categories, e.g. *Conventions & Conferences*. Also we notice that synonymous (here: in their meaning similar) designators for different categories exists, e.g. *Conferences, Events, Conventions & Conferences*.

Within Yahoo's knowledge base the paths along a hierarchy mark a distinct knowledge domain. Every context of a subcategory is a specialization of the context its supercategory represents. This knowledge domains are represented in the directed graph along every path starting with a node that has no incoming edges (the uppermost category) to a node which has no outgoing edges (a leaf-category). For instance, *Business & Economy* → *Companies* → *Computer* and *Computer & Internet* → *Computer* represent such domains (a proposal for the automatic recognition of semantical properties is given in a second example later). Our example contains thirteen, partially overlapping domains. The semantic closure of a knowledge domain – its context – is described with the designators of the nodes along the path. So we can say the first domain contains information about business and economic, more exactly about companies in business and economics and even more exactly about companies in business and economics which are related to computers. For each path in the subgraph we can describe its semantic by the set of designators appearing in the graph. Therefore we create a feature vector $V_j(p_1, p_2, ... p_n)$ for the path P_j where p_i states whether the knowledge domain contains a specific information or not. The values of p_i can therefore be *TRUE* (1) or *FALSE* (0). Thus the feature vectors in the example have a dimension of 17.

	P1	P2	P3	P4	P5	P6	P7	P8	P9	P10	P11	P12	P13
Business & Economic	1	1	1	1	1	1	1	0	0	0	0	0	0
Computer & Internet	0	0	0	0	0	0	0	1	1	1	1	0	0
Science	0	0	0	0	0	0	0	0	0	0	0	1	1
Company	1	1	1	0	0	0	0	0	0	0	0	0	0
Conventions & Conferences$_1$	0	0	0	1	1	0	0	0	0	0	0	0	0
Electronic Commerce	0	0	0	0	0	1	1	0	0	0	0	0	0
Conventions & Conferences$_2$	0	0	0	1	0	0	0	1	0	0	0	0	0
Software	0	0	0	0	0	0	0	0	1	0	0	0	0
Computer Science	0	0	0	0	0	0	0	0	0	1	1	0	1
Events	0	0	0	0	0	0	0	0	0	0	0	1	0
Computer	1	0	0	0	0	0	0	0	0	0	0	0	0
Information	0	1	0	0	0	0	0	0	0	0	0	0	0
Network	0	0	1	0	0	0	0	0	0	0	0	0	0
Cash Flow	0	0	0	0	1	0	0	0	0	0	0	0	0
Digital Money	0	0	0	0	0	0	1	0	0	0	0	0	0
Conferences	0	0	0	0	0	1	0	0	0	0	0	0	0
Databases	0	0	0	0	0	0	0	0	1	0	0	0	0

The feature vectors have certain similarities, which means that they partially describe a comparable semantic. In the directed graph this can be measured with the number of nodes belonging to two paths. The more nodes two paths share, the more do they describe a related context. In the problem scope spanned by the attributes (the designators), feature vectors with similar semantics are closer to each other than to such vectors with different semantics. To obtain a planar map of the neighborhood relations in the input space we use Kohonen's Self-Organizing Feature Maps (SOM). The SOM architecture is an artificial neural network for the representation for semantical and functional relations of adjacent neurons in the human brain.

Kohonen's Self-Organizing Maps

The self-organizing neural network model was designed to map a multi-dimensional input space to a planar output space with preservation of the neighborhood relations of the input space. The output space however, is formed by a number of neurons usually arranged in a rectangular or hexagonal grid. It is quite possible to arrange the neurons in a hypercube and thus have a higher-dimensional output space with obviously better preservation of neighborhood relations. Anyway, most applications use the two-dimensional output for easy visualization and evaluation.

Each neuron has a number of synapse-weights which is equal to the dimension of the problem (or input) space. This specific weight-vector is the representation of the neuron in the input space while its grid coordinates define its place in the output space. The training of the SOM is an unsupervised learning method; i.e. there is no backpropagation of an error value. The learning algorithm itself lets the neurons align each other to represent the input space. To meet that goal a number of training vectors from the input space must be presented to the network. For each input the best matching unit (neuron) is activated where "best matching" here refers to the Euclidean Norm between the training vector and the weight vector.

Let $x \in \Re^n$ be a training vector and $w_i \in \Re^n$ the weight vector of the ith unit. The best matching unit c is defined as:

$$\|x - w_c\| = \min_i \{\|x - w_i\|\}$$

The weight-vector of the unit is adapted towards the training-vector by a certain degree – the learning rate. Additionally, the best matching unit pulls its neighborhood in the same direction but the strength of the neighborhood adaptation decreases with the distance from the center of the activation.

With the timestep t and the learning rate η the weight adaptation is usually calculated with:

$$w_i(t+1) = w_i(t) + \eta(t) * h_{ci}(t) * [x(t) - w_i(t)]$$

where $h_{ci}(t)$ is the distance function describing a *neighborhood kernel* for the winning unit. The learning rate and the affected neighborhood normally decrease over the time. Thus Kohonen proposes a bubble or a Gaussian neighborhood. For computing reasons often the timestep is exchanged with a distance parameter d:

$$h_{gauss}(z,d) = e^{-(z/d)^2}$$

where

$$z = \|r_c - r_i\|$$

denotes the distance of the unit i to the best matching unit c in the grid. r_j denotes the position of unit j in the grid.

For a more detailed description of the architecture and learning algorithm see [5-8]. Unfortunately, today no comprehensive theory exists how to choose the parameters for the map and its training. Obviously not only the number of neurons is crucial for a good representation of the input space but the number of training cycles, the learning rate and the affected neighborhood are also important for the quality of the map as well.

There are several approaches known to improve the basic SOM architecture. To overcome the dilemma of prefixed grid-dimensions several models of growing networks are proposed [10-12]. We also know about approaches, which propose a hierarchical filtering of the input and thus yield several abstraction layers in the output space [13,14,16]. Currently we use a re-implementation of Kohonens original model [4] merely with a slight modification to represent a manufacturing network.

Usually an activated neuron influences its neighborhood in all directions towards the input vector. From this point of view neurons in the corners and edges of the map have only a limited neighborhood. They have fewer neighbors than neurons in the center of the net. This leads to defects in the topology preservation of the mapping in these areas and apparently it appears an attraction of the edges. We often find the best matches to the training set along there and at the corners of the grid. To avoid this effect we view the rows and columns of the rectangular grid as circles – which is a simplification of projecting the map onto the surface of a sphere. Now each neuron always owns a complete neighborhood: Two distances vertically and two distances horizontally between each two neurons of the grid. From these distances we use the smaller one to calculate the weight adaptation. This results in a better preservation of neighborhood relations of the input space as before. However, we have to regard that the left and right border of the map are adjacent as well as the upper and lower border and the four corners which makes the algorithm a bit more complex.

Let $r_{ix} = [0, MAX - 1]$ the x-coordinate of unit i and r_{cx} the x-coordinate of the best matching unit c.

$$d_1 = |r_{cx} - r_{ix}|$$

$$if (r_{cx} - r_{ix} \leq 0)$$

$$d_2 = MAX + r_{ix} - r_{cx}$$

$$else$$

$$d_2 = MAX - r_{ix} + r_{cx}$$

$$d_{cix} = \min(d_1, d_2)$$

$$dist_{ci} = \sqrt{d_{cix}^2 + d_{ciy}^2}$$

The following graphic shows a 20×20 map of our example in chapter 2: First we see the rectangular output space and below our quasi-spherical output space. Units are labeled with the name of a path when their weight vector deviates by less than 20 percent from the feature vector.

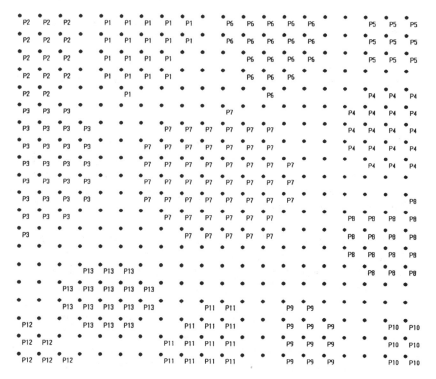

Figure 2: A map of our example with a rectangular output space.

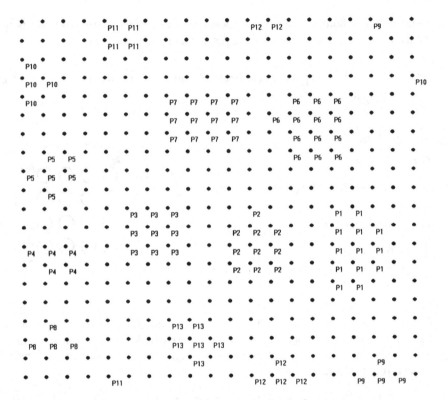

Figure 3: A map of our example with a quasi-spherical output space.

We can see that similar knowledge domains are represented adjacently in the map, e.g. **P2-P3**. Knowledge domains with disjoined context, like **P1-P13** or **P10-P13** are located far from each other.

Where does the adjacent representation of similar input vectors in the output space come from? With the adaptation of it's neighborhood a best matching unit c equalizes the weight vectors of the surrounding neurons to it's own weights. The neighbors of c now represent similar vectors with their weights. Therefore an input vector which is similar to that represented in c, i.e. both are neighboring in the input space, will likely find it's best match in one of c's neighbors.

But obviously there are also domains with disjoined context (**P5** and **P10**) close to each other in our map. This has two reasons. First, each projection into a lower-dimensional space necessarily creates neighborhood relations, which did not exist in the higher-dimensional space. However, the Kohonen-algorithm preserves the most important neighborhood relations. The second reason is the distance measurement between two vectors. With the values *TRUE* and *FALSE* for the feature vectors, the Kohonen-algorithm uses the hamming-distance between two vectors to measure their difference. Hamming-distance means, only such positions count different where one vector is *TRUE* and the other is *FALSE*. Therefore the algorithm treats the originally disjoined paths **P5** and **P10** as equal in the 12 positions marked *FALSE*, where both don't have a certain feature. We could try to avoid this and use a more complex formula than the Euclidean norm for identifying the best matching unit. But the previously mentioned projection problem would diminish the results.

Navigation within knowledge domains

The next step is to exploit the representation in order to find the closest related knowledge base to a given query. Using our trained neural map we assume that the information agent has to find information about *Conferences* for *Electronic Commerce*. Therefore we create a feature vector for this query:

$$\mathbf{Q}(0,0,0,0,0,1,0,0,0,0,0,0,0,0,0,1,0).$$

We provide the feature vector **Q** as input for the SOM and expect that it will arrange the vector between those knowledge domains that contain the desired information, i.e. that this input will activate a neuron which lies topologically in-between the representatives of the most similar context. For testing a vector against the map we only search for the best matching unit with the above described formula and do not adapt any weights. The query **Q** finds its best representation near the cluster for **P6**. **P6** describes the context *Business & Economy* → *Electronic Commerce* → *Conferences*.

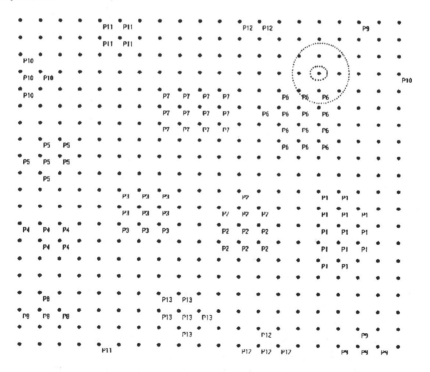

Figure 4: The maps answer for Q. In the inner circle is the activated neuron shown. The outer circle is the search radius for the representative of a path.

As expected, path **P6** contains the closest context to our question. Because in the query it was not asked for *Business & Economy*, the activated neuron is not the center of cluster **P6**. Another query might be to find information about *Conferences* on *Databases*. The feature vector describing this query is

$$Q_2(0,0,0,0,0,0,0,0,0,0,0,0,0,0,0,0,1,1).$$

This input yields the answer **P6** and **P10** from the map. In the example we have no relation between domains containing *Conferences* and *Databases*. For our map the context is disjoined. We also note, that to obtain an answer from the map we have to use a search radius around the best matching unit. The selected radius is merely arbitrary, but the farther away a cluster representative from the activated neuron is, the less is the semantical similarity. For the information agent this means that the

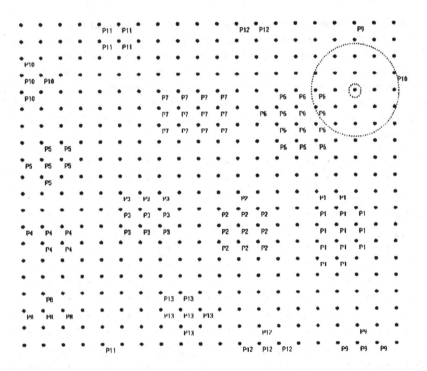

Figure 5: The maps answer on Q₂. We have to increase the search radius to find a representative for a path.

farther removed domains (here Yahoos categories) are less likely contain useful information for his task.

In a last example we look for all information about conferences. Aware of synonyms within the set of designators for the categories, we use a thesaurus to prepare the feature vector for the query Q_3. The feature vector contains questions for *Conventions & Conferences*, *Conferences* and *Events*.

Q₃(0,0,0,0,1,0,1,0,0,1,0,0,0,0,0,1,0,)

yields the answer **P4**. In fact, the category *Conventions & Conferences₂* derived from *Conventions & Conferences₁* in *Business & Economy* (**P4**) contains the most information about conferences.

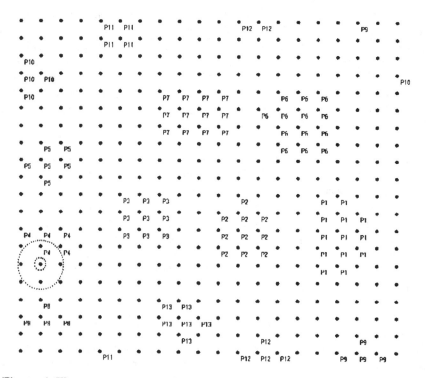

Figure 6: The maps answer on Q3.

Obviously, we did not use the information provided by the hierarchical structure. Instead we only identify paths along the hierarchy and view them as knowledge domains. While the usage of the hierarchy information might have improved the results in some places, we have to be aware of information sources, which are not able to organize their data in this way. Our approach is independent from Yahoos specific structure. To build a semantical map of knowledge bases we only need the description of their data by semantical features. A second application demonstrates this.

Yahoo's classification of categories can not be analyzed automatically. To some extend, the automatic recognition of semantical properties of web pages becomes possible with XML. XML (Extensible Markup Language) is a new improvement on the well-known HTML, the HyperText Markup Language [23,24]. XML introduces a great variety of highly specialized tags. There are special tags for advertisement pages, for forms and so on. Because of this specialization the tags used in a page can be viewed as semantic features of this page. Therefore they describe the semantic content of the page. We could use the set of XML-tags a page consists of and create a feature vector for this site. The dimension of this feature vector equals the cardinality of the tag set. The tag set is defined by a common vocabulary (called profile) the pages share. A self-organizing map trained with a number of these feature vectors will show the semantic similarities of these pages. Additionally, it can also be a navigation base for information agents, which want to visit advertisement sites, for instance.

Unlike other reported applications of SOM's in Information Retrieval, in both described examples we did not aim for a semantical analysis of information and information sources. Instead, we assume the semantics as defined by the features and known. In our Yahoo-example the semantical categorization is manually done with the sorting of sites into categories. For XML-pages the author defines the semantics by using specific tags. With these predefined semantics we map the similarities of objects in a SOM. Our goal is the logical classification of queries into known context of knowledge bases.

There are several questions with our approach we have not yet discussed. First, where do we obtain the data for generating the feature vectors? Supposing we know not more than the location of the information sources. The agents have to go unguided and search for information. When visiting a knowledge base they should not only look for data matching their specific query. Additionally they should retrieve the semantic closure of the knowledge base and with this information complete our own knowledge. This will doubtless require more complex agents. However, after obtaining a satisfying knowledge about the information sources, we can use leaner agents.

Therefore, our approach is suitable for systems of cooperating agents. The acquisition of semantical information about knowledge bases can be shared between agents. Their agency collects and incorporates the knowledge. The acquired knowledge then is available for all agents with the Semantic Navigation Map. Later on, agents can exclusively use this map and do not have to collect knowledge about information sources themselves.

Another problem is the dynamic of the information sources. The training of the map takes a considerable amount of time. So we do not want to rebuild the map when a new information source appears. To solve this problem we tried to train the new vector into an existing map. Therefore we present the new vector a few times to the map. The neighborhood kernel for the winning unit covers the whole map. We choose a relatively small learning rate. Furthermore, we adapt only neurons which are already very similar to the winning unit, e.g. if the weight vectors deviate by less than 15 percent. This procedure moves the already best matching part of the map in the direction of the new vector and leaves the representatives of the other vectors unaffected. Following, we make a fine-tuning of the map. We present all vectors to the map for a much longer training time. In this training we choose a very small learning rate and a neighborhood kernel affecting only adjacent units. With this method we achieved good results. Although for consistency reasons it is recommendable to rebuild the whole map after a number of such additions. Following

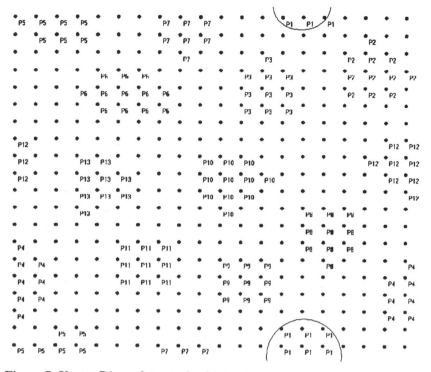

Figure 7: Vector P1 was later trained into the map.

is a map of our example shown where we added the vector *Business & Economy→Companies→Computer* to the trained map. For comparison purpose, below a map which was trained with all 13 vectors.

More often than the appearance of a new information source, an increase of the semantic closure might happen. This means, our map has to cover more different contexts. This results in new dimensions for the feature vectors. Unfortunately, in this case we have to rebuild the map with the completed feature vectors. Here we will use the approach of Merkl [14], who proposes hierarchical feature maps. The speed up for the learning process with this method is even more welcomed, because in the problem scope of knowledge bases we have to handle vectors with a very high dimensionality.

Related work

There are several efforts in applying Kohonen maps in Information Retrieval reported. Lin, Soergel, Marchionini [28] and Cottrell, de Bodt [27] have used SOM's for the semantical classification to avoid misleading interpretations. In contrast to their approaches, we assume a set of knowledge domains whose context is well defined. We expect no misleading interpretation because of the clear semantic of the context designators. Therefore we do not aim for a semantical classification of these

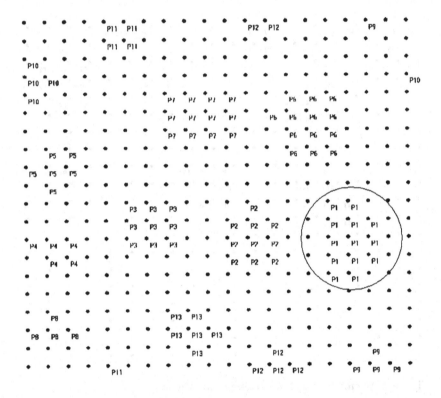

Figure 8: Vector P1 was from the beginning in the training set for the map.

knowledge domains or their underlying information sources. Instead we map their semantic relations and classify queries to the appropriate knowledge domain.

Ritter and Kohonen [5] described a method for the semantical classification of words by their surrounding context. Honkela, Pulkki, Kohonen [2] and Honkela, Kaski, Lagus, Kohonen [3] applied this technique for the classification of words out of natural language texts. The former used the texts of Grimm tales while the latter chose Usenet postings. In all three reports information is retrieved from natural language sentences. We assume that the key words, the designators, are known and emphasize on the mapping of the semantical relations of contexts.

Merkl[15,17] and Merkl, Schweighofer [14] have used hierarchical feature maps for the semantical classification of texts in the domain of international law. Their goal is supporting human readers in the text exploration while we aim for a navigation base to support information agents.

Conclusion

We have proposed a method, which allows to identify information sources for a certain query on the base of their semantical similarity. We used therefore self-organizing feature maps, a special architecture of artificial neural networks. The crucial feature for our purpose is the preservation of topological relationships of a multi-dimensional input space in the projection to a planar map. We showed the application of this method as navigation base for information agents. The semantic comparison between a query and the map answers the question, which knowledge base most likely contains information related to the query. Our approach has several advantages. The map is self-organizing, which means the neural network automatically approximates the problem scope. The map learns unsupervised. Once the map is trained we achieve a very good response time. An alternative to this approach would be the partial or full integration of the knowledge bases schemas. The problems of the integration might be comparable to the maintaining of a map. However, identifying problem related information sources is much more difficult within an integrated global schema than with the semantic map [18,19].

Our approach supports the cooperation of information agents with the navigation map as a shared knowledge base. Agents have to collect knowledge about the semantic closure of information sources. They have to share this knowledge in order to create an extensive map. Each agent contributes with his knowledge about the sites that he visited. Therefore, the total amount of information sources an agent has to visit is highly reduced. Later on, leaner agents can benefit from this work, because they can start their information retrieval at the most promising site. A Semantic Navigation Map promotes the cooperation of information agents with the availability and preparation of acquired knowledge for all agents.

In general, our approach supports the search for semantic similarities in any loosely coupled system where the individual parts can be described and thus compared by semantical features. So far, the description of the involved systems based usually on structural information. Information retrieval had to rely on structural similarities or human interaction. With the completion of the distribution schema on the logical part by semantic maps, we can achieve a distinct improvement in automatic, context related information retrieval.

References

[1] T. Kohonen: *Self-organizing maps*, Springer-Verlag 1997.

[2] T. Honkela, V. Pulkki, T. Kohonen: *Contextual Relations of Words in Grimm Tales, Analyzed by Self-Organizing Map*, in: F. Fogelman-Soulie, P. Gallinari: Proc. of the Int'l. Conf. on Artificial Neural Networks, ICANN-95, EC2 et Cie, pp. 3-7, Paris 1995.

[3]   T. Honkela, S. Kaski, K. Lagus, T. Kohonen: *Newsgroup Exploration with WEBSOM Method and Browsing Interface*, Helsinki Univ. of Technology, Faculty of Information Technology, Report A32, Jan. 1996.

[4]   SOM_PAK *The Self-Organizing Map Program Package*, Version 3.1 (April 7 1995). ftp://cochlea.hut.fi/pub/som_pak

[5]   H. Ritter, T. Kohonen: *Self-Organizing Semantic Maps*, Biological Cybernetics, Vol. 61, 1989.

[6]   H. Ritter, T. Martinez, K. Schulten: *Neural Computation and Self-Organizing Maps: An Introduction*, Reading, MA: Addison-Wesley, 1992.

[7]   S. Haykin: *Neural Networks. A Comprehensive Foundation*, Macmillan College Publishing Company Inc., 1994.

[8]   T. Kohonen: *Self-Organization and Associative Memory*, 3rd ed., Springer-Verlag, 1989.

[9]   H.-U. Bauer, Th. Villmann: *Growing a Hypercubical Output Space in a Self-Organizing Feature Map*, Int'l. Computer Science Institute, Berkeley, California 1995.

[10] B. Fritzke: *Growing Cell Structures – a self-organizing neural network model* (in German), PhD-Thesis, Erlangen 1992.

[11] B. Fritzke: *Unsupervised clustering with growing cell structures*, Proc. IJCNN-91, Vol. II, pp. 531-536, Seattle, 1991.

[12] B. Fritzke: *Growing Grid – a self-organizing network with constant neighborhood range and adaption strength*, in: Neural Processing Letters, Vol. 2, No. 5, pp. 9-13, 1995.

[13] D. Merkl, A Min Tjoa, G. Kappel: *A Self-Organizing Map that Learns the Semantic Similarity of Reusable Software Components*, in: Proc. of the 5th Australian Conf. on Neural Networks (ACNN'94), pp. 13-16, Brisbane, Australia, 1994.

[14] D. Merkl, E. Schweighofer: *The Exploration of Legal Text Corpora with Hierarchical Neural Networks: A Guided Tour in Public International Law*, in: Proc. of the Int'l. Conf. of Artificial Intelligence and Law (ICAIL'97), Melbourne, ACM Press, 1997.

[15] D. Merkl: *Exploration of Text Collections with Hierarchical Feature Maps*, in: 20th Annual Int'l. ACM SIGIR Conf. on Research and Development in Information Retrieval (SIGIR'97), Philadelphia 1997.

[16] D. Merkl: *Self-Organizing Maps and Software Reuse*, in: W. Pedrycz, J. F. Peters: Computational Intelligence in Software Engineering, World Scientific, Singapore 1998.

[17] D. Merkl: *Content-Based Software Classification by Self-Organization*, Proc. of the IEEE Int'l. Conf. on Neural Networks (ICNN'95), Perth, Australia, Nov. 1995.

[18] Y. Chen, W. Benn: *A Systematic Method for Query Evaluation in Federated Relational Databases*, in: A. Hameurlain, A. Min Tjoa: Database and Expert Systems Applications, 8th Int'l. Conf., DEXA '97, Toulouse, France, Springer-Verlag, 1997.

[19] Y. Chen, W. Benn: *Building DD to Support Query Processing in Federated Databases*, 4th Int'l Workshop on Knowledge Representation Meets Databases at the Int'l. Conf. on VLDB, Athens, Greece: IEEE, Aug. 1997.

[20] Y. Chen, W. Benn: *Rule-based technology for schema transformation*, in: Proc. of 2nd Int'l, Conf. on Cooperative Information Systems, Charleston, South Carolina, USA, June 1997.

[21] Y. Chen, W. Benn: *A Systematic Method for Evaluating Queries in Federated Database Systems*, Technical Report/CS-97-03, Department of Computer Science, Univ. of Technology Chemnitz, Germany, 1997.

[22] T. J. M. Bench-Capon: *Why Database AND Expert Systems Applications?* In: A. Hameurlain, A Min Tjoa: Database and Expert Systems Applications, 8th Int'l. Conf., DEXA '97, Toulouse, France, Springer-Verlag, 1997.

[23] World Wide Web Consortium: *Extensible Markup Language (XML) Version 1.0*. http://www.w3.org/TR/PR-xml-971208

[24] *The XML FAQ*. http://www.ucc.ie/xml/

[25] P. Maes: *Agents that can reduce work and information overload*, ACM Communications Vol. 73 (7), 1994.

[26] X. Wu, T. Ichikawa: *KDA: A knowledge-based database agent with a query guiding facility*, IEEE Transactions on Knowledge and Data Engineering Vol. 4 (5), 1992.

[27] M. Cottrell, E. de Bodt: *A Kohonen map representation to avoid misleading interpretations*, Proc. of the Europ. Symposium on Artificial Neural Networks (ESANN'96), Brugge, Belgium, 1996.

[28] X. Lin, D. Soergel, G. Marchionini: *A self-organizing semantic map for information retrieval*, Proc. Int'l. Conf. on Research and Development in Information Retrieval, Chicago, IL, 1991.

Coordination Patterns of Mobile Information Agents

Robert Tolksdorf

Technische Universität Berlin, Fachbereich Informatik, FLP/KIT, Sekr. FR 6–10,
Franklinstr. 28/29, D-10587 Berlin, Germany,
mailto:tolk@cs.tu-berlin.de, *http://www.cs.tu-berlin.de/~tolk/*

Abstract. Mobility is a mechanism to manage accessibility dependencies amongst agents. As such, it is a coordination mechanism in the interaction of agents, users, and information.

The Linda-like coordination language *Mobile Object Spaces* is used to express coordination of entities. It supports the basic operations for coordination by mobility as primitives.

Higher order coordination structures can be captured as *coordination patterns* that describe reoccuring building blocks. We present a template for the description of such patterns and describe some very simple coordination patterns in the area of mobility and information systems.

1 Introduction

Coordination is a phenomenon which pervades our daily life and work. If we are well organized, coordination is invisible and only its absence reveals the necessity for coordinative action. Uncoordinated situations lead to noticeable chaos and to failures of work. Coordination is embodied in human interaction, such as in a discussion where only one participant speaks at a time, in the design of organizations by prescribing workflows, or in computing systems by mechanisms in parallel and distributed computations such as scheduling, locking etc.

The currently most accepted definition of coordination is from Malone and Crowston, 1994:

Coordination is managing dependencies between activities.

We use this definition in the following, as it seems most useful in that it abstracts from the actors involved, from goals they might have and from the kind of dependencies involved. Also it established coordination as an activity of its own right.

The management of dependencies is a complex task that cannot be described by a handful of primitive coordination operations. The structure of such complex coordination activities is of interest, as they are solutions to coordination problems. We could hope to reuse such solutions in different contexts.

In object-oriented programming, the notion of *patterns* has become very popular in recent years. It has been discovered that inheritance alone is not sufficient to express the structure of object-oriented applications and their implementations. This has led to the development of generic software architectures as object-oriented *frameworks* (Johnson, 1997) and of *design patterns* (Gamma et al., 1995) describing known ways to design solutions to related problems in the implementation of software components.

We propose to explore to use a similar approach and to target at the discovery of reoccuring structures of management of dependencies. We see the notion of *coordination patterns* as an attempt to study in an interdisciplinary manner reoccuring and reusable structures of management of dependencies in organizations, economy, and computing systems, etc.

Such patterns can be grouped around common characteristics of interest, that we call *aspects*. In this paper, we will focus on one aspect, namely *mobility* of information, agents, and users. We will look closer at this aspect wrt. coordination and try to detect some simple patterns of coordination.

This paper is organized as follows. In section 2 we look closer at mobility as a coordination mechanism and classify entities of interest. In section 3 we describe the coordination language that we will use for coordination patterns and how its primitives describe mobility of entities of interest. Section 4 is our attempt to describe some higher level coordination patterns that deal with the aspect of mobility. We give pointers to related work in section 5 and conclude in section 6.

2 Mobility in Information Systems

Sources for coordination patterns can be *fields* that are defined by some common context. For example, economics are a field to find coordination patterns. Economics has longly studied auctions as mechanisms to settle prices and to decide on the distribution of some goods. Several kinds of auctions with different characteristics are known and can all be understood as coordination patterns which manage resource dependencies.

Another way to find coordination patterns is by *aspects* which are characteristics that reoccur in different contexts. Mobility is one such aspect of agent and object systems that has attracted high interest recently. The widespread availability of enabling technology for mobile agents and objects – the Internet and Java – has led to a large number of prototypes for mobile agent systems.

It is hoped that applications in the areas of data mining, electronic commerce, and system administration – especially in the field of telecommunication networks – will demonstrate the usefulness of the mobility approach (Milojicic et al., 1996).

Aside from exploring the technical fascination of being able to migrate live agents and objects, we believe that understanding mobility as a mechanism of *coordination* could provide a clearer view on possible applications. Mobility is not a unique characteristic of agents – it is a more natural (and older) characteristic of users and of information.

2.1 Mobility as a Coordination Mechanism

The emerging field of *coordination theory* is characterized as an interdisciplinary enterprise to study how coordination can occur in different kinds of systems. Disciplines involved include computer science, organization theory, management sciences, economics, linguistics, and psychology (Malone and Crowston, 1994). The effort of establishing a separate field is motivated by the observation that the phenomenon *coordination* is apparent in all of these disciplines. It is hoped that the transfer of ideas on coordination amongst them leads to a better understanding of coordination fundamentals and to new ideas in the respective disciplines.

Work in coordination theory has led to a number of studies which aim at identifying categories of coordination processes and management options (Crowston, 1991). The sources for the detection of such processes include computer science, organization theory, management sciences, economics, linguistics, and psychology.

In Dellarocas, 1996 *"accessibility dependency"* is identified as a dependency in resource flows, that states simply that produced resources must be made accessible to users. The placement or movement of activities, and the transport of resources is identified as the basic coordination mechanisms, i.e. the alternatives to manage an accessibility dependency.

The placement of activity in a computing system means configuration, whereas the movement of activities at runtime is the coordination mechanism of central interest in the field of mobile agents and objects.

Transport of passive resources is obviously at the heart of communication based systems. In addition, this activity can also manage a second dependency as it allows for the synchronization on the availability of some data. In coordination theory, this dependency is called *"prerequisite"* dependency meaning that the start of some activity depends on the presence of some result of some other activity.

In the following we will use a coordination language from the Linda family (Gelernter and Carriero, 1992) to express mobility of agents and data. Coordination languages are unique wrt. the dependencies managed as they contain primitive operations that communicate and synchronize processes with data in one operation.

We consider the migration of data or agents from a source to a destination as a primitive coordination mechanism. When aiming at real applications, the question is how to combine such primitives in a useful way. In order to facilitate easy construction of applications with mobile agents, it seems necessary to record such useful combinations as *reusable* higher order structures.

This need has been recognized in the field of object-oriented design as *patterns* (Gamma et al., 1995). The work there has spread to different areas such as object-oriented analysis (Fowler, 1997), or organizational patterns.

In this paper we try to discover some patterns that rely on some mobility mechanism in information systems. As we understand mobility as a means to manage accessibility dependencies, we call them *coordination patterns*.

2.2 Mobile Entities

The notion of mobility can be applied to different classes of entities in information systems. We distinguish passive but mobile information, active and mobile agents, and mobile human users.

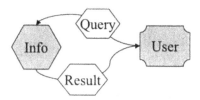

Fig. 1. Moving information

Mobility of information is the very basic requirement to exchange knowledge amongst users, systems, and agents and synonymous to communication. Figure 1 shows this basic kind of interaction: A query is moved from the user to an information source and answered with a result information. In the case of the information source, the result moved to the agent usually is a copy of the information available at the information source.

This pattern of mobility of information is basic for distributed systems that follow a client/server style of interaction. It is the usual way that people access information systems like the Web, Gopher, or databases.

Mobile agent technology introduces the notion of moving an active entity over spatial different places. Such an agent maintains a state across movements and thereby is sort of an active container for mobile information.

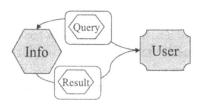

Fig. 2. A mobile agent

Figure 2 shows the classic scenario to demonstrate the benefits of mobile agent technology. Here, an agent is sent to an information source together with a query. The agent can actively interact with the information source, eg. to refine the query. The scenario exhibits a reduced communication load as the interaction occurs at the same place.

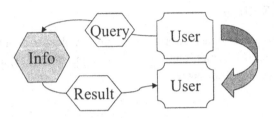

Fig. 3. A mobile user

The ultimate client of information access is the human user who has some information need that shall be satisfied at least in part by using an information system. Considering mobility and information systems has to include *mobility of users.*

Mobility of human users is a given fact. Currently, however, users remain rather stationary with respect to their use of information systems. They are online at some workstation or terminal. However, current technology already indicates that mobility of users will be important in the future. Examples for mobile users are usually given in terms of highly active information managers whose main activity seems to be moving between meetings etc. Two scenarios seem reasonable:

- *The user is relative stationary towards a mobile device.* This includes all well known examples of using mobile telecommunication devices like mobile phones etc.
- *The user is mobile in relation to access devices.* This includes examples of users changing devices with different capabilities – like moving from an ASCII-terminal to a color-workstation – or different location – like moving from the office-terminal to the home.

The first category seems not interesting in our context, as the technology of mobile devices aims centrally at masking the spatial transfer of the device.

The observation of patterns wrt. computing systems usually includes some sample code for demonstration. The following section describes the language we will use for this purpose.

3 A Coordination Language for Mobility

As stated in the introduction, coordination languages from the Linda family are especially interesting to study the implementation and the support of coordination processes. Of specific importance for information systems is that these languages are able to support interaction with multiple information sources, whereas client/server is bound to a two-party interaction.

3.1 Mobile Object Spaces

We define the following coordination model called *Mobile Object Spaces* which is an object oriented Linda (Gelernter and Carriero, 1992) variant implemented in Java.

In Mobile Object Spaces (MOS) we introduce a set of related types of objects. The types of main interest describe multiset collections of elements with different functionalities used as coordination media. These multisets are central to this kind of coordination language. The language itself is given by the definition of the coordination medium, the elements used therein and a set of operations for its manipulation (Ciancarini, 1996).

As in Linda, elements in multisets are accessed associatively. That is, a *matching* relation is defined on objects and object templates. Reading from the multiset is relative to a template that describes what kind of object is sought. It results in one element that fulfills the matching relation.

The definition of the matching relation depends on the kind of object inspected. In MOS, we define a type *Matchable* that is implemented by classes that define an operation *boolean match(Entry o)*. We define a type *Entry* which is basically an empty type used to denote classes that can be stored in a multiset. Thus, tuples as in Linda are one implementation of entries and the matching relation of Linda is implemented by the *match* method in a *Template* class that implements *Matchable*.

Objects of type *Databag* are collections of communicable data. A Databag offers operations for adding, copying and retrieving entries. It is functional in that no notion of processes is introduced. The operations of a Databag are:

- *void out(Entry d)*: An entry is stored in the databag, that is, the entry *d* is cloned at the Databag.
- *Entry inp(Matchable t)*: An entry matching *t* is sought in the databag and retrieved. If none can be found, a bottom element *null* is returned instead. Retrieval means to remove the data object from the databag and thereby moving the found entry to the client.
- *Entry rdp(Matchable t)*: An entry matching *t* is sought in the databag and a copy of it is returned. If none can be found, a bottom element *null* is returned instead. The found entry is cloned at the client.

The type *Objectbag* is a subtype of *Databag*. It introduces a notion of processes that can be blocked and resumed. It adds the following operations:

- *Entry in(Matchable t)*: An entry matching *t* is sought in the objectbag and retrieved. If none can be found, the process executing *in* is blocked, until a matching entry is available. Its execution then is resumed with the retrieval of the matching object which moves it to the client.
- *Entry rd(Matchable t)*: An entry matching *t* is sought in the objectbag and a copy of it is returned. The found entry thus is cloned at the client. Similar to *in*, the operation is blocking.

The type *Objectbag* is not functional, as the execution of operations for reading and writing can overlap. MOS does not define any precedence in the case of race conditions – all necessary decisions are taken nondeterministically.

Objects of type *Agentbag* are collections of agents. An agentbag thus is an environment in which active resources execute. It subtypes *Objectbag* and introduces the notion of starting, stopping and copying a process.

In order to refer to processes and locations therein, we introduce two types. *Future* describes a process which, when evaluated, becomes an entry (see also Jensen, 1993). Thus a future is the target of process creation. Within such a process, a *Continuation* represents a place of execution at which the evaluation of the future can be stopped and resumed.

With these, the agentbag type is characterized by the following additional operations:

- *void eval(Future future)*: The agentbag evaluates the active resource *future* to an entry. It is stored in the state of the agentbag (see below).
- *void move(Agentbag destination, Continuation continuation)*: An agent executing the operation at the agentbag it is executed in (see below) is stopped, moved to *destination* and continued there at *continuation*.

Depending on how they use objects of the named classes, we can classify objects. *Clients* are processes that use a databag or an objectbag. *Agents* are clients that implement an objectbag as their state and can be used by clients. *Hosts* are agents that implement an agentbag. Each agent has exactly one host. *Nodes* are hosting a host. Nodes are not hosted.

With these, we have a model which follows the agent/place distinction usually applied in mobile agent systems, but are able to understand an agent also as a place – in our terminology as a host.

3.2 A MOS Implementation with Java

For experiments, we have designed a simple implementation of MOS in Java. The types of objects that are represented as Java interfaces. They are implemented by objects from certain classes. In our Java implementation we define a set of respective classes that implement the named interfaces.

- *DataSpace*: An implementation of *Databag*.
- *ObjectSpace*: An implementation of *Objectbag*. It contains a *Databag* plus information about currently blocked operations. An *ObjectSpace* is an *Agent*.
- *AgentSpace*: An implementation of an *Agentbag*. It contains an *Objectbag* and a set of processes that execute active entities.

For *Client*, *Agent*, and *Host* we provide a set of abstract classes to be implemented by application objects.

While Java includes an easy to use thread model, the grain size of referring to places within code is that of individual methods. Thus, continuations cannot be used to refer to arbitrary locations in the code. This technical detail does not change the model implemented and is open to changes in future Java versions.

Our classes do also implement the Java specific type *Remote* which allows objects at distant locations to invoke their methods by Javas Remote Method Invocation mechanism RMI. In part they implement the type *Serializable* which makes them exchangeable amongst virtual Java machines.

Each entity in MOS is at a certain location. A location can be logical or physical locality and is denoted by a unique name as a URL. The following rules apply. The logical location of a node equals its physical location. An agent can have a logical location within a host. The physical location of an agent is the physical location of its host. Each resource is located within another resource.

The locality of entities is embedded in *references* to clients and agents executed at some host. These references are matchable objects and thus can be stored in dataspaces. Matching is defined as substring inclusion within the name of the reference.

On each node a MOS environment runs. It includes the top level agent which is the host for all other agents on this node. Also, it includes a special agent, called the *registry* whose state is a collection of references running on that host. The registry is changed by *eval*, *move*, and the termination of an agent.

3.3   Coordinating Mobility in MOS

In section 2 we described mobility as a coordination issue and differentiated between different classes of mobile entities in section 2.2. The previous section presented MOS as a coordination language for experiments. In this section we describe how the different entities are coordinated wrt. mobility in MOS.

Mobility of information is embodied in the MOS coordination model as primitives. Using the operations inherited from Linda, we can move information i to an agent a with $a.out(i)$, copy information matching j from agent a by $a.rdp(j)$, and move information matching j from agent a by $a.inp(j)$. These are the operations that characterize the type *Databag* as described above.

We also find operations to coordinate with the presence of information at a certain location with the Linda primitives as follows:

- We can manage prerequisite dependencies by synchronizing with the presence of information matching j at an agent a with $a.rd(j)$.
- We can coordinate exclusively with the presence of information matching j at an agent a with $a.in(j)$.

In MOS, these primitives characterize the type *Objectbag*.

To move agents with MOS, we declare a class *Future* which instantiates to object that can be evaluated. The respective operations to transfer such a future are to move future f to host a with $a.out(f)$, to execute the evaluation of future f within host a with $a.eval(f)$, or agent a can move from its host h to host i continuing at c with $h.move(i,c)$. In MOS, i has to fulfill the type *Agentbag*.

To coordinate with other agents at locations, we can use the registry. Specifically, we can detect the presence of agents whose references match the partial reference r by $registry.rdp(r)$ or coordinate with the presence of an agent whose reference matches the partial reference r by $registry.rd(r)$.

To coordinate with user, we have to assume that human users are represented by some agent. Such an agent then has a locality and can be referenced. Coordinating with a human user thus is similar to coordinate with agents.

With MOS we have a language which captures actions that we consider primitive wrt. mobility by primitive operations. Our interest is on how such actions are combined and how reoccuring structures of such combinations can be captured as coordination patterns. This is the topic for the next section.

4 Simple Coordination Patterns

In the introduction we referred to the work on *patterns* in object-oriented programming which has established the well recognized notion of design patterns.

The initial focus on mining patterns of program design has been successfully broadened to other domains, such as object-oriented modeling with *analysis patterns* (Fowler, 1997). More recently, the notion of *organizational patterns* develops as an attempt to detect reoccuring and reusable structures in the design of organizations. Our proposal is to collect *patterns of coordination*.

The benefit of detecting coordination pattern is their reuse in different fields. For example, the family of auction patterns has been discovered in *market-oriented programming* as solutions to resource allocation problems and for service trading in distributed systems (see Wellman, 1995).

The goal of our work is to identify coordination patterns that use mobility mechanisms wrt. information, agents, and users. The aim is to find reoccuring structures and to collect them. The patterns could well be implemented as some higher order coordination operations, or as agents that execute them.

To describe patterns, we use a template as described in figure 4. The template is different from the ones used in object-oriented design which include forces, solution, and consequences. With this work, we start to experiment with the notion of *coordination* patterns. It is unclear whether they require the same structure as design patterns, thus we felt it justified to apply a different pattern template.

The most important difference is that we require a coordination pattern to state what kind of dependency it manages. We consider the ability to identify the kind of dependency as discriminating for coordination patterns.

The following subsections describe some simple patterns observed in information systems. The list is not complete at all and shall demonstrate our approach. It could serve as a basis for a coordination pattern catalog, or pattern system for coordination.

Pattern: Name

Also Known As

Other names for the pattern.

Intent

Rationale and intended use.

Motivation

A scenario of application.

Dependency Managed

The dependency managed by the coordination pattern.

Structure

An illustration of the entities involved.

Collaborations

How the entities involved interact.

Implementation

Implementation remarks.

Sample Code

An example for implementing the pattern. We use MOS as the implementation language here. The code only has to illustrate the idea, but does not have to be executable and complete.

Known Uses

Where the pattern can be found in application. The rule-of-three applies: There should be at least three distinct known applications to qualify as a pattern.

Related Patterns

Patterns related to the one described.

Fig. 4. The pattern template

4.1 Pulling Information from a Source

As stated in the introduction, moving information is the basic mechanism of communication in distributed systems. We describe it as a coordination pattern Pull as in figure 5.

4.2 Pushing Information to the User

Pull describes mobility that is initiated by the agent that has a query. The information copied and moved is valid at the time the result was generated, but not necessarily longer. A pattern where the transfer of information is initiated at the location of the information source is Push as described in figure 6.

Pattern: Pull

Also Known As

Query/Result, Client/Server

Intent

To transfer information from an information source to a client. The information has to be in a class described by a query.

Motivation

The information source has more information than the client.

Dependency Managed

Access dependency of client to information.

Structure

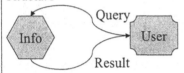

Collaborations

The client moves a query describing a class of information to an information source. The information source selects all information entities in the class and moves a copy to the client.

Sample Code

```
Id queryId=source.in(new Formal(new Id()));
source.out(queryId,query);
Result result=source.in(queryId, new Formal(new Result()));
```

Known Uses

SQL, Web-services, client-server interaction

Related Patterns

Push

Fig. 5. The pattern Pull

4.3 Copying Information to an Index

In Push and Pull the user interacts directly with the information source. This is not necessarily an efficient solution and can be enhanced by an intermediate Index as described in figure 7.

4.4 Visiting Places

In Index copying information to the index is done asynchronously with the access of the index. This might not be appropriate when a timely result is required, or

---

Pattern: Push

Intent

To transfer a stream of information from an information source to a client. The stream is initiated by an agent sent to the source.

Motivation

The information at the source is dynamic. It is not possible to transfer a complete result as an answer to a query.

Dependency Managed

Prerequisite dependency of client to presence of information.

Structure

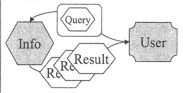

Collaborations

The client moves an agent containing a query to an information source. The agent monitors the source wrt. information entities in the class described by the query and moves copies continuously to the client.

Sample Code

```
source.eval(agent(q,self))

void agent(Query query, Reference dest) {
  do {
    Id queryId=source.in(new Formal(new Id()));
    source.out(queryId,query);
    Result result=source.in(queryId, new Formal(new Result()));
    dest.out(result);
  } while (true);
}
```

Known Uses

Databases, servlets, personalized information services, eg. URLminder, automated mailing-list systems, MBone.

Related Patterns

Pull

Fig. 6. The pattern Push

when queries have to be refined depending on intermediate results collected. In

Pattern: Index

Also Known As

Cache

Intent

To copy information from several information sources at a central and fast place. The place may transform the information, for example by indexing it, or just store it, for example as a cache.

Motivation

The information is of higher accessibility to the user when the information is moved to a fast source before a query is posed.

Dependency Managed

Accessibility dependency of client to information. Index partially manages the dependency by making the access more efficient in terms of interactions and transfer.

Structure

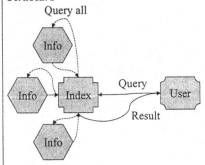

Collaborations

The index retrieves copies of information from several informations sources. It repeats it in intervals.

Sample Code

```
source1.eval(agent(q,self));
source2.eval(agent(q,self));
...
sourceN.eval(agent(q,self));
```

Known Uses

Web search engines, Web caches

Related Patterns

Push, Pull used to access the index and used to access sources.

Fig. 7. The pattern Index

figure 8 we describe the pattern Traveler in which a query or an agent passes by multiple information sources.

5 Related Work

Coordination technology recently started to demonstrate that its high level of abstraction is well suited to support mobility of information and agents (eg. in De Nicola et al., 1997). See Di Marzo Serugendo et al., 1998 for a comprehensive survey on theoretic models of mobile agents.

Freisleben and Kielmann, 1997 describe a simple coordination pattern, namely Master/Worker for parallel computing. Although older, Carriero and Gelernter, 1989 are even more ambitious in describing three patterns of coordination in parallel programming, namely result-, specialist- and agenda-parallelism.

The coordination language Bauhaus support mobility of processes with a *move* operation (Carriero et al., 1997). Processes are thereby able to navigate in a hierarchy of multisets in which they are executed as active entities.

The rich set of work on mobile agents – with the ancestor Telescript (White, 1997) – has focused very much on the technology involved and on finding useful applications for mobile agent systems. For the Aglets system, a set of templates has recently been proposed (Minami and Suzuku, 1997) which capture basic collaborative behaviors of mobile agents as plans. These templates include patterns like spreading a set of agents over places where they perform activities and join later.

6 Conclusion and Outlook

With this paper we tried to explore mobility as a coordination mechanism and to experiment with the notion of coordination patterns. We conclude that understanding mobility as a mechanism that manages dependencies can lead to a uniform model of communication, synchronization and mobility.

From the experiments with coordination patterns we conclude that their description leads to schemas of complex coordination activities above the level of coordination language primitives.

Resulting from this first effort is an agenda that starts with refining and evaluating the proposed template for coordination patterns. In this paper, we proposed a limited form of well known pattern templates and added a description of the dependency managed. It has to be explored whether this structure is sufficient.

Coordination patterns discovered have to be categorized. A first step to do this would be to introduce a classification of coordination goals and mechanisms. Work in coordination theory could provide the frame for such a classification.

We have to look at a broader variety of fields and aspects to find coordination patterns. In this paper, we described some experimental coordination patterns with the aspect mobility and information systems. Coordination, however, is a much broader phenomenon, so fields like auctions, voting, standardization etc. should be examined for coordination patterns.

Pattern: Traveler

Also Known As

Plan, Itinerary

Intent

To send out an autonomous agent that visits several information sources and adapts a query autonomously to the results received.

Motivation

The result is required to be of high timeliness or the query changes depending on partial results.

Dependency Managed

Access dependency for the user and prerequisite dependencies amongst partial results and refined queries.

Structure

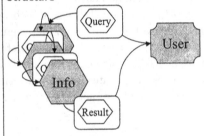

Collaborations

An agent or query is sent to an information source which passes it on to another source. The result is returned at the end to the user.

Sample Code

```
source1.eval(visitor(
 new Plan(source2, source3, self)));

void visitor(Plan plan) {
  Id queryId= in(new Formal(new Id()));
  out(queryId,query);
  result.updateWith(in(queryId,  new Formal(new Result())));
  query.updateOn(result);
  move(plan.next(), visitor);
}
```

Known Uses

Meta search engines, research prototypes of mobile agent systems

Fig. 8. The pattern Traveler

References

Carriero, N. and Gelernter, D. (1989). How to Write Parallel Programs: A Guide to the Perplexed. *ACM Computing Surveys*, 21(3):323–357.

Carriero, N., Gelernter, D., and Hupfer, S. (1997). Collaborative Applications Experience with the Bauhaus Coordination Language. In *Proceedings of the 30th Hawaiian International Conference of System Sciences, HICSS*. IEEE Press.

Ciancarini, P. (1996). Coordination Models and Languages as Software Integrators. *ACM Computing Surveys*, 28(2):300–302.

Crowston, K. G. (1991). *Towards a Coordination Cookbook: Recipes for Multi-Agent Action*. PhD thesis, Sloan School of Management, MIT. CCS TR# 128.

De Nicola, R., Ferrari, G. L., and Pugliese, R. (1997). Coordinating Mobile Agents via Blackboards and Access Rights. In Garlan, D. and Le Métayer, D., editors, *Coordination Languages and Models, Proceedings of COORDINATION '97*, LNCS 1282, pages 220–237. Springer.

Dellarocas, C. N. (1996). *A Coordination Perspective on Software Architecture: Towards a Design Handbook for Integrating Software Components*. PhD thesis, Massachusetts Institute of Technology.

Di Marzo Serugendo, G., Muhugusa, M., and Tschudin, C. F. (1998). A Survey of Theories for Mobile Agents. *World Wide Web*, 1.

Fowler, M. (1997). *Analysis Patterns*. Addison Wesley.

Freisleben, B. and Kielmann, T. (1997). Coordination patterns for parallel computing. In Garlan, D. and Le Métayer, D., editors, *Coordination Languages and Models, Proceedings of COORDINATION '97*, LNCS 1282, pages 414–417. Springer.

Gamma, E., Helm, R., Johnson, R., and Vlissides, J. (1995). *Design Patterns*. Addison-Wesley.

Gelernter, D. and Carriero, N. (1992). Coordination Languages and their Significance. *Communications of the ACM*, 35(2):97–107.

Jensen, K. K. (1993). *Towards a Multiple Tuple Space Model*. PhD thesis, Aalborg University.

Johnson, R. E. (1997). Frameworks = (Components + Patterns). *Communications of the ACM*, 40(10):39–42.

Malone, T. and Crowston, K. (1994). The Interdisciplinary Study of Coordination. *ACM Computing Surveys*, 26(1):87–119.

Milojicic, D. S., Bolinger, D., Zurko, M. E., and Mazer, M. S. (1996). Mobile Objects and Agents. Technical report, The Open Group Research Institute.

Minami, K. and Suzuku, T. (1997). JMT (Java-Based Moderator Templates) for Multi-Agent Planning. In *OOPSLA '97 Workshop Java-based Paradigms for Agent Facilities*.

Wellman, M. P. (1995). Market-oriented Programming: Some Early Lessons. In Clearwater, S. H., editor, *Market-Based Control: A Paradigm for Distributed Resource Allocation*. World Scientific.

White, J. E. (1997). Mobile Agents. In Bradshaw, J. M., editor, *Software Agents*, chapter 19, pages 437–472. MIT Press.

Mobile Information Agents
on the Web

Andreas Gehmeyr
Corporate Technology, Siemens AG
D–81730 München
tel: +49 89 636 51434 (fax: 53319)
Andreas.Gehmeyr@mchp.siemens.de

Jürgen Müller
Computer Science Institute, TU Freiberg
D–09596 Freiberg
tel: +49 3731 39 3116 (fax: 2645)
hjm@informatik.tu-freiberg.de

Albert Schappert
Public Networks, Siemens AG
D–81730 München
tel: +49 89 722 49866 (fax: 21650)
Albert.Schappert@oen.siemens.de

Abstract. Information acquisition from the distributed and rich resources of the World Wide Web is confronted with the following situation: there are only a few entry points for finding the right information, there is too much net traffic for information acquisition, and there is no coordination between different users.

This leads to the well known problems encountered when searching for information: there is a considerable delay time using search engines, the quality of the results is in general poor, it is difficult to access the appropriate information, and the overall costs for complete satisfaction of the user's needs are considerably high. Unfortunately, these problems will not diminish; the situation will even worsen due to the exponential growth of the number of users and the information available. Current approaches handling these drawbacks such as empowering search engines oder raising the bandwidth are not able to keep up.

In this paper we present a new design for distributed information systems using mobile agent techniques. Our approach overcomes the unbalanced structure of the WWW, reduces net traffic in this medium, supports automatic user grouping, information sharing and information space modeling.

Keywords: information agents, information retrieval, mobile agents, agent system design, information systems, user grouping, internet

1 Introduction

One of the central resources of modern economies is information. Information is increasingly becoming an important production factor which will amplify capital and work-force. Thus, activities for information processing (and covering the whole information life cycle) will be crucial for future prosperity. As a first step to support information processes we focus on information acquisition in modern information media like the Internet.

Precise and cost efficient search of required information is one of the major problems in the Internet today. Current retrieval support in the Internet is based on a few retrieval tools (search engines) which satisfy the information needs of many users. But the user has to examine manually the information sources in order to determine their value. Additionally, almost every user builds up his personal information space which is the basis of his personal workbench but which is almost never made public to other people. A solution to these problems or automated support of these activities could result in better information retrieval.

Problems The Internet as an information repository is characterized by distributed information sources and heterogeneous users. It has developed initial means to solve information acquisition tasks, but they are running or will run into severe problems. The situation today is characterized by centralized information sources like catalogues or search engines on one side offering access to the distributed original information. On the other side, single and distributed users are struggling to find the information they need. The granularity of both sides - huge and powerful search data repositories and single personal users - is very imbalanced. There are reasons for this situation but the dynamic development of the Internet will turn it into absurdity. This will be explained in the following.

Solutions The solution to the problems outlined above lie in the adaptation of the granularity on both sides. There is no alternative to decentralizing the access to Web resources. Decentralization can be achieved by specialized information providers focusing on certain issues and offering high–quality service. Users on the other side are forced into higher organization levels in order to reach those sources. Users might either use the service of information brokers or might organize themselves in order to become a considerable 'market force' in the electronic information marketplace.

Both sides will be supported by techniques for different fields of computer science. We propose the use and the combination of agent technology and information retrieval to group users automatically and to realize sophisticated information services.

In the project MIAOW (Mobile Information Agents on the Web) as a part of the InfoSphere project, we are combining well-known information retrieval-methods with concepts of distributed artificial intelligence, especially mobile agents, to make information retrieval more precise and cost-efficient. In our ap-

interests and the filtering of information at remote hosts. Sharing obtained information results in a more precise and cost-efficient retrieval. Dispatching mobile agents to remote hosts and processing information at these places reduces net traffic.

2 Problems

The Internet and the World Wide Web are becoming one of the most important information resources. More and more data are brought directly into that medium or are accessible via interfaces. This huge amount of information can be accessed by a small number of general purpose search programs. The number of active users is steadily increasing. So the situation can be characterized by an enormous number of independent users on one side and by a few powerful search machines as entry points to the information resources on the other.

This imbalance of the information market leads to several well known problems:

- there is a considerable delay in processing information queries
- retrieval quality is very poor
- found documents must be reevaluated by the user
- documents are fetched unneccessarily
- information searching uses up online time

Central information access Even before the WWW there was a need for supporting the user in finding usable information due to the lack of a built-in search component postulated for the design of progressive hypertext-systems (see [Halasz, 1987]). Several tools have been established to master a the global search for documents with miscellaneous topics . Today, common retrieval tools for the WWW are search engines (eg. Lycos, Altavista or Webcrawler) and WWW catalogues (eg. WWW Virtual Library).

Popular search engines receive millions of query requests every day. To offer this service they need high-performance hardware and huge harddisk capacity. To acquire information search engines use Internet robots (also known as softbots, wanderers or spiders). They automatically obtain information from web-servers, but are criticized for their production of about 20 percent of today's net traffic and for the poor quality of query results they deliver.

The client-server scheme for accessing search engines is too inflexible. If a network connection is down, users cannot query the search engine. Also, the results achieved by a search engine do almost nothing to help the end user shorten the time consuming process of separating useful from useless information. They are primarily used as an initial information source to find links that discuss desired topics and which may hold references to more related documents. One can suppose that soon search engines will no longer be able to handle the supply and demand of information on the Internet.

Specialized information processing On the other side of the information acquisition process there are single users. They formulate their information needs and contact information servers in order to satisfy these needs. Users profit from the small number of existing search engines, but they are not able to satisfy their information needs appropriately for several reasons:

- it is difficult to express information interests in standard boolean retrieval language
- each document must be retrieved by the user himself
- each document must be evaluated by the user himself

Users act on their own. There is no history of past sessions, there is no profile containing user preferences or background information on the different servers, and there is no interest matching or grouping.

Poor information quality The interaction between many heterogeneous users and few powerful programs over the Internet is naturally very simple (and it must be so). For instance, the average length of a query to major search engines lies between one and two words. Search engines cover the whole web, they are optimized for large numbers of transactions and small response times; aside from some catalogue services they do not offer sophisticated information services. So the retrieval results cannot be and are not of a high quality.

3 Solution

Since information will continue or even augment to be the central resource of economics, a solution to the problems mentioned above has to fulfill several criteria. It has

- to respect the open and distributed architecture of the Internet
- to provide a platform-independent integrability with existing systems and services
- to support a wide range of activities within information processing
- to automate routine tasks and to adapt to changing requirements
- to presume future development of the entire environment

To–date, our focus lies on information acquisition in an Internet environment, i.e. distributed information sources of highly variant quality. The solution we propose is based in the combination of **information retrieval techniques with mobile agent techniques**. The former handles the unstructured and inhomogeneous information itself, the latter matches the distributed and evolving environment. In the following additional aspects of this approach are discussed.

There are two aspects of our approach. First, it is able to improve the information retrieval right now. But second, it contains an inherent design for more sophisticated information systems which might lie in future development directions (and we suppose it will). So our discussion also presumes such aspects.

Decentralized and specialized information sources Decentralized search catalogues will be able to collect locally or thematically limited data. Universities or research institutions may offer their local resources to the public or industrial community; information providers may sell their information defined by specific topics to clients. We assume that the Web will move in that direction and tailor our solution to such a situation. There will be specific information servers for any kind of knowledge field. These servers will offer more intelligence to their customers. Especially, sophisticated information retrieval techniques and special services of the information providers will be available.

Information sharing Decentralization of information sources will force users into higher organizational structures on the other side. Information interest must be coordinated in order the keep the effort and the cost of information acquisition in an acceptable range. Users will cooperate and this cooperation must be supported automatically. And the information acquisition process will be highly automatic, since the customer has to concentrate more on value-adding activities than on primitive searching.

This situation satisfies the following criteria:

- it is naturally distributed
- it requires a complex interaction
- it is a very dynamic environment.

Thus it is predestinated for the application of agent technologies to solve the problems mentioned above. We follow an approach to combine mobile agent technologies and information retrieval and user grouping technologies.

User grouping

Users normally interact as single entities with the Internet as an information repository. This leads to unnecessary net load, to long response times of information servers, and to additional cost. We propose the grouping of users according to their information interest. Information interest might be expressed by user profiles as a annotated set of keywords describing their information needs. It might also consist in monitoring certain information providers or Internet sites.

Information retrieval techniques

The average query–size to search engines has a length of less than 2 words. This leads to the well known recall size of ten thousands of hits. It is impossible to view all this results. We propose to include a more detailed description of the user interest into the query. The vector–space model [Salton & McGill, 1983] from information retrieval offers a first approach to realize a higher sophisticated user model. In this model, a user interest or a document is represented by its keywords. The keywords are weighted (manually or automatically) according to their importance. Such a keyword builds a dimension in a vector–space. Now, a document is a point in that vector–space, according to its weighted keywords. To get the similarity between user interests, or between documents or between documents and interests, you've got to apply any similarity measure (e.g. the cosine of the angle between the two represented items) on that vector-space.

Query results can be refined at the information provider as an additional service and thus lead to higher retrieval quality.

Information gathering with agents

The final (pre–) processing of query results is normally done by the user on the client side. Due to poor retrieval quality this is tedious work, it costs a lot of time and net resources, since even unnecessary information must be fetched. We propose processing and valuating the data at the information provider. Specialized user agents know the interests of their user in detail and negotiate a value–adding service with the information provider. Such an additional service requires information processing on the server side (i.e. information retrieval or structuring or valuation). The agents pay for the service and return only the results (relevant data or excerpts) to the their user. Moreover, several users may be represented by one agent, sharing resources and cost.

Agents and the Internet

Agents became the basic technology of information gathering in the Internet [Cheong, 1996]. However, the use of the term agent is very broad and there is no standardization for the use of agent techniques. In the following the term agent will be characterized more closely and current approaches which use agents in the Internet will be discussed.

About agent characteristics

The question about what an agent is, has been discussed in the Distributed AI community for over twenty-five years without a generally accepted result. Our view on agents is based on two recent definitions:

The Franklin-Graesser definition is the essence of agency synthesized from a dozen recent definitions discussed in [Franklin & Graesser, 1996]:

An autonomous agent is a system situated within and as part of an environment that senses that environment and acts on it, over time, in pursuit of its own agenda and so as to effect what it senses in the future.

The definition of Jennings and Wooldridge [Wooldridge & Jennings, 1995] is currently one of the most widely used working definition and focuses on more precisely on the agents abilities. It essentially says:

An agent is a hardware or software-based computer system with the following properties:

- *autonomy*: agents operate without the direct intervention of humans or others, and have some kind of control over their actions and internal state;
- *social ability*: agents interact with other agents (and possibly humans) via some kind of agent-communication language;
- *reactivity*: agents perceive their environment and respond in a timely fashion to changes that occur in it;
- *pro-activeness*: agents do not simply act in response to their environment, they are able to exhibit goal-directed behavior by taking the initiative.

This definition also answers the question on the distinction between agents and objects in that agents go beyond objects on account of their minimal properties: autonomy, social ability, responsiveness and pro-activeness. Agents go far beyond objects if the *strong agency criteria* are used for their characterization. In that case agents have "believes, desires and intentions", or in other words, they are knowledge-based (believes), they are goal-directed (desires) and they follow plans (intentions) in order to reach their goals.

In addition to the properties presented above, we are interested in *mobile* agents, i.e. agents which are able to migrate from one computer to another one.

Information gathering with agents

Sycara et al. [Sycara *et al.*, 1996] [Sycara & Zeng, 1996] developed the RETSINA system which uses distributed intelligent agents for information retrieval tasks. These tasks involve

"..locating and accessing informations from various on-line information sources, resolving inconsistencies in the retrieved information, filtering away irrelevant or unwanted information, integrating information from heterogeneous information sources, and adapting over time to user4s information needs and the shape of the Infosphere".

Each user is associated with a personal agent (assistant), who collects, presents, refines and confirms information which is requested by its user. For this task the assistant contacts other agents distributed on different machines. They have different tasks like planning the information retrieval process, monitoring and result composition, and being responsible for special topics.

The main difference to our approach is, that all agents are stationary. The advantage of RETSINA is, that the user is disburdened by his assistant and that the different information retrieval subtasks can be processed in parallel by the respective agent.

Griswold [Griswold, 1996] presents a set of agents used for

"keeping an automatic eye on topics and sites of importance to the user, delivering information and alerting the user when developments require the users attention".

Though terms like "sends out a smart agent" or "agents will visit your book-marked sites" are used to describe the behavior of the information seeking agents, they are stationary. They use the local browser as a tool to analyze the book-marked sites of the user searching for keywords.

Etzioni and Weld gave in [Etzioni & Weld, 1995] an excellent characterization of intelligent agents on the Internet together with their tasks and techniques for their realization. Their consequence is that only the agent technology will be able to fulfill the ambitions tasks to be solved in automatically gathering "interesting" information from the net. Mobile agents that would actively roaming the Internet were (in 1995) tagged by the attribute "Fiction", though they mention the basic technology developed by General Magics Telescript. Our approach not only brings the fiction to reality, in combining advanced information retrieval technology with an agent oriented realization for information gathering, our prototype realizes essentially all aspects for Internet Softbots as discussed in their case study.

The currently perhaps best overview on intelligent information retrieval and information gathering systems is presented in [Oates et al., 1997]. Their cooperative information-gathering approach views the search for relevant information as a distributed problem-solving approach where several agents cooperate in order to reach a global goal, e.g. the update of a local environmental database. Their method is based on the usage of positive relationships between information pieces, while our approach focuses on overlaps of the search criteria.

4 Design

In a first prototype we developed a cooperative information retrieval based on mobile agents. It consists of two agent servers, different types of stationary agents (agents that remain on one server and that cannot be dispatched), one type of mobile agents (agents that could be dispatched), a graphical user-interface for management of agents and presentation of results and a database. It will contain the following features:

- Mobile agents that can dispatch to agent servers and filter information near or at the information source.
- Creation of agent groups based on similar user profiles
- Simple cooperative information retrieval within a group
- Presentation of results for groups of users based on the agent groups
- Local storage of results (links and documents) with relevance values for all groups in a local database
- Maintenance of the local database by agents (dead links, link changes, etc.)
- Access to information providers through agents

4.1 Design principles

We designed our system along the $\mathcal{AWIC}$ design method that has been reported in [Müller, 1997]. The $\mathcal{AWIC}$-method is a hybrid design method for multi agent systems and it is based on various software engineering ideas including strategies of simulation systems.

AWIC stands for *Agents, World, Interoperability,* and *Coordination.* The general idea is to fill the corresponding models in a sequence of iterations. Each iteration is followed by a cross-checking phase where the models are analyzed concerning consistency and over-specification. Here we will just briefly present the *AWIC*-models.

1. Identify the *agents* in your problem domain. Specify their tasks, perception, activities, world knowledge, and basic planning abilities.
2. Represent the *world* (environment) the agents will act in. Make sure that the activities defined in the agents can be performed and that general laws are provided which prevent the agents from acting harmfully.
3. Define the *interoperability* between the world and the agents. I.e. the action requests (from agent to world) and perceptual information (from world to agent).
4. Specify the agent *coordination* by means of agent-agent communication, extension of the planning abilities towards joint planning, and joint activities.

4.2 Design realization

Filling the *AWIC* models for the mobile information gathering task roughly results in the following considerations[1]:

A There will be four types of agents: The *Profile-Agent* who holds the search profile defined by the user. It is a mobile agent. The *Group-Agent* is a stationary agent responsible for grouping similar requests of Profile-Agents. The *Proxy-Agents* are mobile agents generated by the Group-Agents for searching tasks. The *Server Agent* is the representative of the agent server (see below).

W The world of the agents consists of the computer net (in our case the SIEMENS intra-net) including the agent server in that net. The agent server provides different services to the agent, which help them to fulfill their task. The services are provided by *Resource Facilitators, Interface Facilitators* and *Information Service Modules*[2]

I If the agent has been installed on an agent server, it operates in a sandbox realization of the servers information market place. Interactions with this part of his world are registration and unregistration activities as well as packing and sending requests when they are to leave the host. There are no direct interoperations with the net itself, though the agents know about the location of other agent servers.

---

[1] Due to space limitations only the catchwords may be presented. However, the different agent types and their interaction will be discussed more closely in the following sections
[2] Note that Facilitators do not match our agent characteristics. They only provide services on request. Thus they would take the role of passive objects in an OO-approach

$\mathcal{C}$ Cooperation between the agents are on the level of information exchange between agents being on an agent server at the same time. Further the Profile Agents have to negotiate with the Group Agents whether of not they could join an existing group.

In the following the different parts of the system will be deepened.

Parts of the prototype

The basic execution environment is the **agent server**. It is devoted to the management and control of the agents and its tasks are:

- creation of agents (interface facilitator)
- grouping of agents (group agent)
- modeling of the information space
- control over migration

The agent server offers an execution context that will provide agents with a uniform environment independent of the actual computer system on which they are executing. Also, it manages the dispatching and the reception of mobile agents, the communication between agents and the authentification. The representative of the agent server is the

Server-Agent This agents knows about all agents that are on the server. Agents who join the server have to register by specifying their agent types and their names. Other agents can address the server agent for getting these information. In addition, this agent can create new group agents or remove them and profile agents by request.

Profile-Agent This agent type will be created by the user and it will use the profile of a user to search for information. It has the ability to dispatch to different agent servers. When being started it will dispatch at first to the agent server. At this server it will look for agents with similar profiles by addressing group agents which will hold the profiles for a group of agents and comparing the profiles with its own one. It joins the group which fits best the user's interests. If more groups are found, it can clone itself and join several groups. If no similar profiles will be found, it will address the server agent for creating a new group and will give the user profile to the newly created group agent which maintains the group. At initialization of the group a data base entry for the group will be created and filled with some available default information sources on the Internet. The profile agent queries these entries and dispatches to an agent server near or on the information source to access the information. On the Internet-agent server it filters information based on the user profile.After having done its work, it will return home to the server and give his results to the group agent.

Group-Agent Group agents coordinate the information retrieval for a group of agents. By knowing which agent is searching at which place it can give out information sources where no agent is active yet. In addition a group agent maintains the local database. It adds documents and links to the local database given to him by profile agents and supplies the profile agents with addresses of knowledge providers. Also, it holds the profile information of agents and gives them out by request of profile agents. Also, it sends new arrived information provided by profile agents to the interface agent of the users in the group. It computes the group profile and sends out a mobile proxy agent to collect the desired information.

Proxy-Agent A Proxy-Agent is the mobile representative of a group. It has the basic structure of a Profile-Agent. It is created by a Group-Agent to do a concrete and special task, i.e. gathering information concerning a restricted profile on one special agent server.

Interface-Facilitator Basically interface agents are responsible for the presentation of results transmitted by group agents. Results are presented in the graphical user-interface, but they could be re-transfered to another application. In addition, this agent is the facilitator between user and profile agent.

Resource-Facilitator To reduce the size of profile agents, they have the ability to add new functionality dynamically. Resource-Agents offer task modules (classes) for different tasks, eg. information filtering, database accessing and so on. The profile agent can address the resource agent and order task modules.

Information service

The information service module provides sophisticated information retrieval techniques combined with preprocessing of data, so that only relevant information is offered to the customer. It must not not necessarily need control over all the information resources, but they must be accessible.
In our system the basic features of the Information service module are provided by the InfoSphere system.

Interface facilitator

The task of the interface facilitator is the creation and management of agents

Agent-Management-User-Interface The GUI supports the user in managing agents. Agents could be started, retracted or stopped. Also, results are presented in the GUI. In addition the user can send messages to the agent or retrieve them from the agent.

5 Usage

In order to illustrate the behavior of the system described in section 4 we will discuss some use cases from the user's viewpoint. We suppose, that a user needs the system to collect information to a certain topic. Several activities are required in that context:

1. the user must define his information interest for a query agent
2. the user must configure his query agent
3. the agent con join a agent group
4. the group has to determine proxies
5. the proxies must migrate to the appropriate information sources
6. the proxies have to acquire the information
7. the proxies must deliver the retrieved information
8. the results must be delivered to the user
9. the agent server will be updated

We group these activities in three classes:

- configuration (activity number 1 to 4)
- migration and information retrieval (activity number 5 to7)
- delivering and adaptation (activity number 8 to 9)

These main clusters are described in the following. To illustrate the interaction the overall system is sketched in figure 1.

5.1 Configuration

In order to start a query the user has to describe his information interest. He might choose from several templates, adjust a template to his actual needs or he might construct a new from scratch. His information interests are described by a set of annotated and weighted keywords. These keywords are already available in the template, they can be entered directly or they are automatically extracted from a set of specified documents. The information interest can be refined interactively. Synonym lists, word stemming or domain selection can be applied automatically.

The agent needs further specification including life-time, desired cost of the information, preferred information sources and sites, privacy, information sharing, grouping and negotiating strategies, and more. Default values are stored in the templates or might be chosen from prior sessions or selected from lists.

In the next step the agents enters the agent server. An appropriate group has to be determined appropriate group that shares similar interests, the same destination, equal resources like money or life-time or additional criteria. There are different means to compare these criteria with existing groups. They can be evaluated by parameter comparison, by automatic clustering procedures, or by applying information retrieval strategies on the information interests (e.g. by the vector space model [Salton & McGill, 1983] as realized in the InfoSphere system). If there exists already an agent group matching these criteria, the agent joins that group and the group profile will be adapted. Otherwise the agent sets up its own group.

The group creates and configures proxies according to the parameters of its members. Additionally, it uses information about the resources available in the server environment. E.g. there might exist an annotated model of the Web which contains descriptions of information resources or available information servers. So each proxy gets a certain task including a proposed migration path to the most promising information server.

The proxies migrate to information servers.

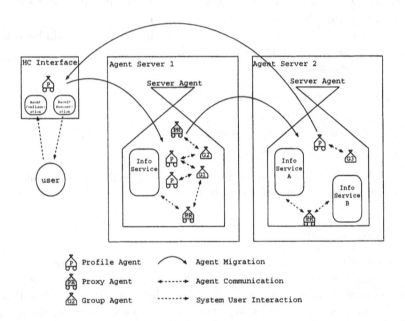

Fig. 1. Architecture of the agent system

5.2 Migration and information retrieval

Entering an information server, the proxy determines the services available on that server. He negotiates the optimal service, the price, the duration and — if successful — passes his interest to the server.

The information server itself is not necessarily the owner of the information. He might access the information by traditional techniques like database queries or search engines. But it is an important point that the server should have cheaper or faster access to the information than the user (otherwise the retrieval could have been done by the user himself).

After processing the query, the results are passed to the proxy. Depending on its mission, the proxy takes the contents of the results or links to the results or meta information about the results. The proxy gets additional information from the information server about available resources or condition to use them.

If the proxy agent meets other agents traveling on information servers, he might exchange information with them. He might get useful hints to promising information sources (servers) or he might even get results, that are carried by the other agent. Payment and negotiation processes are involved in this contact.

He determines whether to return (if his task is accomplished or his resources like money or life-time are insufficient) or to proceed searching and migrates to the next destination. The proxy might also die while fulfilling his task (for instance if the information server needs to long to produce results).

5.3 Delivering and adaptation

Returning to their origin the proxies hopefully bring high–quality results to the original query. They join their originating group and the results are distributed to the group members following a fixed algorithm or negotiating with single group members. The retrieved information is paid (n.b. since the retrieved information is shared, only a partial price must be paid by each group member).

On the local server an annotated list of information servers is maintained. The proxies exchange their experiences with the group or server in order to refine that existing model of information resources. For instance, an information server included in the local model might have changed his policies or might have disappeared. The list can be refined or updated according to the results the proxies are bringing in.

After completing all his tasks the proxy dies.

The single information agents themselves determine, if their tasks are completed or if they have to wait for other proxies to return. They might join other groups in order to satisfy additional aspects of their mission, they might migrate to other servers or the might return the results to their owner.

After completing his tasks (which can or must be confirmed by the user) the agent starts sleeping (e.g. by joining the template list).

6 Discussion

The system and the functionality as described above has been partly realized in the diploma thesis of Kai Kramhöft (see [Kramhöft, 1997]). It operates within the intranet of Siemens Corporate Research as an experimental system. The information services available cover Web search engines and newsgroups, the processing is based on the personalized information filtering system InfoSphere^{TM} (for a detailed description see [Schappert & Kleinhans, 1996]).

The system proposed above by its design (section 4) and usage (section 5) intends to solve some of the problems (see section 2) of the Internet as an information resource. Our approach leads to the following properties:

Advantages

- The cost of information acquisition are reduced
  There will be less net traffic because less unnecessary documents have to be fetched by the user; the costs charged by information providers cut down by dividing them to all group members.
- The coverage of different resources of the web is extended
  Mobility supports the integration of different providers (like databases) that are not covered by search engines; the integration of new and to–date unknown services is supported, because or system adapts to the changing environment and refines his control mechanisms by learning.
- Flexibility and extendibility is guaranteed
  The agent architecture supports an open architecture, that can be extended easily by wrapping existing services; the negotiation concept between agents and providers ensures the operation in changing environments.
- The quality of the retrieved information is better
  Specialized services of different information providers are tailored automatically to the information needs of the users by providing a detailed model of the user interest to the service provider; sophisticated information retrieval techniques can refine the information acquisition.

Disadvantages

- The system does not offer immediate responses
  The complex interaction between agents, their migration and the sophisticated information processing costs time. If the user wishes immediate responses, he can incorporate the services available today into the system.
- There is no optimum solution for single users and single criterion
  The system offers a solution that is better and more economic from the average viewpoint; but since the quality of results is higher, the single user might expect better results than today.
- An infrastructure for the agents is required
  A platform can be chosen that is available almost everywhere (like Java); with the existing approaches services must also be provided (i.e. search engines).

Summary

We have proposed a system for information retrieval, that extends existing approaches in the context of the Internet. It is based on the combination of mobile agent and information retrieval techniques and supports information sharing and decentralized information processing. We believe that our approach will improve the possibilities for information acquisition from the Internet, and, moreover, that this approach is one of the feasible solutions in that context.

Acknowledgment

We thank Kai Kramhöft for realizing a prototypical implementation of the design proposed in this paper.

References

[Cheong, 1996] Cheong, F.-C. 1996. *Internet Agents*. New Riders Publishing.

[Etzioni & Weld, 1995] Etzioni, O., & Weld, D.S. 1995. Intelligent Agents on the Internet: Fact, Fiction, and Forecast. *IEEE Expert*, **10**(4), 44–49. special issue on Intelligent Internet Services.

[Franklin & Graesser, 1996] Franklin, S., & Graesser, A. 1996. Is it an agent, or just a program?: A taxonomy for autonomous agents. *Pages 21–35 of:* J.P. Müller, M. Wooldridge, N.R. Jennings (ed), *Intelligent Agents III*. Springer LNAI 1193.

[Griswold, 1996] Griswold, S. 1996. Unleashing Agents. *Internet World*, May, 55–57.

[Halasz, 1987] Halasz, F.G. 1987. Reflections on NoteCards: Seven issues for next generation hypertext systems. *Hypertext*, Nov., 345–365.

[Kramhöft, 1997] Kramhöft, Kai. 1997. *MIAOW*. Tech. rept. Universität Bremen.

[Müller, 1997] Müller, H.J. 1997. Towards Agent System Engineering. *Data & Knowledge Engineering*, 217–245.

[Oates et al., 1997] Oates, T., Prasad, M.V.N., & Lesse, V.R. 1997. Cooperative Information-Gathering: a distributed problem solving approach. *Pages 72–87 of: IEE Proc.-Softw. Eng.*, vol. 144. Black Bear Press.

[Salton & McGill, 1983] Salton, G., & McGill, M.J. 1983. *Introduction to Modern Information Retrieval*. McGraw–Hill.

[Schappert & Kleinhans, 1996] Schappert, A., & Kleinhans, J. 1996. Personalized Information Filtering. *First International Conference on Practical Aspects of Knowledge Management*, Oct.

[Sycara & Zeng, 1996] Sycara, K., & Zeng, D. 1996. Multi-Agent Integration of Information Gathering and Decision Support. *Pages 549–553 of:* Wahlster, W. (ed), *Proceedings of ECAI'96*. Wiley Pubs.

[Sycara et al., 1996] Sycara, K., Pannu, A., Williamson, M., Zeng, D., & Decker, K. 1996. Distributed Intelligent Agents. *IEEE Expert*, **11**(6), 36–46.

[Wooldridge & Jennings, 1995] Wooldridge, M., & Jennings, N.R. 1995. Intelligent Agents: Theory and Practice. *Knowledge Engineering Review*, **10**(2).

Melding Abstractions with Mobile Agents

Antonio Corradi, Marco Cremonini, Cesare Stefanelli

Dipartimento di Elettronica, Informatica e Sistemistica
Università di Bologna, Viale Risorgimento 2, 40136 Bologna, Italy
Ph.: +39-51-6443001 - Fax: +39-51-6443073
{acorradi, mcremonini, cstefanelli}@deis.unibo.it

Abstract. The Mobile Agent (MA) model seems to provide one of the most suitable technology for distributed systems to integrate the Internet in a synergic way. One of the problems that should be faced when considering mobile agents for distributed applications is the lack of a thorough model capable of describing the Internet world composed of interconnected networks, each of them with their peculiar policies (for administrative, management and security purposes). We propose a Mobile Agent system based on a model designed to consider and favour aggregations of abstract and protected (network) domains: the use of this model makes easy the development of Internet applications. The paper describes the MAMA system (Melding Abstractions with Mobile Agents) and its implementation in the Java language. An application for distributed monitoring provides an example of the results achieved within the MAMA system.

1 Introduction

Distributed programming is obtaining increasing importance due to the widespread diffusion of internetworking. The large dimension of Internet and the huge amount of information already available has focused the attention on code mobility as an alternate solution to simple message passing solutions [3].

Instead of traditional client/server programming, emerging models are the Remote Evaluation (REV) [18], the Code On Demand (COD) [3] and the Mobile Agents (MA) [15]. The first two models can be considered as complementary. In the REV model, any client can send the code to a remote server that can use this code both in the execution of the current operation and to add up new behaviours to its features at run-time. The COD model can make possible for the client to enlarge its capacity of execution by dynamically downloading code from the server. The typical

Work carried out under the financial support of the "Ministero dell'Università e della Ricerca Scientifica e Tecnologica (MURST)" in the framework of the Project "Design Methodologies and Tools of High Performance Systems for Distributed Applications".

COD application configures the server as a code repository and makes the client load the code by need. This is the model followed by Java Applets.

The distinguished point of the MA model is to allow the mobility of entities, even in execution. The agent is the execution entity - composed of code, data, execution state - that has started on an initial node. Agents are capable of moving autonomously to a node different from the current one and to resume execution there. The MA model can be considered as an extension of the REV one with enlarged functionality.

The MA model could be applied to many areas, such as electronic commerce, network management, information retrieval, CSCW, etc. It can describe distributed applications, but lacks a comprehensive framework which permits to model some common Internet situations, composed of a very large number of interconnected LANs with their peculiar policies for network management, resource administration, and security. We argue that this scenario should be considered in the definition of a general programming model for MA. In addition, MA applications, dealing with insecure interconnected networks and mobile executable code, are forced to take into account the security issue since the first phases of the design.

This paper presents a system called **MAMA** (Melding Abstractions with Mobile Agents) for the development of Mobile Agent applications. MAMA follows a model that considers the Internet heterogeneity and provides several abstractions to suit the common localities in the Internet. In particular, we introduce the place as the abstraction of an execution node, and the domain as the locality considered an abstraction for one LAN belonging to a single organisation. Different domains can be connected by gateways that represent the interconnection points for different LANs. We consider this framework suitable to assist the definition of all the policies necessary to develop MA applications over the Internet

MAMA led the design of the MA system architecture, where any abstraction of locality finds its concrete counterpart. Java is the language chosen to implement the system architecture. Java addresses the requirements of typical Internet applications: portability, interoperability, rapid prototyping and easy integration with the Web scenario. Our programming language choice seems not to address the efficiency issue; however, the growing interests Java receives ensure that efficiency is also dealt with by all implementors and it is going to be more and more improved.

MAMA assisted in the rapid development of several applications. The paper reports a distributed on-line monitoring tool that is employed in the MAMA system to ascertain the global application and system state: applications can exploit monitoring information to enlarge their knowledge of the dynamic state of the system, for instance, for load balancing.

2 The MAMA Model

2.1 Overview

MAMA permits to face the requirements of a typical Internet distributed application by following a few guidelines:

- the execution model is based on agent mobility;

- several locality abstractions in a hierarchy model Internet LANs and their interconnections;

- security is considered as an integral part of the design and is integrated at any system level.

MAMA represents everything as either an agent or a resource. The agents can move to a different node, wholly re-establishing there, by migrating their code and copying their execution state [3]. The resources represent the logical and the physical entities available in any node where agents execute: examples of physical resources are printers and local devices, of logical ones are blackboards and tuple spaces.

Agents interact with resources by means of interfaces which assume a fundamental role for security and extensibility of the MA systems. In addition, the MAMA framework has a layered structure composed of places and domains mapping the local environment and the interconnection among nodes of a LAN. These levels of abstraction permit the development of many different security policies in the MAMA model.

2.2 Interface

The concept of interface is a uniform abstraction for handling both physical and logical resources. Agents can not directly access to resources; they make use of resource interfaces.

The interface is very useful from a security viewpoint, since it can control the actions of agents on resources: interfaces provide a safe access to resources, and filter the permitted operations. Agents may be granted/denied access to the local resources depending on the security policy adopted. As an example, consider an interface toward a local database: it is available through the permitted operations to all currently residing agents. Let us note that the same resource can provide different interfaces to different agents, depending on the security policy. As an extreme policy, the resource can become private to one specific agent. In this case, the agent itself becomes the resource manager, and anyone in need of one operation from the resource should issues its request to the manager agent.

2.3 Place and domain

A very important feature of the MAMA model is its structure composed of different levels of locality abstraction that describe the real structure of an internetworked environment (see Figure 1).

The first abstraction is the place, where agents execute and are enabled to tightly interact by directly cooperating with each other. At a higher level of abstraction, there is the domain, a logical entity that groups a set of places that shares common policies and privileges: inside one domain, places have the visibility of one another and can exploit locality to provide common management policies and to adopt uniform security policies.

The idea of structuring the system in locality of different levels of abstraction, with domains containing set of places, is of paramount importance in granting security. In fact, different locality may have peculiar security policy: each place may have a proper strategy, to satisfy, for instance, the security needs of the place owner, while the domain models a common strategy of a group of places, to enforce the security policy of one department of an organisation. A set of domains matches the internal structure of an organisation. The two levels of abstractions create a double enforced protection: any action is checked first against the domain security strategy and, if it is authorised, is passed for control to the final place of execution. We believe this layering of security policies be fundamental for the modelling of real agent applications.

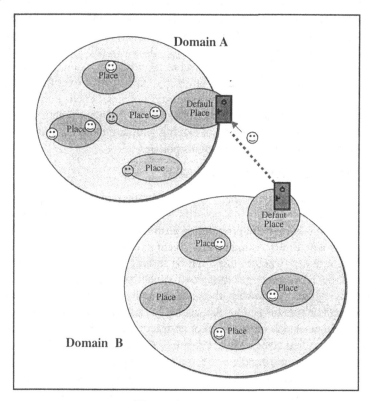

Figure 1. The MA model

The MA model takes into account security both for the agents and for the current locality. Agents should be granted integrity and privacy of their internal information, while both domains and places must be protected against malicious code operations.

With regard to agent coordination, we have already stated that agents inside a place can interact by sharing common resources. Whenever an agent needs to share a resource with another agent residing in a remote place, it is forced to migrate to the remote place. Mobile agents can directly migrate from place to place inside one domain. Whenever an agent needs to move outside the domain, it needs to rely on a specific entity, the gateway, in charge of the inter-domain routing functionality. The gateway is part of the default place of a domain. One agent that migrates to a new domain is constrained to move to its default place.

Outside the scope of the place, agents can interact only by means of message exchange. The MAMA model assumes that messages can be eventually delivered to agents even when they migrate.

3 The MAMA Architecture

The Mobile Agent model described in the previous section is naturally mapped in the architecture of the MAMA system. The agent execution environment is the realisation of the place concept and the allocation of each agent execution environment is constrained into a single node. There cannot be an agent execution environment spanning over different nodes (whereas there can be several agent execution environments in the same node) because its goal is to provide an interface to the physical machine. At a higher level of locality abstraction, the domain concept is mapped in the network domain that can contain several execution environments sharing common management and security policies. Each network domain is embodied in a default place containing the gateway for inter-domain communication. The default place is also in charge of dealing with and handling the agents entering or exiting the domain and of enforcing its policies.

3.1 The agent execution environment

The agent execution environment is the realisation of the concept of place: this locality is where agents may interact with each other and with node resources. Each agent execution environment provides an abstraction of the physical machine, and it is then constrained into a single node. Agent execution environments can not span over different nodes (whereas there can be several agent execution environments in the same node). An agent execution environment contains the resources that can be accessed by agents. Following the model, each resource is represented by the interface that controls the actions that agents can perform on resources.

A possible extension of this level of abstraction could be the realisation of a new type of agents, called static agents, providing the functionality of Resource Manager in order to control and mediate the interaction between mobile agents and local resources. The interaction style between mobile agents and local resources evolve in the sense of introducing a higher degree of abstraction in the system.

The agent execution environment offers agents services by means of the modules shown in Figure 2:

- the **Agent Manager** offers the basic functionality for agent mobility and for communications outside the place. Mechanisms for agent mobility are offered by the MAMA run-time support. This module provides message-passing style of communication for agents residing into different places and even different domains. It also manages the local naming of agents and the possibility of defining several aliases for the same agent;

- the **Local Resource Manager** is the interface for place services and for the node resources that agents may access. This module makes possible the agent access to local resources via their object interface. This makes possible a tight form of interaction between agents in the same place by means of shared objects. For instance, agents can share a blackboard object and a tuple space. This module controls the authorisation of agents accessing to local objects and ensures the respect of the place security policy;

- the **Distributed Information Service** is responsible for looking up information about agents and places in remote nodes. The visibility is limited to one domain which is logically viewed as a unique context composed of places mapped on different physical nodes. In particular, it provides a Domain Name Service and a Directory Service functionality. This module is an application service currently implemented as a set of dedicated agents. However, its functionality could be also implemented in terms of agents interfacing with traditional Directory Services (X.500, NIS, etc.) and Internet DNSs.

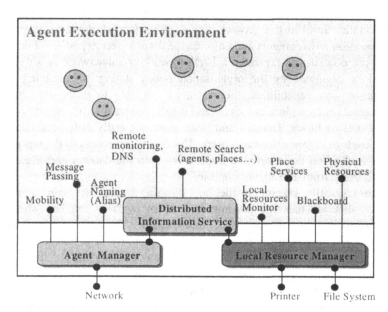

Figure 2. The agent execution environment

It is important to examine the security issues raised by the interaction of an agent with its current agent execution environment. Both parties of the interaction need to be protected against reciprocal malicious behaviour. On the one hand, it is necessary to protect the execution environment from agents that could cause damage or steal information. On the other hand, it is necessary to protect the agent against possible unauthorised actions by hostile execution environments.

The design of our architecture addresses the security requirements for both the place of execution and the agents. Privacy, integrity and authentication are required for protecting the place of execution. Authentication is necessary in order to authorise agents to interact with local resources of a place. Privacy and integrity aim to protect both the information carried by agents and the ones stored on the host.

In addition, we allow for the definition of layered security policies. Agents entering the domain are authenticated and authorised to interact with places. At the place level, agents are granted a set of permissions to invoke operations on local resources. Domains and places are the structures that permit an efficient definition of policies derived from Access Control models. A general policy for the system can be defined first at the domain level, by controlling the interaction of agents with places on the basis of user identity or role. Then, policies for the specific resources can be defined at the place level by different managers, by refining the domain policies. Coherence between domain and place policies must be granted by the MA system which is in charge of detect all conflicts between the policies at the two levels [16] [11].

3.2 The network domain

The domain concept presented in Section 2 identifies a logical locality mapped at the implementation level in the network domain. The network domain groups a set of agent execution environments and enforces the domain security policy. For instance, the network domain can represent a LAN network or subnetwork of a department, and will be regulated by the organisation policy stating and defining the user authorisation and capabilities, the resources available to users, etc. Inside the network domain, each place can have (and usually has) a specific security policy that rules the actions inside. Domain and place policies usually differ, representing the distinct needs of organisations and users. The agents can access to the resources of a place depending on the restriction imposed by both the domain and place security policies derived from user identity or role.

Agents typically execute inside one domain, where they can communicate asynchronously via message passing: each agent owns its mailbox where it can receive messages when moving from place to place. The agent support guarantees message delivery even in the presence of agent mobility. It is not possible for two agents to open stream connection, instead they can decide to move to the same place of execution, where they can share some common objects.

Message passing and agent migration are performed directly between places belonging to the same domain, because places inside one domain have the visibility of all the others. Messages and mobile agents crossing the domain boundaries involve the default place (containing the gateway), that is responsible for:

- routing all messages to/from the domain, acting in a way similar to traditional IP gateways; it is worth to stress that the gateway handles only messages exchanged between agents belonging to different domains, that produces a usually limited traffic of messages;

- handling the incoming/outcoming agents; the gateway receives agents arriving from other domains and it is in charge of performing all the security checks required by the domain policy on the newly arrived agents. Agents exiting the domain are sent to the gateway for further routing to the new destination domain;

- dispatching the agents arriving in the domain to the correct destination place; in practice, it contains a name server for the other places of the domain. This functionality is required only locally to the gateway and only for agents entering the domain and thus it does not represent a bottleneck;

- physically separating the domain from all others; in this case, it acts as a proxy, capable of transferring agents and messages between the domain and the rest of the world.

4 The MAMA Implementation

The MAMA architecture has been implemented by using the Java language [2]. Java provides an intrinsic portability and inter-operability in heterogeneous environments. The object-oriented nature of the Java language is suitable for the design of MAMA: the encapsulation principle suits the abstraction needs of both resources and agents; the classification principle makes possible to inherit behaviour from already specified components instead of starting the design from scratch.

We use the Java Virtual Machine without modifications and, like other MA systems, we introduce a new operation (go) allowing an agent to move itself during the execution. The go operation requires as a parameter the method that has to be activated after the migration.

The support for migration has taken advantage of Java object serialisation. When an agent migrates, it moves also all its private Java objects (they are copied to the new location and then destroyed in the old one). All other objects one agent has references for are left in the current place where they can be later found if the agent comes back; in particular, Java non-serializable objects maintain their allocation.

The MAMA system, composed of places, domain and gateways is implemented in Java (JDK 1.1.5) [8] with a very limited number of class (175). All the current MAMA features are based on the current JDK version and some of them are going to be changed to adhere to the new model of the JDK1.2.

5 The Distributed Monitoring Application

Mobile Agents can improve performance in many distributed applications, because they can take advantage of the network bandwidth availability, and they carry on execution in case of disconnected situations [19]. Mobile Agents can be useful also for achieving fast prototyping of applications, if they have been developed in a rapid prototyping environment, available also to applications.

Mobile Agents are commonly indicated as a good solution in the field of electronic commerce, for information-retrieval applications or in network management and in the support for cooperative works.

This section describes our agent implementation of an on-line distributed monitoring system [17] to collect information about the agent application at run-time. The monitoring system is capable of inspecting the configuration of the whole system to provide information for system upgrades, for load balancing policies, and, in general, any dynamic strategy.

The monitoring system architecture is completely distributed. There is no centralisation point and there is no single point of execution: the monitoring system is not only distributed but also even mobile, being composed of only mobile agents.

Monitoring agents are assigned to specific domains and have the duty of gathering the information collected by moving from node to node inside one domain. We restrict the scope of monitoring agents to one domain in order to provide a light implementation of the agent, avoiding the problems of mobility between domains with different security needs. In addition, it is possible to assign a variable number of monitoring agents to each domain, depending on fault tolerance, time latency of the information to be gathered, etc. The higher the number of agents per domain, the higher the consistency of monitoring information with the current system state.

The monitoring agent looks for information about the configuration of each place (in terms of services available) and the load distribution in the system, in terms of both mobile agents and object-resources present in each place.

We have compared the results obtained by the agent solution with a more traditional one where a single monitoring entity (the master) resides in one node and gathers the monitoring information of the whole domain by message passing with the slaves, one in each controlled node.

Figure 3 shows the results obtained in monitoring a domain composed of a network of 12 SUN workstations (Sparc 4, Sparc 5 and Ultra-1) Ethernet-connected. The figure shows the total time (in msec) to obtain the complete situation over the whole domain. This experiment considers average monitoring information: the master/slave solution requires a number of messages equal to the number of observation (per each slave); the agent solution dispatches a variable number of monitoring agents that compute the average in place. The time measurement shown in Figure 3 is an average measurement over a high number of executions.

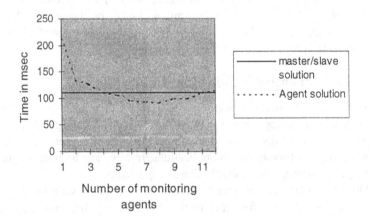

Figure 3. The agent-based monitoring solution compared with a traditional master-slave monitoring approach.

The obtained results show that the agent solution can perform the same of a traditional one and can achieve better performance with a limited number of monitoring agents in the given domain. The presented results refer to the first prototype of the agent support, whose successive versions tend to achieve better performance. Apart from the performance, a mobile agent monitoring application offers a more flexible solution than traditional distributed ones. In particular, when dealing with mobile computing, network bandwidth limitations and unreliable communication scenarios.

6 Related Work

While many proposals of MA systems have been presented recently, we compare only a few of them, chosen because of similarities in goals and application areas. The distinguished features of MAMA, if compared with the other systems, is to present a comprehensive framework, the hierarchy of places and domains, suitable to apply patterns of security policies integrated at the design level.

In the class of Java-based mobile agents projects, we compare our system with *Aglets* [10], *Odyssey* [12] and neglect efforts such as *Sumatra* [1] because they have chosen to change the Java Virtual Machine, loosing its portability.

Aglets uses an event-based programming model, where examples of events are the agent migration, its dispatch and its arrival. It provides only a weak mobility model, because any moving agent must start its execution from the beginning in the new node. Aglets currently has only a primitive form of agent authentication, but a new security architecture for this system has been proposed in [9]. With respect to Aglets, we support a stronger form of mobility.

Odyssey has a simplified structure if compared with our system but also implements a go operation. Odyssey go operation differs from MAMA go because it permits only to specify the destination and the routing of an agent by means of the Ticket constructor. For this reason Odyssey agents are restarted at each destination. Otherwise, if a particular method must be invoked at a specific destination, a subclass of the main Agent class must be used, the Worker class that supports only one task per destination.

Ara [14] adopts a different approach compared with us and the other systems, providing a core Java-based module that supports multiple agent languages like Tcl and C++. Agents move between locality called "places". We extend the concept of locality present in Ara.

In the class of mobile agents systems based on script languages, *Agent Tcl* [6] provides a support for agents written in Tcl (in the near future also in Java and Scheme) which communicate mainly by using an RPC mechanism. Our system, instead, supports message-passing between agents and a direct access to shared objects in the same place.

Other works address the issue of standardisation. A group of MA systems developers (Crystaliz, General Magic and IBM among the others) has submitted to OMG a proposal to achieve interoperability for different architectures and implementations [5]. This proposal standardises some aspects of MA technology and its integration with CORBA [13]. A similar effort is the FIPA one [4] where the focus is on the standardisation of communication and management of agents. Another standardisation effort is the Open Distributed Processing (ODP) [7], that is a joint activity of the ISO and ITU and provides a framework to develop architectures with an integrated support for distribution, internetworking, and portability. In addition, it focuses on the use of formal description techniques for specification of the architecture. Our proposal follows the guidelines presented in the different standardisation efforts: we adopt a layered structure with different abstractions, and we agree also on the importance of the integration of MA systems with other technologies. Our paper presents also the realisation of an MA architecture in a Java environment.

7 Conclusions

The paper presents an MA model with locality abstractions (place, domains and gateway), introduced with the goal of making easier the design of global and non traditional applications for the Internet scenario. MAMA provides a layered framework in which agents can move depending on their needs and their accesses to different services. Our system considers fundamental the enforcing of security, for both the agent and the place of execution, to preserve all entities, introducing a structure that permits to apply patterns of policies at different levels and with different scopes.

The Java implementation, apart from the a priori granted interoperability and portability, has been carried out in accord with the possibility of rapid prototyping. This approach makes possible to vary the behaviour of several system components and to experiment different policies.

The first experiences, coming from the implemented applications, exhibit acceptable performance, if taking into account Java efficiency limitations. In any case, we believe that Java will grant higher level of efficiency in a little time.

References

1. A. Acharya, M. Ranganathan, J. Saltz: Sumatra: A Language for Resource-Aware Mobile Programs. In Mobile Objects, J.Vitek, C.Tschudin (Eds.), Springer-Verlag, Vol. 1222 Lecture Notes in Computer Science, 1997.
2. K. Arnold, J. Gosling: The Java Programming Language. Addison-Wesley, 1996.
3. A. Carzaniga, G.P. Picco, and G. Vigna: Designing Distributed Applications with Mobile Code Paradigms. 19th International Conference on Software Engineering (ICSE'97), 1997.
4. L. Chiariglione: FIPA 97 specification, Foundation for Intelligent Physical Agents. October 1997.
5. Crystaliz Inc., General Magic Inc., GMD Fokus, IBM Corp.: Mobile Agent Facility Specification. Joint Submission. Supported by: The Open Group, OMG TC Document, June 1997.

6. R. Gray, G. Cybenko, D. Kotz, D. Rus: Agent Tcl. In W.R. Cockayne and M. Zyda: Mobile Agents: Explanations and Examples. Manning/Prentice Hall, 1997.
7. ITU Recommendation X.901-904 - ISO/IEC 10746 1-4. Open Distributed Processing - Reference Model, July 1995.
8. Java Development Kit, Version 1.1.5. Sun Microsystems, 1997. http://java.sun.com/products/index.html
9. G. Karjoth, D. Lange and M. Oshima: A Security Model for Aglets. IEEE Internet Computing, Vol. 1, N.4, July/August 1997.
10. D. Lange , M. Oshima: Programming Mobile Agents in Java - With the Java Aglet API. IBM Research, 1997.
11. E. Lupu, M. Sloman: A Policy Based Role Object Model. Proceedings of EDOC'97, IEEE Computer Society, October, 1997.
12. Odyssey, version beta 2, General Magic, 1998, http://www.genmagic.com/agents/odyssey.html
13. Object Management Group: The Common Object Request Broker: Architecture and Specification. Rev 2.0 (OMG Document 96-03-04), 1995.
14. H.Peine: Ara - Agents for Remote Action. In W. R. Cockayne and M. Zyda: Mobile Agents: Explanations and Examples, Manning/Prentice Hall, 1997.
15. K. Rothermel, R. Popescu-Zeletin (Eds.). Proceedings of the First International Workshop on Mobile Agents, Berlin (D), Lecture Notes in Computer Science, Vol. 1219. Springer-Verlag (D), April 1997.
16. R.Sandhu, P.Samarati: Authentication, Access Control, and Intrusion Detection. The Computer Science and Engineering Handbook, 1996.
17. B. Schroeder: On-Line Monitoring: A Tutorial. IEEE Computer, Vol. 28, N. 6, June 1995.
18. J.W.Stamos, D.K.Gifford: Remote Evaluation. ACM Transaction on Programming Languages and Systems, Vol. 12 No. 4, October 1990.
19. J. Waldo, G. Wyant, A. Wollrath, S. Kendall: A Note on Distributed Computing. In Mobile Objects, J.Vitek, C.Tschudin (Eds.), Springer-Verlag, Vol. 1222 Lecture Notes in Computer Science, 1997.

Data-Security in Heterogeneous Agent Systems [*]

Piero A. Bonatti[1], Sarit Kraus[2], Jose Salinas[3], V.S. Subrahmanian[4]

[1] Università di Torino, E-mail bonatti@di.unito.it
[2] Bar-Ilan University, E-mail sarit@umiacs.umd.edu
[3] Army Research Lab, E-mail salinas@arl.mil
[4] University of Maryland, E-mail vs@cs.umd.edu

Abstract. In this paper, we describe: (i) how agents can protect information from other agents and (ii) how servers that support agent cooperation can help in this process. We show that agents' data security policies can be encoded through three structures called *metaknowledge*, *history* and *agent security tables*. We develop a framework that allows arbitrary metalanguages and history maintenance policies to be "plugged in", and develop complexity results, including polynomial (efficiently computable) approximations.

1 Introduction

Developing a platform for the interaction of multiple agents requires contributions from several areas of computer science, ranging from systems software to support interoperability, network software to support multiagent communications, heterogeneous data and software integration to meaningfully exchange data, and artificial reasoning to support intelligent reasoning and decision making tasks. With these goals in mind, we are conducting a joint research effort between the US Army Research Lab, the University of Maryland, Bar-Ilan University (Israel), the Technical University of Vienna, the University of Torino (Italy), and the Universities of Gießen and Koblenz in(Germany).

An ever-present, and important issue in the area of agent based systems, is the need to provide a wide range of *security services*. Such services range from:

- *Authentication* of agents ("Is Agent A who is requesting a service really agent A?")
- *Network security* services which ensure that network packets do not get improperly read by unauthorized intruders, and
- *Data security* in which each agent wishes to hide some of its data (and/or capabilities) from other agents.

In this paper, we will focus on *Data Security* only. We make the following contributions:

First, we will precisely identify how each agent enforces data security. For this, each agent must specify three types of information: (1) metaknowledge it

---

[*] Partially supported by the Army Research Office under grant DAAH-04-95-10174, by the Air Force Office of Scientific Research under grant F49620-93-1-0065, by ARPA/Rome Labs contract Nr. F30602-93-C-0241 (Order Nr. A716), and by an NSF Young Investigator award IRI-93-57756.

has about other agents ("what do I believe agent A knows?"), (2) historical information it has about past interactions with other agents ("what did I tell agent A before?") and (3) an agent security table that specifies how it will respond to other agents' requests. Metaknowledge may be expressed in many languages as exemplified in the vast quantity of work in the area of knowledge and belief [28]. We show complexity results for the problem of meta-reasoning when the meta-language L is allowed to vary.[5] We identify classes of languages L that allow polynomial computations.

Finally, Historical data: An agent that stores entire histories is liable to get quickly overwhelmed by physical storage requirements. On the other hand, storing detailed histories is often desirable from the point of view of data security. We provide a general framework to specify and maintain historical archives. The semantics of the history specification language may be obtained through an encoding into a *fragment* of logic programs under the well known stable model semantics [16]. Even though the complexity of stable models is well known to be NP-hard, the fragment we identify yields polynomial time results under some simple conditions.

The organization of this paper is as follows: first, we overview our IMPACT system for supporting multiple interacting software agents. The architecture consists of two parts – a set of IMPACT servers, and agents themselves; security must be maintained on both sides. We describe, in sections 3.1 and 3.2, servers' and agents' data security, respectively.[6] Finally, in Section 4, we relate our work to the few existing works in this area.

2 Preliminaries: IMPACT Architecture[7]

A platform to support the creation and deployment of multiple software agents will need to interoperate with a wide variety of software sources. Any definition *Def* of what it takes for a software package S (in any programming language) to be considered an agent program, must come accompanied with tools to augment, modify, or massage S into an agent according to the definition *Def*.

In IMPACT, an agent is built on top of a piece of software code S, represented by a pair $S = (T_S, F_S)$ where T_S is the set of all data types manipulated by the software package S, and F_S is the set of all pre-defined functions of the package S that are provided by the package's application programmer interface.[8] For example, the Oracle DBMS may be viewed as a body of software code S where T_S consists of a set of attribute domains, tuples over these attribute domains, and relations (sets of such tuples), while F_S consists of the classical relational operations.

---

[5] This flexibility in allowing the language L to vary is particularly useful, as in most real-world applications, we expect different agents to reason differently.

[6] Section 3.2 – the heart of this paper – contains the key new technical contributions.

[7] The contents of this section are not new, see [7, 1, 24, 21, 22] for more details.

[8] This assumption is consistent with all well known object based software interoperability frameworks such as CORBA/ODE [12] and ODMG's ODL [10].

An agent is built on top of S by adding: (1) a service description (in a special language described in [3]) which describes the services provided by the agent, (2) a message box that handles messages to other agents, (3) a decision layer (described in [14]) specifying how the agent takes actions, and (4) a security layer that describes the security policies associated with the agent. Due to space reasons we are unable to go into the full details of these layers – the interested reader is referred to [3].

The IMPACT architecture contains a set of replicated, mirrored servers that provide a variety of services, including agent yellow-pages (to find agents that provide a requested service), an agent ontology service, as well as type/thesaurus services.

Notation. Let $S = (\mathcal{T}_S, \mathcal{F}_S)$ be a body of software code. Given any type $\tau \in \mathcal{T}_S$, we will assume that there is a set $Var(\tau)$ of variable symbols ranging over τ. If $X \in Var(\tau)$ is such a variable symbol, and if τ is a complex record type having fields $f_1, \ldots, f_n$, then we require that $X.f_i$ be a variable of type τ_i where τ_i is the type of field f_i. In the same vein, if f_i itself has a sub-field g of type γ, then $X.f_i.g$ is a variable of type γ, and so on. In such a case, we will call X a *root-variable*, and the variables $X.f_i$, $X.f_i.g$, etc. *path-variables*. An assignment of objects to the variables is a set of equations of the form $V_1 = o_1, \ldots, V_k = o_k$ where the V_i's are variables (root or path) and the o_i's are objects – such an assignment is *legal*, if the types of objects and corresponding variables match.

Definition 1 code call. Suppose $S = (\mathcal{T}_S, \mathcal{F}_S)$ is some software code and $f \in \mathcal{F}$ is a predefined function with n arguments, and $d_1, \ldots, d_n$ are objects or variables such that each d_i respects the type requirements of the i'th argument of f.[9] Then $S : f(d_1, \ldots, d_n)$ is called a *code call*. A code call is *ground*, if all the d_i's are objects.

Definition 2 code call atom. If cc is a code call, and X is either a variable symbol, or an object of the output type of cc, then $in(X, cc)$ is a *code call atom*.

Intuitively, a code call atom succeeds (returns *true*) just in case X is in the result set returned by cc. As an example of a code call atoms that we have implemented, consider $in(X, oracle : select(emp.rel, salary, >, 150000))$. This code call atom would succeed, instantiating X to any single tuple in relation emp that has a salary field of over 150,000.

Definition 3 code call condition. A *code call condition* is defined as follows:

1. Every code call atom is a code call condition.
2. If s, t are either variables or objects, then $s = t$ is a code call condition.
3. If s, t are either integers/real valued objects, or are variables over the integers/reals, then $s < t, s > t, s \geq t$ and $s \leq t$ are code call conditions.
4. If χ_1, χ_2 are code call conditions, then $\chi_1 \& \chi_2$ is a code call condition.

---

[9] In general, each function $f \in \mathcal{F}$ has a *signature*, specifying the types of inputs it takes, and the types of outputs it returns.

A code call condition satisfying any of the first three criteria above is an *atomic code call condition*. (Intuitively, the operator & is just logical *and*.)[10]

3 Security in IMPACT

In this paper, we will concentrate on *Data Security*, i.e., keeping a designated set of facts secret.[11] We observe that security may be violated in the following ways.

First, the IMPACT Servers may have some data that may get compromised. For example, information about which agents provide which services. In general, the fact that an agent A offers some service s_1 may only be disclosed under some conditions (e.g. A may provide code for the RSA public key cryptosystem, but this may only be disclosed to agents in the US).

Secondly, agents may have security requirements on their own data, so that in general, agents with different clearance levels may obtain different answers to the same service request. Existing agents may have their own security protocols, and need/desire nothing else. By contrast, our results in this paper apply to a situation where an application developer who builds some of his own agents, wishes to include some security/access control methods in his system.

Third, we must be sure that through the *Interaction* between agents and the IMPACT Servers, no secrets are "leaked" by an agent to the IMPACT Server (or vice versa).

In the rest of this section, we tackle each of these three parameters, by providing a simple security architecture. Our solution is quite generic, and applies to a wide variety of languages and architectures.

3.1 IMPACT Server Security Services

Suppose A is an agent, which offers services $s_1, \ldots, s_n$. A *non-disclosure agreement* between the IMPACT Servers and agent A specifies that *the fact that agent A offers service s_i will only be disclosed to other users/agents if they meet certain specified conditions*. In this section, we show how non-disclosure agreements can be articulated and enforced within IMPACT servers.

Throughout this section, we assume the existence of a partially ordered set, $(SL, \sqsubseteq)$, whose members are called *security levels*. If $\ell_1 \sqsubseteq \ell_2$, we say that security level ℓ_1 is "lower" than ℓ_2.

A *service description* consists of a service name, a set of mandatory inputs required to use that service, a set of inputs (not required) that may be provided, and a set of outputs generated by the agent providing that service. A service name consists of a verb (e.g."plan" and "sell") and a noun-term, defined as: (i)

---

[10] The current implementation, based on our HERMES platform [24, 7, 21, 8, 1], supports Ingres, Dbase, Paradox, packages for face recognition, nonlinear planning and terrain reasoning, operations research software, a GIS and a text indexing system.

[11] Further important issues relate to access control and authentication protocols [23] that we do not address here for space reasons.

if n is a noun, then n is a noun term, (ii) if n_1, n_2 are nouns, then $n_1(n_2)$ is a noun term (e.g., "route" and "tickets(opera)"). See [3] for more details.

The IMPACT Server maintains a Verb Hierarchy and a Noun-Hierarchy that are weighted directed acyclic graphs. Each node in the graph is labeled by a set of synonymous words. The edges denote ISA relationships. When a service $v_Q : nt_Q$ is requested (where v_Q is a verb and nt_Q is a noun-term), the IMPACT Server conducts a k-nearest neighbor search through the verb and noun hierarchies to "relax" the query. Then it may return agents which provide services within a given distance from $v_Q : nt_Q$ in the hierarchies.

The IMPACT servers' data structures and algorithms (cf. [3]) can be easily extended to incorporate security paradigms. When an agent A registers a service named $v : nt$ with the IMPACT Server, it also provides a set of conditions specifying to whom the fact that agent A offers this service may be released. The IMPACT Server maintains two tables (implemented in Oracle DBMS):

- An *agent table* having the schema (`AgentId,SecLevel,ConnectionInfo`) where `SecLevel` is the agent's security level, and `ConnectionInfo` is a specification of how other agents may connect to this one.
- A *service table* with four attributes – Verb, NounTerm, Agent, and Condition. The last column specifies a condition that must be satisfied by a client in order to access this information. For example, the tuple:

$(retrieve, surveillance(video), agent1,$

$in(T, \texttt{oracle:select}(emp, dept, =, security)) \,\&\, = (T.name, U) \,\&\, ts \sqsubseteq Level(U))$

says that "Agent-1" provides a service called "retrieve:surveillance(video)" that may only be used by individuals in the Security-Department having a top-secret (ts) or higher clearance.

In order to precisely define the syntax of the "Condition" field of the service table, we need the following definitions:

Definition 4 ordering terms/atoms. 1. If U is either a variable over user-ids, or is a user-id, then $Level(U)$ is an ordering term.

2. Every member of SL is an ordering term involving no variables.

If t_1, t_2 are ordering terms and $\underline{op}$ is any binary relation in $\{\sqsubseteq, \sqsubset, =, \not\sqsubseteq, \not\sqsubset\}$, and if at most one variable occurs in both t_1, t_2, then $t_1 \underline{op} t_2$ is an *ordering atom*.

Definition 5 service table condition (STC). 1. Any ordering atom is an STC.

2. Any code-call condition over the Oracle software system maintained by the IMPACT Server is an STC.

3. If $\mathcal{A}_1, \mathcal{A}_2$ are STCs, then so is $(\mathcal{A}_1 \,\&\, \mathcal{A}_2)$.

The IMPACT's algorithms for k-nearest neighbor and λ-range search presented in [3] may be easily modified to incorporate security checks such as those represented above (we do not go into details of these algorithms here). For example, one of the operations which is used by the $k - nearest neighbor$ algorithm is *search_agent_table*, which originally took three arguments – a verb V, a noun term NT and an integer K. It originally searched the Agent Service Table to find at most K agents that provide the exact service (V, NT). To maintain security, a new argument – an agent name U– should be added to *search_agent_table*. U is the name of agent that requested the $k - nearestneighbor$ information. In addition, the SQL query executed by *search_agent_table* (see [3]) should be modified as follows: SELECT agents

FROM AgentServiceTable

WHERE Verb=V AND NounTerm=NT AND Eval(Condition,U).
Eval(Condition,U) will return True if the STC Condition is satisfied.

3.2 Security in IMPACT Agents

We are now ready to go to the heart of this paper. In addition to the security policy associated with the IMPACT Server, each agent A in the system may have an associated policy that it uses to handle requests from other agents.[12]

For example, suppose an agent B asks agent A (police database) to execute the code call condition ψ. For instance, ψ may be the request: "Find all records associated with student criminals at Walt Whitman High school." Agent A may treat such a request in any one of the following ways:

- Agent A may refuse to execute the request (e.g. this could happen if agent B is not a police officer);[13]
- Agent A may execute the request (e.g. this could happen if agent B is a personal software agent of the local FBI Director);
- Agent A may execute a *modified* request ψ' and return the result of ψ' to agent B (e.g. a low level police officer may only get a partial answer, since juvenile criminal records are kept confidential).

In order to facilitate such requests, each agent maintains three types of information.

1. **Metaknowledge Component:** Each agent maintains some *Meta-Knowledge* about other agents, possibly including statements of the form "Agents B and C share information", "Agent B was created by agent C" (and hence, agent C can access B's information), "Agent B is a Univ. of Maryland agent", etc.
2. **History Component:** Each agent may maintain a *History of interactions* with other agents, expressed in some language.
   Specific programs implementing meta-knowledge and history manipulations may be implemented as an instance of our general definition of "software code".

---

[12] As mentioned earlier, the work reported here is applicable to agents that do not have an existing security policy in place and wish to incorporate a policy.

[13] Note that B may hear about A's services from another agent (even if the IMPACT server protects this information) and thus A should check the eligibility of B before executing the request.

3. **Agent Security Table:** Each agent maintains an Agent Security Table
   built on top of the previous two. It has the schema
   (`Condition, ReqService, ViewToUse, OutVars`).
   When another agent requests agent A to execute an operation op, this table
   is consulted to determine how to proceed. The `Condition` field of this table
   may include conditions over the data structures managed by agent A, as well
   as over the History and Meta-Knowledge components managed by A. The
   `ViewToUse` field may involve several variables. The `OutVars` field specifies
   which of these variables are to be returned.

For example, a very simple quadruple in the Agent Security Table is given by:

- `Condition`: $\text{in}(X, \text{oracle} : \text{project}(\text{police}, \text{name})) \& = (X.\text{name}, U) \& \text{Level}(U) \sqsupseteq s.$
- `ReqService`: $\text{in}(X, \text{oracle} : \text{select}(\text{criminal}, \text{type}, =, \text{juvenile}))$
  $\& \ in(X.name, whitman : rolls()).$
- `ViewToUse`: $\text{in}(X, \text{oracle} : \text{select}(\text{criminal}, \text{type}, =, \text{juvenile}))$
  $\& \ in(X.name, whitman : rolls()) \& \underline{X.age \geq 15}$
- `OutVar`: `X.name, X.crime`.

The above quadruple says that if a police officer with security level greater
than or equal to s (secret) requests information on students from Whitman High
School who have criminal records, we must evaluate this query *only* with respect
to individuals over 15 years of age – younger criminals will not be reported back
to such a police officer. The `OutVar` field specifies that the police officer will get
back, a single table having two fields – a **name** field, specifying the name of the
student, and a **crime** field, specifying what he was convicted of.

There is a tradeoff in the choice of languages for expressing meta-knowledge
and historical information. Increases in expressiveness are usually accompanied
by a corresponding increase in computational complexity. We now go into these
three components in greater detail and analyze some of the possible choices.

3.3 Meta-Knowledge Component

The MK component of our framework allows an agent A to use metaknowledge
about other agents to decide how to process their requests. As different agents
will use different types of metaknowledge about other agents, we propose a general architecture for "plugging in" different metalanguages into our framework.
We do this through a special body of software code $S_{mk} = (\mathcal{T}_{mk}, \mathcal{F}_{mk})$, defined
as follows:[14] $\mathcal{T}_{mk}$ consists of a *metaknowledge program* (MKP) defined in any of
the several languages listed in the next subsection; $\mathcal{F}_{mk}$ consists of the following functions (these functions' interfaces are independent of the metaknowledge
program language above, though their implementation may vary):

1. `getall(agent − id)` : This function returns all information that agent A
   has about the specified agent. The output type of this function is a set of
   formulas, in a suitable logical language.

---

[14] Different agents may use this single body of code, though of course, the data (metaknowledge) will vary.

2. `verify(fact)`: This function returns "true" if agent A's metaknowledge entails the specified fact, and false otherwise.

3. `update(agent_id, service_request, output)`: This function updates the body of metaknowledge concerning the specified agent, by recording the fact that the given service requests has produced the specified output.

4. `consistency_check(agent_id, service_request, output)`: This function checks whether the above update would violate some integrity meta-constraints (see below). It does not modify meta-knowledge.

5. `witness(agent_id, fact)`: This function returns the set of all substitutions θ ([26]) that cause agent A's metaknowledge to entail fact $F\theta$ where F is the input fact.

Possible Languages for Metaknowledge The languages for expressing metaknowledge will have a set of basic *meta-predicates* that capture the aspects illustrated in the previous section, e.g.: `UMD_agent`, `level(ℓ)`, `share_info(agent_1)` and `created_by(agent_2)`.

Moreover, the language may have a meta-predicate `Bel(agent, fact)` that expresses information that the specified agent is deemed to believe. In general, this predicate may be modified by the `update()` function introduced in the previous section.

In the meta-language, the agents' beliefs can be restricted through integrity meta-constraints of various sorts, based on *meta-conditions*:

Definition 6 meta-condition. An *atomic meta-condition* is defined as follows:

1. Every atomic code call condition is an atomic meta-condition.
2. If p is a meta-predicate of arity n and $t_1, \ldots, t_n$ are terms of the appropriate type, then $p(t_1, \ldots, t_n)$ is an atomic meta-condition.

A *meta-condition* is either an atomic meta-condition or a conjunction $\chi_1 \& \ldots \& \chi_m$ of meta-conditions

Definition 7 integrity meta-constraint. An *integrity meta-constraint* is a formula of the form $\Phi \to \texttt{Bel}(A, F)$, or $\Phi \to$, where Φ is a meta-condition and where the variables in A, F occur in Φ.

Definition 8 meta-constraint satisfaction. An integrity meta-constraint $\Phi \to \texttt{Bel}(A, F)$ is *satisfied* if for all substitutions θ such that $\Phi\theta$ and $\texttt{Bel}(A, F)\theta$ are ground, if $\Phi\theta$ evaluates to true, $\texttt{Bel}(A, F)\theta$ is also true. An integrity meta-constraint $\Phi \to$ is *satisfied* if for all grounding substitutions θ, $\Phi\theta$ evaluates to false.

These linguistic facilities are simple but powerful. For instance, they suffice to express: *closure conditions* on agents' beliefs, as in

$$\texttt{Bel}(A, F) \& \texttt{Bel}(A, G) \to \texttt{Bel}(A, \texttt{and}(F, G)),$$

belief inclusions among different agents, as in $\texttt{Bel(A,F)} \rightarrow \texttt{Bel(B,F)}$, *general rules* depending on other meta-predicates, e.g. $\texttt{Bel(A,F)} \& \texttt{created\_by(B,A)} \rightarrow \texttt{Bel(B,F)}$, *forbidden beliefs*, that cannot/should not be believed by the agent: $\texttt{Bel(A,F)} \rightarrow$.

Example 1. The code call $\texttt{getall(ag1)}$ may return the set: $\{\texttt{umd\_agent(ag1)},$ $\texttt{created\_by(ag1,ag0)}, \texttt{created\_by(ag2,ag1)}, \texttt{Bel(ag1,criminal(student259))}\}$. Meta information of this kind may be exploited in the Agent Security Table as follows.

- $\texttt{Condition:}$ $\texttt{in(X,oracle:project(police,name))} \& = (\texttt{X.name,U}) \& \texttt{Level(U)}\sqsubseteq\texttt{s}.$
- $\texttt{ReqService:}$ $\texttt{in(X,oracle:select(student,id,=,input.id))}.$
- $\texttt{ViewToUse:}$ $\texttt{in(X,oracle:select(student,id,=,input.id))} \&$
  $\texttt{in(false,mk:verify(Bel(U,criminal(input.id))))}$
- $\texttt{OutVar:}$ $\texttt{X.name}.$

The above $\texttt{ViewToUse}$ condition ensures that $\texttt{ag1}$ does not receive the name of any student under 15 who is already known by $\texttt{ag1}$ to be a criminal (in this example, $\texttt{student259}$ would be omitted).

The generality of meta-constraints can be proved formally. Consider the following set of constraints:

$$\texttt{true} \rightarrow \texttt{Bel(A,true)},$$
$$\texttt{Bel(A,P} \leftarrow \texttt{Q)} \& \texttt{Bel(A,Q)} \rightarrow \texttt{Bel(A,P)},$$
$$\texttt{Bel(A,P)} \& \texttt{Bel(A,Q)} \rightarrow \texttt{Bel(A,and(P,Q))}.$$

These three meta-constraints are equivalent to a well-known logic program called *vanilla meta-interpreter*[20] which is known to be a sound and complete meta-interpreter for arbitrary logic programs. Thus, since such programs constitute a general computational mechanism, the same is true also of integrity meta-constraints. As a corollary, we obtain the following upper bound for the complexity of the MK component's deduction procedures.

Theorem 9. *The value of the functions* $\texttt{verify, witness, consistency\_check}$ *is only semi-decidable, in general.*

Thus, in practice, the expressiveness of the MK component should be limited, in order to meet computability and efficiency requirements. In the following we show how different restrictions affect the computational complexity of the MK component. For this purpose, we need a few preliminary assumptions.

We assume that the the metaknowledge of an agent can be regarded as the closure of a logical theory T in some (arbitrary) logic with language L and entailment relation $\models$.[15] A *metaknowledge* program is a set of formulas in L. As is common in work on abstract entailment relations [25], we assume that the logic has suitable notions of *open/closed formulas*, *instantiation*, and *consistency*. Formally, this means that the following conditions hold:

---

[15] Remark: the internal data structures need not be sets of sentences, and the actual implementation can be chosen arbitrarily.

1. $\mathtt{verify}(F) = \mathtt{true}$ iff for some closed instance F' of F, $T \models F'$;
2. let T' be the theory corresponding to the new state produced by $\mathtt{update}(\mathtt{A, Req, Out})$; then $\mathtt{consistency\_check}(\mathtt{A, Req, Out}) = \mathtt{true}$ iff T' is consistent;
3. (soundness of $\mathtt{witness}$) for all substitutions $\theta \in \mathtt{witness}(A, F)$, and for all closed instances F' of $F\theta$, $T \models F'$;
4. (completeness of $\mathtt{witness}$) conversely, if for some closed instance F' of F, $T \models F'$, then there exists $\theta \in \mathtt{witness}(A, F)$ such that F' is an instance of $F\theta$.

Recall that a *Datalog* program is a logic program without function symbols [20]. The *extensional* (resp. *intentional*) *part* of a logic program is the set of facts (resp. rules with non-empty bodies) contained in the program.

Now we are ready to state formally how the complexity of the MK component varies as a function of some possible restrictions on the meta-language L. Due to space limitations, here we show the effect on $\mathtt{verify}$ – the complexity of the other functions is given in the full version of the paper.

Theorem 10. *Suppose that T is a Datalog program and F is an atomic metacondition, and U is an agent-id. Consider the following decision problems:*

P1: *deciding whether $\mathtt{verify}(\mathtt{F}) = \mathtt{true}$ when only the extensional part of T is allowed to vary;*

P2: *deciding whether $\mathtt{verify}(\mathtt{F}) = \mathtt{true}$ when only the intensional part of T is allowed to vary;*

P3: *deciding whether $\mathtt{verify}(\mathtt{F}) = \mathtt{true}$ when both parts are allowed to vary.*
Then we have the following results:

1. *The complexity of P1 is polynomial in the size of T, while P2 and P3 are NEXPTIME-complete.*
2. *If all the rules of T are meta-constraints, then also P2 and P3 are polynomial in the size of T.*

Next suppose that T is a set of arbitrary quantifier-free F.O. formulas.

3. *If the set of predicates of L is fixed, or, more generally, the arity of metapredicates is bounded by a fixed constant, then deciding whether $\mathtt{verify}(\mathtt{F}) = \mathtt{true}$ is NP-complete.*

Summarizing, the tradeoff between the expressiveness of MK and its computational complexity can be balanced under a wide spectrum of choices.

3.4 History Component

In general, we will assume that the historical archive associated with an agent A consists of *some* set of dialogs involving A. For instance, these could include requests that have been made to A and the results of those requests. Agents differ based on how they answer the following questions:

- *Which requests should be stored in the historical archive?* In general, agents may choose to store only certain types of requests. This may increase the efficiency of history manipulation, but may lead to future security violations, because an agent may "forget" what it previously disclosed.
- *Which attributes of these requests should be stored?* Among the possible attributes are the requested service, the sender, the answer, the time at which the request was made.

By analogy with the Meta-knowledge component, we introduce a general framework where different *History Specification Languages* (HSL for short) can be plugged in.

We assume the existence of a fixed set, $\mathcal{A}$ of message *attributes*. Each attribute $A_i \in \mathcal{A}$ has a fixed *domain*, denoted $dom(A_i)$, and a fixed set $\mathcal{B}_i$ of binary "comparison" operations on $dom(A_i)$. The *interface* functions provided by the history component of an IMPACT agent include:

- `retrieve_reqs(Sender)`: Retrieve all messages sent by the sender to the agent in questions.
- `find_srvc_reqs(Service)`: Retrieve all messages requesting a given service.
- `attr_retr(Attr,op,Val)`: Retrieve all messages m such that the specified attribute of m exists, and such that $m.\text{Attr}opVal$ is true. For example, the invocation `attr_ret(SendTime, >, 20 : jan : 95 : 1900)` may retrieve all messages whose `SendTime` field is after the specified time.
- `insert(Request, Sender, {AttrEquations})`: Insert the fact that `Sender` sent the specified request, and state the values of the attributes involved.
- `delete(Request, Sender, {AttrEquations})`: This has the opposite effect. For example, `delete(req1, ag1, {date = 20 : jan : 95 : 1900})` means to delete the statement that the date of the request is 20 : jan : 95 : 1900.

Definition 11 history conditions. Suppose `f` is one of the above functions, not equal to insert or delete, and `args` is a list of arguments for `f` of the appropriate type.

- Every code call condition is a *history condition*.
- `in(X, hist : f(args))` is a *history condition*.
- If χ_1, χ_2 are history conditions then $(\chi_1 \ \& \ \chi_2)$ is a history condition.

Example 2. Suppose that one of the possible answers to a service request is: "Request rejected: attempted security violation". In order to discourage such attempts, the agent may refuse to provide any service for 10 days after an attempted violation. This policy can be expressed by means of the following entry in the Agent Security Table, whose `Condition` field checks previous security violation attempts through the history component.

- `Condition:` $in(X, hist : attr\_retr(output, =, attempted\_violation))$ &
  $\quad\quad X.Sender = Agent \ \& \ (now - X.SendTime) \leq 10days.$
- `ReqService:` $\star$ (denoting any requested service.)

- ViewToUse: X=reject
- OutVar: X.

The notion of an HSL-program below specifies how to update the data structure in which historical information is stored.

Definition 12 HSL Programs. A *History Specification Rule* is a rule having one of the two forms listed below:

$$insert(Request, Sender, Attr) \leftarrow \texttt{history} - \texttt{condition} \qquad (1)$$

$$delete(Request, Sender, Attr) \leftarrow \texttt{history} - \texttt{condition} \qquad (2)$$

An *HSL Program* is a finite set of history specification rules.

Example 3. An agent may only save requests made by police officers. In addition, the requests of police officers with security level not higher that "secret" are saved only for two years. This policy can be specify using the following HSR program:

$insert(Request, Sender, [sender, header, date, response]) \leftarrow$

$in(X, oracle : project(police, name)) \& = (X.name, Sender)$

$delete(Request, Sender, [sender, header, date, response]) \leftarrow$

$in(X, his : attr\_ret(SendTime, <, now - 2years) \& Level(X.Sender) \sqsubseteq s.$

Let R_1 and R_2 be the ground instances of two history specification rules. If R_1 and R_2 have conflicting heads (e.g. insert(r, s, a) and delete(r, s, a)) and their bodies are simultaneously satisfied, then one of the two heads must *not* be derived. The set of all possible such choices can be characterized formally through a simple transformation of an HSL program P, into a logic program P^+. Every rule of forms (1) and (2) above is converted, respectively, into the following rules:

insert(Req, Sender, Attr) $\leftarrow \neg$delete(Req, Sender, Attr) & hist-cond

delete(Req, Sender, Attr) $\leftarrow \neg$insert(Req, Sender, Attr) & hist-cond,

In addition, we add to P^+ all the true instances of the atomic conditions contained in the above history conditions. The set of *stable models* of P^+ coincides with the set of all possible ways of disambiguating conflicting directives. The formal definition of stable models [16] is omitted here due to space limitations.

Theorem 13. *Suppose P is an HSL program. Then P^+ is guaranteed to have at least one stable model.*

In general, the reader will easily note that P^+ is not a stratified (nor a locally stratified) logic program [2, 29]. Not much is known about existence of stable models for non-stratified programs – yet the above result guarantees existence of stable models for logic programs produced by the above transformation.

Clearly, the logic programs P^+ generated by the above transformation, may have multiple stable models, corresponding to different disambiguations. We would like to guarantee that one stable model is picked *deterministically*. One way to accomplish this is to assume the existence of a selection function f (not described here). For example, f may select a stable model, based on lexicographic order (more interesting selections can be conceived).

Theorem 14. *If f can be computed in polynomial time,[16] then the stable model of P^+ selected by f can be computed in polynomial time w.r.t. the size of P^+.*

We remark that this is one of the few results known on polynomial computability of stable models. Past results have proven to lead to exponential computations [17, 18]. The identification of this *polynomial fragment* of logic programs under the stable semantics is a contribution of this paper.

3.5 Agent Security Table

Recall that the agent security policy is specified by the Agent Security Table, whose schema is: (Condition, ReqService, ViewToUse, OutVar). Both Condition and ViewToUse may contain code calls to: (i) the body of software constituting the actual service of the agent, (ii) the meta-knowledge component, and (iii) the history component. (It is precisely for this reason that we have chosen to define the agent security table last.)

Example 4. The table in Figure 1 lists one entry of the Security Table of an agent which is a police database. The entry indicates that any FBI officer having a security level of at least **top-secret**, can obtain a list of the names of all juvenile criminals.

Condition	ReqService	ViewToUse	OutVar
$ts \sqsubseteq Level(U)$ & in(X,oracle:project(fbi,name)) & =(X.name,U)	in(Y,oracle:select(criminal, type,=,juvenile))	in(Y,oracle:select(criminal, type,=,juvenile))	Y.name

Fig. 1. An example of an Agent Security Table

We say that a tuple in this table is *active* (with respect to agent A who submits the request) if the Condition field of the tuple evaluates to true when the special variable U (which may occur in the code call conditions) is bound to A.

ReqService (the requested service) is the primary key of this table. Let S be the given service request. If none of the tuples whose ReqService field matches S are active, then the agent refuses to provide the requested service. If exactly one such tuple is active, then the corresponding output is returned. Otherwise, let $t_1, \ldots, t_n$ be the active tuples of the agent security table that match S; the request can be processed according to any of the following options:

1. (Nondeterministic choice) One of the t_i s is chosen randomly, and the corresponding output is returned to Agent.

---

[16] It is easy to see that polynomial selection functions can be easily created by choosing a function that takes as input the set of conflicting heads and removes one atom from each conflict.

2. (Prioritized service) Suppose that $t_1, \ldots, t_n$ is the actual order in which the above tuples are listed in the table. This order is taken as a preference ordering over possible service executions. Accordingly, the output of t_1 is evaluated and returned to Agent.

3. (Conservative combination) The output is the intersection of the outputs of $t_1, \ldots, t_n$.

4. (Union of results) The output is the union of the outputs of $t_1, \ldots, t_n$.

The appropriateness of the above policies depends on the representation conventions adopted by the agent designer. For space reason we have to defer the discussion of when each policy is appropriate to a longer version.

4 Related Work and Conclusions

Most of the research on security of agents deals with issues related to the usage of agents on the Web. Some researchers try to answer questions such as, "Is it safe to click on a given hyperlink"? or "If I send this program out into the Web to find some bargain CD's, will it get cheated?" (e.g., [11]). Others try to develop methods for finding intruders who are executing programs not normally executed by "honest" users or agents [13], or deal with problems of identity verification and protecting message exchange in multi-agent environments [30]. Others tackle the problem of protecting mobile agents from their hosts [31]. In contrast, we focus on data security in multi-agent environments.

The problem of security in databases has been studied intensively, e.g. [4, 5, 6, 9, 19, 27, 32]. While this work is significant, none of it has focused on agents. We attempt to build on top of existing approaches. However, data security in autonomous agents environments raises new problems. In particular, no central authority can maintain security, but rather participants in the environment should be responsible for maintaining it. We deal with this problem and present a detailed model for autonomous agents which are responsible to maintain their own data security. They can obtain some help from the IMPACT Servers.

Foner [15] discusses security problems in a multi-agent matchmaker system named Yenta. The matchmaking done by the IMPACT Server is much more limited. IMPACT servers do not have access to the agents' data as Yenta's agents have. Thus, IMPACT Server's security tasks are simpler. Each agent is responsible for its own data security. We believe that this approach will lead to more secure multi-agents systems.

Other distributed object oriented systems provide some security services. CORBA [12], an object request broker framework, provides security services, such as identification and authentication of human users and objects, and security of communication between objects. These services are not currently provided by IMPACT, and their implementation is left for future work. CORBA provides some simple authorization and access control. Our model allows the application of more sophisticated security policies using the ViewToUse idea.

Summarizing, in this paper we have split the problem of security in agent systems into two parts – dealing with security in the servers that facilitate inter-agent interactions, and with the individual security mechanisms of each agent, respectively. We have given a simple solution to the former and presented a *generic* and *flexible* solution to the latter problem. We identified three components – metaknowledge, history, and agent security table – that an agent must have in order to express and enforce its security needs. Our framework allows different agents to use different meta-reasoning mechanisms and different types of histories. Similarly, through the agent security table, agent designers can flexibly specify what information must be protected from whom, and how to react to service requests. This reflects the reality that the security requirements of different agents will probably differ. Both the history component and the metaknowledge component are transparently implementable on top of commercial object data interoperation mechanisms such as CORBA/ODE and ODL. We provide interface definitions for these components. Our results describe the complexity of metareasoning and reasoning with histories, and identify polynomial fragments for efficient reasoning.

References

1. S. Adali, K.S. Candan, Y. Papakonstantinou and V.S. Subrahmanian. (1996) Query Processing in Distributed Mediated Systems, in: *Proc. 1996 ACM SIGMOD Conf. on Management of Data*, Montreal, Canada, June 1996.
2. K.Apt, H. Blair and9 A. Walker. (1988) *Towards a theory of declarative knowledge*, in J. Minker (ed.) "Foundations of Deductive Databases and Logic Programming", pps 89–148, Morgan Kaufman.
3. K. Arisha, S. Kraus, F. Ozcan, R. Ross and V.S. Subrahmanian (1998). IMPACT: The Interactive Maryland Platform for Agents Collaborating Together (submitted).
4. E. Bertino, C. Bettini, E. Ferrari and P. Samarati. (1996) A Temporal Access Control Mechanism for Database Systems, *IEEE Trans. on Knowledge and Data Engineering*, Vol. 8, Nr. 1, pps 67–80.
5. E. Bertino, P. Samarati and S. Jajodia. Authorizations in relational database management systems, *Proc. 1st ACM Conf. on Computer and Comm. Security*, Fairfax, VA, Nov. 1993.
6. P. Bonatti, S. Kraus and V.S. Subrahmanian. Foundations of Secure Deductive Databases, *IEEE Transactions on Knowledge and Data Engineering*, 7,3, June 1995.
7. A. Brink, S. Marcus and V.S. Subrahmanian. Heterogeneous Multimedia Reasoning. *IEEE Computer*, 28(9):33–39, Sep. 1995.
8. K.S. Candan, S. Jajodia and V.S. Subrahmanian. (1996) *Secure Mediated Databases*, in: *Proc. 1996 Intl. Conf. on Data Engineering*, Feb. 1996, New Orleans, LA.
9. S. Castano, M.G. Fugini, G. Martella, and P. Samarati, *Database Security*, Addison-Wesley, 1995.
10. R.G.G. Cattell. (ed.) (1993) *The Object Database Standard: ODMG-93*, Morgan Kaufmann.
11. D. M. Chess (1996). *Security in Agents Systems*, http://www.av.ibm.com/InsideTheLab/Bookshelf/ScientificPapers/.
12. The CORBAservices Specifications, 1997. http://www.omg.org/library/corbserv.htm

13. M. Crosbie and E. Spafford (1995). Applying genetic programming to intrusion detection. In Proceedings of the AAAI 1995 Fall Symposium series, November 1995.

14. T. Eiter, V.S.Subrahmanian and G. Pick. (1998) *Heterogeneous Active Agents*, draft manuscript, 115 pages.

15. L. N. Foner (1996). *A Security Architecture for Multi-Agent Matchmaking*, Second International Conference on Multi-Agent Systems (ICMAS96), Japan.

16. M. Gelfond and V. Lifschitz. (1988) *The Stable Model Semantics for Logic Programming*, in: Proc. 5th International Conference and Symposium on Logic Programming, ed R. A. Kowalski and K. A. Bowen, pp 1070–1080.

17. G. Gottlob (1992). *Complexity results for nonmonotonic logics*, Journal of Logic and Computation, 2(3):397-425, June 1992.

18. G. Gottlob. (1995) *The complexity of default reasoning under the stationary fixed point semantics*, Information and Computation, 121(1):81-92, 15 August 1995.

19. S. Jajodia and R. Sandhu, Toward a Multilevel Relational Data Model, in *Proc. ACM-SIGMOD Conf.*, Denver, May 1991.

20. J.W. Lloyd. (1987) *Foundations of Logic Programming*, Springer.

21. J. Lu, G. Moerkotte, J. Schue, and V.S. Subrahmanian. Efficient Maintenance of Materialized Mediated Views, in: *Proc. 1995 ACM SIGMOD Conf. on Management of Data*, San Jose, CA, May 1995.

22. J. Lu, A. Nerode and V.S. Subrahmanian. Hybrid Knowledge Bases, *IEEE Transactions on Knowledge and Data Engineering*, 8, 5, pp 773–785, Oct. 1996. Released as a University of Maryland Technical Report, Summer 1993.

23. T. F. Lunt. Access control policies for database systems. In C. E. Landwehr, editor, *Database Security II: Status and Prospects*, pages 41–52. North-Holland, Amsterdam, 1989.

24. S. Marcus and V.S. Subrahmanian. Foundations of Multimedia Database Systems, *Journal of the ACM*, Vol. 43, 3, pp 474–523, 1996.

25. W. Marek, A. Nerode and J.B. Remmel. (1990) *Non-Monotonic Rule Systems 1*, 2, Annals of Mathematics and Artificial Intelligence, pps 241–273.

26. A. Martelli and U. Montanari. (1982) *An Efficient Unification Algorithm*, ACM Trans. on Prog. Lang. and Systems, 4, 2, pps 258–282.

27. J. Millen and T. Lunt, Security for Object-Oriented Database Systems, in *Proc. of the IEEE Symposium on Research in Security and Privacy*, Oakland, California, May 1992.

28. R. Moore. Semantical Considerations on Nonmonotonic Logics. *Artificial Intelligence*, 25:75–94, 1985.

29. T. Przymusinski. (1988) *On the declarative semantics of deductive databases and logic programs*, in J. Minker (ed.) "Foundations of Deductive Databases and Logic Programming", pps 193–216, Morgan Kaufman.

30. C. Thirunavukkarasu, T. Finin and J. Mayfield (1995). *Secret Agents – A Security Architecture for the KQML Agent Communication Language*, Intelligent Information Agents Workshop *held in conjunction with* Fourth International Conference on Information and Knowledge Management CIKM'95.

31. T. Sander, C. Tschudin. Protecting mobile agents against malicious hosts. In G. Vigna (ed.) *Mobile Agents and Security*, LNCS, to appear.

32. M. Winslett, K. Smith, and X. Qian, Formal Query Languages for Secure Relational Databases, *ACM-TODS*, 19, 4, pp. 626–662, December 1994.

Author Index

Lecture Notes in Artificial Intelligence (LNAI)

Lecture Notes in Computer Science